THE
DISSENTERS

THE
DISSENTERS

Voices from Contemporary America

JOHN LANGSTON GWALTNEY

Random House New York

Copyright © 1986 by John Langston Gwaltney
All rights reserved under International and Pan-American
Copyright Conventions. Published in the United States by
Random House, Inc., New York and simultaneously in Canada
by Random House of Canada Limited, Toronto.

Library of Congress Cataloging-in-Publication Data
Gwaltney, John Langston.
The dissenters.
1. Dissenters—United States—Biography.
2. United States—Social conditions—1945-
3. Oral history.   1. Title.
HN65.G89   1986   303.4'84   85-28113
ISBN 0-394-52725-9

Manufactured in the United States of America
Typography and binding design by J. K. Lambert
2 4 6 8 9 7 5 3
First Edition

If a man does not keep pace with his companions, perhaps it is because he hears a different drummer. Let him step to the music he hears, however measured or far away.

HENRY DAVID THOREAU

ACKNOWLEDGMENTS

*Who paid for my freedom and what the price and
am I somehow beholden?*

CARL SANDBURG

The heart and soul of personal and national liberty is freedom of thought. The pursuit of this indispensable ingredient is an imperative good habit which a phalanx of winter soldiers of conscience from Anne Hutchinson to Muhammad Ali have passed on, often battered but unbroken, to the American people. Many in that company, living and dead, have passed that habit on to me. I am profoundly indebted to a staggering profusion of ageless sages, but am even more beholden to those who sustained my body and opened my mind to the often troublesome necessity of respect for other people's opinions. People like my mother, whose life and parables taught me that justice is the ultimate mercy; people like my sailor father with his vivid tales of Nagasaki, Marseilles, and Veracruz; people like Margaret Mead, whose School of the Air radio broadcasts taught me, long before I left my parochial corner of the world, that differences were fascinating, nonthreatening elements of humanity; all inclined me toward the life of the mind.

This journey among American principled dissenters was materially assisted by a fellowship from the National Endowment for the Humanities and a Senate Research Committee Grant-In-Aid sabbatical leave from Syracuse University. The support of Vice Chancellor John J. Prucha and Dr. Robert G. Hill, Vice President for Program Development of Syracuse University, was particularly instrumental.

Professor Morton H. Fried of Columbia University, Dr. Mary L. McDonald of the Indian and Northern Affairs Branch of the Canadian Government and Dr. Bernice Johnson Reagon, Director of the Program in Black American Culture at the Smithsonian Institution, have been gracious supporters of this research since its inception.

A number of other people assisted this inquiry in many important ways. Special thanks are extended to Mss. Gail Arsenault, Nancy Bartow, Polly Hovemeyer, Dora López, Naomi Millender, Janet Pennissi, Evelyn Rodriguez, Josefina Rodriguez, Thérèse Rossignol, Peggy Sabatier; Messrs. Scott Cunningham, Bob Hughes, Eddie Negrón, Fulton Oursler, Jr., Ben Thacher, James Yohannan, Peter Zicari; Professors James Bartow, José

López, Joan Nicklin; Attorney John M. McEachern and Reverend Frank Haig.

It would be impossible to overestimate the contributions of my wife, Judy, to the forging of this project and volume. In addition to all the typing, she also did much of the drudgery of tape transcription. A sagacious and probing interviewer with a genius for rapport, her editing and research skills are manifest throughout the entire work. For her general discernment, intrepidity, and aplomb in a very serendipitous field of endeavor, I am profoundly grateful.

Needless to say, I acknowledge a surpassing debt to the contributors, whose tolerance, courage, equanimity, and candor made this anthology of principled dissent possible.

Contents

"We are not terrorists. We are captured combatants in a decolonization war."

"I believe there's a moral law in the universe, and if there's a
state law that significantly denies that moral law, then I have to
choose the moral law."

"We don't need any laws, we don't need any constitution, we
don't need the Declaration of Independence. All we need to do
is treat people with respect."

"Unburdened by the torments of the time—I reach for a happy
heart, and pray."

"I don't think most people feel that they can question the Henry
Kissingers of the world."

"The blood of a Palestinian child and the blood of a Jewish
child are equally precious."

"Save Our Sisters!"

"An indecisive person is not a reliable person."

"Going along with the medical profession does not necessarily
mean you are in good hands because drugs can have lethal side
effects!"

"With a high level of honesty, there's a better chance of people
being able to face up to each other and their differences."

INTRODUCTION

*We have not really budged a step until we take up
residence in someone else's point of view.*

JOHN ERSKINE

I worry a good deal about the soundness of the national mind and heart.
Even if I were not an anthropologist by profession, the degree of genuine
tolerance in the national marketplace of ideas would be a matter of prime
importance to me.

I was born into a large extended black American family with a well-
earned reputation as spirited defenders of unpopular or outmoded positions.
My grandfather remained serene and unswerving in his devotion to his
huge, patient workhorses long after the motorcar, that piece of technical
impudence, had demonstrated that it was here to stay. That devotion was
infinitely more than quirky eccentricity. It was the practical imperative of
his belief that reward should follow faithful service. His fidelity to those
deserving beasts was a duty that he felt bound to fulfill, often at considerable cost to his own living standard and domestic peace.

One of my shadowy but oft-mentioned antebellum cousins is said to have
burned down a polling place on the premise that if *she* couldn't vote, no
one should. The politically inspired arson of that violent ancestress was
seen as a wholly justifiable act of patriotism. The worthy seniors who
acquainted me with her exploits were plainly aware that Euro-American
authority regarded her protest as an indefensible act of terrorism. Heroism
such as hers is a part of the unwritten constitutions of successful resistance
to discrimination that inspire and guide most black American families
through the wilderness of caste. In many a house on many a street in many
a black American town, pieces of the master's silver, a nightstick wrested
from an agent of repression, the cherished memory of some act of righteous
defiance are esteemed relics of resistance. The hushed tone with which
these trophies and memories are explained and recalled reflects more than
patriotism and reverence. That lowering of the voice also says, "Be careful,
child, there is still the very real probability of grievous hurt, harm and
danger in the knowledge you have just acquired."

One of the best friends I have ever had lived in a large, clean packing
case, espoused his own very personal religion and maintained the goodwill
and respect of most of his black neighbors. His alienation, profound though

it was, never carried him beyond core cultural limits of communal loyalty, civility and personal cleanliness.

For the whole of its historical life, the black American nation has been institution-poor. It had to make one large institution, the theology, serve many purposes. The relative scarcity of mass institutions has meant a necessary expansion of the importance of the dealing individual among black people. The dealing individual is expected to stand firmly upon the ground of precedence and personal experience.

The black towns in which I grew up were lush and varied gardens of diverse opinion. My first barber-shop haircut was enlivened by animated but civil discussion ranging from the advocacy of the religion of the Black Jews to vegetarianism. The barber, as staunch a member of the African Methodist Episcopal Church as could be found, and a man who had raised the noble art of barbecueing to new heights, insisted that the purveyors of strange doctrines be given a decent hearing. It is a rare black community that is not home to at least one woman who is nicknamed Sis Pluck because she *will* speak her mind. Life for the people of these black towns is immeasurably richer and more satisfying despite the troubles they endure because of this tolerance and courage. The well-being of the entire country is no less dependent upon them.

The courage to maintain unpopular views is a vital resource in any society striving for plural democracy. Principled dissent, though a troublesome treasure, is the most vital of social fluids. Without it the free marketplace of opinions is an arid sham. Standing up and out for unpopular causes divides families, strains friendships, threatens jobs and even menaces lives. Nevertheless, a decent respect for difference of opinion is crucial for any society that really means to avoid the deadly extremes of total anarchy and the tyranny of the majority.

Principled dissent is a subject that has never really been far from my thoughts for all of my conscious life. Long before I read that Senator J. William Fulbright had characterized the American people as "ill at ease with dissent," I knew that difference was regarded by many people as bad in and of itself. I remember from elementary school days an Italian-American youngster who was generally ostracized and occasionally pummeled primarily because he liked poetry. I remember an Anglo-American girl who was equally suspect because of her "excessive" interest in literature and foreign countries. My attempt to relate civilly to both of these youngsters caused them such acute embarrassment among their peers that we were all sorry it was ever made.

Once on a hot early autumn afternoon as the school bus was parked at an elementary school, something happened that has given me pause for thought ever since. The driver had gone into the school to consult with a janitor and I was the last passenger left on the bus. A sizable group of little white children took it into their heads to be mildly menacing toward me. As I had attained the magnificent age of seventeen and was twice their size, I was not afraid of them, but I did not want them to board the bus, so I attempted to close the door. Just then a very small white girl sprang onto the high step of the bus and placed herself between me and the other children. She delivered a short condemnation of the deportment of her schoolmates and then said to me, "*I'll* help you, mister." The fact that I was eventually obliged to protect my diminutive protectress has little to do with the case. I remember that little girl, whose name I never knew, because she had learned a degree of valor and tolerance which many adults never develop. As the pint-sized mob lost interest and wandered away, I asked myself why that little girl was different.

I have encountered many examples of courage and tolerance since then. Now, forty years after that event, I have been able to conduct research which permitted me to ask a variety of wave-makers and boat-rockers how they got that way. I traveled as far as my finite resources would permit and listened to people who have risked the ill opinion of friends, neighbors, and officialdom to do what they think is right. I followed media, correspondence and word-of-mouth leads to people known to stand on their rights and follow their consciences. With a tape recorder, a braillewriter and a pair of attentive ears I recorded these dissenters' stories in their own words. I have never believed that the world is unbridgeably divided between people to whom things happen and people who know the meaning of what happens. There is far more truth and poetry in ordinary speech than is commonly imagined, and the best judge of the meaning of a life is very often the person who is living it. Most people are their own best storytellers and reporters.

The opportunity to talk to all kinds of Americans about principled dissent was a sobering challenge. Oral history, like everything else, is the art of the possible. I have worked primarily among my own people or among other nonwhite groups. Could I talk civilly but candidly with white Americans of widely differing ethnic backgrounds about very important personal things? The principled dissenters I talked to, of all races and ethnicities, extended to me the same degree of courtesy I gave them. The people I listened to and talked with admitted me to their homes and shared their confidences and genuine hospitality. Fortunately for the national good, there is a strong current of willingness to challenge authority on principle. Following that strong, complex stream of diverse opinion has led me from a prison in Illinois to a convent in New Hampshire.

This journey among dissenters has obliged me to look to the state of my own respect for the various opinions of humanity. Listening, and the very occasional appropriate questioning, are the heart and soul of the oral historian's art. The truly neutral human observer has not yet been born, and I am keenly aware of the strength of my own convictions and antagonisms. I am not in agreement with every dissenter I listened to, but I believe that all these dissenters are principled in that their sincere beliefs have prompted them to radical advocacy and action.

The personal narratives comprising this work represent a microcosm of national diversity. The narrators range in age from their twenties to their sixties, and a wide variety of occupations are represented. There are, among others, civil servants, clergymen, professors, a bus driver, a radio broadcaster, a union official, a soccer coach, a bookkeeper, an engineer, and a number of people who for a variety of reasons are unemployed, but who are by no means uninvolved. The national ethnic and religious mosaic is made manifest by the contributions of an American-born black Buddhist, a Japanese-American Episcopalian, a German-born, naturalized American Quaker, a convinced Catholic Native American, a Muslim, and a general assortment of Catholics, Protestants, Jews and atheists.

The people who speak for themselves through these pages are politically very diverse. They have advocated and acted from radical positions ranging from what would be seen generally as conservative to liberal and even socialist political perspectives. Some, like Sisters Catherine and Justine Colliton and Bill Ansley, were born into families with deep commitment to a labor union orientation and to the dissent implied by solidarity. Others had the distinction of their respective advocacies and actions thrust upon them by crucial experiences in their lives, such as war, blatant injustice, or some painful incident that brought home to them the lamentable gap between how things are and how they are generally said to be. Pat Muñiz' Republican stance is her intrepid attempt to find an alternative to entrenched Democratic Party monopoly in her neighborhood. Both Maude DeVictor and Charlie Sabatier exemplify, along with many others, Mrs. DeVictor's contention that "Revolutionaries are made, not born."

The women and men I have listened to have one thing in common. They have all been willing to suffer the consequences necessarily attendant upon taking unpopular stands. I tried to remember their suffering and the strength of their sincere commitment as I listened. The pain and distinction of their advocacies were very often unsought. Maude DeVictor, the black civil servant who discovered the causal connection between Agent Orange and cancer susceptibility, could have remained silent and spared herself the studied harassment of one of the largest bureaucracies on earth. Elizabeth Barrett demands an accounting and compensation from the United States Army for the death of her father, who was a victim of a "chemical warfare" experiment. She is still a firm adherent of the American doctrine that persistence and hard work are ultimately rewarded, and her life is now largely devoted to a quest for the whole truth.

The hunger for accountability touches ecclesiastical authority also. The four Sisters of Mercy who sued their bishop for an explanatory hearing after being summarily dismissed from their jobs are sadder but wiser for their standing upon their rights and are in no way sorry that they demanded justice. Vietnam veteran Charlie Sabatier was just sitting in his wheelchair aboard a Delta Airlines jet when a stewardess and a pilot tried to make him sit on a blanket. His refusal to comply with a policy he deemed needless as well as demeaning got him arrested. The American people, living up to their best impulses, granted Charlie and other disabled people freedom from discrimination on paper, but it is the willingness to dissent that secures the actual benefits of those good impulses. The price of personal and national liberty is still eternal vigilance.

There is a strong desire in the American character for happy endings and ultimate resolutions; but in real life, virtue is all too often its only reward. When spunky Gloria Arsenault drove her school bus to the police station because she was unable to put a stop to pot smoking on it, the national wire services picked up the story and she was lionized, but when another school bus driver did essentially the same thing only a hundred miles away, she was reassigned to a lower-paying job!

Many of the issues still generating principled dissent in this country are recurrent. The Reverend James Robinson and I were thinking about this when we met at my house to talk about the decision of his church to grant sanctuary to a number of refugees from Central America. We were briefly interrupted that afternoon by a phone call from a friend of mine, the ninety-three-year-old daughter of a slave. Hundreds of years ago some of her ancestors, or mine, might have posed the same dilemma to that same New England white congregation that Central American refugees now pose. The right of freedom of association figured very largely in the principled dissent of young Irish-American Tim Manley. Instrumental in the founding of a Black Culture Club at his predominantly white college, in the face of considerable white opposition, he became the only white member of that campus organization.

Questioning authority is a sign of social health, and conscience is prompting all kinds of Americans to demand that all kinds of authority be accountable. It is the more than occasional dream of all authority to be beyond accountability, just as those who are subject to authority fantasy about a life beyond restraints. When I was a very young child, I told my mother that I would be very glad when I was old enough to cut the ham. Sensing that it was greed which prompted my desire for adulthood, she said, "Don't you know being old enough to cut the ham means being old enough to take less than your share?" Another very wise black elder told me that the power to do one thing is never the power to do all things, and that if anyone can oblige you to use your power, then you are not powerful enough. Authority, as practically vested in real human beings, is basically ambivalent about limitations imposed upon it. Authority, like Cupid, likes no law but its own. Absolute power is a corrupting illusion cherished by all but the wisest of us. Many of the instances of principled dissent recorded here would not have occurred if authority on many levels had been mindful of its limitations. The Sisters of Mercy who sued their bishop originally sought only an explanatory hearing. The Delta Airlines captain who insisted that Charlie Sabatier sit on a blanket cost his company avoidable negative publicity and an out-of-court settlement. Both Ms. Barrett and the Reverend Yasutake are frustrated but undissuaded by the consistent attempts of agencies of their own government to evade the clear intent of the Freedom of Information Act.

The contempt of the powerful is sometimes a spur to principled dissenting. The rhetorical question "Who do they think they are?" comes hotly to the lips of those who provoke and those who wage the often very personal war of principled dissent. Professor Thorburn was stung irrevocably out of her attempt to reconcile traditional medicine and dietary therapy by the contempt of a prestigious gynecologist. The Sisters of Mercy were hurt and angered to hear that they had been airily dismissed as "big fat zeroes" by elements in the clerical bureaucracy that had commanded their years of faithful and meritorious service. The knowledge that they are being dismissed as worms is often quite enough to turn people into principled dissenters. The simple visceral insistence that authority explain its arbitrariness has probably generated more principled dissent than the insistence upon redress. Hubris, that rash, overweening arrogance of office, is the source of an incalculable but substantial amount of standing up and out. "Who do they think they are?" often precipitates the response "I'll show them!"

Certain preoccupations and themes have surfaced over and over during the course of my listening. The momentous themes of war are much upon the national mind. The fears, guilt, resentments, and birth defects generated by the Vietnam war are still destroying domestic tranquility. Beyond the tormenting legacy of that war, Armageddon scenarios loomed large in the thinking of the people who appear here. The goad of their Vietnam experiences drives Joe Bangert and Charlie Sabatier to social action which is in large measure restitution and Nurembergian penance. People like the Reverend Robinson and John Bangert are moved to active principled dissent by a strong sense of obligation to do what they can to prevent a fatal repetition in Central America of the Southeast Asian tragedy.

Strong forebodings about the ultimate nuclear disaster galvanized Sarah into active demonstration against the proliferation of lethal weaponry. The same dread strengthened Margo Koch Ruthe's resolve in her campaign to acquaint young people of draft age with alternatives to military service.

War is the most immediate of Damoclean possibilities that prompt people to principled dissent. The toxification of the habitable globe through the excesses of a technology seen as fatally frivolous and vain is another powerful spur to direct principled action. This view of technology as a kind of rogue robot inundating the earth with diminished living and eventual death through chemistry has heightened the yearning for utopian alternatives. Andy Mager's more humane republic is small, free, and open. Professor Thorburn is receptive to accounts of lost continents and extraterrestrial philosopher kings and better living through spiritual alchemy. Ahmad El-Hindi is strengthened by his vision of a Pan-Arab United States of the Middle East. An ex-Roman Catholic, Irish-American asked a Wampanoag medicine man to officiate at his wedding, and Puerto Rican nationalist political prisoners draw sustaining solace from the vision of a more agrarian, purer Marxist motherland of the future.

All the principled dissenters I talked to entertain occasional doubts about their own ability to persist in their principled dissenting. These doubts do not generally extend to prolonged reservations about the rightness of their causes or the eventual triumph of those positions. Common to many of these principled dissenters is the idea that there is an operating necessary cosmic or historical agency working for the ultimate success of the ideas for which they are standing up and out. Maude DeVictor is armed in her struggle by her belief that she is a vehicle of the Buddhist cosmic law of cause and effect that pervades all life, retributively restoring harmonious balances throughout. Staunch Roman Catholic Alice Thompson believes quite literally in angelic intervention in some of her moments of extreme trial. For Margo Koch Ruthe, great nature itself is a vindicating, retributive force. Injustice for her is essentially antinatural. Injustice, like murder, will out. She likes to illustrate this conviction by alluding to the Goethe poem "The Cranes," in which those birds are the only witnesses to a murder which they expose. The bumper sticker on Bob Sampson's car tells the world that God is his copilot, and his conventional speech is punctuated with references to God as an honest, alternately severe and merciful judge.

It would be difficult to overestimate the importance of the media in determining the success of some principled dissenters. National circulation periodicals, television, and radio were all instrumental in disseminating the vital awareness of the dissenting of Maude DeVictor. Had it not been for the publicity accorded her whistle blowing, the Veterans Administration would have been free to move against her much earlier. Her firing came during a period of decline in media interest in her campaign to alert the world to the very present and future perils of dioxin poisoning. Many of the other principled dissenters I talked to have extensive press files in which the details of their activism are carefully preserved. Principled dissenters are frequent contributors to the often polemical to-ing and fro-ing that enlivens letters to the editor pages. The favorable attention of the local press certainly facilitates the efforts of law professor Richard Schwartz and engineer Ahmad El-Hindi to strive for rapprochement between Arabs and Israelis. Bob Sampson keenly feels the lack of press interest in his campaign to expose what he regards as the arrogant, summary, and extralegal bureaucratic treatment of his hearing to protest his firing from the Massachusetts Probation Department. One of the prime considerations in the general willingness of principled dissenters to face my tape recorder was the expectation that their positions would receive greater publicity if they were aired in this book.

I was not permitted to tape-record the four Puerto Rican nationalist prisoners I interviewed at the Dwight correctional facility in Illinois. Since the arbitrariness of authority makes it impossible to represent the principled dissenting of these young women as other participants in this inquiry are represented, I must present their views as deduced from their letters and published writing, my braille notes, and conversations with them and their kin and friends.

It is plain that principled dissent ranges from generally pardonable oddity to strongly abominated behavior. No one who participated in this project saw this arc of principled dissent exactly as any other contributor. Contrary to conventional wisdom, there is nothing which "everybody" knows is right or which "everybody" agrees is wrong. A principled dissenter who is reluctantly prepared to permit the American Nazi Party to march in Skokie cannot countenance a similar demonstration by nudists. Another is quite unperturbed by the advocacy of incest, but irrevocably opposed to the public espousal of violence as a means toward any end. Nevertheless, he is convinced that violent advocacies of all kinds should be violently suppressed by the established law. The very same person also feels that the established law is a source of arbitrary, partisan excess that must be guarded against.

Some varieties of principled dissent are relatively easily tolerated or even generally praised. When senior citizen Simon Geller takes on powerful commercial interests and the Federal Communications Commission for the right to his own eccentric classical music programming, he becomes the center of what almost amounts to a cult of admirers and well-wishers.

Popular opinion, however, as I experienced it, was most hostile to the dissenting of the four Puerto Rican nationalists. In my opinion, it is precisely because of the unpopularity and general lack of understanding of their positions that they should be heard.

No one I spoke with, whether in passing or at length, denied the existence of principled dissent, but beyond the general recognition of a kind of altruistic commitment, precise definition was extremely elusive. Morton Fried compared it to the sun's corona, implying that we could only come to terms with something less than the pure concept itself. Charlie Sabatier thought that arriving at a definition would be as difficult as isolating a single atom. Everyone made a clear distinction between doing the right and honorable thing for reasons of conscience and charlatanism, the imp of the perverse, and doing well by doing good. It was generally agreed that principled dissent implies suffering of significant degree. "Reasonable courage," "giving right the glory," and "being a fool in the eyes of the foolish" are but a few of the many definitions I heard during the course of this inquiry. Some people do seem to be more affected than others by what can only be seen as a moral imperative, an altruistic drive, the simple inability to turn their backs on what they perceive to be wrong or unjust.

Principled dissenters tend to belong to circles of kinship and friendship and advocacy centering in part on the issues they advance. Maude "Mother of Agent Orange" DeVictor and Joe "Dioxin" Bangert had been drawn together by the amity of common interest before I met either of them. Margo Koch Ruthe's daughter Eva and Al Davidoff both published in the same United Auto Workers' magazine. Most dissenters had numerous suggestions about others they thought would make valuable contributions to an oral history anthology of principled dissent. Professor Schwartz facilitated my meeting with Mr. El-Hindi. John Bangert suggested that I speak with his brother Joe. I met the Reverend Yasutake through my interest in the Puerto Rican Prisoners of War.

The narratives and ideas presented here are intended to afford an impression of principled dissent in this country. There is an element of the fortuitous in the discovery of some of these contributors. Serious exchanges emerged from casually initiated civilities with Jefferson City, Missouri taxi drivers, Chicago waitresses, and Atlanta art-gallery owners. Conversations ranging from minutes to hours with scores of people refined and expanded my insight into the myriad variations upon the theme of principled dissent. A truly infinite variety of changes is being rung upon the theme, and diverse as this collection of advocacy and action is, it might have displayed an even wider spectrum of divergent commitments. No single anthology of principled dissent can be comprehensive. Some readers may not see some contributors as principled dissenters. Others may feel that no collection of this kind can possibly be complete without reference to this or that issue representing their own personal preferences and priorities. There are many people who might have contributed worthy narratives to this collection who are not represented in it. My daughter Karen's loss of employment several years ago because of her opposition to the lie detector test as a condition of employment might very well have been the exemplar here of a very important current issue in principled dissent. A staggering assortment of T-shirts, buttons, banners, and bumper stickers proclaim the insistence of numberless dissenters upon their rights of advocacy. Right-to-lifers, free-choicers, animal liberationists, single taxers, zealous defenders of the reputations of historical personages long past caring—are all maintaining with tenacity their different views. In my opinion, this counterpoint of conflicting causes does not add up to cacophony. There is a kind of indispensable harmonious noise generated by a society struggling toward plural democratic life. In a life and profession very largely devoted to the consideration of different perspectives, I have yet to encounter any position so bizarre as to rule out at least a respectful hearing. The final complement of this book is the consequence of a number of circumstances. I was, of course, influenced by my own beliefs and interests, and the workings of chance favored some interviews and ruled out others. The absence of the views of the Ku Klux Klansman who says he lost his job because of his beliefs is occasioned by the infeasibility of an interview, not by any personal judgment that his ideas are unutterable.

The spontaneous discourse I recorded is the expression of deep thinking in every instance. Most principled dissenters have thought long and hard about their standing up and out and tend to draw their exemplars from personally analogous sources. Law professor Richard Schwartz mentioned jurist Oliver Wendell Holmes as worthy of emulation. China scholar and anthropologist Morton Fried chose ancient Chinese scholar and historian Ssu-ma Chien as a dissenting hero. Sarah picked Jane Fonda, a woman of similar class background and protest orientation, as her exemplar. Al Davidoff, a union leader, chose William Winpisinger, veteran labor leader. In addition to particular choices that varied from Olympia Brown, the first female Unitarian minister, to Elder Nathaniel Turner, who led the Southampton, Virginia, black revolution of 1831, Mohandas Gandhi and Martin Luther King, Jr., headed all the lists of principled dissenters.

In assessing the reasons why they were inclined toward principled dissenting, many mentioned a variety of significant triggering incidents. These incidents occurred very often in childhood or early youth and are almost always some very personal permutation of the general theme of the tyranny of the majority. Margaret Avery traces the origin of her concern with principled dissent to an act of childish unkindness for which she still feels great shame. Very often, principled dissenters perceive their positive activism as a kind of equal and opposite compensatory reaction to some early participation in or tolerance of unfairness or acquiescence to unreasonable authority. Grady Cassidy's thinking about principled dissent is strongly influenced by his awareness of his own youthful unfairness in love and war. Decades after the event, a principled dissenter still remembers with fresh chagrin his inability to break a kindergarten teacher's edict of absolute silence to say that he had to go to the bathroom, even when it meant soiling his clothing. The beating of some minority classmate, the shunning of some girl thought to be too popular with the boys, the pretended acceptance of detested ideas and attitudes, seem to incline principled dissenters to a very strong "never again" position. Never again to be found wanting in the courage to follow the truth wherever it seems to lead, never again to bend before prevailing opinion, never again to countenance injustice in concerns dear to them.

Oral styles vary in mighty degree. They reflect the life and work of the contributors. Some are natural raconteurs, easy in the grammar of the spoken word; modern rhapsodes, with folk-inspired powers of evocation. Such people have the ability to so lose themselves in their storytelling that their narratives flow quite naturally from affecting rapture to moving pathos and back again. Others warm slowly to the use of the spoken word, immersing themselves gingerly in its currents, acquiring competence as they acquire confidence in the interview context. Professors, lawyers, and other people whose livelihood involves the constant reliance upon the conventions of the standard written form tend to approximate more closely the grammar of the written idiom. By those standards the oral discourse of such people appears more polished than the speech of people less bound by formal speaking and writing.

A consistent striving for candor was common to all of these narrative donors. Contributors literally took pains to render a true account of their principled dissenting, not only during the hours of initial taping but in their review of their respective narrative manuscripts, which they minutely examined for weeks or sometimes months. Contributors resisted the impulse for unbridled self-serving and pointed out balance-restoring personal weaknesses and errors. Everyone who participated in this inquiry wished to do so. None availed themselves of the opportunity to withdraw at any point and all were extremely helpful in facilitating the work. This assistance went far beyond the minimal courtesies and materially improved the quality of the interview context. We met informally in my office, more often in my home or the homes of contributors. Sometimes we met in mutually agreed upon intermediate places such as hotels, motor inns, or restaurants. A high standard of hospitality was an essential element in establishing rapport. Good food was almost invariably a prime element in that relaxed, confidence-inspiring social environment that fosters good talk. Charlie Sabatier's heroic sandwiches and worthy beer, Gloria Arsenault's tangy meatballs and good coffee, Margo Koch Ruthe's tofu and lemon squares, Bob and Betty Anderson's potato salad and Serrano ham, the ham and chicken salad sandwiches and noble cake of the four Sisters of Mercy, Morton Fried's diced creamed ham and mighty millet liqueur, and my wife's creamy, chunky fish stew—all indicated a degree of civility beyond the perfunctory. Getting beyond the mechanical civilities is an absolute imperative of profound exchange. The time and hospitality Bob Sampson and I shared at the Howard Johnson Motor Inn was vital to our subsequent estimation of each other. The Reverend Michael Yasutake and I got to know each other at a long leisurely hotel breakfast. A Third World buffet, a Puerto Rican Nationalist Presbyterian church supper, and a Hyatt Regency champagne brunch made listening and talking infinitely more amiable and empathetic mutual experiences.

The assistance and general cooperation of contributors extended to the vital area of documentation also. Many had neat xeroxed packets of the most relevant correspondence and newspaper and magazine articles pertaining to their instances of principled dissent. Sister Catherine lent me her extensive file. Gloria Arsenault produced a huge cardboard box crammed with letters and clippings, as did Margo Koch Ruthe. The Reverend Robinson sent excerpts of local press coverage of his congregation's Central American Sanctuary Program. Simon Geller directed my attention to the relevant issues of *Broadcasting Magazine*.

Most contributors were emphatic in their preference to appear in this anthology under their own names. In the very few instances where donors are anonymous, that option was invariably chosen out of regard for the feelings of colleagues, near kin, or dear friends. After long deliberation, Bob and Betty Anderson chose anonymity essentially out of consideration for the feelings of her parents.

Once conditions of amity, security, and trust are established, the narratives flow quite naturally with a minimum of formal questioning. The general aim of talking and listening is to ascertain a description of the respective examples of principled dissent and to gain some insight into the lives of the dissenters. A second prime goal of these conversations was to acquire insight into the perceptions, definitions, and range of principled dissent.

To test for the limits of permissible advocacy and action, I often solicited the reactions of the contributors to four examples of extremely unpopular dissenting. In one example frequently alluded to, I briefly detailed the trials and general ostracism suffered by a person who insisted upon the advocacy of the premise that incest should be a prime means in the sexual education and socialization of children. In a second example of controversial dissenting, I cited the case of a member of the Ku Klux Klan who maintained that he had lost his job because of his advocacy of the beliefs of that organization. A third example was the action and advocacy of Puerto Rican Nationalists who will not forswear the use of armed force to secure independence for Puerto Rico. A fourth frequently discussed example centered on the right of the American Nazi Party to conduct a street demonstration in the Chicago suburb of Skokie, which has a large Jewish population. These examples triggered much valuable discussion about the frontiers of the free marketplace of ideas. They were the issues most frequently raised to get beyond the rhetorical question "It's a free country isn't it?" In mythic theory, according to the impossible, ideal, democratic dream, Americans are free to act and advocate as they please. These four instances of very unpopular dissenting were often catalytic in that they facilitated personal, practical thinking about personal practical limits of permissibility. We also considered literally scores of other generative issues and questions. The notions of Flat Earthers, the League Against Animal Nudity and the ideas of Goethe, Nichiren, Dickens, Luther, Humboldt, Ibn-Khaldūn, and Fats Waller kept our exchange fluid and fruitful.

This inquiry has carried me from a consideration of principled dissent in my own particular core-black ethnic corner of this nation of ethnic nations to a general consideration of principled dissent drawn from many other national ethnic corners of our common country. I have found beleaguered but perennial traditions of principled dissent everywhere I have been privileged to look. Senator Fulbright's characterization of the American people as ill at ease with dissent is certainly valid, but this is a generalization which is well founded in any nation. Principled dissent never flourishes for long anywhere. Its indispensable merit is not in occasional hundred-flower bloomings but in its persistence, which is more like the tenacity of grass in urban places whose will is to grow.

The principled dissenters who attract media attention are a very small part of the vast number of people who choose decency over expedience in daily life. The millennium is probably just as far off as ever, but there is a vast reservoir of conscientiousness that makes American life more than mere survival. Wherever I have gone in this land I have seen unprovoked malice, but I have not known a corner of it which is not also brightened by men and women honestly trying to do the right and honorable thing as they see it. There is an astounding range and variety in this striving. Much of it is anonymous. The Swedish-American waitress who gave me a sotto voce warning against the beef stew risked her job for a stranger. The two quiet grandmothers who sat in my living room and told me of their fear and anguish at the prospect of an ultimate nuclear holocaust have suffered the indignities of picketing and arrest to impress upon the consciousness of their fellow citizens the imminent danger of the arms race.

The quality of our national existence has been enriched by a legion of rebels for a profusion of unpopular causes. These nameless demonstrators have been willing to endure contempt, confinement, and even death to warn us against every peril from atomic proliferation to cruelty to animals. There are a number of regions on our globe where difference of opinion is the primary cause of death. Boat-rockers are a threatened species everywhere, but the insistence of all kinds of Americans on following the truth wherever it leads them is still instrumental in guarding the democratic way of life. At the very core of our very best nature, the American people have always known that we owe a debt past reckoning to friends, relatives, and fellow citizens who make us think beyond our comfortable orthodoxies.

Following the high rocky road of free thought is an experience beyond price. A host of the illustrious and the obscure have marched along it in every age. It leads from Harpers Ferry and the sublime heroism of Captain John Brown to Lower Manhattan's Union Square Park where once, within the brief space of a quarter hour, my attention was demanded by partisans of Palestinian nationhood, the Jewish Defense League, and legalized prostitution. While it is as true as ever that one person's advocacy is another's abomination, my odyssey among the wave-makers has reassured me that an often grudging, but durable sense of elemental fairness is still a significant aspect of American national character.

THE
DISSENTERS

Bob and Betty Anderson

"We've got a different set of circumstances, so that means that all the rules are changed."

□ □ □

How glorious it is—and also how painful—to be an exception.

ALFRED DE MUSSET

In a more reasonable society, Betty Anderson's severe physical disability would not be seen as the most important aspect of her character and personality. In a more perfect nation Bob Anderson's blackness would not sentence him to the severe social disability of racial discrimination. The decision of these sensitive, intelligent people to marry and have children would not have caused them additional gratuitous social harassment in a land where freedom's holy light gleamed less fitfully.

Because they are intelligent, sensitive people, they are not unmindful of the insensitivity and downright malice of some of their near kin and neighbors, but the Anderson home is no bastion of gloom and doom. Our conversation proceeded to the welcome accompaniment of freshly baked bialies, potato salad, prosciutto, tuna salad, artichoke hearts, milk, juice, beer, and wine. Angela and Carla, the Anderson children, provided a musical prelude for the good talking and eating. They are lively, curious, gifted girls of nine and seven who demonstrate, quite unconsciously, that the dire predictions of necessary tragedy for children whose parents are not color coordinated are by no means infallible. It will require a horrendous amount of social spite and malice to teach those girls to hate themselves. The society that means to make "tragic mulattoes" of them has got its dirty work cut out for it. The taped reflections of their parents were occasionally graced by the faint happy sound of singing from the children's room as the youngsters reluctantly but respectfully prepared for bed.

The principled dissent of the Andersons consists in doing what should be considered the most natural of human cultural acts. Many people in their world have chosen to shun and stereotype them, but the wholesome ordi-

*nariness of the family Anderson in their extraordinary circumstances is
plainly manifest. Bob and Betty Anderson are not their real names; their
anonymity proceeds from regard for the feelings of their near kin.*

———

BETTY I think we are very unhappy with any kind of dissent in this
country. I think the sixties were clear on that. Anyone who sort of had a
different way of looking at something was classified by the powers that be
as, well, crazy, I guess. Really totally aberrant in terms of their idea of
what things should be. And even now when you see some of the things that
Reagan has done, the whole idea of dissent at this point is that people are
afraid in some ways, I think, to say, "I can't live with this." There's a
whole feeling that if I say something against the rule at this point, somehow
we're gonna be looked upon as not quite on the track. But as for advocating
incest, I don't understand why someone would want to advocate it. You
could really turn that incest thing around, you know. You really could. I
mean, there are people who have said to us, who said to me before we got
married, "It's very nice that you want to get married, but why don't you
wait until you're past the child-bearing stage? How are you going to do that
to your kids? You can't take care of them, physically, in the way that someone else can. Are you going to give them the kind of experience that they
should get? Are you going to be able to hold them? How are you gonna do
all the things that need to be done, since you can't do it?" Now there may
be some people who say that the fact that I have two children is a crime in
the same way that incest is a crime because they feel that I would be hurting
my children, they wouldn't have a good experience. Now I don't believe
that. I think that's a lot of hogwash. Angela went to a class, Operation
Explore they call it, a three-day trip with her class, and a woman came
over to me and said, "I'm anxious because my daughter's going away for
three days and she's never been away." And then she says to me, "Your
girls really help you a lot at home don't they?" and I said "Yeah, they do,
they are really good kids." She says to me, "It's so wonderful that Angela's
going away—she'll get a rest." I mean, I felt like I was Simon Legree! And
here was my daughter, who works in the coal mines all day, who is going
on a three-day trip to get away! There's an expectation that our kids are
gonna get an experience that not only is lacking, but is painful to them,
and that somehow it's criminal that I could do that to them. I think that
there are people who really think that way. And that's happened to me on
numerous occasions. You know, I can remember carrying Angela in a
pack on my chest when she was about a month and a half old and we got
out to the store and shopping and, you know, the baby was crying, babies
do cry. But because *my* baby was crying a woman passed me in the street
and turned to her friend and said, "Oh look at that! Isn't that disgusting.
How could that woman do that to that baby?" Well, I went home and
cried for like three days, and I told Bob, "You carry the baby from now on,
I will never carry her again." And he said, "You gotta be kidding! Are you
gonna listen to these idiots out on the street? You know what you're doing."
It bothered me so much, I think, because you get ingrained with certain

kinds of stereotypical ideas. Mothers are supposed to be X, Y, and Z, and fathers are supposed to be A, B, and C and somehow if you turn it around in some way, like we've done, where I work and Bob stays home, it's not quite right, and so instead of feeling comfortable with the decision that you make 'cause you know deep down inside that that's the right decision, you question it when someone else questions it. It makes you think, wait a minute, am I really? I mean, when this woman said that to me when Angie went on the trip, the first thing I thought was, wait a minute, am I really—? It gets to you at certain times. There's an expectation that a woman has a certain role. I can't fulfill the role that to some extent should be the traditional role of a woman. I can't clean my house, lift my babies and change their diapers, and do the things that they need done. The reality is that probably had I not had polio, I would do very much what I do now anyway, but the attitude is, what do you want to do this for? What are you doing to your children and don't you think it's going to be a very hard life for them and don't you think that they are going to have difficulty? Yeah, they are. But that's okay because we all have different difficulties that we deal with and that hopefully help us to be the people who we are. I'm not going to say better than we are, because I've heard that a lot too. You know, "When you come through the struggle you're gonna be so terrific." I don't want to hear that anymore! But it's that kind of attitude. Or they are amazed that I have children. Somebody will say, "Oh, how are your girls?" and the other person will say, "Oh, you have children? Oh, I didn't know that." Like somehow it's totally unexpected that I should have children. I think that anyone questions when you're ready to have children. You know, am I doing it quite the right way? I mean, that's a natural kind of response. But I think that when you have people like this person who said to me, "Why don't you wait till you're past the child-bearing age until you get married," she's someone I felt really knew me very well, and when she said that to me, it negated everything. I mean, at first I thought, wait a minute, this is crazy, am I crazy or what? And then I thought, she doesn't know me at all. When I told my mother I was pregnant for the second time, with Carla, the response was not one of joy, which I would certainly have if my children came to me and said that they were in a loving relationship and they were gonna have a child, it was one of "Oh my God! Are you crazy?" It's that sort of response.

BOB   I've been getting a different reaction lately from people and I'm not sure why I'm getting this reaction. But a lot of people that I know who were probably married around the same time Betty and I got married, which is eleven years ago, are not together anymore. And for some reason people think that it's wonderful that after eleven years we're still married. Now I'm not sure if that's only because of the fact that so many people are getting divorced, or if it's because Betty and I, with all these mountainous problems, are still married. I'm not sure, but I think that the point of view is that, Wow! You mean even with all your difficulties, even with some of the different things that you have to do, you're still married? These people, it almost sounds as if it's amazing to them. And I don't even know what to say when they say, are you still married? I go, what do you mean? am I still married? They don't really say, "Are you still married?" but it almost comes out to, "Are you and your wife still together?" And so it's amazing. I guess people thought, well, you know, they'll try and do it as long as they can, and if it gets to be too hard, the guy'll just say, "Hey, I can't do it anymore," he'll say, "I'm sorry, I gotta leave." So many of the people that I've come in contact with recently had this point of view but now a lot of them are divorced and separated. And it's like people, whenever there's someone who doesn't fit right into the same slot that everybody else fits into, you could almost feel people looking at you and say, you know, "They've got two kids, how the hell did they *do* that?" It's almost as if they look upon you as being so different that it's not possible.

BETTY You're being nice. The way they look at it is that somehow Bob is my quasi-attendant and we could never have a sexual relationship, so they can't imagine where those two kids came from. I mean, people have asked me, "Did you adopt your children?" Which is really bizarre. Because somehow they cannot imagine that I could have a sexual relationship. It's very hard because on the one hand you think, am I being paranoid? On the other hand, as a person, as a human being, you feel so negated, because it's like no one can look at your accomplishments or achievements in any real way. It's always, "It's so terrific because . . ." Not, "It's so terrific."

BOB We've got a different set of circumstances so that means that all the rules are changed. All the rules have changed because this person who's said to you about not having children or not even thinking about getting married until you were past child-bearing age, this is a person who would normally have said to a woman of your age, "Congratulations, you're getting married, you're having a child, very nice." But because Betty's in a motorized wheelchair, Betty had polio many years ago, well, this person suddenly decides, "Oh, this will be terribly difficult for her to have a baby." I didn't know that the woman had said that about Angela taking the trip, but what I would have said to her if she'd said it to me was "Yeah, you know, we even took off her ball and chain to let her go on this trip!" I mean, people have this point of view. Our children are helpful in a way that a lot of other children never try to be helpful because their parents don't need for them to be helpful or they feel that it's not necessary. But you have to teach them to be helpful and you have to teach them to do things they can do. Normally you would be teaching them this in any event, unless you might be too lazy to be bothered. They were probably worried that this poor woman in a wheelchair with a baby would have a child growing up who would not have a normal life, like everyone else, whatever that is, and the life is obviously going to be filled with sadness. People get to have such strange points of view. We've seen a lot of it in our eleven years, well, more than eleven, about seventeen years all together. But it's been all kinds of stuff. Ridiculous, some of it. You know what's amazing to me? The girls are in the gifted children's program at the public school here and they get to have some additional things that the others don't get to have, or to do, and people for some reason are amazed. They are *amazed* that our kids do so well. I don't know why. Coming from this background that is so filled with so much sadness, their perception is that it is *so* difficult and it must be *so* sad and there must be, I mean, they must think we have our own personal cloud that comes inside and hangs over the house every day. And after a while it just gets to be sickening.

BETTY   When we got married I think that my parents felt, particularly my father, although my mother was very supportive of my father, that you know, they had sort of taken care of me, was I now going to get into a relationship which might not last 'cause maybe Bob didn't know how difficult some of the physical aspects would be? I mean, I really can't feed myself, I've got to be dressed, I have to be washed, I have to be, you know, taken to the bathroom, that whole thing, and did he really know what he was getting into and would he eventually decide it was too difficult and leave me? So I think there was an aspect of genuine concern, but I think the overriding factor was that Bob was black. Without a doubt, that was the overriding factor. My father said to me, "How could you do this to me?" My mother told me I was going to kill my father by marrying Bob, that it would absolutely kill him. It would give him a heart attack, or he would take a gun and I would be the one who was pulling the trigger. I mean, that was the kind of feeling. This was actually said and we had planned to get married two years before we actually did. But we didn't because, I mean, I think otherwise we would have done it, but partially because my feeling was, how could I do this to my parents who had been so terrific to me? You know, they hadn't institutionalized me and they had taken care of me and was I gonna hurt them so much. I mean, they really laid a guilt trip on me and I accepted all of it. My Aunt Jane is Cuban and my Uncle, who is Italian, married her and when they first got married my grandparents didn't speak with them, okay? On the grounds of color. She was very dark-skinned and you didn't do that in those days, and my father came out of that whole background where you don't do that. If you said to me right now how does my father treat Bob, I'd tell you that my father treats Bob as well as and sometimes better than his own sons. He loves him tremendously, 'cause he's gotten to know him. I think the color issue certainly is still there, it's a question he has and maybe it's somewhat more based on reality that, you know, Bob could be hurt, or might not get as far, or we won't be able to buy a house in the suburbs. Who wants one anyway, but that's my father's dream. And that my children will have problems when they grow up because people won't accept them. Italians won't accept them and therefore whites won't accept them and black people won't accept them and so if you look at that in terms of where he's coming from now, I would say that he has some facts and he's used them maybe in a way that I don't really agree with. I think that when people get to know my children they will love them 'cause that's the kind of children they are, that's the kind of people they are.

My father is very closed, close to the chest. Very unable to really talk about his feelings. If he's angry he won't talk to you. That is a real cultural thing. Bob and I have been married, as Bob said, eleven years. After two and a half years my father talked to us again. Like he had never *not* talked to us. He met Bob in the supermarket with Angie and I was at work and he said to Bob, "Um, Betty's aunt is here." I mean after two and a half years! Not, "Hello, how are you, how's Betty?" but, "Betty's aunt is here from Canada, why don't you two come over at night?" I got home, Bob told me and I thought I would die, I mean, it was like absolutely unbelievable. I could not believe that this had happened. And we went to the house and there were tears and then it was, "Come over next week and we'll have dinner" like nothing had happened. They were a little cold to Bob and I was always on pins and needles that something was gonna happen that was gonna once again destroy this relationship, and I think Bob was too, but finally things were much better. It bothered me tremendously that it was a strained relationship, but it didn't bother me enough at that point. I knew what I wanted and I knew that Bob was what I wanted and I don't think anything could have made a difference in that. I mean, I was willing to say, look, if my parents never talk to me again, so be it. You know, this is what I want, I know what I want. It was very scary for me because it was a feeling of, who do I turn to if this doesn't work out? What happens? And I didn't know. But nobody knows anyway. There are other people who don't know, and they do it. They deal with it. But the interesting thing and the reason that I say that I don't understand, it's so unreal to me, is that after two and a half years, we began this relationship again and at this point Bob has really established a relationship which he didn't have at all when we were going together, or very little, and my father absolutely loves him. I mean, I cannot tell you the way that he treats him. He can talk to Bob better than he can talk to me! And yet, my sister fell in love with and married a Jamaican, who's also very dark-skinned, okay? And then my father wouldn't talk to my sister!

BOB   But he talked to me! I think that he feels that he's supposed to do exactly what he does and that is to sort of when you're angry just ignore everybody until it's over and when it's over then you can treat everybody the way that you treated them before, and that's pretty much the way he deals with me even now when he gets a little upset about something. We were talking recently about the fact that their reaction to our having Carla was so subdued, and that's his way of dealing with things he doesn't really want to talk about. It's as if he doesn't really hear them. And then a day or two later when you're talking about what's on sale at the supermarket he'll speak, and he catches you totally off guard because you're not ready for it then. That's his way of dealing with something difficult for him, and when he brings it up, you just got to be ready to talk about it.

BETTY   I think it has more to do with how they feel about themselves, or how my father feels about himself. It has more to do with how he perceives others will see him. The reality is that in my entire family, none of us have married Italians. I think this really relates to that. We grew up very early with people of different backgrounds, of different cultures and we really all got into that. Our friends were a potpourri of whatever and my parents always taught us from when we were very young that you play with everyone. You invite everyone, we can have anyone for dinner. I mean, many times we had friends, my father's friends from work who were black, over for dinner, or, I remember going to one of his friend's houses a long time ago, when I was maybe ten years old, and they were black and we had dinner with them and whatever, and he had Puerto Rican friends, Jewish friends, and we really believed in that. And I think one of the most hurting things was, in a lot of ways, we all feel it was a lie. It was like, you know, it's okay until it got to some kind of sexuality. But you see, somehow sexuality has a lot to do with that too. I mean, somehow the fact that you're married is very different than that you're having a baby. It's absolute craziness!

BOB   It's all in their minds, that's what it is. It's ridiculous. I was going to say before that probably the thing that's been most dominant in my life for a very, very long time has been the fact that I was always involved one way or another with some sort of religious experience. Part of it was that I felt that my father-in-law was probably having more difficulty than I was. Not just dealing with me and Betty, but he was probably having more of a difficulty in trying to deal with other members of his family. Like I said, the religious point of view came in because I always felt that all of us are in the same boat and that we're the same. That's the way that my parents raised me and that's what I believe. So, when it came time to make a stand for that point of view I was willing to say to my father-in-law, you didn't agree with me, you didn't feel the same way that I felt, but I think that we can come to some sort of an understanding, and I felt that he would be willing to do that. I felt it was a difficult position for him to be in. I didn't like what he was doing to me, I didn't enjoy it. I felt this was a person who was telling me that I didn't really exist the same as everyone else existed. It was an individual experience for me, but I think that as a group, black people have been experiencing this for a very long time. I never really felt it was him not liking me, I'd never really felt that way. I felt that if he didn't like me, that would be one thing, but I didn't think it was that. I just felt that there were these other pressures coming to bear on this man who had this family who had all these other relatives who were then going to say, "Hey, there must be something really wrong with your daughter if she has to go and get herself a second-class citizen to marry."

The thing is, you've sometimes gotta be willing to make your move based on the other person. It could be regarded as weakness, but it's all according to how you look at it. I feel that I got what I wanted for Betty and me and for our whole family based on the way that we dealt with the whole situation. Some people might feel that I gave in. Some people might feel that Betty's father gave in, but I don't really care about who gave in. Like they say, you can lose a battle but you don't lose a war. You don't look at who gave in to who and who didn't give in. The point is, what's the end result? And the end result has been very, very good for us. You know, my children have a very good relationship with their grandfather and are having a good experience with him and so we're very happy with it.

My parents would not, well, they were vocal about it, but they didn't come out and really say what they wanted to say. I mean, they sort of skipped around the point, but they felt that if we had children, who was going to stay home and take care of the children? And so we told them that we would work it out in the best way that we could. I would say it was sort of a strong thing. My parents are both from the South and so am I, and so I think maybe in the back of my mind I thought they might have some racial feeling about it, but I never really felt that it was that strong a feeling, the racial aspect of it. It was more on a practical level about what Betty could do and what Betty could not do in terms of being home with the children and taking care of them. And so it was difficult. It was just something you had to do and it's just that you have to make up your mind about what it is that you're going to get out of this whole relationship. Oh, I think it was the correct thing to do. I always felt it was the correct thing to do because Betty and I wanted to be married to each other; we weren't going to be married to the rest of the family. We were going to be married to each other and we felt all along that as long as we were serious and as long as we were committed to each other, then no matter how difficult it would be, we could always be together and there were not any problems that we couldn't overcome as a couple.

BETTY   I think that Bob's family had a lot of feelings that *they* weren't even sure about maybe, okay? And I'll give them the benefit of the doubt that somehow I was this white, rather well-educated woman who was first of all taking their son, brother, away from them, and Bob had a rather important place in his family in that his mother was not always there. His mother and father were separated and they relied upon him a lot. And I took him, I *took* him away from them in some way. But they were never honest with me in any way. I mean, I thought they were very warm and very accepting and they were very glad that we were getting married, and so forth, and until we got married I don't think either of us really had any indication of some of the feelings that they really had. They would make comments. We lived here and they lived on the other side of the city, and we said, you can come and visit us any time, but we would like you to call before you come. We decided together this was our home and we didn't want people to be just dropping in any time. Well they saw that as *my* rule. 'Cause I was from a different place, and the reality is that in some sense maybe that's true. They had a home where people always dropped in. Some people they didn't *want* to drop in just dropped in! You know, and I didn't want that. I don't want to have to watch the jewelry and the record player, you know? That kind of thing. And some of Bob's cousins were into drugs and that kind of stuff and I was concerned about that, as Bob was also, but they saw this as my sort of uppityness or whatever. This has become Bob's and my joke. They'll ask Bob a question and they'll say, "Well, we know you have to check with Betty but—." And we would say, "Well, you know, we'll discuss it and we'll let you know." And I think there were really a lot of feelings about it and about the fact that Bob was working very hard and somehow they see us as having lots of money, which we certainly don't, and somehow not giving to them because *I* don't want to.

Or that somehow our style of living when we got married was very different from the style they had, and it was more like that's what *I* wanted and somehow Bob sort of gave in.

BOB   I think that people will never ever get used to the idea of people from different cultures marrying. It's just something that's so different to many, many people, and it's ridiculous. When you first move into a neighborhood, no one knows what you represent, no one knows how you're going to keep your property, they don't know how clean you're going to be, they don't know anything about you. Then after they get used to you being around, they start to treat you like everyone else. And so it really doesn't matter.

BETTY   Well, I'm not so sure about that. I don't think that it has so much to do with people accepting you, as much as it has to do with you accepting people and therefore their attitude changes. I mean, my husband can walk down the block and say hello to fifty people within three minutes, sincerely, with warmth. It's a phenomenal kind of experience. It sometimes freaks me out because we're walking down the block and these thirty-five old ladies are saying hello, how are you, how're you doing, how's the kids.

I think, Bob, it's more than people just seeing you. I think you could be here and almost be invisible too, but you're not the kind of person who's gonna be invisible. I think that's probably what you did with my father too. He was saying, "I'm gonna treat you as invisible" and you were saying, "Damn! I'm not invisible, I'm a person and I'd like to have a relationship," and he finally responded to that. That's how you respond to people. You know, some of the very closed societies, the Hassidic Jewish community, who don't say hello to anybody but themselves, will get on the elevator and they'll say hello to Bob? I think, wait a minute, am I hearing this? I mean, it's true because he says, "Hello, how are you?" They'll ask him how his children are, you know, how's your wife? I think that's part of who Bob is. He reaches out and people reach back. Needless to say, I think he's terrific.

BOB   After eleven years I've convinced her, right? Eleven years of indoctrination! But you know, even still today my family see the way that we live, they see the way that we approach things as somehow meaning that we think of ourselves as being better than what they are. We don't feel ourselves as being better than anyone else. We simply have the standards we have for our family and feel that the things our children do are the things we want for our children and are important, and we want to do as much for our children as we can. We want to live our lives in a way that we feel is beneficial to them. If that doesn't go along with the way someone else wants to live, then that's not our problem. I mean, they have to come to some resolution about the way they want to live and not the way *we* want to live. We understand the way we want to live.

Bill Ansley

"The nature of what I'm dealing with forces you to get involved with the legal aspect and the terminology and familiarize yourself with the law, but when you get right down to it, there is right and there is wrong."

□ □ □

I want women to have their rights. . . . I know that it is hard for men to give up entirely. They must run in the old track. . . . When woman gets her rights man will be right.

SOJOURNER TRUTH

Names and places in this narrative have been altered because the issues that provoke the controversy are as yet unresolved. Large and likable, Bill Ansley is a quiet bachelor, "happily single," with the courage of convictions that are strange and new to the comfortable, established patriarchal hierarchy of his town and region. I first became fully aware of his persistent efforts to secure equity for young women in his high school's sports program when I was a guest lecturer in that institution.

Bill risks much by opposing an elite that has come to look upon influence as a kind of prerogative. It is plain that he loves the town and region he serves. He is an expert boatman who draws a great deal more than purely recreational dividends from sailing. My general impression of him as a tranquil, considerate, deeply committed person basically at home in his environment builds steadily. Nevertheless, I sense a kind of tenacity and intensity beneath his casual demeanor that is an indication of the importance he attaches to this or any other fight he determines to wage. He says that he will persist, and I believe it.

I guess each of us has our own concept of what we think is the right thing to do. The particular area in which I've been working is with public schools and athletics, and you have ways of dissenting. In fact, before I go any further, I might share a little story. When I first got out of college and was at least as naïve as your basic just-out-of-college person, I was tending bar here at night and substitute teaching during the day, hoping to get a full-time teaching job. This was the early seventies when teaching jobs weren't that easy to come by and I was working for a former teacher who had bought this old inn. Finally I was lucky enough to get a job teaching. A fellow quit at the end of September, got in a spat, resigned, and there I was, hired at first as a permanent substitute, but later it evolved into a regular full-time position. This fellow at the inn, who apparently thought a lot of me, said, "There's one thing I want you to watch out for when you start working in the schools. It's like they sneak up behind you with chloroform on the rag and they just put it over your mouth and nose and before you know it, you're just going along with the tide." And I've never forgotten that, and I tell you, the more I'm there, the more I see what he meant. He had taught in New York before he purchased the inn, so he was familiar with that. And there are all those wonderful reasons to not make waves. When you're young you think, well gee, these people have been doin' things for years, what do I know? Right? And then you're there a little bit longer and you say, well hmmmm, maybe I *do* know a little bit more than some of these people. And then, depending on your circumstances, you know, how many mouths you're trying to feed or whatever, you've got better reasons to maybe not speak up. I teach social studies, more particularly I have a class called Sociology, but it's really sort of misnamed in that it's more an Introduction to Social Sciences. We do anthropology, psychology, economics, political science; I teach ancient history and United States history. There's six of us in the department but two of us have made a habit of changing off every couple years just to stay refreshed.

I always played sports and I was interested in coaching at the school and I started off coaching boys and wound up coaching girls. In the seventies women's athletics had certainly taken off quite a bit and by the late seventies I was aware that women at the school were getting the short end of the stick. We have an old-school athletic director and coach of men's sports and he happened to have all sons for offspring, and he has his own very different view of things from somebody who grew up in my era. One of the sports he coaches is soccer and we have two soccer fields at the school. By most any measurable standard they're both very, very good fields, but one of them happens to be better than the other and it's better partly because of its size. It's a little bit bigger and he's on record as saying, "Well, the girls just can't kick the ball across there and I just can't believe, Bill, that you want to make an issue out of this." I said, "Well, believe it." I mean, it started very tactfully, I just said we'd like to share that field for practice, we'd like to share that field for games and so on. Our principal happens to be cut from the same cloth. The way the school is situated, you would first come out to where the girls play, and then you would walk past that to the boys. The principal walks right by the girls, doesn't even break stride, and goes out and watches the boys play. This happened a few times and it takes a little courage on the part of a staff member, but I finally go and speak to him and I say, "You know, there's a certain psychological effect on the girls when you walk right by them. They tend to feel like they're dirt." "Oh they never said anything to me," he says. I said, "I can believe that." So you know, Ansley goes back and he mentions this to the girls and says, "Maybe a few of you should say something to him." So they do and he's on my case. "What are you trying to do, turn these kids against me?" The most he ever did was come by at half-time of the boys' game and watch the girls play. He told me, "Well, I just don't find it as interesting." I said, "Well, I can accept that, but it seems to me, in your position, that's not the point." I maintain that he should try to see at least one of the field hockey games too. I don't care for field hockey, but I go over when there's an opportunity. If they're having a game and our practice ends or something, I go over and watch, 'cause I know the kids care that Mr. Ansley is there watching. To my thinking it's such a narrow view. It's an illness, it's a sickness. It's something that really does permeate the whole society. I mean, there's no question about it in my mind, but I think if that sort of thing is gonna change, it's gonna start changing in schools. So that's one example.

There are more subtle things. If we looked at the budget, as of course I have, the dollars seem equal, but when you try to find out where is the four hundred dollars spent on the girls' uniforms, you can't find those uniforms. So if I'm on the School Committee and I look at that, I say, "Oh we're in heaven here, everything's fine," but it doesn't always work out that way. The athletic director ultimately decides how that money is spent. And say it's four hundred dollars for each, and say that person decided, well, I'd really like to have this for the boys, who I happen to coach, and we need five hundred for their uniforms so maybe we've only got three hundred for the girls this year. And then the only place that would show up is on the individual vouchers, if somebody wants to go dig that out, and that hasn't happened. The system would suggest that somebody should check to see that the money is spent there, but in fact, until somebody like me makes waves, nobody's gonna check. And so it rolls on and on and on.

I consider myself to be a relatively reasonable person so I tried talking about these things with the athletic director. I did my little time for Uncle Sam in the military so I'm acquainted with chain of command, and I got nowhere, so I went and I talked to the principal and he said, "Well, you talk to the athletic director." So I shuffled for a while and I saw I was getting nowhere. So I started to put things in writing. Another example. Here I am, I'm coaching women's soccer, I have forty students, forty athletes, okay? We have one team. We have a varsity women's soccer team. At this time there were sixty boys playing soccer; they had four teams. Four paid coaches. So I finally put this in writing to the principal. The answer I got was, "When there's need for another position, I'll be expecting a recommendation from my athletic director." Now the athletic director not only coaches soccer, he has a vested interest in those four teams for all the experience his players get on the way up. He's also dealing with the number of fields, and if there's another girls' team that means that much less field for the boys, and the whole thing is fraught with what anybody would call a conflict of interest.

I read recently, "Never attribute to malice what can be attributed to ignorance." So let's say it is an honest mistake. But to further answer your question, in terms of dissent, a couple of things happened in just the last year. Number one, there's a fellow who coaches and teaches at the middle school who has similar interests to mine and does not think that everything is as it should be. Number two, there's a parent who happens to have a keen interest in equity, I would say on every level, and also happens to have some daughters, some of whom play sports, some of whom don't, and so the three of us put our heads together and we found this group called Network and they serve this area. They're federally funded and their job is to help implement sex equity in any kind of institution, and they do this basically in a nonconfrontational way. They help familiarize both aggrieved parties and administrative parties with the law. We're fortunate here that we have a state law that is roughly parallel to Title IX of the federal legislation that demands things such as equal funding, equal support, and the like. So they were a big help, mentally, first off, 'cause I don't have to tell you that you can get pretty frustrated. I've seen a lot of good coaches leave in six years because they don't want to deal with this crap. Some people still continue to teach but just don't coach because they don't feel that the hassle is worth the remuneration. And others leave for other schools or just leave for other things. Because the fellow at the middle school and I made so many waves and have written so many letters, the superintendent instructs his assistant to meet with myself, the fellow from the middle school, the principal, and the athletic director to clear the air. So we had this afternoon meeting last November and the principal has a stomachache, he can't go. Hand to God. The principal has a stomachache. So he doesn't go! So we're there, the athletic director, the two coaches, and the assistant superintendent, who is also the Title IX supervisor. In other words, any complaints about sex equity he is supposed to deal with. So we had our meeting and you know, I come rolling in with a manila folder that's chock-full of correspondence from the last several years. But, getting back to the power aspect, the assistant superintendent, all his information for six years came from the principal and the athletic director. So his view, and I don't have any doubt about this at all, was that we two coaches are troublemakers. Like, "What are they tryin' to do?" In fact, I had people say to me, other coaches, people who were once close friends but they're starting to put a little distance between us now because I'm making waves, they say, "Bill, there are some people who think you're seein' shadows here. They don't think there are real problems here." And I'm saying, "I know there's some people like that, that's why I do these things." And I'm also thinking if I were in the Soviet Union now, I'd be in there with all the crazies. Anybody who's challenging the system—and this is the attitude we're dealing with—there's something wrong with you 'cause you don't think everything is wonderful here. And I see this in the public schools generally speaking. There's a real reluctance to criticize, to self-criticize, or to accept criticism, and it's back to the whole chloroform thing, the status quo. People are used to it. Every once in a while I get the most wonderful note from a totally unexpected source on the faculty that says there are some people who think I'm really doing the right thing. They're signed and everything, and it will be from somebody that I have not even talked to or that I've never seen at athletic contests, but who is clearly aware of the issue.

The boys' basketball coach gave me a five-minute finger-pointing tirade because, and I quote, he said, "What are you doing, disrupting my whole season!" Let me tell you what this issue was about. At the school we have cheerleaders, you know. Well, one year when I had coached soccer, the varsity cheerleaders led cheers for the girls' soccer team and for the boys' soccer team. Seems logical enough to me. Well, I went on sabbatical for one year. I was away and things, I must say, slid backward in that year. So I came back, you know, slowly picking up the pieces, as it were, as far as sex equity is concerned, and among the issues I raised at our November meeting, which was before the basketball season, was this. I said, "One thing that bothers me is that last year the women's basketball team had junior varsity cheerleaders. The men's basketball team had varsity cheerleaders. This does not seem to me to be the right message to be giving these women—you're second best." And to me that's just so apparent. There's a guy who coaches the women's basketball team. That issue does not bother him. Now that's what he tells me. Does that mean he doesn't want to make waves or does it mean he genuinely sees no difference? I have to wonder. I'm sure the girls see the difference. I know they do. This is a situation that's so easy to change. I guess that's what's so annoying to me. So this one issue came up at our November meeting and the assistant superintendent agreed. He said, "That's not right." But they start again this year with the same thing! So that was when I filed my first formal complaint. I felt certain, since he had said it was something with which he didn't agree and he didn't think was right, that he would have no choice as the Title IX officer but to act in such a way as to stop that procedure. Either the girls would cheer for both or there're lots of alternatives. They can just cheer for home games. One alternative that I didn't particularly want to see, but that would have been equitable, was for them not to cheer for any. So they decided not to do anything. And not only that, he's required by law to respond to me and his answer said, among other things, he didn't think my technique, or my way of going about this was proper. You can't use the law as a club, you must educate people, and I mean, this just knocked me for a loop. He said things are more equitable here than in other schools. I'm thinking, more equitable! I mean, what does that even mean? Either they're equitable or they're not. This is just this past November. And it was at this point that we contacted the people at the Network and this lady came down to visit. She met in the morning with the assistant superintendent, who thought she was coming for a five-minute chat about cheerleaders. She wound up spending a few hours with him. She wound up telling them that she thought they needed an eighteen-month intervention program to really get squared away. She left him with his head spinning! And that's pretty much where we're at right now. She wound up telling our assistant superintendent, "We would love to work with you on this," and after his balking and hesitation, she says, "but you should be aware that we will proceed in any case, whether you care to work with us or not." The Network people have, first of all, the knowledge of both the state and federal law, and they have worked in so many other institutions that when I start to tell her specific incidents, she's filled in the end of the story. She's seen it all.

I've felt very safe on one count in that as a teacher I've always had the best of recommendations. I'm tenured. I've been teaching for—this is my twelfth year—and you wouldn't have to be much of a lawyer, I don't suppose, if all of a sudden I started to get these horrible recommendations, to have any trouble making the case that that's only happening because I'm bringing formal complaints against the school system. The other thing I thought about and chose to disregard was what happens if you find the people in the administration just don't say hello to you in the morning or they ignore you. You know the subtle things that they can do. To an extent, yeah, they can mess with your money. I think more they can mess with your mind. I guess that through the years of trying to deal with these people I've come—I have to be honest—I've come to feel superior, in that they can't mess with my mind. I just don't think they see this issue, or if they see it, for some reason they're not dealing with it. For example, there have been a few days when I've gone past the principal in the morning and said, "Good morning," and I have not perceived an answer! Now, maybe he answered. Maybe I mumbled and he didn't hear me. And part of it is there are enough mornings when he does say hello or good morning that I'm honestly not sure. The boys' basketball coach in his five-minute tirade that I mentioned earlier, one of the things he said was, "You'd just better look out in the spring. I hope I have a chance to mess up a championship season for you." That bothered me. It bothered me that he said it and it bothered me that he was so narrow, that he would even feel that way. It bothered me that he wouldn't let me explain when I started to, that he cut me off and kept ranting. This was going to ruin *his* season because word had filtered down by this time to the cheerleaders, the varsity cheerleaders, which *he* had to cheer for *his* teams—the boys, and somehow if they were forced to cheer also for the girls, they were gonna quit, 'cause they weren't gonna be told who they had to cheer for. My view is that the reason they want to be cheerleaders is they enjoy the socialization aspect of it and presumably they're heterosexual and want to socialize with the boys. They may have sister feeling for the girls, but it's not enough. And that brings to mind another thing in that letter I mentioned earlier that I got from the assistant superintendent, who told me things were more equitable at our school. He said that I was trying to force the issue, use the law as a club, et cetera, and these girls were *only* cheering because of intense school spirit. And all I could read after that was, *for males*. I mean, what is this, Oldham *Boys* High School? Oh! The thing was just so fraught with loopholes that I'm really amazed an educated person, an assistant superintendent, would even sign his name to it. And I know that if we get to a point where we do have to take legal action, he's gonna be sunk on things like that.

You know, talking about power, another thought that comes to mind is that it's considered, I know it was when I played sports, and it still is by the kids today, considered a real *treat* to play a night game. You know, under the lights, with the crowd, and there's something about it. You just feel a little more special, and over the years the boys have played a couple of night games a year, maybe not every year, this is soccer we're talking now. So, we're back to my AD—the athletic director and men's soccer coach, same person—and they play down at the field in town, which is the only field here that has lights. Now he happens, in the last few years, to also coach the town baseball team, okay? That's in the summer, it's an NCAA team. And I went to him two soccer seasons ago and said, "What do I have to do to get a night game for the girls?" You know, how do you pay for the lights—we're dealing, again, with financial restraints—and he says, "Oh, we pass the hat and we get enough money to cover the costs." And he rubs his chin and says, "I don't know if you'd get enough crowd at a girls' game to be able to do that." To him I say, "Oh, okay, thanks," you know, but to myself I say, "I've been to the boys' games at night and the hat's always missed me! I don't remember ever seeing this!" So that's one year that goes by and I bring it up again the next year and he apparently has forgotten our conversation and I asked him again, "Well how do you pay for the lights this year?" 'Cause now, by this time, I'm convinced there is no hat being passed, so I'm not going to buy that. That's what I was expecting to hear again and I was going to confront him and say, listen, I was at such-and-such a game and I didn't see the hat passing. But he says, "Gee, you know the Ravens, the NCAA baseball team they have in the summer?" he says, "I just put that night on their bill." Now they pay the electric bill for those lights. So you know, it's another one out of twenty-five nights. They don't *know!* 'Cause they get their electric bill, you know, who the hell knows, twenty-four games, twenty-five games, so I look at this and I say, "Well, shit, he's gonna put his neck out for his boys' team, but he's sure not gonna put his neck out for *my* team!" I don't know how much it is, sixty dollars, a hundred dollars? We're probably talkin' petty larceny.

So this was one of the things in our big three-hour November meeting. This was an issue that I raised. I'm putting my cards on the table. The assistant superintendent hears this and I see him looking at the AD for a denial and he doesn't get one. It's just silence is all he gets and he says, "Mack? I don't want to hear this. I don't want to hear this again." That was it. This guy Mack Sullivan, he gets tremendous press. The thing he got bad press about was the year I went on sabbatical and he waited and waited and waited until after the soccer season started to hire a coach for the girls and it was a shambles and it wasn't the fault of the coach they hired. Anyway, two weeks ago there was this article in the Sunday paper. There's two pages, two photos, and it's this homage to him. He's been AD I guess for twenty-something years, coached three sports, and there's no doubt he's a very good coach. But if you read that article and you knew nothing about Old-ham High School, you would say, oh there's just boys' athletics teams at this school. It did not one time, in two pages, mention girls. And they had just won a championship in basketball, our softball team has been eight straight years to the state tournament, and that's really beside the point. Even if they had only shoddy programs, they should still get some mention. But that's what I'm saying. You would think it's even harder to ignore successful programs, but he didn't have any trouble with doing that at all. So at first I said, this is just outrageous, but then I'm thinking, well, in a sense, it's really very good journalism because it really reported the story just as it is. That's what it's like there. So I've got my copy and that's another thing I'll have when we start talking Title IX and intervention and people start coming here to look at what's wrong.

There's a woman who was hired this year to teach who had coached very successfully at a bigger school and she took a program I don't think had won a game in three years, and they had a close to 500 record and the kids loved her. She was a motivator and she did a great job and I like her, even though in the fall we're competing for the same athletes. This lady is well thought of as both a teacher and coach, but she doesn't want to deal with it. She recognizes the differences, she's given me a lot of support mentally. She says, "I'm really glad you're doing this, but I just can't deal with it. It's too frustrating for me." There are other women who coach. I can say without any hesitation that I'm the one who's been willing to take the steps to be in the vanguard, or however one would term it. I would feel comfortable in having many of the women who coach on the group that's going to be analyzing what's happening at the school.

I've never really tried to account for the hours I've spent on this, but there's a hell of a lot of things I could be doing with my time besides writing letters, copying my letters, and going to the Network, and ta-da, ta-da, ta-da. But on the other hand, there's *nothing* I could be doing that would be more worthwhile. And if I didn't feel that way, I wouldn't be doin' it. I don't know if I can give a better answer as to why I'm doing it than to say there's just a visceral feeling that there's right and there's wrong. The nature of what I'm dealing with forces you to get involved with the legal aspect and the terminology and familiarize yourself with the law, but when you get right down to it, there is right and there is wrong. And that's really what's motivating me. And because I feel the situation as it exists is wrong, I'm going about the rigamarole to put it right. It's not that I'm really fond of the law, or that I want to learn a lot about the legality of it; that's all secondary; that's the means to the end.

I probably owe a lot of that to my parents. I grew up with a pretty keen sense of what's right, what's just, especially where individual persons are involved. Whether they're women or men or white or yellow or black or whatever. I don't know if it's the earliest, but it's maybe the strongest influence, and I've only come to reflect on this recently. I can't say I felt this when I jumped into all these things, but it was my parents. They both worked all the time. I was brought up at a time when they both were involved in unions. My dad worked in the thirties with building service employees both in organizing and being a leader in the union. Not top level, but high level. My mother was a shop steward and in a different business entirely. She worked at a big, big retail store and so a lot of the talk at home centered around grievances. This person's doing this, this person's doing that—whatever. And I remember probably when I was eight or nine going to union meetings with my mother because they were at night and she didn't want to go out alone. So those things, I guess, permeated my consciousness.

The other thing is, and I can't believe I haven't mentioned this word yet in how long I've been talking, but the thing that I've come to see as at least as important as an awareness of all of these issues is *persistence*. You know, once you make up your mind that you're gonna see something through, the individuals involved, in my case the principal and athletic director, they can shuffle me back and forth right now, as far as I'm concerned, as long as they want, because I just don't have any problem smiling and saying, okay, I'll go and I'll write another letter or I'll write another memo and I'll get my copy of it. And I don't think I'd do that unless I had the feeling that somewhere down the road somebody was gonna do somethin' about this. Now at one point I thought, well, the assistant superintendent will do something about this when he hears about it. Now I'm not so sure. Maybe he has, for whatever reason, his own concerns. He doesn't want to buck the guy who's been there twenty years, or whatever. Maybe he thinks I'm wrong, maybe it's an honest disagreement, but apparently he's not anxious to move or he's not moving very quickly, that's for sure. But I have this feeling that somebody's going to pick up on this and I have this feeling that I'm not gonna invest all this time I have invested and just be like some of the other people and walk away from it. And also, you know, you can tell me no, and you can tell me it's not gonna change, and you can tell me you think I'm being wrong and I'm stupid and whatever, but I'm just gonna keep smiling at ya and I'll be back here tomorrow and I'll be saying, "How come the girls can't play on the big field?"

I've always, for whatever reason, been pretty analytical, and I could look at a situation and say, okay, what's the worst thing that can happen here?" You're not always right when you do that; sometimes things can get worse than you ever thought! But you get to a point where you can be pretty comfortable with your decision. We're talking about just a lot of immobility here. It's a tough system and there are lots of reasons why people don't want to change. Some have to do with their own vested interests, some have to do with laziness, some have to do with ignorance. Yeah, let's not leave that out, just plain old sexism. See, there's such a resistance. I remember when I first raised that term. The term I raised was "equal opportunity" and Oh! Man! You could see the color come to the AD's face and he said, "We can settle this, we don't have to, this isn't a question of equal opportunity, this is a question of whether or not they can use the field." That's the attitude! Yeah, oh jeez!

Well, I was in student government in college. Not the student body president or anything like that, but student senate. There were issues then that, being in a parochial school the issues seem ludicrous to anyone who went to a nonsectarian school, but there were issues, nonetheless. In terms of being a subject person, a student, and being able to speak up for your rights, now that I think of it a little bit, I remember that it wasn't an easy thing to do. It took a certain amount of intestinal fortitude. Well, yeah, I can give you an example. Real easy. At this time I was living off campus. I think it was junior year and my roommate was the student body president. I had always certainly been active in issues, I didn't have much trouble expressing myself, and at the time the hot issue was whether or not we were gonna have what was called intervisitation. That meant not coed dorms, but just members of the opposite sex being able to visit in the dorms. I mean, people were picketing and demonstrating and everything else. I guess I should say that prior to that local issue, probably fifty percent of the people at school—this was 1970—were involved in the antiwar movement and so on and so forth. So people of that era, many of us, were certainly no strangers to protest. Anyway, Bobby came home one night and said, "We're having this new meeting and I need three students and the other two are so-and-so and so-and-so." So it wasn't so much a conscious choice on my part to get involved. It was like, well, here you are. I certainly wasn't going to say no. Well partly I felt that way because you feel there's an element of just feeling good, that somebody you respect thinks enough of you to say you're on this committee. And I also thought enough of myself that I felt I could probably express myself and the views that we wanted presented as well as anybody else they would pick. The risks were that these people in this private school were liable to feel unkindly toward students who participated in this issue. But, on the other hand, you're thinking, well, they have agreed to meet with us, and they're willing to talk about this, so we went ahead and as it turned out, it was pretty fruitful. We were able to get some measure of intervisitation. I don't think anybody felt any bitterness over it. Obviously I can't speak for everybody, but I think that the process, the negotiating process, went relatively smoothly, and I enjoyed it. I guess the idea of problem-solving was attractive, you know, to be able to be the negotiator. Maybe that has somethin' to do with your question, John, about heroes. You know there are all kinds of heroes, and if you can come in and resolve a problem, it doesn't have to be a crisis, really, but if you can do that and people go away feeling comfortable, then you're a hero of sorts.

How much principled dissent we should allow is something I've certainly thought about. And I won't say that my position is fixed in stone. I've felt, oh, I don't know, certainly since college, and I've felt it ever increasingly through the years, that the First Amendment is one of the most beautiful things we have in this country. I've been involved with the ACLU and I can remember not too long ago a really awkward situation where the ACLU wound up defending the right of the Nazis to parade in Skokie. My feeling is, let the Nazis parade in Skokie and let them stand on their own merit. If anything, they're gonna awaken the consciousness of many people. I don't like what they're saying, but I guess I don't feel threatened by them saying it. I think some of it is a function of perhaps an overly honed concept of logic. But I don't have any trouble at all seeing a logical progression from the Nazis can't march, to Protestants can't march, to Democrats can't march, to you know, where's it stop? A lot of people think you're *crazy* to say that. I mean, everybody knows the Nazis are wrong! You know, you couldn't stop the Nazis and not worry about stoppin' somebody else. But I can't buy that. Maybe I'm a victim of my own logic in that regard, but that's what it tells me. I don't like the idea of somebody drawing the lines on who can talk and who can't talk or who can do anything, I guess, for that matter. I don't know about whether they are principled dissenters. Gee, if you would just ask me if I considered them dissenters, it would be so much easier to answer! I'm sure *they* feel they're principled. I suppose, yeah, I feel they're principled, but obviously, I disagree with their principles.

As to the Klan marching, without giving it any more thought than the few minutes here, I think I'm leaning that way. I'd have to feel that anyone who did stand up for their principles was a principled dissenter. I suppose we're going to have to get to a definition of principled, you know. And if we get to that, it seems that in a democracy, if we could use that word, we've got all different ideas of what principled means. There's no doubt about that. I think of my own situation and what we've been doing, and democracy plays an interesting function here, 'cause a few times along the way I've been asked by people in authority, well, what if we put such-and-such an issue to a vote of all the coaches? And suppose they said—we'll use this issue as an example—no, the girls should not play on this larger field. Well, I damn well wouldn't shut up about that issue. I know I wouldn't. And I don't think that standing up for what one thinks is right is something that democracy should prohibit. You know, I don't buy, say, the idea of ancient Athens that if you raise this issue so many times and it's voted down by the council, you're gonna be exiled for eight years. I think you should still have your right to stand there and talk about it and pursue it. My own principles are such that I don't think I'd ever get to the stage where I would pursue violence against these people who disagree with me, and yet I think just about anything short of violence I might consider pretty seriously. I wouldn't say I would permit the Nazis to act on their principles. The idea of having their parade and if they want to talk and express their views, that's fine. I would think that we're just as free to disagree with them, we're free to walk away from them. And yet, this is one of the thoughts that crossed my mind even as I said that. Sure, I'm one who's gonna walk away from them, but what about someone who isn't?

When we talk about principled dissent, there's an implication that there is a higher goal than self-involvement. I have an aversion to violence and yet I suspect we could hypothesize here long enough and at some point I would say, yeah, I think that might provoke me to violence. I don't know what the issue would be, but I think there probably is a point at which I could probably do that. My first feeling about Puerto Rican nationalism—it's not just a feeling, there's thought involved—it's a legitimate issue, okay? I believe it's even been a ballot issue in Puerto Rico within the last decade maybe, I'm not sure when. The ballot box certainly doesn't solve everything, but in some ways, presuming elections are fair and not like, let's say; I perceive Salvadoran elections, or Nicaraguan elections, or lots of others, but presuming it's fair, there's room for those people to work for a nationalist movement. Even if they're defeated there's nothin' to stop them from continuing the fight in a nonviolent way. Just like there's nothin' to prevent people from pursuing ERA in a nonviolent way, and I guess that's what I would prefer. I guess I wouldn't say that these people were not principled dissenters just because they had, say, resorted to violence. It takes a lot of guts and I'm sure the thought occurred to them that they could very well wind up in jail. I would hesitate to say they were unprincipled. They're certainly dissenters. I guess I would just say I disagree with the means with which they chose to express that. I wouldn't see them as unprincipled because they used violence. Not necessarily. I mean, that's why this is the United States now, right?

I don't think of myself as a pacifist, and yet I think the last time I ever struck a blow I was about twelve years old. Well, *I* might say that the blow was for principled dissent! There was this kid on my block whose father was a cop and the kid was a bully. Not too much with me because I was always pretty good-sized, but certainly with a lot of other kids on the block. I remember comin' home one day upset and it must have been a Saturday or a Sunday 'cause my dad was home and he asked, "What's wrong with you?" And I told him, "This kid is just pushin' us all around." And my father said—my father used to box; he was an amateur boxer—he said something to the effect of, why don't you smack him one and then he won't do it anymore. And I said, "But his father's a cop!" My father says, "So what? You're not going to get arrested for somethin' like that." And I said "NO?" I went right back downstairs and we had a quick little fight and I got in a few good shots and it was all over and I never had another problem with him. But at the same time, I didn't really feel good about it. I've been in a few confrontations, growing up in the Bronx, but that just happens, and honestly, I talked my way out of every one of 'em. Part of it, I think, was perceiving tense situations, whether on the street or in school or wherever. I think most people who grew up in a metropolitan area would agree, there's a lot to be said for confidence. When you're confident on the street, people don't bother you. But here I am, a big white kid walking across 155th Street into Manhattan, maybe people are thinking, this guy must know somethin'! I made that trip hundreds of times and it never went the other way. I didn't talk to my parents too much about where I hung out. My parents used to say "no" too much for me to say a lot, and they were worriers. My mother was a worrier so why trouble her about where I was spending the time.

I'm not forgetting that you said when you tell on yourself you don't tell much, but Sally Grosman smacked me in the head with a roller skate once when I was eight or ten and I whaled on her! But it was more a reaction than anything else. And you know how every neighborhood has the one lady who was always lookin' out her window? Well, Mrs. Crosby was there and I mean, I was no sooner *home* than my mother was saying, "What are you doing punching Sally Grosman?" Well, before she could even finish askin' the question she saw the egg I had on my head. She never officially condoned the act, but she also didn't carry out the prosecution. It was just sort of left that way. I had enough goin' on with holding ice on my head.

One thing I came to really appreciate about my parents was that, for as long as I can remember—you know how parents always have their constant themes, however right, wrong, or useful they may be—and one of my parents' constant themes was, "Make up your own mind, don't be a follower." And I know there have been times when I'm sure they've regretted that. I have a brother and three half sisters, but the next closest is eleven years older, so for practical purposes for a long time I was home alone. I can remember the gist of one occasion when I was told that. The gist was me using as an excuse for doing something wrong, "Well, everybody's doing it." And I got the old, "Well, if everybody jumped off the Empire State Building, well sucker, you ain't gonna jump, are you?" "Well no, I guess I wouldn't." "Well, make up your own mind." Oh yeah, I'm sure they meant it. I'm sure that in their own lives, and especially as I mentioned earlier, with their work in unions, they faced a lot of uncomfortable situations. I really can't say when I started to become aware, but I remember them grappling with difficult issues. I can't remember the specifics, but I remember tone. I remember people really feeling that they had been mistreated, and on the one hand you're looking at these individuals you knew were struggling just to be there at this meeting, and on the other there was this guy called "oppressor" or "ownership" that was bigger than every individual. But apparently these people as a group were dealing with it and they were at least making enough headway so that they could feel good about it.

I'm reminded for no particular reason of something I read that really struck me. I've come to look at women's athletics and the entrenched athletic director and his good press as, you know, he's a giant, he's an empire unto himself. I was reading in ancient history about this fellow who lost an Olympic event and it was bad enough that he lost, but he was absolutely bullshit that the people in the city constructed a statue to the victor. So this guy goes out at night after the people have constructed the statue and he's working to topple the statue and it's massive and heavy and he's inching it off its pedestal and he finally succeeds in toppling it and it falls on him and crushes him to death. And I couldn't help think, there's a moral here, Bill! You don't want to be standing underneath when it goes. I suppose there's a valuable message there for anybody who's trying to topple anything big.

With all the hassles that this has entailed and may entail in the future, I know that I'm happier doing this than I would be sitting there being conscious of the injustices, or what I perceive as injustices, and not doing anything about it. I mean, there's just something in me that I just could not *tolerate* that. I really believe they are injustices. I'm willing to concede the chance that I'm wrong about this, but of course, I don't really think that's the case. I'm willing to concede they might be right, but I'd be willing to bet just about anything I can bet that they're not. This was a gradual thing. The issues, the things I've told you about, as you take them one at a time, are really trivial. Who plays on the field, who cheers at this game, who plays night games, these are not of themselves earthshaking issues. But the thing is that as you look at six of these or eight of these, twelve of these, you can't escape the fact that there's a real pattern here and the pattern is, we care about the boys and the boys are important to us and it's nice to have the girls here and they can do this, but they're just not as important. And you don't have to look too far to see that same thing every-place in our society. I guess to sit and know that is happening and not do anything about it just sort of goes against my grain.

One of the things that made it easy to care, I'd say the single most im-portant reason for me caring about all of those issues, was just lookin' at the kids who played soccer when the principal would walk past them and go out to watch the boys play. I mean, it got to the point where you could see the looks of disgust on their faces and I don't think it was a contemp-tuous thing for them, it was like, "How could you do that to us?" And of course, when you're coaching kids most coaches get pretty close. You're coaching and you feel what they feel, whatever it is, and so that made it easy. I'd say that was the single most critical thing that made me want to really try to do something about it. So what are your choices in a situation like that? Well, there aren't many choices besides going to the guy and talking to him about it. The kids didn't verbalize much at first. After that time I told you I went and he said, "Well, the kids never said anything," I came back and talked to 'em and said, "I think you ought to go talk to him, he really thinks you guys don't care." Obviously not all of them were gonna go talk to him, but a couple of 'em were gutsy enough, or innocent enough, or whatever, and they said something. And they live near him and they saw him every day and they went over to talk to him, and when he still didn't come, then it was fair game. Anything related was an open topic for discussion. Then they said, "Well, how come the boys have those nice warm-up suits and we don't have any at all?" I'm sure that before I ever talked about it, in one sense I was their coach and just another authority figure.

I guess one thing that's been a help is that there have been enough good signals in the rest of society, in the 1970s. There's enough reinforcement other places that females of school age feel they actually are somebody, so it's not that hard a thread for them to pick up. I'm reminded of another quote from my athletic director. In one of the very few lengthy conversations we've had—usually they're foreshortened because one or the other of us would not want to blow our stack—but in one of the lengthy conversations he said, and I know he was genuinely serious, "You know, Bill, I don't think the girls would even be cognizant of these issues if you didn't bring them to their attention." I said, "I'm a *social studies* teacher! These issues are a lot more important than coaching soccer or softball!" And he looked at me like, What are you talking about?

There are many reasons, most of them selfish, why I would just love to go to the School Committee and blow the whistle, so to speak, on some of these things. I think if they were a good Committee, I wouldn't be carrying this fight. They would be more cognizant of the issues. It's certainly partly their fault that they're in the dark, and partly the administration's fault that they are in the dark. But the only reason I haven't done that so far is if I do go and make this more of a public issue, or if I went, say, to somebody in the newspaper—and there are plenty of people on the newspapers around here I could go to—what I see happening is entrenchment. The other side digs in, we dig in, and then instead of really dealing with correcting the issues, everybody's trying to cover their own behind and say I'm right, you're not right. I see where that might happen. But at this point, I don't think that would be the most effective. I guess one of the things I'm also convinced of, besides persistence, is that you have to remember what your goals are. There have been lots of steps along the way where I could have gotten momentary satisfaction out of a letter to the editor or something like that, but in terms of remembering what you want to accomplish, that's not the best way to go about it. But I'm not giving up, I'll keep writing the memos. Part of my mind-set is the determination that what I'm interested in is going to prevail over the nickle-and-dime stuff. There have been days when I've gone home saying, not believing, but saying to myself, "Forget this. I'm not gonna coach next year, I'm gonna chuck this out the window." It is wearing and at times, although not often in my case, it can be frustrating. That's where the support of people with mutual interests is really important.

At our meeting in November, I was sitting there taking notes. Everyone else was just talking. I just did that because when I'm in a free-for-all discussion, I tend not to interrupt, but also if a thought comes up relative to something, I'll just jot it down. I don't want to lose that thought. So I was just sittin' there and Mack says to me, "You know another thing, Bill, this is a small school here, we don't need all this paperwork. You got a problem, we can talk about it. You don't have to be writing all these memos." And I just remained impassive and inside I'm saying, "Ooooh, I really got to that sucker, didn't I?" So for next year he's already on the stick. He talked to me this week about a better schedule for the girls. And again, it's not a change of attitude, it's pressure. And like the cheerleaders, I don't think they can be completely comfortable with just cheering for the boys and not for the girls from now on. At least they're going to have to think about that now.

Gloria Arsenault

"When I believe something, I firmly back that up
with what I do."

□ □ □

We boil at different degrees.

RALPH WALDO EMERSON

*Despite her hectic circumstances, school bus driver Gloria Arsenault was
a spontaneous and gracious hostess. I was aware that the privilege of entering her neat home was rarely extended to strangers. Quite apart from the
matronly modesty that makes her reluctant to admit even long-time friends
to her home during her husband's absence, Mrs. Arsenault was very busy.
She was deeply immersed in plans for her daughter's wedding and pre-
paring to be flown, with her husband, Arthur, to Kansas City as honored
guests of the National Insurance Companies of America, who had named
her their Good Citizen of the Year. Some months prior to our meeting,
finding herself unable to stop the students from smoking pot on her school
bus, Mrs. Arsenault had driven the bus and its junior high school passengers to the local police station. This decisiveness has earned her the praise
of such notable personages as the President of the United States and Dr.
Rupert von Trapp. Her exacting job notwithstanding, Gloria is a homebody in the sense that her home and family are extremely important to her.
The letter from President Reagan assuring her that she has "earned the
respect of the national community" stands framed on the parlor organ,
next to a photograph of one of her grandchildren.*

*Our far-ranging conversation was rendered even more agreeable by
Gloria's tasty little meatballs, and cup after cup of her excellent coffee.
She is a small, active grandmother who doesn't look or sound as if she
were entering her sixth decade of life. Her passion for what is right pervades and complicates her Roman Catholicism, her conservatism, and even
her strong family orientation. Her Bay State Irish-American convictions
are far less doctrinaire and conservative than they appear initially.*

Gloria has thought profoundly about the action that projected her to national prominence. Her voice became even softer and more serious as she acknowledged the critical role of the media in that prominence. Her account was given added somber emphasis when I read later of the fate of another woman school bus driver in a town only a hundred miles away. She did what Gloria did and the reward for her civic-mindedness was re-assignment to a lower-paying job.

––––––

You know, I'm not usually a star! I was really elated, honored, to think you would think that much of me that you would want to interview me. The award I was telling you about is given by the National Insurance Companies of America. The President of Holyoke Insurance submitted my name and the news clippings that had appeared in the *Salem Evening News*, who gave me excellent coverage. They were very, very kind in the stories they wrote about the incident. Frank Story, President of Holyoke Mutual Insurance Company, submitted these stories to the national con-vention, and each year they give a Good Citizenship Award. Last year they said they had given it to an airline stewardess who had stopped a bombing in a plane, and for them to put me in that category, was just—it overwhelms me! I just don't feel as though I am that great a person. I'm just an ordinary person. Oh, the issue is certainly a very important issue because I first heard about it, you know, kids using pot, back when my children, Arthur and Billy, who are now in their thirties, were kids. I ob-jected to it then too. Now the older boy didn't bother with it, but the second oldest boy did and he was given a choice. He could either quit it or leave the house. I just wouldn't have it in my house. He was in high school. He was probably about sixteen or seventeen and he'd been using it, but I was not aware of the fact. He wouldn't use it in the house because I certainly would have smelled it here. He was using it outside and when I found out about it he was out of high school then. He was eighteen, and I said, "No way. Either you give it up or leave." So he says okay, he would give it up.

And then when I started driving the school bus, smoking was not al-lowed. I did not allow smoking on my bus. I started driving the bus I guess about eight years ago, and mine was one of the few buses that would pull into the yard without a butt on the floor. How did I manage that? It wasn't easy! It was a fight all the way. There were many ways. I would report it at the school. And say, you know, this one. And the kid would be expelled from the bus for two or three days and it would stop. These are just regular Marlboros, you know, but there is a no smoking policy on school buses. Apparently there were enough drivers who just ignored the rules that when they found one who did try to enforce it, she was a very dirty name! We won't put that name on tape. I wasn't the only woman driving a bus at this time. The majority of the school bus drivers are women because we are a group of people who can tolerate kids and their noise, and believe me, it gets noisy, extremely noisy. And the noisiest group on the bus are the kids that are in the third, fourth, fifth, and sixth grades. Junior high are the toughest. They don't want any adult telling them what to do or how to do it. They don't like hearing me say, "Not on my bus. You can do that if you want to, but not here." In the beginning the other drivers would just say to me, "You're making your own life miserable. What are you doing it for? Why are you being upset?" Well, kids in high school, I'm sure if they are smoking, at that point, there's not that much you can do about it, but I felt as though in junior high these kids are learning to smoke and it is addictive. I know, I learned to smoke. I did smoke for fifteen years. I know how damaging it can be. I was out of high school when I started to smoke. I was earning money. I was through school and of course, it was the thing to do.

I found razor blades on the bus—they had slashed a seat—and I figured that was the only reason they were there. And even the principal said to me, what do you think they're doing with razor blades? I said, "I imagine they're usin' 'em in the art class." They may have in some instances, but this is why they're carrying the razor blades: to cut their cocaine. I didn't know that's what they were doing. This was the principal. Whether he knew or didn't know, he just wondered what I thought. And dumb me, I always give my opinion. I should find out theirs first.

I think most of the drivers were pretty tolerant, because buses would be pulling out of the school yard with the smoke blowing out the windows. It was against school rules but it wasn't enforced. I think it wasn't enforced perhaps because the teachers received the same type hassle I received when I tried to stop it. After a while, if you're not getting parental assistance on this, if the parents say, "So, if the kid wants to smoke, let him smoke," and the teachers say they're there to give the children an education, they're not there to discipline children, well, I don't know, I've never tried to teach school, but you give up. You're not getting the backing. I believe the school was lax because the parents wanted it that way. I think that the school systems have received enough parental pressure that they are backing down from their principles and their rules. One teacher in particular said to me that when he tried to stop a child from breaking a law, dealing with drugs, the parents said to the teacher, "You pursue this and I'll sue you." You know, the man's out earning a living, he has a family, he can't be sued and harassed, so he backs down.

I didn't back down because I have a very responsible job. I'm responsible for the safety of every kid on that bus from the time he steps foot in my bus until the foot steps out of the bus. I am responsible for him. I'm driving this bus through traffic, through dangerous intersections and if I'm being made sick by an odor on my bus, just how safe a driver am I? So I felt as though that was intolerable. Completely intolerable. Furthermore, it was only a week before that I had found the razor blades. How safe am I or the other students on the bus with razor blade–carrying students? I mean, you know, if this kid is taking a drug and he's carrying such dangerous things, how safe are my other students on this bus? How safe are they if I'm sitting up there in the front seat of this bus being nauseated by the odor, and in some instances, you are also intoxicated by this odor. Even though you're not smoking it yourself, the aroma is intoxicating to other people. Why do all these kids have to leave their homes clean, showered, shampooed, and walk into school reeking like that? Why? It's not right. Maybe it's my Irish temper, but I felt, well, the ones that are doing it should be taken off the bus. That's what I went to the police station for. Get those kids off my bus. I didn't know which ones. You don't know, and to go down and confront them is not a wise thing. Other drivers have been abused by walking to the back of the bus. You're apt to be physically accosted. One of the other drivers knew that a window was broken down in the back of her bus so she pulled the bus over to the side of the road and went down to investigate. There's a rubber casing that goes around the outside edge of the window and in this rubber casing were pieces of glass. They took this rubber casing and put it around her neck and dragged her to the front of the bus and said, "You f—ing so-and-so, drive the f—ing bus and mind your f—ing business." And they put her in the driver's seat. She got taken off the route. But as far as I know, nothing was done to those kids. No, it wasn't all the kids who did this. The other kids sit there, they don't dare do a thing. I mean, they're only kids. She knew who it was but as far as I know, the whole thing was hushed up.

Other drivers have reported pot-smoking to the police. There is a Sergeant Witwicki, who is the crime prevention officer in Peabody, and he's the one that handles the pot-smoking incidents. Very often when I would report these things to him, he would speak to whoever and it would stop on this bus. Other drivers have stopped their buses by his car, I have done it, and said, "Come in and take care of this situation for me." It has been done before. I wasn't the first. I was the first to get publicity about it, not the first to object. It didn't seem like any earth-shattering experience to me. I just smelled the pot again. The week before when I had smelled the pot I had called the school. We have a radio because the kids were slashing bus seats, and buses that were having trouble were supposed to radio back to the company and say, "I have a problem. I'm returning this whole busload to the school." If the school were not open, if it was a late bus and the school were not open, it was to be returned to the police station. So you see, that thought had already been put up in my mind, to take the bus back to the police station if there was nobody at the school to handle the problem. 'Cause we do not handle discipline. So I was on my way to school in the morning the week before and I had called in and said, "Would you call the school." I'm picking these kids up at 7:15, 7:20. The school switchboard doesn't open until 7:30. Well, I'm radioing dispatch, "Would you notify the school?" They can't get through to the school. So I said, "Well, get ahold of Ronnie." Ronnie is our safety manager. He's the one that gets the kids if they're having problems, you know. If what we're doing isn't handling the problem, Ronnie would go out and speak to the kids. And very often it worked. Sometimes it didn't, and in this instance it didn't because the week before Ronnie had come out and told the children, "This is against the law, it's gonna be prosecuted. Now this bus is on the books and it's gonna be watched and if we see kids smoking on the bus, the bus is gonna be pulled over and the offenders are gonna be taken in." The very next day somebody smoked pot on my bus! And I radioed in and the dispatcher said she couldn't get through to the school. Sorry, Ronnie wasn't available. So, you know, my hair was standing up, my brain is about to explode, because I'm upset. This is going on on the bus, there's nothing I can do about it and nobody else is doing anything. So when one of the last kids got off—and they knew that I had called in for help and hadn't gotten it—as he got off the bus he said to me, "See? Nobody does anything." I think that was the last straw. I think right there, that was the straw that broke the camel's back. I said to myself, "You know, he's right." I was furious about that. But then for the rest of the week, for a full week, everything was all right. Then it was the morning of December 22, which was one week after this incident. And I smelled the pot again and of course that particular day a week ago when I had gone back in and turned in my keys the air was blue in that office. I was furious because I read the riot act to everybody that would listen to me. Including the president of the company. You know, I was really upset that nothing had happened. So the following week, as I said, the minute I smelled the pot I radioed and they said to me the same thing, nobody could be reached. I said, "Would you please advise?" She said, "Gloria, why don't you take them to the police station?" And I said, "Ten-four!" And off I went. And the kids knew we were going because they heard this conversation. I'm speaking into a radio and my speaker in this bus was up over head. We had a good ten-minute ride and the thing that amazes me is, we stopped at two railroad crossings, the bus came to a complete stop. I can't understand why those kids didn't go out the back of the bus. The pot did go out. They put their cigarettes out, but the thing is, I didn't care. I wanted those kids off the bus, or I wanted those kids to get a three-day suspension. I felt that the police would know, because I'm sure they have a pretty good idea who it is that's involved. No, things weren't quiet on the way. There was a big hubbub. The bus was extremely noisy. The conversation was really at a high pitch, but what they were saying, I couldn't tell you. I was driving and I knew that I was upset so I had to be very cool and very calm and watch the road and make sure I didn't smash the bus up. On our way to the police station I didn't want to go to the hospital instead! You know, when we got there, Sergeant Witwicki was waiting. Captain Costello was waiting and they were very firm and very stern. Sergeant Witwicki told me to secure the bus. Which I did. Put it in neutral, put the brake on, locked it, and pulled the key. The Sergeant said "We'll take over from here."

I don't mind driving. I like it. I get tired, there are times I get *very* tired, but I like being out there. I don't like hangin' around the house. And I like being with kids. And my kids are all grown. But driving is an easy job—it really is easy! I don't care if you sit in an office, there are things that are difficult. No matter what kind of job you have, there are frustrations. It's confining, but you're moving. And not all the kids are pot-smokers. A lot of 'em are really nice kids. I would say the majority of them are terrific. It's just a few rotten apples that make your day miserable. Oh definitely, most of the kids are okay, and maybe this is why you scream at the kids that aren't because you are protecting those who are. The day the pot was on the bus, there were only two kids smoking pot. I didn't know how many then, I had no idea, I found out after.

Other drivers have said to me that they wouldn't have done what I did and if they had been told to, they wouldn't have faced the barrage of reporters as I did. The other drivers felt that *that* took courage. I *know* it took more courage to face those reporters than it did to go to the police station! It was amazing.

So anyway, the next day when I picked up the kids they were *very* good. You could have heard a pin drop on the bus the next day. So as far as I was concerned, it had been dealt with. It had been solved and there was no big deal. And then came Christmas vacation. People who had seen me over Christmas vacation and then saw this in the news said, "Gee, she never said anything." It was no big deal. How it got to be a big deal was that Captain Costello filed a report to Mayor Peter Torigian. I think it was he who conducted the search and they found hashish pipes, they found razor blades, they found marijuana cigarettes, there was a cache that they showed on the TV of the things that were taken off this bus because they couldn't search the children. The children were all asked to leave the bus and, thinking that they might get searched, they left everything on the bus. They can legally search the bus. So they found all this stuff. This is a junior high crowd. There was a report put on the mayor's desk in two hours. The police department, the school department, the mayor, and Travel Time, the company I work for, had a meeting. On the bus they had asked the kids to identify the smokers and the kids wouldn't. They asked the smokers to identify themselves; they didn't. So because they didn't know who the offending parties were, it was decided at the meeting to suspend the bus for three days. But because of school vacation they didn't notify the parents until the third of January—and the parents were very irate. Suddenly they're confronted with a problem of transporting their children to school. Some parents felt as though their children weren't involved. Well, ninety-eight percent of the parents were right, their children weren't involved and they felt it an unjust punishment. They therefore called the news media, the TV, the mayor. The parents all called to complain that their children were being unjustly punished. The newspapers that were there were the *Boston Globe*, the *Herald Traveler*, *Peabody Times*, *Salem Evening News*, *Daily Evening Item*, as well as WBZ-TV. These were the barrage of reporters that I faced on January fifth. And was I lucky, my hair was all done. It was my anniversary! It was our anniversary and we were going out. Jack Belli, the President of Travel Time, had said to me that the reporters wanted to know who the bus driver was. He says, "I wouldn't give out your name. You have a right to be a private citizen." I said, "Look, if they want to hear about this, I'm *glad* to tell 'em." Because the more people who are aware of what's happening in the schools, the more apt we are to get somethin' done about it. You know, it's the squeaky wheel that gets the oil. I don't feel the parents who are bringing the pressure on the school are the majority of parents. I think it's a few very noisy people and very dominating people and you know, their children do no wrong. I would think they are wealthier. I would think so. West Peabody is the wealthy part of town. I would say that the drivers who drive in West Peabody know that these parents are more knowledgeable as to the rights and privileges of their children.

I could have gone to the school later and said, "Who was it?" But I felt I didn't want to know. I'd rather not know because I know I'd hold a grudge. I really feel that I might have held a grudge against this kid and I was better off not to know because I would rather treat each child on my bus the same. I don't want to know who has the money, I don't want to know who doesn't. To me, every kid on my bus is important. I don't care what house they came from. That's not important to me. What's important to me is how this child behaves on my bus.

Oh, the kids didn't confess, somebody reported who it was. Some parents and their children went down to the school and came forth and told. I am sure that in every home after this incident there were discussions! I am sure there were many, many discussions! And during somebody's discussion, the children admitted that they knew who it was and the parents and the children went to the police and went to the school. The police didn't identify the offenders either. I have no idea if there was any punishment. If they were further suspended from the bus, I don't know because sometimes they're there and sometimes they're not. If a kid's out of school, I don't question it.

No, they don't smoke pot on my bus now. As a matter of fact, if I just smell cigarette smoke I yell, "Put it out! You know better!" And they do. They do know better. And they've known all these years and they'll say, "Are you really serious?" And I'll say, "Yes, I am very serious!" After the publicity, anybody who wanted to enforce the rule at that point did and it has stayed in force. Other drivers have said to me that this made their job easier. But those who just don't want to exert the effort are still having problems. And I just look at them and say that's too bad. You missed the boat because we had it, we had it. When we had that publicity and all of those reporters were there, we had it and that was the time to make your move and put your foot down and they had the opportunity and they didn't take it and it's too bad. It's really too bad. The *Boston Herald Traveler* story says, "Grannie puts the lid on pot!" I thought that was funny. Do you know that there was a knifing in Boston just about the time that all of this was getting that publicity? It was in Roxbury. A knifing at a bus stop. And there was another student that was beaten up badly and these are all drug-related incidents and these are junior high school kids! As far as I know, the black kids on my bus aren't involved. It's the white kids. That isn't important. In West Peabody they can even afford cocaine! It's funny, but it isn't.

If this had happened twenty years ago I probably would have whacked the kid! Right over the knee. You know, a good pat on the back low enough and firm enough for you to know I mean it. I guess I got that maybe from my mother. I can remember coming through the door late and she would be on the other side of the door and my ear would be ringing loudly as I walked by her! In other words, you know, I knew that at nine o'clock I had to be in, 'cause if it was five minutes after I was gonna get a whack. And my mother was a very sweet person, she was a lovely person, but she also had my father's razor strap and I felt it low enough and firm enough to know *she* meant it. You do what you're told. I knew my mother loved me. I really did. I also knew when she said no, that's exactly what she meant. Other than that, she was very generous, very loving and very giving. She never did for herself, never. She was doing for us. And I was the youngest of three. She was good to me.

I can remember being in the navy and being at a hygiene lecture and I was sittin' there silently saying the rosary so I wouldn't listen to the filth that this guy was telling all these WAVES. Oh yes, he was a gynecologist and really explaining but I didn't want to hear it. I was shuttin' him out because I believed this was wrong. I really believed that and when I believe something. I firmly back that up with what I do. I know a lot of people don't do that. I know an awful lot of people who say one thing and they live another thing, and to me, that's hypocritical. My mother raised me with "What you don't know won't bother you," and I thought I was too young to know that stuff! I just sat there and concentrated on the rosary and didn't listen!

When I was growing up, if I didn't like what the crowd was doing, I went home. I can remember doing something that I'm very ashamed of where I should have gone home, I should have left, but I stayed. I didn't participate, but I didn't run away either. And to this day I shamefully feel that I should have protected the boy who was being abused by the rest of the kids. They were abusing him because he was Jewish. Isn't that awful? That was a terrible, terrible thing. You know, I was maybe about twelve or thirteen, but you go to church and they teach you that the Jews crucified Christ and we are taught to love Christ and these Jews crucified him! It makes you hate them. It's wrong to teach a kid that. I think that was wrong to believe. Further, we were told that the Catholic Church is the *only* church. If you don't belong to the Catholic Church you're gonna go to hell. Gee, I don't know, in my life, I've met a lot of people that I just assumed were Catholic 'cause they were good and then I turned around and found out that they weren't Catholic. What a shock!

To this day, I don't even know who that poor Jewish kid was, but I remember the incident. It was different in the bus. I was in charge. As an observer, a passerby, I never felt that it was my responsibility to interfere. I live and I let live. I live the way I believe I should and my friends, close friends, are people who share my views. People who don't share my views I just stay away from.

I can't be physically abusive to somebody. I mentioned paddling a kid's bottom. To me, that's not being physically abusive. You know, to take a fist and punch is a lot different than takin' someone over your knee and paddling them because, there again, you're the person in charge and it's your duty to do this and therefore you do it. Whether you like it or not, you do it. Yes, I guess I felt responsible during the war. This is my country! This is my home and I would feel protective about it. This is my neighborhood. I'd feel protective about it. This is my country and I feel protective about it as a citizen. But I don't go around trying to solve all the ills of the world! I think I know my place and try to keep it.

People should be free to express their own views as long as they're not offending somebody else, physically or mentally. In the privacy of your home, with your own friends, what you do is your business. You come out into the middle of the street and what you do is *my* business. When my next-door neighbor starts usin' filthy language and I hear it, I get mad. Someday I'm gonna go over and *tell* him how mad I get. This is what I feel.

Well, I suppose the Ku Klux Klanner has a right to do what he wants, but he has no right to impose his religious beliefs on me, or to stop you from progressing in your life. I would like to be able to say to him, go jump in the creek, you know, take a long walk off a short bridge. I think the First Amendment protects us on those levels. I think he can say whatever he darn well pleases—to those of us who choose to listen to him. I mean, I wouldn't listen to him, I'd turn him off. I wouldn't have sanctioned the Nazi march. No, I really wouldn't. You're really gettin' me because it would be inflammatory and it certainly would be very offensive to the people whose neighborhood they were walking into. Yeah, what about free speech. My foot's goin' under the table 'cause I'd want to give 'em a hit in the head! But you see, their principle is against other people's freedom and I don't think these people should suppress the freedom of somebody else. Yeah, they can say what they think, but I would hope that everybody would walk the other way. I certainly would.

It's my personal opinion, maybe it's because I was in the navy and I have a son who is now a lieutenant commander, but I feel that everybody who enjoys the freedom of this country owes this country. I think I wouldn't mind seeing it being obligatory for every person in this United States, before they reach a certain age, to give one year of their life. Not that you'd have to do it diggin' ditches, but to give your service in whatever *you* do well. To give a year to your country. I feel *we owe* this country. I really do. We enjoy its freedoms, we enjoy its benefits, and I think that people should do that. If I had to, and I told you I am not an aggressive person, but I would take up a firearm and I would defend my country against the Nazis. And I would defend this country against the Ku Klux Klan because I feel as though these people are a danger to our country. I would also defend this country against the pot-sellers in this world because I think they are a danger. I think we have the right to defend ourselves against people who go in and rob banks. I mean, supposing *they* form a club and say, "Oh boy, we're bank robbers, and this is what we believe in." Why should these people have rights? They are suppressing the rights of others. Well, if the Nazis take up arms to defend themselves, I'll tell ya! I'd be in line to defend my principles against them. I really think if these guys are comin' after my grandchildren, and this country is being turned around and turned upside down and these people are taking over our country, yes, I would fight. Maybe I wouldn't if I was twelve or thirteen years old, but believe me, today I have a vested interest!

How about the dissent for Vietnam? I didn't understand it at the time because I'm sure I didn't understand the Korean war either. I knew there was a war and I felt that we were helping to protect the principles of a suppressed people and I felt that this is why we were going in. Therefore I agreed with it, but I have since learned that the truth was not being told to us. I don't like not being told the truth. I think that was very, very wrong. I don't think Nixon should have been exonerated and I don't agree with his pardon, but I don't know what to do about it either. You know, it's there and it's bigger than all of us. When you go up to the ballot, and you go to vote, you look at the two and you wonder which is the lesser of two evils sometimes. You sit there and so what do you do? You don't vote at all? It's too bad that this one person that rules this country is being moved by big money. Big money is power and in order for a person to get themselves elected by the entire nation, they have to have money and power behind them. And therefore it is greed that is ruling the world and not human dignity. We really don't know what to do about it.

My mother always wanted me to be with good people. So that goodness, I guess, would rub off on me. Because it was important to her that I be good. And I think it's important to me that *my* kids be good. Good is pleasing other people, doing things to make the people happy, for other people's well-being. Bad is taking away the rights of somebody else, taking away something that they have earned. I think we should work. I think it's good to work for what you have. I think it's wrong to expect somebody else to give it to you or to pay you off or for you to cling to somebody else. I don't like that. As far as the bus thing, that was like running down the street and there's a baton and someone says to you, "Here, carry it." It's got to get down there and we all know it and someone passes it to you. Would you drop it? I wouldn't. I'd run with it. So it isn't that I stand here at home and say, "Oh, I'm gonna go out and get that baton!" I don't do that, but if suddenly faced with an issue that's got to be dealt with, yeah, I'll deal with it. But I'm chicken. I'm not gonna go lookin' for it!

But my mother was a very prejudiced person. To be Irish Catholic was perfect. Other than that, there were an awful lot of imperfect people around! I can remember her meeting Art and saying, "Well, he's a nice boy, but it's too bad he isn't Irish!" But she found out, I'm sure, by that point in my life, that just because a person was Irish didn't necessarily enkindle me to that person. I think it was Arthur's gentleness that attracted me to him mostly. He is a very gentle man. He puts up with me, he has to be! He works as a foreman in a shipping room and he works very, very hard. Very long hours. He's proud of me and when something comes up he'll go, "Did you hear about Gloria?" And then they'll come over and say, "Oh!" And I tell them all about it. I don't have to announce it, you know. I think the kids, too, at work hear, "Hey, your mother was in the news again," or "Are you related to *that* Gloria Arsenault?" Arthur Junior was the funniest, I think. Well, maybe that's 'cause he's my first born. He was, at the time, in Bremerton, Washington. He said that he was reading the newspaper in the ward room with a bunch of other officers and there was a little story about a bus driver. And he reads the first few lines and—at this point my name had not been revealed—he says, "Gee, this sounds like something my mother would do!" And the other officers went, "Aw, go on." He says, "Travel Time, Peabody. I know that was my mother!" So he called home and my daughter Gail answered the phone and he says, "Has Mom done anything to get herself in the newspapers lately?" Gail says, "She sure has!" I told you, that story was flashed nationwide. It was on TV. I think it was because people object strongly to dope being peddled to kids in school.

Well, how my son would know it was me—ask him about the day he took a popsicle from some other kid and mother took him by the hand to his piggybank and said, "Get a nickel!" All right. So now he's got the nickel clutched in his hand and he gets *dragged* down to a store. "Go in there and buy a popsicle. You give that back to that kid and don't you *ever* do anything like that again!" He knows. Ask him about the day he wouldn't tell me where he was goin'. I took every bit of his laundry out of the hamper and I threw it right in the middle of his room. When he comes home from the weekend, "What's this pile of dirty clothes in my room?" I says, "You're too big to tell me where you went for the weekend, you're big enough to do your own laundry." So for two weeks he did his own laundry. At the end of two weeks he says, "Ma, I'm goin' so-and-so and I'm goin' with so-and-so, would you please do my laundry?" This is my naval hero. He said boot camp was easy after living with me! When my kids came home from school and they did somethin' wrong, in school, they didn't want me to know about it. They would rather I not find out. People used to say, "You expect too much. You expect too much."

Years ago if the cigarettes had not been allowed to be smoked on the bus, we wouldn't be dealing with pot now. Before I drove the big bus I drove a station wagon. I started out driving a station wagon and it was special education and I used to insist that the kids wear their seat belts. Other people would say to me, "Why fight the seat-belt issue, the kids don't want to wear them." I said, "Yes, but if I fight the seat-belt issue, I don't have to take it any further." So I would tell 'em, "You ride in this car, you wear your seat belt. It's a law. I got my seat buckled up, you buckle up." And if I heard any language, and you did hear it, 'cause they're sitting right next to you, I reported it at school and it would stop. They'd just say, "The hell with it" and I'd say, "Watch your language!" So you know they're not going to come out with anything stronger. Yet "hell" and "damn" are used on TV they're so acceptable today. When I was a kid you swallowed your tonsils if you heard it. When I started driving the bus I said if I had known, I would *never* have let my kids take a bus to school. With these goings on, I would have let them walk!

The letter from the President, that was very big. The junior high school was in such a to-do. You know, "She got a letter from the White House!" It's true, when I speak to the principal now and tell him I have a problem —boy! He goes over and says two words to that kid and I don't know what those two words are, but they work! It makes me feel proud. I feel proud, but I don't feel as though that day I did any really big thing. A reporter said to me, "What do you think about this? Is this much to do about nothing?" And I said, "About me, yes. About kids smokin' pot on the school bus, no." That issue is very great and big and real and I will do anything, I will talk to anybody to keep that in the public mind. If I took time from getting ready for a wedding to talk to you, and if something I have said to a kid will make him stop and think, this is not a way to go, it's not going to improve my life, it's not going to make things better for me, well, this is why I'll do it.

Margaret Avery

"If a thing is very important, like principled dissent, it is probably a complicated thing and a simple thing at the same time."

□ □ □

To make your children capable of honesty is the beginning of education.

JOHN RUSKIN

I have known Margaret Avery since her first few months of existence. She is now a tall, statuesque, thinking woman approaching her middle thirties. Her choice of anonymity is a predictable product of her native caution and esteem for privacy. Her personal reserve notwithstanding, she has suffered insult and risked bodily harm to follow her conscience. Her participation in school integration as a child and later as a college student acquainted her with the spit, verbal filth, and physical harassment of adult antagonists.

Margaret is a deliberate person with a well-earned reputation for candor and kindness. Her participation in this inquiry and her enlisting of the assistance of several other interested people are what her friends have come to expect of her, just as her provision of a supper of thick-cut country ham sandwiches and coconut mocha black walnut cake was predictable. Margaret and I and her lively minded twins met in a midtown Manhattan motor inn, and as we ate her delectable alternative to an extremely unprepossessing array of motor inn menu offerings, we caught up on the main events of our lives since our last meeting. We talked together and sang together and explored at length the dimensions of the complicated issues of principled dissent. I do not know anyone who has made principled dissent more a part of their everyday life. Margaret is massively but quietly involved in the well-being of her neighborhood. She is the implacable enemy of those elements that diminish the quality of life where she lives. She has chased down numerous juvenile grocery snatchers, organized grass-roots groups of young women to discuss birth control, and made two citizens' arrests. Her friends and neighbors will tell you that if you don't want to know the truth, don't ask Margaret.

Like most really important things, principled dissent is one of these things you think about very often very deeply, but not in the concentrated way you are asking people to think about it. If I had to define principled dissent, I guess it really comes down to thinking and acting reasonably on important convictions.

When I was a child, my father and my mother and aunts and you all found many ways of telling me that I would be nothing at all if I were not my best self. I know that's what you were doing when I was a very small girl in disgrace of family fortune. You were saying, "Look, little Margaret, you shouldn't do anything just to be popular, but I, the most injured party, am fond of you and believe in you." I never forgot that. You gave me silver that day and now you have given my children silver and I am very close to tears for all kinds of reasons. Now this is what principled dissent is all about. If it does get to be a big public number, it has to be about this also. I am going to talk about that day because that is how I tend to think and talk. I mean, for me and probably most black people I know, examples without some kind of grounding in what actually goes on or has gone on are time-wasting exercises.

Now, when I was a very little girl, I did what we call—well, there's no way to say it but to say it—I mocked you. I imitated the motions of a blind man. I'm still very ashamed that I did this but I did do it and I did that because the other children had done it and because, quite frankly, I could do it better than any of them, and even then I wanted them to know that I could do it and a lot of other things much better than any of them could. This was the top of something very big. Much bigger for us kids, I'm sure, than it was for you. But not for my grown-ups because they were ashamed and they cared. It was a very complicated thing and since I am talking about it to talk about principled dissent, I really have to dwell on it. My grown-ups were scared because they were asking themselves questions about my independence of mind and also about my cool, which really means my civilization. They were ashamed because you were a friend of the family, a guest who had shown more than the expected interest in me and there I was seemingly leading the very people who had insulted you. And that was extremely unusual and troubling to them because I was not generally a leader among neighborhood children. So they did that number on me that every traditionally brought up black child could give you examples of. My family and some of the families of some of the other mockers got together and worked out a few lessons so we would understand what our mockery really meant. I mean what it said about us and how we would feel if our disabilities were thrown in our faces. It was my father who organized the whole number.

Then there was me. I was ashamed and thoughtless, but I was also disloyal, arrogant, and expedient. It is cowardly and thoughtless for parents to imagine that children cannot understand when they are being and doing these negative things. Children are young, of course, but they are not stupid. Now that I am bringing up two of them myself, I understand the great temptation to think of children as blank pages, but when I remember how it was with me when I was a child, I know that the highest obligation I have to them is to teach them to think and act in such a way that they do not deny their own best natures. Someone else could put food in their bodies or a roof over their heads or even give them more things than we can, but to make them decent human beings who will think for themselves, neither individuals nor agencies are probably going to have the time or desire to try to do that for them. I said *try* to do that for them because life has shown me that you can't be sure whether what you put in will necessarily come out in reason and decency. But I know that the activity of all those parents was designed to show us kids something unpleasant about ourselves which we needed to have brought out into the light of our powers to reason and feel. They knew how much we could bear and that we should know what we were doing and how it felt to be treated that way. And when we knew, and what is far more important, when we *felt* what they were trying to teach us, they gave us a little party to welcome us back into the company of those who win more than they lose. That was important to us kids partly because we felt uncomfortable being out and being faced with imitation ad nauseum of our own mispronunciations, foibles, and errors. Correction was generally heavily spiced with understanding and illustrated with examples on our kid level. To have it pitched in language which made no concession to our age, or to tease us about habits we were trying to acquire; well that was hard on us. Well before they were half done with their lessons, I understood what grown-ups meant when they said that they'd "rather take a beating" than some other kinds of punishments.

I guess black people have been doing these morality play punishments for a long time, but that was the first time that it happened to me. I think that my days of principled dissent really start from that incident and the things associated with it. It showed me in a kind of limited, less lethal form, what life has shown me. You can do things which qualify or even destroy the ability of people very close to you to remain close to you. Some of these things should be done and others should not be done. Your mother's friendship or your father's good opinion is not worth the price of your own reasoned approval of your best self. I learned then, in the way that children learn, that thoughtlessness is probably the first and last refuge of scoundrels. Just before I did my ultimately costly and instructive piece of mockery, I was conscious of not feeling right about it. While watching D.J. and Sarah and Kirkland do their numbers, I was uneasy about it, but narcissism got to me and I was more anxious to carry that particular part of that particular day than I was to figure out why I felt funny about doing this mockery number. I can still remember the act of will with which I consciously dismissed my better nature. Very often it is not that we are incapable of thinking beyond our immediate circumstances, but the fact that we choose to be bemused by a particular moment. In really big things, this is fatal for our self-respect. I have a few principles and sticking to them is what has made life worthwhile and difficult for me, but learning to stick to them is something you have to be taught, or what in rare instances you can teach yourself.

Most people just cannot be bothered to do anything more than teach you right from wrong—if they take the time to do that. That is not the same thing as teaching you principled dissent. Everyone has some ideas about right and wrong. Also many people have the courage without having any convictions which they have reasoned out themselves. That is why a principled dissenter is not necessarily a hero, at least not most of the heroes I learned about in schools. I mean that people like the Trojan crowd and the American Revolutionary set were brave, but not very reasonable people. Robert E. Lee was probably brave enough but he used his courage, which was probably considerable, for what a reasonable person, even in his time, would have to regard as a reprehensible cause. I think there must be a certain amount of reasonable soul-searching and the courage to face unpopular or strange ideas before you can close your mind and act upon the convictions you have decided to advocate or challenge.

When I was in school I could see that the white and black traditions of heroism were separated by this question of the importance of the right of the question. I wanted to know about the irresponsibility of the Greek women gods which started the whole Trojan thing. In some kind of automatic way, most of the kids who were white were automatically for the Greeks and against the Trojans. All through school and other parts of life, wherever I have to deal with white people, I see this general impatience with the roots of the matter. I don't mean that there are not white people who can and do think and act things through reasonably. I don't mean that there are not heaps of black people who are also dangerous, uncritical conformists. I mean that in general terms, the more you have to lose and the longer you have had more to defend, the chances are that you will go to greater lengths to keep and acquire, right notwithstanding. Every serious black school child has to have questions like mine about basic things that we sing about or read about or places we go to as we learn about our heritage, whatever that is.

I was once in a position to make a boy do almost anything for me, but this was a case of someone—him—wanting something—sex—with someone—me—so badly that he lost sight of vital questions like: Should I have this thing I want? Should the person who has it be expected to give it to me? What will it cost both of us to give and receive it? What will it cost people close to me to have this thing given and received by the giver, me, and the receiver, him. I have found that my father was right when he told me that most things people find difficult to talk about are the things they cannot afford to be silent about. I tried to talk about why I felt the ways I felt about giving sex and I wanted the boy to talk about the ways he felt which made him want to have sex with me. He didn't want to talk and I guess I understand that, but he wouldn't talk, so we went our separate ways for years and years. I always loved you because you would listen to me and, at least as important to me, you talked to me as if my opinions about important matters meant something. I don't think children ever really respect people of whatever age, unless they, the children, feel respected. Most of the adults I knew behaved toward me in such a way as to train me to think that not to answer a civil question was a kind of insult. People who wouldn't answer my civil questions were saying that I was not worth taking up time with. They were saying that they couldn't be serious or that I was too dumb to be serious.

I do not like feeling like dirt. I learned through being forced to live up to the meanings of my arrogances and indiscriminate passion for popularity. I learned to control my greeds as much as I have because people who had gotten theirs under control took the trouble to show me my faults and their consequences and to tell me of theirs. Now I could have treated their lessons like dirt, but I didn't like how I felt about that. My mother told me things about herself which I will never tell a living soul. I know how hard it must have been for her to tell me those things and I know that she must love me a great deal to tell me these things. You see, my mother, as you know, is the last person who would call a talk show or just go around confessing all over the place. I guess all us neighborhood kids thought of our parents, especially our mothers, as saints or devils. They were certainly nothing less than queens. When they spoke, we were right there, or got there as soon as humanly possible. I always knew in more than some off-handed vague ways why the really important things were happening. I knew because people told me and because I was made to feel that I could ask any question I really wanted to know the answer to.

My father was the only person in my family who ever talked baby talk to me and he only did that when I was using curiosity as a means toward some trivial end. I remember that he kept me up hours past my bedtime talking in baby talk about some dumb thing I had asked him just to avoid bedtime. "You know, Shug," he said, "I'd have respected you a great deal more if you had just asked me if you could stay up a little longer." Now I know that he needed the sleep more than I did, and I know, because he made me think, that his punishment was instructive and a great sacrifice to him. My father worked hard and he was not well, but he gave me four hours of his precious leisure to get me to deal honestly and master my greed. I could see that he was tired and I knew he was not well, but I wanted what I wanted, even after he had already given me a break in the bedtime number. Now somebody reading this might say, well, she is just being goody-goody or self-deprecating or something, and I could tell you something about that kind of reader. I am mentioning these simple things because they are the things I remembered when I was lying awake last night thinking about what principled dissent is, and whether I am a principled dissenter. I decided that I was and what it is and then I tried to figure out how I got to be one, and these are the things which came to mind.

Everybody has some experience that could be called principled dissent, but that does not mean that principled dissent is their dominant style. It is mine because I prefer it over other life-styles I have tried and observed others trying. It is, like every other style of life, a habit. Something you will do with reasonable consistency and frequency once you get used to doing it. You have to try to get to the bottom of things. You must learn not to take things on face value. You must try to know with all your heart and mind the real truth of things. These things are very hard to do because most people do not like to be questioned about important things, or their versions of important things; things like sex, patriotism, religion, money, their word, God's word as they understand it, their principles. If a thing is very important, like principled dissent, it is probably a complicated thing and a simple thing at the same time, because that is generally the way things are in nature and that means human nature also.

Joe Bangert

"There's a certain balance on this earth and if you mess with it, it's gonna mess with you."

□ □ □

A man who specializes in killing other men—regardless of ideology—is an assassin. Forcing youths to do this is a crime.

JORGE LUIS BORGES

Joe "Dioxin" Bangert is fluent in Vietnamese and steeped in the inglorious mysteries, abundant fantasies, and anguished lessons generated by the Vietnam War. The war experience is central to his life now. It has filled him with guilt, pride, shame, and nostalgia. His activism revolves around alerting the nation to the perils of Dioxin poisoning, but that is only one central issue of many that prompt his principled dissenting.

We sat and talked at a large, round refinished table that has served me since graduate-school coffee-house days. We ate good Scandinavian cheese, beef, veal, and pork sausage, and drank dark beer and ale from Norway, New Castle, Hamburg, Tsingtao, and San Francisco. Joe relived his central experience and the experiences generated by it. As he remembers, the reasons for his sense of political mission become apparent. The importance of solidarity of veterans and the responsibility of veterans to warn their fellow countrymen against the mortal dangers of unquestioning obedience and jingo fever are constantly elaborated themes.

Joe is the active president of Chapter 117 of the Eastern Massachusetts Vietnam Veterans of America, and he recently organized a Vietnam veterans weekend encampment, "Operation Justice," to call attention to the class action suit filed by Agent Orange victims against the federal government and seven chemical companies that manufactured the herbicide. He is unhappy on principle with the out-of-court settlement of that suit and feels the settlement is paltry and unmindful of the principles that generated the whole Agent Orange protest movement. He feels that the abandonment of those principles may mortgage the futures of unborn generations. Joe is very much aware of the demands of future generations, as he and Vicki have just become the parents of Christopher Robert, an eight-pound, four-ounce, healthy baby boy.

I was raised in an orphanage in North Philadelphia. I came from a poor background but I was shocked at the degree of injustice in the country, you know, just about the time that I was coming into puberty. At the time I was a Catholic and I remember thinking, "Hey! It must be hot shit that Jack Kennedy's running for President," because they made much of the fact that he was a Catholic and came from an Irish background. But I never forget the fact that he was also a millionaire and his old man had a big store in Chicago. So there were class lines too that didn't fool me that I was cognizant of at an early age.

I remember that the newspaper used to have world trouble spots on large maps, not just of the United States, but of the world. To be sure, I was being educated in the good old Catholic, anti-Communist way, which inevitably set me up to go to Vietnam, but I do remember siding with people who wanted the right to vote, who wanted to sit any damn place they wanted to on a bus or at a lunch counter. It had to do with some other imagery in that my father had been dragged out of our house when I was very young. He was literally pulled out of our family and I guess I knew then that when cops intercede it causes pain. I knew that psychologically, but in 1963 I was seeing it on a massive scale. I think that if I had been old enough, I would have gone down South in the Civil Rights Movement, but I was too young then. I was only about eleven or twelve, but my senti-ments were there. I was grounded in principled dissent because I saw that the people were acting nonviolently and acting in their own right. I don't know if I was all that sophisticated, but I knew something stunk in America when the President of the United States was assassinated. I knew that it had something to do with all those world troublespots I was reading about, but I was too unsophisticated to put it all together. Anyway, I found out at an early age that although there's the line you get in your civics class, there's also the ultimate truth that one level of politics in this country is dirty and based on violence. That demonstrated itself over and over again in my lifetime. That's even before Vietnam. And then I watched what was basically a civil war break out in Philadelphia.

One time my brother and I and Eddy Schwartz came up out of the sub-way at Sixteenth and Allegheny in Philadelphia and we're walkin' back to the Home I was raised in—which was a white institution in a completely black community, with the exception of medical students at the Temple University Medical School and they were mostly upper-middle-class white Jewish—so we're comin' out of the subway and we look up the street, and there were a lot of young black men, about eighteen to about twenty-five years of age. So Eddy and my brother said, "Shit, I ain't goin' out there, that's crazy. Those niggers'll getcha!" Well, I was fifteen, and I figured I could walk down the street with impunity and nothin' would happen to me and I certainly wasn't gonna cross the street because of an unwarranted fear. And that's truthful, that was in my mind. I wasn't lookin' for trouble, I was the last person in the world that wanted trouble, but at the same time, I didn't want to be an actor in an unwarranted fear. My crass em-

piricism said, walk down the street and see what happens! And so I did.
And I got outside of Bob Evans's funeral home and about three guys
grabbed me and started working me over. They had brass knuckles and
worked me over pretty good, and while they were doin' it, Eddy and my
brother were across the street feeling helpless and started screaming, "You
niggers, you niggers, stop!" I'm not grateful to them for that! And afterwards I made it back to the Home and what evolved after that I think
really taught me a few things in my life. When I got back I was put in the
infirmary and I had been stitched up and been given some downers, and
I was layin' in bed and I heard this big rumble throughout the orphanage
of these older boys. They were all white, the older boys that never really
gave a shit about us younger kids but used this incident as an occasion to
organize a rumble. So I just heard this activity throughout the Home, of
guys gettin' chains and gettin' their knives. Their testosterone was flowin'
and I heard, "Donahue got a gun!" And they went out. I heard there were
some bad rumbles in the neighborhood and the next day the Philadelphia
police department come up there with their picture rogues' gallery, and
they sat by the bed and they were goin' through page after page of black
faces. Kept goin' through them and it was none of the individuals that
attacked me, and after about an hour and a half of this, the detective that
was at my bedside turned around and said, something to the effect—I'm
just trying to remember, it's been years now—said something like "Come
on, just pick any of these niggers." And I turned around and said, "Well,
I can't. They weren't the ones that hit me." And he said, "That's all right,
just pick three of them because any three of 'em probably will have done
it already to somebody else. Just pick three of 'em." And I turned around
and I couldn't. And I know they left in disgust. But for me, that taught me
somethin' about the larger injustice that existed, and I think the Philadelphia police department did an excellent job in teaching me attitudinally
why blacks started to become quite militant at that point in Philadelphia,
because it was only a year or two after that that there was the first so-called
riot in Philadelphia. But I can tell you that I did have black friends in the
community and in the school who called me up when the so-called race
riot was going on in North Philadelphia in 1965, and basically hinted that
it was a grand occasion for me to go down to all those stores whose windows I'd looked in but never had money to buy anything, and get anything
I damn well wanted. There were plenty of whites that shopped during the
great black urban uprising in Philadelphia in 1965!

You know, to me, when I was a kid, if you had a mother and father and
lived in a house, you were middle class. That was my class consciousness.
It's terrible how sophisticated I had to get later. I guess the beginning of
my understanding of dissent was really born with the Civil Rights Movement at a very young age. I remember seeing something about dissent too
in Saigon because that was on television. I remember the Buddhists rising
up. I'll never forget the monks immolating themselves. I'll never forget
that there were Americans immolating themselves too, but in the quasi-
revisionist history of the Vietnam war that was on Channel 2, they never
talked about the fact that early on during the war there were Americans
who knew what was going on and in their outrage all they could do was

to consume themselves in an act of protest and defiance. I was shocked when GBH had their program on that they never paid homage to those Americans. In sixty-three and sixty-four Quakers, Catholics, and Unitarians torched themselves. One guy stands out in my mind, Norman Morrison, a Quaker who did it in Washington on the steps of the Pentagon practically. So I guess those world trouble spots kept coming up.

One of my best friends at school was Timmy Hannigan. We were seniors at Roman Catholic high and I knew his brother. His brother, Tommy Hannigan, was a year before us. Timmy was my best friend in high school and he came to school one day very disturbed and I said, "What happened?" He said, "Tommy was killed in Vietnam." This was the first time a death brushed close to me and it was the first funeral I went to. I remember having revenge on my mind because he was a friend of mine and all I knew was that Communism killed him. That's what they told us. You know, he went off to South Vietnam to fight Communism and they killed him. That was enough! That was enough for a lot of us. A year later I graduated from high school. I was seventeen, I couldn't get a job in a factory. You have to be eighteen to work around machinery. I tried and I did get jobs. I got a couple of jobs. They would last about two weeks before they would check out my birth record and then it was, "Hey! You ain't eighteen, take a walk, screw!" I had a lot of good jobs. To me then, they were good jobs. Warehouseman at Sears, warehouseman at the General Electric appliance store. The fact that I was A-1 meant that I could never get a company to put me in a training program. That was my class lot. This is something that a lot of middle-class people can't get through their thick, stupid heads. They think that Americans went off willingly to Vietnam. They don't understand that the dice were thrown and the great majority of us who went there never had a choice. But I wasn't afraid to do my duty either. I was raised in that post–World War II era and the myth in the cities was, if you ever put on the uniform for the Uncle and something happened to you, the Uncle would always take care of you. Within working-class districts, that was our answer; socialism for soldiers. You just have to go in and put in your time and they'll give you your free ticket to college, you know, if you survive the holocaust. Then too, machismo entered into it. That's why I joined the marine corps. They said, "Two, three, or four years?" And I remember looking at the recruiter in Germantown and saying, "Ah, what the hell! Give me four!"

So I went to Vietnam but I went in the marine corps. Then the sixty-eight Tet Offensive broke out. It was January of sixty-eight and my long-lost dad popped into the scene again. He found out that I was at Camp Pendleton. We had a rendezvous—my old man's a bit of an actor. It was just before I was about to go to Vietnam and sure as hell, they would have sent me to Hue and if they had, I wouldn't be here tonight talking to you. I was dug in in the hills of Camp Pendleton for maneuvers and it was the last night, called staging battalion, where they really brutalize you that one last time. They had this little mock Vietnamese village. A couple of days before we heard about this staff sergeant who was training green recruits in the art of hand grenade–throwing and he pulled the pin on the grenade and pulled it into his chest and blew himself up in front of a whole bunch

of recruits. I guess they'd write that up now as post traumatic stress disorder, but that wasn't in the books then. I'll try to get off this subject.
How I was saved from the jaws of death was, long-lost dad pops in. I'm
dug in in this position and this lieutenant runs up to me and the sun was
going down and he said, "Lance Corporal Bangert, report immediately to
the commanding general. He just landed in his helicopter out on the main
road." I went, thinking, Jesus Christ, what's going on now! So I run up
there and there's the commanding general sitting in his helicopter and
there's my old dad sitting on the other side. I said, "Oh God!" Dad was
always a shaky character, you know. He was a con man and an artist, but
this showed me his art. So I get there and my dad says, "I want you to
meet the general, Joe." So we go flying back mainside and we have a big
dinner in the general's chow hall and have drinks and everything and I'm
just thrilled. Pop had found out that the general was a two-star general and
he had told him that he was a three-star general in the air force, which
wasn't true, but the general didn't know that. Generals as a group of people
are pretty stupid. So he was trying to ego trip to my dad and show him his
power by pulling me out of training. Of course, Pop told another lie and
said that I was brilliant, and can we do anything to get this guy out of
going to Vietnam? I was upset then because I wanted to go. I thought,
"God, Pop, what are you doing to me? I'm ready to go!" The general said,
"I think I can fix you up. I want you to take the Army Language Aptitude
Test because your father tells me you used to be an altar boy and you
speak Latin." So I said, "Yes, sir!" Being a lance corporal, I better say
yes, sir. Well, I aced the test, got a hundred percent in it, so they gave me
orders. "Report to Defense Language Institute, West Coast Branch, Pre-
sidio, Monterey—to Vietnamese Language School." I said, "Great!" Not
only am I going to go to Vietnam, but unlike everyone else in my unit
and in my service, I'm going to go to Vietnam with a working knowledge
of Vietnamese. That will probably pay off in my own survivability. So I
was thrilled. I studied Vietnamese as I was ordered by the military and I
didn't mind getting paid doing that work. I loved school and I went to
work eight hours a day. There were two hours a day mandatory study. My
teachers were Vietnamese. Some were from Hanoi, some of them from
Saigon, some of them were from Hue. The guy who specifically taught me
was minister of agriculture under Ngo Dinh Diem. Here he is teaching me
Vietnamese as we're watching the Tet Offensive in 1968 on television at
the same time. It was a pretty good ego trip for me. Here I am a lance
corporal and I'm sitting here with colonels and majors and generals and
CIA spooks. So did I get an education! Very quickly I found out something
about the dynamics of military power in the country. I also found out how
stupid the officer corps in the U.S. military was too, because they weren't
very good at learning Vietnamese. If a guy with a high school education
could learn Vietnamese like a crackerjack and these officers were like
picking their noses and didn't know what the hell was going on, it told me
that no matter what my social lot was in life, I had brains and I could
excel. And to prove the point I did. I studied Vietnamese with a passion.
I loved the culture. I was being taught by Vietnamese professors who
would come up with quotes like this: "When you Europeans were trying

to get King John to give you the right to petition and redress your government, we in Vietnam had to fill out civil service forms to get jobs"; or, "When you folks in Europe were finding out that it was probably a good idea to put pants on, we in Vietnam had bureaucracies and kings to contend with." It was my first chance at higher learning and I loved it. The history was incredible. It impressed me more than the language! So off I went.

Dad didn't get caught. That was one of the few times he didn't get caught. I never had much interface with my dad. In retrospect, whether other people in the family like it or not, in my own particular case because of the circumstances, my father was there when I needed him, even though I might have been embarrassed when he first showed up. It turned out that he delayed my entry into the most virulent part of the war. The benefit that I got from going to Vietnamese language school and meeting Vietnamese people before I went to Vietnam has meant that I have the benefit of coming back from Vietnam a human being. A lot of people came back home as animals. I think the purpose of that act of my father's was to let son know his dad was resourceful. The marine corps probably never found him out, not at all. To get in their officer corps, you have to have a diminution of your mental processes in the first place. Otherwise, how are you going to hit the beaches when some idiot in his striped suit in Washington tells you to?

I'll tell you one thing that happened to me when I was at language school. They did make me a corporal—and a corporal in the marine corps is a noncommissioned officer, which means you're in charge of leading troops. One night I had some boot recruits come into the barracks that I was in charge of. They were screaming and hollering and they woke me up and I remember looking out the window and I saw a car pull up. I heard a Southern voice say, "And if you open your mouth about this I'll kill you! You understand that, you bastards? Fuckin' doggies!" And the car drove away with people screaming. And I remember one other voice, but I was half asleep and he went, "My God! He's bit my ear off!" That's what woke me up. It turned out the next morning I found out that two army Vietnam veterans that happened to be stationed at Fort Ord had been brutalized. They were at the enlisted men's club and they saw some marine recruits at language school get drunk. Out of the kindness of their hearts they offered these guys a ride home to their barracks. The marines turned on these army MPs in the car on the way and started a fight. One guy I think had his eye put out and the other MP had his ear ripped off. It was a terrible, dirty fight. And then they forced the guys they beat up to drop them off at their barracks. I was a conscientious marine so I went the next morning to my commanding officer and said, "Captain, I got a terrible situation on my hands . . ." He said, "What's that?" "You probably heard about the two army MPs that were brutalized and attacked and I know the people who did it. They're right in my barracks!" The captain said, "Marines stick together." I was so outraged that I walked out of his office. I marched down to the provost marshall's office. I was on an army base, ultimately under army supervision. I said to the provost marshall, "I'm horrified and sickened about what happened to the two army Vietnam veterans, the MPs that were beat up last night, and I know the people who did it." The army captain said, "What would you need to point them out to me?" And I said, "Give me a forty-five and a gunbelt and we'll go right now and we'll get them." So they gave me a gunbelt and a pistol and they followed me and I walked right into my barracks and I walked right upstairs and pulled out the pistol because those guys were intimidating, and I said, "You and you, fall out." I pressed charges and I got at least three or four eyewitnesses that were up at the time of the incident and we turned them over. I went through hell. I went through terrible hell. Well, it's important to remember that it was in June of sixty-eight that this occurred. I remember being an East Coast kid and a kid that loved the Kennedys. I started to change politically since I was imminently going to Vietnam. I remember Bob Kennedy started opening his mouth very honestly, saying that the war was stupid, that it was a waste of lives, especially after the debacle in Khe Sanh and Hue where the marines were actually chewed up and destroyed by General Giap. General Giap graciously withdrew and didn't take them as POWs, and he could have. I remember that the order was given that no marine in or out of uniform was to go to hear that "Communist" Robert Kennedy speak. I got so pissed off. I'd had it. I knew then that I was in the wrong business, but I was kind of stuck to a four-year contract. I went nonetheless, and I was impressed by Bob Kennedy, but I was shocked because what he was saying was what students were saying. That the war was stupid, was ill-conceived, and the Americans ought to get out. That was before I went to Vietnam that I had that experience. That was in June. I was waiting in the barracks for a transfer. They were going to send me to San Francisco to the marine barracks at Treasure Island to await the court martial of the guys who beat up the MPs. We just got our orders to go to San Francisco when they said that Bob Kennedy was assassinated in Los Angeles. In April of sixty-eight Martin Luther King was assassinated. I was at Monterey when that happened. So most outrageous things were happening at home. I realized that although I might be missing Hue and Khe Sanh, there was a war at home. I would go on liberty with some Chicano marines. We'd go to East Los Angeles—I'm a marine in uniform—but they would say, "Be careful" as we crossed the street into El Barrio, because there was warfare going on. So that was a pretty heavy experience and I'm not even in Vietnam yet!

I want to tell you about my fight with the Klan. In the marines I'm stationed in Memphis and we're staying at the Hotel Tennessee. I knew something about the Klan, I knew they were down on black folks. I knew they were down on Jews and Catholics, so I didn't think very much of them. They were down on trade unions too. Here I am in Memphis, I could not believe that the Ku Klux Klan was having a rally in downtown Memphis. I said, "Jesus, I'm a Northern boy! I gotta check this out!" I wanted to get right up front. I was with some marines from New York, Boston, and some black marines from L.A., and I see these guys with the TV cameras setting up and making their speeches and I start learning all this shit like there's a cyclops and there's wizards and all this crap. I remember saying to some guys from Atlanta, "You know, these guys are a disgrace to the white race!" They said, "Jesus! That's what *they're* gonna

say about *you!*" I said, "Look, we're marines! I ain't puttin' up with this
shit!" So here's a good fight. We can practice our training right here! Someone came up with a football and we started playing football between the
TV cameras and the Great Cyclops. Sheldon was speaking, I remember,
you know, before one of his own got him. The Klan didn't like that, but
we were baldheaded marines, we were dying to fight. We were ready to
take on the Klan right there! Not for politics, just for the hell of it. We
were in good shape, lean prime shape, and I remember we ran to the Hotel
Tennessee in Memphis where we had rooms. They started picketing the
hotel. We said, "Ah, shit!" We knew about what happened down South in
the Civil Rights Movement. Philadelphia, Mississippi, wasn't very far. We
said, "Damn! We're the enemy now!" So we went upstairs, I think we
were on the eighteenth floor and we weren't into drugs then but we were
certainly into macho. I remember we had a couple of bottles of Jack
Daniel's. We said, "These boys are going to come in and get us!" There
was a sense of adrenaline going in the room and it was very clear that the
police weren't going to intercede because the police were there guarding
the Klan. We did get a little scared, but if you're ready to go to war, you
don't care. We drank the Jack Daniel's, we were celebrating the fact that
we disrupted a Klan rally. We kind of laughed at them. We didn't know
what was going to happen. I didn't have one iota of politics that I could
say was politics then, except that I didn't like the Klan. We downed about
two bottles of Jack Daniel's between about five of us and got good and
drunk. We found out that with a slight tap on the hotel room doors you
could be in the next room and then the next room. We went over about
three rooms. All these rooms were empty so we opened up the window,
ripped the color television off the wall, and we threw the color television
down there where the Klan guys were picketing. We were trying to repro-
duce the scene from the *Hunchback of Notre Dame.* We didn't have any
hot oil but we certainly had a color television. They wanted to be on television so we said, "You want television? We'll give you television!" From
the eighteenth floor! I don't know if it hit any of them, I don't think it did,
but it shook their shit!

I'll just tell you one more story. It was the Fourth of July in 1968 and
I decided to go to Berkeley because I hear these goddamned students that
don't give us the time of day are going to have a demonstration, and they're
going to have a Viet Cong flag and I'm going to go up and see this. I'm
still a reactionary and I went up to Berkeley with some friends. It was our
idea to catch some of these students with that goddamn Communist flag
and we'd beat the shit out of them. I remember that was the first time I
ever saw hippies. They had holes in their jeans, you could see their asses,
women with no brassieres and their blouses were open. It was like total
anarchy! There was something attractive, but something very repugnant.
But the fact that I was there! I knew I was going to drink in some exotica,
you know, tit America. I know that's where free speech started. People
could say "Fuck you, fuck you, fuck you" and people would say that's
the right to free speech. I thought that was a bit nuts because I was from a
conservative background, but I wanted to see it. Again, empiricism drove
me on. It was the first time that I was ever in a university place and of

course I was a pariah with my short hair. I knew I was purging some remnant innocence. Just before the march began down Telegraph Avenue I looked on a roof and I saw a whole roof full of naked people and they were screwing. I said to myself, "Jesus! These people are selling Marxism-Leninism and I'm going to Vietnam to fight Communism. There's something very confusing here." The march was beginning on the street and I saw this punk with a Viet Cong flag. He had a whole bunch of Viet Cong flags and he was putting them up on the telegraph poles. Here was the moment. There were all sorts of hippies, dope was being smoked all over the place; I was afraid even to take a breath. Somebody said to the kid, "What are you doing with them goddamn flags?" "I'm putting them up." He was really smart 'cause he said, "Hey! Don't be so worried about the flags. Why don't you smoke a joint?" Then all of us just stopped dead in our tracks. He said, "Yeah, yeah, before you do something rash, why don't you just smoke a joint and think about it?" The guy turned out to be a Yippie. So we said, "You got one?" He said "yeah" and gave us a big bomber and we got good and toked. I said, "Jeez, you got another one?" "Yeah, yeah," and he gave us another one. "Yeah, you need it. Here's one with the American flag on it." Oh my God! This is fun, smoking another one. This guy's doing agitation propaganda, killing us dead cold in the street with marijuana attacks, right? He gave us a third one, gave us a fourth one. We were good and loaded. Now I was ready to look around for the naked bodies. I wanted to see everything. So the kid with the flags turned around and said, "Hey, this shit don't grow on trees! I tell you what, you help me to get rid of these flags and I'll turn you on to four more joints." So we said, "Okay." We had met the enemy and had been smashed. This is *before* Vietnam, right?

Meanwhile at the base I'm still dealing with these big pig bastards from Texas that were scaring the shit out of me in the pending court martial. One night while I'm duty NCO, they come in from liberty and they hand in their cards and I can't believe it! The fingernails of one of the defendants were all stained with dried blood. I woke up the next morning and I found that there was a busload of returning Vietnam vets. And the story goes that there was a corpsman on this bus and these same assholes that I was trying to prosecute were also on this bus and they passed a snide remark that this corpsman was a "squid," which, as you know, is a derogatory term for a sailor. So this corpsman stood up and said, "I'm as much a marine as you are and maybe more. I've had thirteen months in Vietnam so shut up." He was tight with a bunch of other marine corps vets that were on the bus. The corpsman made the terrible mistake of getting off the bus at the navy barracks before they got to the marine barracks and these Texas guys got off the bus, doubled back, beat him up, and he died the next morning. And I was the only one who knew that these guys had committed murder. About two days later, the legal officer comes up to me. This kind of explains how a change took place in my life. I mean, this is the first time I've had a chance to tell you or anyone about this—the raw material for my metamorphosis in Vietnam. In a sense, Vietnam was my escape from an outrageous, untenable situation. I didn't know what to do. I knew the deck was stacked against me. Finally a marine corps legal officer came up to me and talked to me about the pending court martial. I didn't know whether I should open my mouth about the murder of the corpsman. I had been terrorized a couple of times by these same individuals and I was in fear of my life. The legal officer said, "Corporal Bangert, you know marines usually stick together and I'm not going to let you into the courtroom unless you give an affirmative answer to this question. I think it's only fair. I want you to compromise. It's no use sticking to your guns, otherwise you're not going to have a chance to give testimony. That's the way it works." I said, "What's the story?" He said, "Well, I'm going to ask you before we proceed in the court martial tomorrow, whether you would be willing to serve in combat with these men that are accused." So I went back to my barracks and thought about it. I saw him the next morning and I said, "Okay, I got the answer. I'll answer in the affirmative." He said, "Okay, you can come to the court." So I went to the court and the first thing the legal officer said to me was, "Corporal Bangert, before we proceed, I'd like to establish something. Being a marine, would you be willing to serve in combat with these accused marines?" And I said, "Captain, I'd like to answer that question. I was approached by you yesterday and you told me that if I didn't answer this question in the affirmative I wouldn't be allowed into this court martial and I told you yes, I'd answer the question in the affirmative and now I'm here in the court martial. I would be willing to serve in combat with these marines that are accused, with one stipulation, Captain, that they would be permanent point!" They kicked me out of the courtroom. I immediately put in for leave. I wrote a letter to the Eleventh Naval District telling them all the facts that I knew about the corpsman who was killed, took my leave, and then I was on my way to Vietnam. I hear there was a court martial and they got off lightly and they were sent to Vietnam and the reason was that they were connected with LBJ's politics in some way. They were family friends or something like that. During my leave, the Democratic National Convention was held in Chicago and at that point, I knew that it made more sense for me to go to Vietnam than to try to figure out what was going on in this country in 1968. But the spirit of rebellion had entered into my soul.

So finally I'm on the first leg of the Vietnam trip and I can remember what was on my mind. I could be killed in Vietnam, but I knew, secretly, you know, psychologically, that after what I'd been through, Vietnam would be a relief. We had to stop in Honolulu and it was a cruel stop because Hawaii is a beautiful place and we only had thirty minutes to lay over and I remember that everyone piled out of the plane and went in and ordered their Mai Tais. I was sitting with a sergeant, it was his second time over and he said, "This is terrible that we have so little time. We could have such a good time." I didn't say anything to him, but I told you that the rebellion had already entered my heart. I dropped a dime in the phone and said in a clandestine voice, "There's a military air force plane that just landed from California. There's a bomb aboard. Good-bye." Click. Then I went back to the bar. My Mai Tai was there and I drank it very slowly and other people forced them down real quick. I'm sitting there just smiling, didn't say a word. Had another Mai Tai. Forty minutes go by, fifty minutes go by. They finally assembled us and they said, "All people from the military air transport service plane that just landed forty-five minutes ago, please return to the aircraft." They made us stand outside the aircraft. They unloaded all the baggage and they made us stand with the baggage on the parade deck for about a half hour. I'm thinking, as the perpetrator, "You bastards! You want the guy with the bomb in his bag to blow up the guy next to him! God! You're cold!" Nothing happened so they said, "All right, you people are going to be taken to Honolulu. You'll be here for two nights. You folks have two days' liberty so we'll put you up in hotels." I was thrilled. Now I have a chance to see Hawaii and I'm getting all my revenge on the military. I don't know if it was principled, but it certainly was nonviolent and I got everyone a benefit. I think, even retrospectively tonight, I'm not ashamed. I take responsibility for that act. I know that there were at least fifty people on that plane who are not walking the earth tonight and I take some, you know, misplaced gratitude that at least they had two or three days in Hawaii before they died. I don't give a damn! I had a right to do it! Let the bastards know who they're playing with. I was nineteen then, okay? Now I'm thirty-five. They better be careful when I'm forty-five and fifty!

All the Memorial Day and Fourth of July speeches lost all their significance for me in Vietnam. All my religiosity lost its significance for me in Vietnam. When I was a gunner, I saw a Protestant minister and a Catholic priest take off in a helicopter to do gun missions, and a doctor too. Just because they wanted to have that macho experience. I became a gunner on a helicopter for the same reason. There was a lot of frustration in Vietnam, which brought out a lot of cruelty, but let's face it, what went down in Vietnam and what went down in military training before Vietnam among young men was a veritable mind fuck, if you'll excuse my language, but that's what it was. They indoctrinated most people to believe that in the name of anti-Communism any kind of behavior could go! That's real clear in El Salvador today, isn't it? I've changed because of my Vietnam experience, and it was a bit schizophrenic for me to work it out, but I worked it out directly. I worked it out within two years. I'm not one of the walking wounded from Vietnam. I purged myself and I know that one of the criteria to receive aid for post traumatic stress disorder is to manifest an "obsession with justice"—which I have. I should get fifty percent disability from my Uncle Sam and I can prove it. I've been obsessed with justice since I walked out of the Vietnam jungle. "Obsession with justice" is recognized by the American Psychiatric Association as one of the conditions of post traumatic stress disorder, which they consider a serious mental disorder. There are more things taking place in my life than the Vietnam War, but the Vietnam war experience kind of set them off.

I had a garden in Vietnam. I used to go down to the riverside, the Thach Han River, and I used to take the silt from the river. The area I was stationed in had been so heavily defoliated it was like a desert. I'd go get the silt and I had seeds that my family sent me from the States. I planted some flowers. I think there were marigolds and some mums and I used to try to plant some banana trees. Bananas to me, coming from Philadelphia, are the ultimate in exotica. They still amaze me. I love them. Some place I even have a photograph of one of the flowers, I think. The flowers would grow up, let's say within seven days, and blossom to a total blossom within four days and then shrivel up. It was absolutely speeded up, the growth process, and the bananas always wilted and died. Nothing grew, nothing! When I saw my garden going through these weird changes I knew something was wrong and I remember that one of the ideas which went through my head was, "We're smoking pot and they're worried about that! And yet, I knew that they had declared war on the land itself! Come on, give me a break!" I remember when C-130s would fly over my base spraying the Orange. I had a good sense of paranoia because I had read Rachel Carson's *The Silent Spring* when I was a sophomore in high school, so I knew something about DDT and I just knew they were spraying DDT in Vietnam. I also saw with my own eyes what was happening to the jungle. I saw the destruction. I saw exactly what the bastards were doing and I was part of the bastard force, but I was an American doing my duty!

My impact with dioxin started in Vietnam, but it really came to light in 1977, when I had a chance to chat with Maude DeVictor for a while on the phone, and then I finally got to see her and I helped organize the National Veterans Task Force for Agent Orange and brought the first group of national leaders of Vietnam vets and environmentalists together in St. Louis. I hear a lot of old guys, World War II vets I work for, they say, "Joe, Joe, Joe, aren't you going to get over Vietnam? Why don't you get over it?" I mean, it's really a major point of reference in my life and they say, "Why don't you get over it?" I think I at least have a responsibility to humanity and trees, to the people I knew and befriended, both Vietnamese and Americans, to my good American friends who were my comrades-in-arms and died there, I'll always honor the memory of humanity that was lost in that war on both sides by at least telling the truth about that war. I'm learning as much as I can about the truth as a person who was in a war, a most horrible experience. You know, the final lack of communication is war.

Militarists are the ones that have these idealistic phrases, "contain Communism," "eliminate with extreme prejudice," "neutralize." That's why the American people have to stop and look at their English language, stop and look at those words and ask people, and do the search themselves, what do these words mean? Eliminate with extreme prejudice means smash those human beings into soil, smash them into guts and viscera, and that's what warfare is about and that's what the mission was in Vietnam. "Body count." "Get a body count." These were concepts and they didn't come from enlisted men off the streets of America because we were mostly citizen soldiers. These were concepts that came from military academies in this country and from the general officer corps. They're the ones that brought those concepts into Vietnam. I refer to it in my own terms as the Auschwitzification of the workplace, and the Auschwitzification of the military service. And the cheapest commodity are the humans that they send out to kill. They're cheap, they're finite, they can't sue, we can extinguish their lives for thirty thousand dollars, okay? And that's no problem. We give them all a flag and a letter from the President.

Do I expect my fellow Americans to listen to me? Yeah! I want them to go through the same painful reexamination that I had to go through at twenty years of age about what country I live in. People have gotta take the responsibility because it's being done in our name. I think the most painful thing is that people with some consciousness in this country are almost cursed. You become like an expatriate, the victims of a kind of soft fascism.

The Klan guy that you were talking about is just in the wrong area. He should go out to Southie or Belmont where the rest of those coneheads live. Personally, I'd like to see the Klan all sent back to Caucasia. Yeah, I would restrict the marketplace of ideas to some extent. How would I justify principled repression? Well, I think people manipulate the loopholes, you know, the Jeffersonian loopholes in democracy, to their own volition. I do believe, to a certain degree in home rule, and I think that if people in the community of Skokie decide that they don't want the Nazis to march, that's a two-way street. Before Nixon jammed the Supreme Court, I think these cases could be taken to wise people who knew something about law and wisdom and justice. Somewhere you gotta draw the line. The weight of each argument has to be looked at in the light of other things happening in the community and you have to come to a decision. I'm not into dragging it out like twenty years. You make a decision and you try to use common sense. I think common sense is something that's missing. Like if the Department of Environmental Quality Engineering decides a guy in Orleans can't have tree stumps in his yard because you have to cover them with six inches of dirt, they're nuts. Common sense tells you that. But they can find a drum of 2,4,5,T and not really get excited about that.

I've been a dioxin detective on Cape Cod and found plenty of it. I could tell you about Mike Galuska, who worked at Naushon Island from 1979 to 1982 and was ordered by the trustees to use 2,4,5,T on the range lands and now he's into acute kidney failure and I'm trying to fight for his case. He's got constant kidney syndrome with a nephrotic condition. He happens to be a Vietnam-era veteran who never set foot in Vietnam and he's an acute dioxin victim, and the state has stacked their case against him 'cause they said they don't know nothin' about dioxin to relate it to his worktime exposure. I think the dioxin question is sort of a major cutting edge to the whole question of legitimacy of the powerful. I've got evidence that possibly many drums of 2,4,5,T are clandestinely being stored on the very watershed of the Quabbin Reservoir, which feeds most of the water going into Boston.

Apart from my own observations of my botanical experimentation in Vietnam, as a Civic Action Officer, I had the occasion in 1969 to see children with what turns out in hindsight to be very serious cases of chloracne. I'd seen some of the birth defects myself in Vietnam but never related it to anything. I remember the first time I ever thought about Agent Orange was when I was with a group of young Americans in Detroit, Michigan, in January of 1971. We had decided that, in the wake of My Lai, that the American people should know what they were buying in Vietnam, or what they were being forced to buy in Vietnam—and that was in fact, to use Maude's word, genocide. We gave testimony at the Winter Soldier investigation conducted by the Vietnam Veterans Against the War on January 31, 1971. After we gave testimony of war crimes, I remember we had interaction with Ike Pappas of, I think it was, CBS News. He's a Pentagon correspondent and Ike said to me, "Do you expect the American people to believe your testimony when they see that you have long hair and beards and look the way you look?" I told him, "I don't know what you're gettin' at, but everything we said, as far as we're concerned, is true. And he asked me, and this was on tape, "Well, your appearance. You lose credibility with the American people." And I remember I said as an aside, 'cause he was tryin' to get our goat by attacking our veracity, "Well, Ike, you know there were a lot of things sprayed in Vietnam that the American people will find out about in the future and I think that our behavior has somethin' to do with it." I was being a smart aleck, but little did I know, and I found this out later when I did my research into Agent Orange and the effect of phenoxy herbicides on the physiology of the human body, that it in fact causes hirsuteness! So that was my first discussion of it and we gave testimony to that effect, some of us. But I think it was really the work of Maude DeVictor that brought it out in 1977. She is a heroine!

I've a number of things I could throw up that have never been said about Agent Orange. Being a fundamentalist—ten years ago I would have used the word radical, but I'd like to wordsmith Ronald Reagan's speech-writers—so being a fundamentalist, I decided to look at the roots of this whole problem and I read a couple of interesting books. One was, *The Crime and Punishment of I. G. Farben*, by Joseph Borkin, which really illuminated the ideology of chemical and biological warfare in the United States. It was there that I found out that part of World War II was the technological rush to synthesize organic chemicals and to synthesize rubber and to synthesize petrol, and I began to see these names across the Atlantic. Dow Chemical and Mobil and Bayer, back and forth, and I saw this pattern. And then I read in Borkin's book the fact that the first use of herbicide for basically warfare purposes had been with the Third Reich. And that was in their quest for the final solution of the Jewish question. They found that carbon monoxide was not cost effective, and they'd come up with this notion of using prussic acid, which was a primitive herbicide that was used in Germany. Prussic acid with the odor taken out of it was called Zyclon B, which we all know was used for a great part in the elimination of six million people. And then in my research I found that the March 21, 1951, copy of *Time* magazine describes the military operation called "Operation Paper Clip," which was the "liberation" of over six hundred mad Nazi scientists, chemists, and germ warfare specialists from the Third Reich directly into the bowels of the U.S. military establishment. And a lot of them either went into the Army Chemical Corps directly, or many of them went to Texas to an air force unit called, I kid you not, the United States Air Force Global Preventive Medicine Unit! Agent Orange was a fifty-fifty mixture of two commercially available herbicides that were brought to this country in 1945 at the end of World War II, when I believe those Nazi scientists, along with the rocket experts, the chemical scientists, came to this country. That fifty-fifty mix was sprayed, along with other herbicides, over some six million acres of southern Vietnam, which is the land mass of the Commonwealth of Massachusetts and Rhode Island put together. The air force loves to say that they were doing it to prevent the guerrillas from using the bush to their advantage, but knowing that so many Nazis came from Germany and this year being 1984, I'd like to just dispel myths and be vulgar. I believe that they knew at that point in time that there was a snowball's chance in hell that they could contain the Indo-Chinese brand of Communism and they had a dog-in-the-manger attitude and basically attacked the food supply of the guerrillas, but more importantly they attacked the land itself. And it is ironic that by the time the Yanks were done, South Vietnam had to import rice from Texas and Arkansas, and that rice is still being treated in the United States with 2,4,5,T. It's one of the few crops that are still being treated with one of the ingredients in Agent Orange that wiped out the arable land in Vietnam so effectively.

I think the Agent Orange issue is finally bringing out what I guess our Native American brothers and sisters have been trying to get into the new arrivals' heads for about four hundred years, and that is that there is a certain balance in this earth and if you mess with it, it's gonna mess with you, and whether people like to take that in theologically or not, I think it's certainly coming home to roost. The whole Agent Orange operation was born out of a covert nature. The first couple of test missions were even flown by the CIA. And generally the secrecy was to keep the American people in the dark about what was being done in their name. Today a great controversy is going on and it's been going on for years. Vietnam veterans are angry, the American people are angry about this involuntary toxic insult to their society, to their balance, to their whole environment, and it's all secret.

One day I found out that the man that actually went to Vietnam in 1961 and began the first experimentation of spraying this Agent Orange ingredient on plants, and then studying the effects of plants and judging what dose should be used per acre, is a man who lives right here, and I don't know how it happened, but in the middle of my research I was looking through the Cape Cod Telephone Directory and there the son-of-a-bitch was listed, right in my own home town in Harwichport! I almost jumped! So I keep an eye on him.

I've always put forward—it's known in Agent Orange circles where my nickname is "Joe Dioxin"—Bangert's One Point Peace Proposal between the U.S. government and Vietnam veterans, and that is my equivalent of forty acres and a mule. They give us $600,000—a $100,000 housing allowance tax free, $500,000 in the bank tax free—and we sign a chit with the U.S. government that we'd never come back and ask for anything based on our war damage, and we could pick up our lives and go. A lot of people think that's outrageous, but I don't think it's outrageous because it's probably the cost of one or two aircraft carriers. I mean, what do they have to lose? It was their President and a Republican, I might add, Abraham Lincoln, who said that the U.S. government should care for him who bore the brunt of battle and for his wife and orphans, and that is the slogan of the Veterans Administration.

A lot of people ask me, they say, "You poor bastards that went to Vietnam, I really grieve for you cause you are really in some shit." And I turn around and I think of that Biblical passage, "Weep not for us but weep for yourselves and your children." And I say, "Listen, don't think I'm a chump. Were you born in the post–World War II period?" And they say, "Yeah." And I say, "Were you born in a hospital?" And they say, "Yeah." And I say, "Well chances are the second you were born you were pulled out of your mother's body and washed off with hexachlorophene, including your testicles, and you were covered with dioxin the second you entered the world, so I'm not the only one at risk."

I think this is interesting: Dioxin spelled backwards is Nixoid! And I think that's like a hemorrhoid but it's worse 'cause it's covert! You just feel the pain but you get no skin manifestations. Yeah, I still don't like the man. That's why I named him Nixoid. But to get back to my point of why Americans should be concerned, we're being bombarded with dioxin, and it's interesting that the first application of dioxin was for military purposes, okay? And it was at Fort Detrick that they took the little German secrets and found out that this stuff that killed six million Jews could certainly be used to take care of Communism, or so they thought. Then they found that they had a commercial application too, that it could wipe out those nasty dandelions, the bane of the middle class. And it's so widespread now that there's dioxins in the process of synthetic textiles. Dioxins are present in the tannery business; dioxins are present in all wood preservers. I mean, right here, you and I are sittin' at a wooden table and the table in front of you has some kind of preservative on it.

An interesting case is Binghamton, New York. I love this story. People got together and they said, "Let's rebuild Binghamton. We want to make it an urban redevelopment scheme." And they got old Rockefeller to come out and put a state office building in downtown Binghamton, and it was the centerpiece of redevelopment. They had these transformers for the air conditioner and heaters and they turned them on one day and the damn thing caught on fire and the PCBs inside the transformers caught fire. The ventilation ducts were right next to the generator—this building hadn't even been opened—and they blew this contaminant of PCB everywhere. Later they found dioxins all through the building. So you've got this monument to anti-science and the quest for technology sitting in the middle of Binghamton, New York. It's a monument to dioxin in the domestic application. And then the other aspect is that 2,4,D—the other half of Agent Orange—is the most widely used herbicide for agricultural purposes in the United States, and no one cares to check whether there's traces of 2,4,D in the food that we eat. And then, irony of irony, is that since the environmental movement has been able to stop some of these toxic herbicides being used on our food, the corporate mentality has been to dump it on the Third World, ironically in Central America, and you know these same people that make these decisions, every morning they're cuttin' up them Honduran bananas and putting them right on their cereal, *every* morning. And they're peeling into that stuff and there's a book called the *Circle of Poison* and it *is* a circle of poison. I think the first book I ever read about sociology documented in the black community in, I guess, Chicago, that slogan, "What goes around comes around," and I think that's what's happening now. And it's gotta stop.

John, you just brought another memory to mind 'cause I met a man at

Love Canal that I interviewed. He had six children, five sons, one daughter. All of 'em were in Vietnam. His daughter worked for the CIA, and I was looking over his house and he was in the danger zone and was told to move out and I'll clip the story and send it to you, my interview with him, and he said to me, and I don't think he was conscious of it, "Why there's chemicals all over the place. Why, without chemicals life itself would be impossible." Completely lifted it from Monsanto you know, without losing his consciousness. But I begged to differ with him because I say, without chemicals life itself *is* possible. When the utilities were talking about the efficaciousness of using herbicides in 1984 along the railroad rights of way, at a recent hearing I attended, I turned around and there was a moment of truth between me and this guy that was a pseudobotanist workin' for the utility companies and I just raised the question ('course I'm looking for my Nazi pattern), "But when did you-all start using this stuff?" And he said, "Oh, right after World War II." Better living through chemistry! They used to *cut* the brush when it was an obstruction! Prior to World War II.

I'll tell you one last story. When Sabra and Shatila took place, because I was against the marines going into Beirut, I knew it stunk. I knew that those cluster bombs, antipersonnel weapons that were first researched and tested and dropped in Vietnam were now being sold throughout the United States military's client states around the world, specifically Israel, and then dropped on the Palestinian people, and I was outraged. But you can only do so much with your outrage. What we did on the Cape is, we organized a memorial service for the victims of Sabra and Shatila, and I was really glad to take that negative energy that I felt for my government, and we had demonstrations—all four of us, right? People said we were crazy and stuff like that, but we found another thing to do and we contacted all the religious leaders that we could get and I'm proud to say that I had a role, along with my brother, in bringing together the imam from the mosque in Quincy, the Catholics, the rabbi from Hyannis, the Protestants, of all stripes, the Baha'is, the Greek Orthodox, and we brought them together in one church and we had a memorial service and raised the whole question of our religious indignation at what was going on in the name of America and in the name of Israel and the name of whatever at that time, and then we raised money for Oxfam Lebanese relief. Afterwards there was this virulent Zionist on talk radio in Boston. He'd just come back from Israel and he thought it was just great that the road signs in Southern Lebanon were now in Hebrew and I turned around and I got on the radio and I said, "Look, I'm a Vietnam vet and I think that the alternative to what you're saying—which is the policy of internecine warfare for the forseeable future —the alternative is, I think it's possible for Jews and Moslems and Christians to live in peace in a pluralistic society and to do that you gotta cut this religious exclusivity of the Israeli state and they've gotta open up to other segments of society." And basically I was accused of being an apologist for the Palestinian people, and I said, "Why not? Someone's gotta apologize!"

I think the American people would like to perceive themselves as innocents, but we're not innocent, you know. American society lost its virginity a long time ago. Some serious errors have been made by our society, individually and collectively, and we have to address that and if I can sum up with one thing, it's the greed factor. If people decide they could really live with an old sixty-three Chevy as opposed to a Mercedes Benz, then we could turn on the real problems of the world. American people do not understand what they could do to change things. To start with, they could get off the notion that they are passengers on the *Titanic* and they're just waiting for an order to be barked out and in the meantime, they're just listening to the music. They gotta know there are icebergs out there. A lot of them have enough money to travel abroad and they know that the causes of the United States have been fairly identified with evil throughout the world. They should feel really bad about that and try to do something about it! Like I do and like a lot of folks do and be bad Americans— which means speaking out at the most inappropriate times about the most appropriate things. Take some part in calling attention to the egregious errors that are going on. How come this whole world of peoples and nations can't stop that internecine warfare that's killing kids? How come people with more bread and diets than you can think of can't get some food to Africa where two million people are starving? My right-wing friends would say "You're a bleeding liberal." I'm not a bleeding liberal, but I'm a human being with scars on me, physical and psychological, with five senses and that gets me into the dioxin thing. You can do what you can do and I do think that one person can make a difference. If you scream alone, you'll be in the nut house. You gotta get a large number of people screaming and then you're a movement.

John Bangert

"You have to take responsibility for your life; quit
pissing and moaning."

□　□　□

*America is not always right, but we have the right
to protest for the right. That's what makes America
great.*

JESSE JACKSON

---

*The most important aspect of John Bangert's life is his heavy commitment
to the causes he is convinced are vital to a new birth of social health. He
works as a church sexton and has described himself as a "househusband,"
but his advocacies have carried him to Nicaraguan coffee and cotton fields
and veterans' Agent Orange protest encampments. He was instrumental in
the decision of his church to offer sanctuary to Central American refugees.
Heavily involved in the Reverend Jesse Jackson's campaign for the American presidency, with "very reddish-white" skin from his German-Irish
background and "a little bit of Indian" from his father, John is moving
away from his natal creed and diminishing those loyalties and legitimacies
of ethnicity and race and sex that are still so massive in most lives.*

*A large, urban man with an appreciation for small-town life, John is
also a missionary with all his mind and heart for his vision of a new future.
He does not suffer the slow-hearted with much alacrity and will put the
pointed questions that decorum, expedience, and even prudence would
hesitate to raise.*

*We talked long and sincerely through the evening and night and into
the morning of a cold winter night at my house. Freshly brewed coffee,
freshly squeezed orange juice and natural apple cider made the talking
even easier. John is a sentimental man who is also ring-wise in the culture
of protest. He is aware, sometimes poignantly, of the cost of full-time
participation in the culture of protest and alternative life-styles. His house
is often not as warm as he would like it to be and some of his friends speak
ominously of the inevitable season of rainy days for which he is not pre-
paring. But John Bangert's longing for the conventional existence is ambivalent. He knows that reentry into the middle-class mainstream carries
with it the possibility of corruption and a dulling of his vital, wider concerns.*

The first time I heard the term "principled dissent" was when you spoke
to me about it. I think you ought to copyright that word. I think that's
Gwaltneyan English. When I first heard it from you I did think about it,
and I have thought about it a great deal. As a matter of fact, understanding
what it means has affected me in a real positive way. I see that principled
dissent is dissenting from the norm. Change is good, and if you don't
foment dissent, then we're never going to have changes. I believe that my
definition of principled dissent would be that when you conspire with a
group of people—meaning "breathe together," according to Marilyn Fer-
guson's book *The Agrarian Conspiracy*—that you breathe together to
breathe new ethical life into our materialistic culture.

I believe that the human rights situation in Central America, as it is in
other places on the globe—in South Africa, in Palestine, in Saudi Arabia,
in Iran and Iraq, in India, well, we could go on forever—is very wrong.
But the fact is that in those places are going to be people, hopefully, that
have what you are now calling—and I agree with you—principled dissent.
Where people will stand up to change the status quo, the government or
the movement of people in a positive direction by principled dissent. I'm
not going to say that everything in the governments of Central America is
wrong. Just like I'm not going to say that everything in the government of
Nicaragua is right! But there are certain things—no matter what the government is doing or is not doing—that are wrong and they are the human
rights violations. In El Salvador and Guatemala those human rights violations cause people to flee their countries and come to the United States. I
don't care what their agenda is. I don't care whether or not they are all
fleeing for the same reasons. The fact is, when they get to the United
States, they are forcibly returned to their government of origin.

I didn't bring any notes because I didn't want to clutter this up with
notes. I wanted to talk from my heart as well as from my mind, but Sanctuary, with its biblical understandings, is when a group of people, usually
church people, say that this is a holy place. What I understand that to mean
is that at one time people who were being threatened by their government,
or by their moneylenders, or by any particular group of people who were in
power, could find sanctuary in a house of God. Here in America there is
a separation of church and state, so our government has never really been
confronted with the idea of Sanctuary. So I think for two reasons Sanctuary
is a very viable alternative for Salvadorans and Guatemalans. First of all,
it puts the government on notice that people are going to implement Sanctuary whether it's viewed as being within the legal framework or not. Just
as they did during the Holocaust, which was the despoiling and killing of
so many millions of Jews and other people in Europe, as well as the
Underground Railroad of the 1860s in the United States. It was against
the law to harbor a man who was owned by another person. It was legal
to actually forcibly return people. But a group of people stuck together
and said—for whatever reasons, and I'm sure that some of the reasons
were not as noble as they would like us to think they were—maybe it was

chic to be an abolitionist in New England, but anyway, the fact is, that this idea is the one we've adopted and that idea is that no government should return people who are refugees for whatever reason. No government should forcibly return people if they are, in fact, in danger. And the people who are returned to Central America, notably to El Salvador and Guatemala, are returned to certain fear, if not death and torture. So I see Sanctuary as giving those people an option that they might not have if a group of us were not conspiring together.

I think that if you're going to offer Sanctuary, you've got to not just pick the downtrodden and oppressed. I think that you have to stick to your guns. If you want the change that Sanctuary is, then sure, if someone asked for sanctuary, asked for safety, you have to give it. You're talking about a human being. I'm sure that even if Ronald Reagan came into my house and somebody was after him I would give him solace. I would give any man or woman who is in need solace. I don't particularly have to like them. I would find it hard to give that sanctuary to someone who had perhaps killed members of my family. I don't know if I could manage that. I mean, I'm thinking about it. I'm thinking about it and reading about it in different literature. I suppose I take it back to my father. My father has spent a great deal of his life in prison. That has sort of ripped our family apart and I'm not fond of my father. I'm sure that there are factors beyond his reach or my reach that caused that, but in fact, my father wasn't in our home. A lot of people ask me if I hate my father. No, I don't hate my father; I dislike my father. I don't hate Ronald Reagan; I dislike his policies. But if it's the butcher of Beirut who went into Sabra and Shatila and now doesn't have guns and is in trouble himself, I wouldn't like it, but I would hope that I would be able to extend sanctuary to him also. If it was right-wing death squads of Roberto D'Aubuisson trying to come here, I would hope that I would reach out to the person and the soul if they were in danger. But I have no feeling that Roberto D'Aubuisson will come to Harwichport and knock on my door and ask me for sanctuary.

No, I didn't regard my father as a principled dissenter. That's a good question, but my immediate response is no. That would be very comfortable, wouldn't it? To regard him as a principled dissenter. I don't know my father. I just discovered in the past year that he is alive and that he's sort of semiretired in a sort of a rest home. I'd like to see him, but I've lots of other things to do.

What do I have to do to act on my advocacy of Sanctuary? That was the question I asked myself last February, as a matter of fact. When the concept is put out and I see other people doing it, what do I have to do? I realized in a very strange moment at night that, in fact, there was no blueprint. That when you do it you have to conceptualize it yourself and tailor it to see how Sanctuary can fit in a community that's not like the ones in the books and pamphlets that are written about Sanctuary. What I found was that I needed other people. I needed some conspirators— coconspirators. That was the most important development because I've always been able to work by myself. At least, I thought I had, but I realized that if we're going to do it, then I needed to have other people who were committed to it and were willing to do the work, to suffer the failure, and possibly to go to jail for it. I wouldn't want to do that. That's not my thrust. My thrust isn't to do an action that gets us arrested. The thrust is to do something that I feel will help people who are in trouble and in pain. People who are hurting for some sort of safety and at the same time willing to use that safety to come out and talk about their oppressors. So that's why Sanctuary is pretty unique. It's not just social service. There are lots of people who want to plug into it from a social service point of view. They want to take the good little brown people from El Salvador and Guatemala and give them sheets and T-shirts and clothes and canned food that has been left in the back of their cupboards. I *do* mean to be smart because that's what happened. I do realize that there were a lot of people who helped, but I realize that a lot of that help was really not a very good commitment. But, nevertheless, I do see that the most important ingredient I needed to implement Sanctuary on Cape Cod was a commitment of a small core of people. I realized, after the fact, that we didn't all have to see eye to eye on the whole development and there was something new to my life called accommodation.

There's one common binding point. The cohesiveness of our group is the water we swim in and that is our concern for Central America. There are front-runners and doggy paddlers and the timid, who are just willing to jump into the water and get their feet a little damp, and many, many side-watchers. That's how I would describe it. Some people were upset when I used the word "solidarity," thinking that it was a Communist word. A Boston *Herald American* reporter did some reporting on us. I ran into him this week at the Democratic Senate hearings and I asked him, "You're well-known in Nicaragua and other places. The clipping that we got from the *Herald American* read, 'The First Parish Brewster Socialist Action Committee.'" He said, "Well, I didn't write that." I said, "I didn't say it and if I didn't say it and you didn't write it, how did the newspaper get it?!" The fact is that we're talking about Nicaragua and it said, "Anti-Reagan Cape Codders go to Nicaragua." That was the headline for that article. As a matter of fact, the ten people who went to Nicaragua are not appreciative of the Reagan policy, but I wouldn't say they were anti-Reagan. That was just a way of selling their stupid newspaper. That was an unethical decision that someone made to sell his little piece. I realize now that this is how a lot of people act because that's how they get a piece of the action. No, they weren't anti-Reagan. The purpose in going to Nicaragua was to first of all see a Third World country, but not just to see it from the air-conditioned hotel, but to live with the people, to smell and to touch and to sleep in the same conditions the people have, and to realize that after you leave those people are going to be there for the rest of their lives in those conditions. I was upset. I was embarrassed. I thought the piece was going to read, "Historic Cape Cod church rings bell on freedom again." What appeared in print as "The Socialist Action Committee" should have appeared as The *Social* Concerns Committee.

I know that in 1942 it was illegal for Jews from Europe to migrate to the United States. It was illegal for Americans to house such Jews in the 1930s in our own country. In the abolitionist days and the preabolitionist days, it was against the law for people to house self-liberated people. I

feel that those laws were immoral and needed to be disobeyed. I think that
if Rosa Parks had not used your concept of principled dissent, she might
still be sitting at the back of the bus. In historical terms, you can look back
and say, well the defiance of the fugitive slave laws must have been very
carefully planned; but Sanctuary was not carefully planned. It was a little
spit, a little hope, a little organization, and a lot of trust! To view Sanctuary
in the same light as Sojourner Truth with a group of people coming North,
I was going to be as bold as to say that Sanctuary is the same thing, but
it's not. It was desperately different, but the roots are not different. The
source of oppression has changed in some ways. The oppression of the
people of El Salvador and Guatemala has its origins in the same oppression suffered by blacks and poor whites in the South and different parts of
the United States.

People who wish to help a group of people nonviolently can do that,
and it would be wrong for them not to help these people. I feel that if
you're not helping, and you know about it, then you're immoral. If you
don't know about what's happening in Nazi Germany, then that's ignorance. If you do know about it and you don't do anything about it, then
that's immorality. I think it's justifiable to break a law that a group of
people you respect, after having studied and prayed about it and thought
about it, believe is immoral and that hurts people, hurts human life. If that
law is implemented and it hurts human life, then it ought to be changed
and one way of changing such a law is to challenge it.

I see myself as an active pacifist. I mean that if someone came to my
home, first of all I would look at it as being really not my home—I have a
problem with people saying that because they promised to pay thirty
thousand dollars to a bank they own a home—but if someone came to my
home and wanted something in my home that I'd worked real hard for, I
would realize that what this person wanted to take from me was a thing,
and I've departed from things a long time ago. It's my own conviction
then, that things are not important, no matter if it's a color television or
something else. It might piss me off to lose this thing, but what I'm saying
is, I've made a decision long ago that I would never ever hurt anybody
just because they took things from me. I would not help them, but I would
not hurt them.

Since I came back from Nicaragua, somebody called me up and said,
"I'm going to shoot you." I didn't hide, but I certainly called the police
after thinking about it for a long time. I believe the police gave me more
difficulty than the threatening caller. The fact is, they made me feel guilty
because I had called them. I think that I did protect Gail, my wife, but I
wouldn't be protecting her as if she were my property. She's a human
being and my child is a human being. I would defend their lives. My intent
would be to stop anyone from hurting my family. Maybe it's academic and
maybe if I were faced with such a situation today I would throw the sofa
at them, or have a complete change of opinion, but now, if I was asked
this question, and I have been asked it, I would say that I would not purposely hurt anyone or take a life or harm anyone if they were just after
property. I think human life is more valuable than property. In viewing
the films of Greensboro, the reality of that anti-Klan march was horrible.

To see it happen so quickly—somebody comes out and shoots you and you see somebody that you love with their head all busted up and their life spilling out on the streets—that's a whole different story. That can change people I'm sure.

My reaction to the guy who called me up and said he was going to shoot me was, well, that's nothing new. They did that to me in Nicaragua, but a guy called me up at another time and said, "What are you Communists doing? You communist bastards," he said. I said, "Wait a minute. First of all, my mother and father were married before my conception. Don't hang up so we can have this discussion." And I think I disarmed him with this approach. I spent forty minutes on the phone. He raised point after point which I responded to without being pissed off. The only thing that would have pissed me off would have been if he had hung up. I had a conversation with a human being. Somebody I disagreed with a great deal, but I was tired of having hate put on me—of somebody hating me for not knowing me! Hating me just because of what they thought I represented. They didn't get down, they didn't touch me, they didn't know me as a person and I cared about that. I wasn't going to say, "Well, you stupid asshole, don't call here again," or anything like that. I wanted to talk to him. I didn't have to sell him my bill of goods. I said, "Well, let's agree to disagree, but let's get on, let's have another point." I disarmed his anger. I disarmed him somehow by having a conversation with him. The greatest reward for that whole Nicaraguan trip was for him to say that although he didn't agree with me, he thought that I didn't fit into the category. Those were his exact words. He admired me because I could defend myself in conversation without putting anyone down. Without putting him down. I was glad that I got a chance to talk to him because I couldn't let him give me a ration of shit. I was just tired of people doing that. I received pictures of the people in the group that went to Nicaragua with nooses drawn around their necks. Written on these hate drawings was, "You stupid bastards." I'm sure that they were not sent by this guy who called me a "Communist bastard." Here, we got that stuff right here.

Just last week someone called me and said, "John, we have to talk about poverty and I don't know any poor people." She said "Oh! I didn't mean that. What I meant is that I would like you to talk about the Third World." She said, "You're the only one I know who knows anything about poor people and I thought you could come and talk about that to our class." I laughed and said, "Oh!" She said, "Oh, I didn't mean it that way." My friend, who has the two cars, who has the house, who has the workshop, who has her own copying machine, who has her own fancy typewriter, who has everything that's materially fine, said to me, "John if you had what we have, can you imagine how much more work you could do?" I said, "Yeh, but I might be distracted."

When I was speaking to the high school kids about Nicaragua, I was saying that I had talked to this woman who said, "Well, I've gone to Nicaragua and no one's ever told me that the people eat the parrots when times are very hard." So I said, "Well, maybe you've never asked." The high school kids laughed so I asked them, "What do you do when you get up in the morning?" "Well, I get out of bed." I said, "Okay, that presupposes that you have a bed. It presupposes a room." I said, "What do you do next?" "I go to the bathroom." "Okay, that presupposes a bathroom. What else do you do next?" "Well, I have some orange juice, some break- fast." "Well, that presupposes that you have a way of keeping food in your house." I said, "Let me take you and exchange you for a time," and I made a role-playing model with a Nicaraguan kid. "It's 85 or 90 degrees when you get up, maybe even a hundred, and you're not going to go into the bathroom or the room next door to take a shit because there is no room next door. So you have to walk a good twenty minutes because in 110- to 120-degree heat, you don't want to have an outhouse real close, do you? So what we have is a shack with ten holes on one side and ten holes on the other with a roof over a great big dugout and that's the bath- room. Now picture it. Smell it. You're there, no water is coming through. It was built maybe ten years ago. That's your bathroom all your life. So you come back but you've spent forty minutes just going to the bathroom. Maybe you're going to have water for four hours a day, if you earn it." So I walked them through that. I said, "Now I was trying to tell the Nica- raguan kids that in our country and elsewhere in the world there are people that poop in little pots and then they use drinking water to get rid of that waste. Now in Nicaragua people have to carry that water. Now picture that kid in Nicaragua and picture how most people in the world live. Not the European tradition, but most people in the world live that way. Think about that!"

Until you actually get down, until you're with these people, you just don't look and observe. Then you realize that they are not doing these things because of some quirk in their tastebuds. They're doing it because it's their reality! The pigs live in the house because there are no fences and if you don't take care of your pigs they are going to run away or somebody's going to steal them. Behavior modification for the bulls in Nicaragua is death. They don't misbehave too often. These North Americans were ask- ing, "Where is this bull that was being ornery?" Somebody pointed, "It *was* that one." Next morning there was beef in that kitchen. They said, "They're killing that poor bull!" So I said, "Hey, if you go to a slaughterhouse, what do you think you're going to see?" I was talking to someone who was opposed to the cock fights down South. I said, "Yeh, but at least one cock has a chance. Look at the chickens in McDonald's."

It is real interesting to bring this to the attention of people who don't view it that way. Most of the people in the Third World live just the way that the people in Nicaragua live. Maybe some live better, but basically life is like that. "Oh!" they said, "They wash in their own excrement!" I said, "Well, we do too—it's called recycled water. We have the technol- ogy, we can move things." I said, "The people in Nicaragua are not poor because they want to be poor, they're not sick because they want to be sick, they don't die at age forty-two because they want to die at age forty-two. Their living standard is caused by a combination of things which are be- yond their control."

I come back here and I'm in culture shock. There are more lights in that one high school classroom than there are in the whole town we were in. There were seventeen fluorescent lights strung up and that was the only electric light in that town! That was a lot better than it used to be. Think of it! There are three hundred people in that town and there are more lights in one high school classroom here than they have in that whole town! I asked these students what revolution was and I asked them if at any time there was any benevolent king or person in charge who ever said, "We are wrong and you revolutionaries are absolutely right. Here's the kingdom; take it!"

I think that if you can teach someone to think critically, even about your own teaching, then you are giving them a tool that they can use for the rest of their lives. I like to challenge students. I like to challenge Julie, my daughter. In talking to the kids about Nicaragua, I didn't want it to be a monologue, you know, me telling them about how people live. I wanted to give them the experience of putting themselves in a Nicaraguan's shoes, and, more importantly, of putting Nicaraguans in their shoes too. I just wanted them to see that there can be another way of looking at things.

When I came back and talked at the church where you heard me speak that night, some of the women were very annoyed. They called a priest and the priest called me and said, "How dare you say anything anti-Catholic to a Catholic group!" I said, "I know. If I went to a temple and criticized Israel I'd probably get the same reaction, but the truth is the truth is the truth is the truth." They thought that my saying that the Nicaraguan Church was divided and that there was a revolution within the Church was a bad thing because it made American Catholics feel that the Church was in schism. It is, of course, and I gave them the proof that I could muster. Now that's more palatable to them because it's not just me saying this. It always has to be legitimized by documentation other than me and my conclusions, and I think I'll probably spend the rest of my life doing that. I'll raise an issue and plant the seed in someone, and they're going to fight me and fight me and fight me and someday they're going to say, "Well, he wasn't really that wrong was he?" But by that time, I'll be moving on to something else. I don't know, I wish I could look into a crystal ball and see what kind of shit's going to come down in my life. I'm sure that there are going to be periods in which there will be lots of trouble. It's my little part of life that I feel that I can tantalize people, educate people, piss people off, but not piss them off so much that they're going to run me out of town. I feel that I'm a catalyst for change. I don't mean to be presumptuous, but I see that there are some things I can do.

I needed the time to do what I'm doing so I'm a sexton for eighty dollars a week. But eighty dollars a week gives me more power in a certain part of my life than I would have if I were working for IBM for three hundred dollars a week. I can be with Julie, whom I love, and I love to be with her. I feel this time with her, these two years, in which I'm not teaching and in which I'm doing this Sanctuary and Central American work, are a very positive time in my life. I'm having a fellow from the El Salvador Human Rights Commission come to talk on Sunday. He's flying in from Louisiana. His name is Ivan Escobar. I can get that done. A lot of people wouldn't do that. I can get him a forum, I can get him a place to talk. I can get him media exposure and I can get him and his message to be a seed in someone else's mind. My greatest reward for Sanctuary is not the doing of it, because that's fun, even the bullshit that goes along with it. My greatest reward is to see people, to a certain extent, liberated. Mostly North Americans, not the Salvadorans. I got a letter from someone, his father's a great big real estate person on Cape Cod, and he wrote to me and told me that he was glad that I got him involved and that he was taking his dissertation and going to Central America to study agribusiness manipulation. I felt that the reward I got was just like the reward you sometimes get in teaching. You know, dropping a seed in someone's mind.

I'm a teacher. I just graduated two years ago from Boston State. I had been in the seminary for eight months. I had problems with authority there. I had to take the vow of poverty, chastity, and obedience. I wrote a short story on that called, "For Christ's Sake, or, How I Became a Gourmet on the Vow of Poverty." I left inner city Philadelphia and went to Mainline Philadelphia. The people at the seminary, lots of them, were from inner city Philadelphia or from the Irish neighborhoods. We had one black brother the year before I got there and they made him leave before they made me leave! Basically, I realized then what happened. I didn't have a dowry. My pastor wrote me a letter stating that I was in a state of grace. You see, to be in a Catholic monastery you should have a dowry or some sort of financial offering to the group of people you're with. I guess the size of this dowry depends. In 1968 I guess it would have been anywhere between twelve hundred and four thousand dollars. It's a sort of a token. It doesn't cover the cost of your education, it's a gift. It behooves you to have that token, I can tell you! What happened in the seminary is that I met this French troublemaker, Guy Merveille. He was a Walloon. He was my friend. He was my inspiration. He was handsome. He was wonderful!·

What happened was, Joe, my twin brother, went to Vietnam and I was living with my mother. I graduated from high school in 1968. I was a slow learner. Obviously, I wasn't really a slow learner, but I had some vision problems. When we were raised in the Catholic orphan home, if my glasses got broken, I would be hit or beaten up by the professors—they called them prefects. When my glasses were broken, I would not tell them. They would think I was Joe. Therefore, there's an awful lot of schooling I didn't get because I didn't see. So I fell behind two years. So Joe went to Vietnam because he graduated in 1966 and got caught in the Vietnam syndrome. When I graduated, I was antiwar. I didn't want him to go because, first of all, I didn't want him to die! It wasn't anything political, I wasn't that sophisticated. I just didn't want my twin brother to die. So I probably made some sort of deal. "Lord, if you'll keep my twin brother alive, I'll give you my life." Something like that, I don't know. It was in my Catholic roots. Joe and I were both raised in the St. John's Orphan Asylum in West Philadelphia. It was an awful name to an awful institution that was in an awful part of Philadelphia for awfully poor people. When we got to a certain age, we were moved from that home to a home with a teenaged population, starting at seventh grade, which was called St. Joseph's House for Homeless and Industrious Boys. It was sort of like the Catholic Boys Town in the archdiocese of Philadelphia. So Joe went to Vietnam and I stayed in Philadelphia with my mother and made this kind of deal that if

Joe survived—he was, after all, my roommate from the womb—I would do something great.

When Joe came home I had a real nice job at Hallmark Cards, and I gave up that job and went into the seminary. I checked out the archdiocese seminary and I didn't feel I could fit into that, but the one I attended was a sort of modern community of men with some attributes that I thought were different. I had never left Philadelphia except to go to the seashore and we always went by bus so I never had bags, you know, luggage in my life. I went to the corner supermarket to get these big boxes because that's what we always used. Here I am, twenty-one years old and I never owned a suitcase in my life. So I borrowed my old girlfriend's car to go to the supermarket to get these boxes to put my things in. I told her about my commitment to the seminary. She didn't understand it, and maybe in retrospect I didn't understand it either. So she lent me her car and we went to the supermarket and the only boxes we could get were old Kotex boxes. I was very naïve. I just didn't think about it. Now when you enter this seminary, the novice master as an act of humility comes out to greet the postulants—the novices. So the novice master comes out and says, "Where are your belongings?" That was priest talk for your clothes, and I said, "They're in the trunk of the car." So he opens the trunk and says, "Jesus Christ! I can't believe it!" So as an act of humility he has to carry these Kotex boxes through these corridors filled with visiting priests and nuns and other religious who are there at the abbey for the Feast of St. Augustine. He carried the working-class kid's clothes in Kotex boxes in and said, "It's going to be an interesting year." So I did have some problems, but I had met this priest, Father Merveille, and that was one of the reasons I joined. He was working with gangs in Philadelphia—the people I was very much afraid of, although I was raised with black and white Catholic kids, the gang kids were less fortunate than we were. They lived on the streets. This was the late 1960s. It was after the riots and people were breaking down into runners, into gangs, into that tribal system. I was going to go back and work in that environment and find out what I could do.

This one woman I was working with gave me a whole ration of shit. She said, "You're just nothing but a Mainline honky come here to feel good on us." I said, "Oh, wait a minute!" And I just got right down. I said, "That's a ration of shit! I was raised right here and I'm part of this area." I talked back to her instead of smiling politely. I went back but I missed her for a couple of weeks and then one night I got a call and found that she had attempted to commit suicide. I rushed to the hospital and there she was, talking to this Baptist minister, and she said, "Oh! You're here!" And she said, "Excuse me" so the minister left and I went over to her and said, "What did you do?" She said, "I did what lots of people do in my position when it gets real painful, we kill ourselves." And she said, "But obviously I didn't kill myself too much, I'm still here." So we talked and that did something. I realized that it wasn't a game. That people were surviving and people were dying, and that the city that I was raised in was at war. Frank Rizzo was the mayor and it was just a horrible war. I organized with this French priest, the troublemaker Guy Merveille, and we decided to go to the white men because we were white. So he said, "Maybe what we should do is ask for it at the convention." We had a thing called House Chapter and our approach was to ask if we could bring X amount of poor kids from Philadelphia, knowing very well that poor meant black. You know, bring them to our great big estate in the Mainline to give them fresh air, even if it was just for two weeks, so they could have the sense of walking with trees and seeing nature and just being away from the kind of activity that I had been involved with in Philadelphia where you hear trolley cars, you hear guns, the urban sounds. Being novices, we had a voice but no vote. Guy didn't have enough influence with the older priests to influence the vote. They talked about our proposal in House Chapter but they certainly didn't pass it. Father Guy said, "It would seem to me an excellent idea, dear Fathers and Brothers, if we would open our house and bring the youth of Philadelphia here to have some sustenance." You know, he used these big words. Then finally the polite denials came. "Fathers and Brothers, the idea is marvelous, but the facilities that we have are not suitable." I said, "Yes, but we have many toilets." They said, "Yes, but we wouldn't want people running in the hallways and the priests have to use the bathrooms." So it went on and on and finally I was getting red, I was getting angry. I stood up and the abbot recognized me. I said, "Dear Brothers and Fathers, if Christianity works anywhere it should work here and it's not working here. What you are saying is you don't want niggers on your property." I left and I was crying. They just went, "Oh!" There was more discussion and I left and Guy came out and said, "They will cut your balls off tonight!" I went and stuffed myself with a sandwich. I was getting very heavy there, very depressed. I had more food than I ever had in my life. The jobs I had there! I cleaned the trash, I cleaned the bathrooms. I realized that I was doing the jobs that the kids with dowries never did. This was in retrospect, I didn't know it then. Anyway, so I went up to my room at about eleven-fifteen that night. This meeting had taken place around nine-thirty. When I got up to my room the abbot's representative and two other priests were there. They said that it would behoove me to decide to leave that night quietly. I was stunned. I mean, priests raised me and it was like the ultimate rejection. I didn't know what it meant so finally I called somebody and the somebody I called was Joe and I said, "What does the word "behoove" mean?"

One of the last things that happened before I left was that one day during the Superbowl I was on duty and a sick call came in—on Super-bowl Sunday. So I went in to Father Cortez, Francis Cortez. Now he was supposed to be my novice master, my mentor, and I went in and I said, "Father, there's a sick call." Frank was watching the Superbowl but I persisted. I said, "Father, it's a sick call." He said, "Take the number and I'll call back." So I went back to the phone and lo and behold it was a neighbor of my mother's! She said that my mother asked her to call, but she didn't know it was me and that another neighbor of my mother's was very sick. She was a very old lady and my mother was afraid that this neighbor was dying. My mother had called the neighborhood parish priest but because this woman had not contributed to the block collection she was considered not Catholic, or she was excommunicated, or she wasn't on the rolls as being a practicing Catholic, so the priest wouldn't administer to her. My mother called us because she knew we were liberal and would try to get Father Guy to come out because Guy was a renegade who would minister to her. I went and frantically looked through the house for Guy but I couldn't find him. He was nowhere in the house. So what I did, it was just one of those things where I didn't think about the ramifications. If I had thought about the ramifications I might not have done it. I took my habit off, ran to the tabernacle, and I realized something in doing that. The tabernacle is like the epitome of Christianity. It's like *the* power of God. It was the ark of the covenant, the veil would rip. I put the key in, it was very sexual the key's going in, the door's opening, very sexual in retrospect. And you take the ciborium off and the ciborium has a little skirt on it because the nuns handmake this cup holder. The cup has the wafers in it and you take the cup with the cross like the one on King Arthur's helmet and you take this sort of sugar bowl lid off the cup, which covers the gold, and there is this beautiful cup filled with the wafers. And I took some of the wafer in a pax. A pax is what a Roman Catholic priest wears around his neck when he takes on sick calls. It costs around four hundred dollars. It's pure gold because nothing but gold can touch the body of Christ. So I filled it with the blessed sacrament, as they called it, snapped it closed, put the ciborium back the way it was and nothing happened! I expected thunder and lightning to come, but nothing happened. I left the church, went to the back. My mother said that this sick woman was poor and didn't have much food. So I went to the back of the monastery kitchen, took some frozen steaks, soup, fruit, whatever I could find, took a car without permission, threw the food in, and drove to this woman's house. My mother was there and the other neighbor who had called for my mother was there and here's this woman, Helen her name was. She said, "Oh Father, I want to go to Confession." I said, "Well, since Vatican II they changed things around. You don't have to confess your sins anymore, it's called the General Absolution." What I wanted to do was get rid of all her guilt so I said, "I want you to think about all your transgressions against God. Think about all the transgressions that you were afraid to tell anybody. Think about them, you don't have to tell me, just think about them and get rid of them. Accept your forgiveness, accept your forgiveness, don't beg for your forgiveness, accept your forgiveness." And I said, "In the name of the Father and the Son and the Holy Spirit I absolve you from all the sins that you ever committed in your life." She was in bed in this one goddamned garage that's cold even in my mother's neighborhood. This woman is living in a garage that they rented out to her and it had a bathroom and that's it. Her only windows were facing the gas tanks of two cars. She had emphysema and my mother would buy her cigarettes. They took her to the hospital where they had diagnosed her as dying of incurable cancer. They didn't want her on the welfare rolls so they just sent her home to die. Here's this woman dying, my mother didn't see her for a couple of days. My mother was on welfare because of her illness and because my father left. My mother shared soup and other things with her. So I said, "Here, Mom, here's a couple of steaks for you and why don't you make a good meal for her and here's a lot of fruit for her, cook it up." This woman kept her food in my mother's refrigerator. So I gave her

Communion and I gave my mother Communion. It was a real happy little time. Gave myself Communion. She wanted to do an Act of Contrition, which is a Catholic little number they do at Confession, and I said, "Oh, no, no, don't! You're too weak, just stay there." This light came, it was like a sacrament or something. Theologically I won't get into it, but she was, in fact, spiritually renewed. She hugged me and she said, "Oh, thank you!" And I'm feeling, Oh, if she only knew—I'm not a priest—I'm a charlatan. So right afterward, my mother makes her some food and I'm talking with her, you know, being charming with her and she gets up and she gets into the death wheeze and dies in my arms. I never had anyone die in front of me before. Then I knew that everything I did was right. I had no doubt at that point. But I did have uncertainty and fear. I had no doubt personally but I needed another opinion. So I went to someone I respected, an old priest who was the theologian in the house. He wasn't Guy Merveille, Guy said, "You are fine! Don't tell anybody!" This older priest said, "Let me say this. Very few priests in the priestly life of forty or fifty years actually have that kind of experience. Perhaps your priestness was from the spirit." I didn't know if I could reconcile that, but that was a very important part of my development. I realized that there was a lot of hocus-pocus that was only hocus-pocus. There was a sick call and this so-called priest who was supposed to go was watching the Superbowl. I did that thing and I got in trouble. They know about it, I'm sure it got out. So it was one and two and three strikes and they asked me to leave. Three strikes and you're out of the ballgame. Joe took me to Washington and who do I meet but John Kerry and a group of other Vietnam vets? So that was that development. Being at the right place at the wrong time or being at the wrong place at the right time, I don't know. I certainly don't look for it.

I see that I'm doing something at First Parish Brewster that's a little different. Look, I came here in a car and the heat feels fine, so I don't think that industrialization is too bad. But the fact is, the reason that you and I have these things right now is costing some people right now also. We are living in a world that's so comfortable that we won't change it. We won't change it unless we get real pissed and I don't think there's anyone that mad. I don't think there's anyone here as mad as the people in Nicaragua. I see what's happening in Central America—the Sanctuary movement—as a transmigration of souls and men. I see that I have a small part to play in that and it's real comforting. I'm at this crucial point of doing something that I can live with. When I did Tom out, or Tom up, it would only last for three months and I wasn't very happy. Selling insurance—I couldn't keep doing that because I knew the people I was talking to. I knew they couldn't afford it. They were buying the American Dream on the death of someone in their family and the company always won. When I sold cars in San Diego I knew that the car dealer and Bank of America were going to make money no matter what I did and make money in a way that an honest man would not like.

The only thing that I might lose is that I might be wrong. As the Guatemalans I know tell me, "You Americans lose nothing except a sense of pride when you talk about what's going on in my country. We have faced death and face it again. You do not face death." He's right. I don't face death every day. I faced death one day, maybe two days in my life. Maybe every day cosmologically speaking; but in fact, I've only had a couple of close calls. I think it might affect people if they have close calls more often than not. I think American people are distracted by corporate capitalism, by television, by commercials, by music. I think American people are afraid to smell their own farts, their own under-arm smell. I think they've been taught to back away from their own goddamned humanity!

This year I was touched by the deaths of people that I loved very much. And I realized that if I could only have some organicness, shall we say, a Gwaltneyan word again, if it was a bathroom smell or a word that they left, I would want that just to hang on to that part of life. That's not the way it is, folks; our culture has made us fit into the material realm so much that we don't even listen to our own voices. That woman who came with me when I first came here, Carolyn, her voice is her instrument. She doesn't need an instrument to accompany her singing. If we would listen to ourselves and develop our own voices, they might not all be as beautiful as hers but we would realize that our dance or our song or our music is, in fact, our life. It is not in the machines that are behind us, or in radio stations or in the perfect jaw or the perfect skin, which just doesn't exist. The ultimate aspiration of humanity is the humanness of us, not the likenesses of us. Too often we have been sold the bill of goods and have willingly bought it. Behind the best television production of the gaudiest, most beautiful, lankiest people are wheeling and dealing human beings. Juan Valdez takes his sackcloth off after his commercial and goes home in a goddamned Mercedes Benz. The sun is not always shining at four o'clock when they film that commercial because it's filmed in Hollywood. There is no Juan Valdez selling Colombian coffee. The myths that we have permitted to infiltrate our lives are committed on us by a group of real human beings who stink just like we do. The one salvation that we have is that there is the human element and I believe that element is not all bad. I might die saying that, but I believe it. I believe that there is a sense of hope in people, in their own humanity and that before this whole solar system goes back to a spot of dust, after it's gone as far as it can, we might learn that together—all together. If we don't, then we're all going to go back to something the size of a pinhead, back to, back to the dust.

I was just talking about this to Gail. For some reason we went through the psychodrama of my childhood. One of my first feelings, I realized, was that when we had visitors at the Catholic home where my brother and I were raised they would take the 1930 knickers out and we would spend one or two hours with our parents or whoever came to visit us once a month in these nice clothes. These nice clothes were only on for that visiting hour, then they got folded back up and they went back into the box until the next visiting day. I think all that had to do with our development, Joe's and mine, both in a positive and a negative way. The people who were in charge of us had absolute control over our destinies. We could be beaten and many times we were, but I think our childhood was a childhood that gave us certain strengths, tests of endurance that have not all been negative. As a matter of fact, they have, in some respects, been real positive. Not very comfortable, but certainly positive.

Through all the experiences I've had that have brought me to today— you know, being raised in a Home, my seminary experience—I think the culminating and most joyful experience has been my marriage to Gail and the birth of my child, and the value of doing what I need to do. I guess I experience in this phase of life what the psychologist Carl Rogers called the sense of wonder. I mean that point where I can start giving back to humanity. I still squeeze as much out of life as I can, don't get me wrong, but I like to give back to humanity something in return for some of the greatest gifts I've had. I've had good health; I've had the good fortune to see things in a different way; I've had love and I didn't have that much hate. I've seen other countries, other lands. I've seen other people, and I hope to see more and use that in a positive way to share the humanity that we have. I don't think I've ever been bitter. I've been mad, I've been angry, but I've never been bitter. Even with my father. I see that my mother and father, because of their economics, were distracted from child-rearing. I see two routes that I can take. One is that I can spend the rest of my life doing what I consider very middle class, and that's digging up my past with layer after layer of psychodrama to try to understand why I am the way I am or why I was the way I was. Or there's my approach, which is this: You have to take responsibility for your life; quit pissing and moaning. I have to take the responsibility for my own life and quit blaming it on conditions and implement a life that's going to be different for my children or people my children's age. And let them see that not everyone sold out. Someone said to me, "Oh, Mr. Bangert! You were so brave to go to Nicaragua!" I said, "Katie, I wasn't brave. I wasn't brave at all!" But there's something in what she was saying. I see bravery as maybe being on the bridge at Selma or perhaps being a Bolshevik in the twenties or an anarchist in the thirties. To be against the Vietnam war in the sixties, against U.S. intervention in Central America, South Africa, Lebanon in the seventies and eighties. To be so against the status quo that they would kill you, now that's bravery.

There are some people who can pretend not to feel the rest of the world. If they can pretend not to feel the rest of the world then they can live that life, but I'm there taunting them with my pencil. I'm there telling them what it's like. I see myself sort of running between two worlds, and I'm finding that very enlightening, but unfortunately I also see that my wife's clothes aren't the best. I see her wearing old corduroys—and she doesn't want anything else—but I see other people all dressed up in the mall, and I say to myself, "What are you doing?" The young woman who said that she thought I was brave is working in Filene's and wearing all those good shirts. I just hope what I'm doing is not for naught.

Elizabeth Barrett

"If I ever have an epitaph, I would like to be remembered as a catalyst."

□ □ □

The price of justice is eternal publicity.
ENOCH ARNOLD BENNETT

Elizabeth Barrett is the very personal embodiment of irrepressible indi-
vidualism. Her libertarian principles are very apparent. Because she was
weaned on traditional Euro-American beliefs that the striving, persistent
person can move bureaucratic mountains, the murder of her father by the
very army charged with the defense of the Euro-American way has made
her understandably wary. That is why we talked where she felt most
comfortable—in a hotel overlooking Central Park West—and why she was
accompanied by her friend Scott Cunningham, whose sensitivity and in-
sightfulness facilitated our exchange.

To Elizabeth, the law's delay and bureaucratic arrogance are perhaps
even more personal, profane affronts than they are to most. She is an
intense, intelligent woman with a passionate belief in the primacy of the
individual and the obscenity of injustice. She is heavily engaged in an often
maddening campaign to extract information and recompense from the
United States Army. A part of that campaign is to raise $50,000 to pay
legal fees attendant upon her suit against the army. She has raised almost
half of that sum and is angry because of the "piddling $27,000 that stands
in the way." Talking with and reacting to Elizabeth was like relating to the
late Dr. Margaret Mead, my graduate school adviser. There was the same
positive energy and certainty that the will to accomplish is paramount.

Elizabeth is determined to live in this world on her own good terms. She
mentioned the possibility that the weight of human malevolence and the
tyranny of institutions might make suicide a viable alternative for her. The
disposition of her life is, of course, primarily a matter of her own judgment,
but this world would be an immeasurably more banal and degrading place

without people like Elizabeth Barrett. Their visceral abhorrence of the wrong and their hunger for the right are prime elements in principled dissent.

—————

I found out in 1975, eighteen years after the fact, that my father was murdered during an army drug experiment while he was in the hospital. He was given a dose, an enormous dose, of a synthetic mescaline derivative, synthesized, I understand, at Edgewood Arsenal. And, I also understand, tested on only approximately twenty rats before it was given to him. And he died. Went into a coma immediately and died two hours after they gave him the injection. The testimony from the man who gave him the injection said, specifically, they were looking for a means of immobilizing a large group or changing the behavior of one or more individuals. For example, a spy to try to get him to tell you what was really happening, or something of that nature. So, they were definitely trying, I mean, the name of the contract was "Chemical Warfare!" I found out about it in 1975 after some Congressional hearings by the Rockefeller Commission covered the Olson case. Frank Olson was given LSD by the CIA during a cocktail party and subsequently jumped out a window. When that was revealed President Ford apologized profusely to the Olson family and promised them that they would have all the information and he would work with them to make sure that they had some kind of financial compensation. And indeed, they introduced a bill in Congress to do just that. Unfortunately it was a private bill, which has to be passed unanimously, and one Congressman from California objected to the figure of a million and a quarter for this woman and her four children, so it was reduced to $750,000. Subsequently the CIA decided that it would subtract from that $750,000 all the money that had been given to her to date, which was something between seven and eight thousand dollars a year, which they told her was due to one of Olson's insurance policies. So she is now, I understand, poorer than she was to begin with— which is not my idea of justice. At any rate, when this was revealed, somebody, apparently knowing about my father's case, went into a safe at Edgewood Arsenal, retrieved his file, and brought it to the attention of the army. I theorize that the army was afraid, due to the tenor of the times, that if they didn't say something about it, that it would be leaked and there would be worse publicity than if they just braved it out. So they told me and the press at the same time. They told me very little. Almost none of what I have just told you. They told me he'd been given a drug, it was part of an army contract, and he had an allergic reaction to it and died. When I asked for more, they first told me there was no more, and then I said, "Well, look. There are gaps and being in medicine myself, just looking at the records," I said, "there are gaps and you said this is all the information you have." "Well, we thought you meant about the injection," they said. So then they gave me a little bit more. But that only raised more questions. I have been trying to get those questions answered since 1975 with almost no success. And the Carter administration, subsequent to an article in *Rolling Stone* that detailed Warren Burger's involvement in the case, tried to settle with me, and when I said I would be delighted to talk about settlement as soon as they told me what really happened, they refused to talk to me. So I don't know whether it's principled dissent or raging curiosity, or a feeling that I've had since I was born. I was always told that I could do anything I wanted if I was willing to work for it enough. And that this was a great country and that whatever needed to be changed could be changed by people who were willing to work to change it, if it was change for the better. And, indeed, I've found that to be true all my life up until now, which is why this was such a shock.

In 1965 I was working and I had a small child of two and a half. I went to work and the following year when I went to fill out my income tax form I discovered that the money I'd spent on child care, according to the income tax form, could theoretically be put in two places. Either a child-care deduction, which I was not eligible for because my combined income with my husband was more than $6,000—I don't know anybody who's making under $6,000 who can afford to hire a babysitter! Or it could be classified as a business expense. I felt it could be classified as a business expense. The IRS definition of a business expense is money spent in the production of income. When I looked for a job, the first question I was asked was "What are you doing about child care? What arrangements have you made?" So my feeling was that this was money spent in the production of income. I had to have it in order to make an income. So I did take it as a business expense and the IRS disallowed it so I fought the Internal Revenue Service alone up to the tax court. At which point my husband became what turned out to be fatally ill. And I went to the National Organization for Women and they referred me to the American Civil Liberties Union, who then referred me to a big, major, very old-fashioned, conservative Wall Street law firm, and they took the case pro bono. They took it up to the Supreme Court, but long before it got to the Supreme Court, after it was at the tax court level, the publicity it engendered landed me on the Brinkley show and the "Today" show within a day or two of one another, and the morning after the Brinkley show, this was during the time he was making essay kinds of interviews and he had said, specifically, "This is a stupid thing," and explained what he thought should be done about it. Senator Russell Long, who was chairman of the finance committee of some kind of tax committee, introduced a bill the next morning quoting what had been said on that program! And, unfortunately, our Mayor Koch introduced a bill when he was then a representative that simply raised the amount from $600 to $750 a year. A couple making $7,500 a year could take child care as a deduction off their income tax. So that just left the theory the same, raising the money only slightly, still making it terribly impractical for anybody to use as a business expense on a realistic basis. So, it had to go to committee and it was changed in committee to be neither bill. Long wanted to make it a flat-out business expense and he didn't get that, but it certainly was a lot better for everybody in the country than it had been. I felt really proud! You know, I'd done this pretty much on my own and it worked! Things got better because of an effort that I made. I thought, this is really neat!

This is fantastic. I'm having a great time! I was working in medicine. I learned a lot and I started persuading my employers in my drug company that teaching doctors was not the only answer. One had to teach patients too. One had to communicate directly with patients about what was going on and it really meant a difference in their bottom line if drugs were used properly by patients. They were becoming convinced. Indeed, I was starting to do programs that were making a difference both to the consumer and to the company. I was really pleased! Then this thing hit me and I don't know where I am anymore.

I couldn't accept the official explanation about my father's death because it didn't make sense. For me, everything has to make sense. I try to make as much sense out of my life as I can. I will admit to you that every single lawyer that I have ever had sooner or later has said to me, "The trouble with you, Elizabeth, is that you're too logical." I learned somewhere early on in life that if you don't clean up your own environment, you can't really complain when other people don't clean up theirs. And whether that means your bedroom or street, or your city or your country, it all comes down to the same thing. It means that if you don't take care of the problems that you can take care of, or fight the problems you can fight, then you're as guilty of causing them as the people who actually perpetrated them. I've felt that way all my life. I can't remember feeling any other way. Yes, it caused difficulties for me as a child. Always. I don't know whether that particular business about cleaning up my environment caused problems because I lived in a pretty clean environment, in every sense of the word, but the fact was that I was different. My father was a tennis professional and my mother liked to move, I guess. I don't know, we never owned a home. We always moved from one rented place to another. I spent most of my life on Long Island, moving from the North Shore to the South Shore. The longest we ever spent in any one place was three years. So I was always odd child out in a group of children who had stayed together since they were tiny, who knew each other intimately, and whose families knew each other. We were strange. I was the new kid. I was the tallest kid. I was the brightest kid. I was the youngest kid in my class always, and the skinniest. I'm not the skinniest anymore, unfortunately, but I had all these very different aspects. I also had a father who was extremely strange. Tennis was not the thing in the fifties! And here my father was, teaching tennis, which is totally outside of the environment of anybody that I grew up with! And my mother, I mean, she just wasn't a mother of the fifties! She was just very different and very strange. She didn't stay home and bake cookies. She read a ton, was informed about everything, but I guess actually involved in nothing. She didn't have an outlet. So she spent, I guess, most of her time alone. At any rate, all this made me very, very strange in the eyes of my classmates. It's interesting because there's a drastic difference between me and my sister. I was content to have one or two really good friends and I usually did make one really close girlfriend. My sister went so far as to become a Jehovah's Witness because her best friend was a Jehovah's Witness. She wanted to blend in, to be exactly like everybody else. Every time we moved, she was miserable. Every time we moved, I was delighted!

So I guess I inherited a little of my mother's delight in new experiences, in variety, and exploration.

When my father died, my mother sent me off to a school in Ithaca, which turned out to be a school for rich juvenile delinquents, but she didn't realize that. We were not rich. Her father's brother recommended the school and pulled some strings to get me admitted. And when I wrote home and called and complained and said, "This is terrible! This is awful, please get me out of here!" it was put down to the fact that my father had just died and I was lonely and away at school and I would grow out of it— whatever. Finally, after I'd been there for two months, my mother came up to visit me and was so appalled by what she saw that she packed every bit of everything I had. It was spread over this enormous campus because there was a gym and all these different buildings where I had stuff. She packed the whole thing in an hour and a half in tissue paper! God knows where she got that! And off we went. So that was my first school leaving, and then we went to Mexico and I was put in an English school. And it was so bad for somebody like me who was used to being a loner that at one point, to get away from constantly being with people, I went up to a roof where clothing was put to dry and disappeared! I mean, I didn't tell anybody I was going up there and the next thing, I mean, I wasn't up there fifteen minutes before I heard people screaming all over the courtyard! For me, missing me! At one point, I got so desperate I literally tried to climb over the gates and the guard had to pull me down. So I finally left there and my mother put me into a Mexican Catholic school where the mother superior was the only person who spoke English! That was really terrible. I did manage to get out of that school periodically and wander around the city. I learned absolutely nothing! The classes were all in Spanish and I think it was just a total disaster! Finally, somebody told my mother about this other school and I went there and that was wonderful. It took a while to settle in, but this woman, instead of using any of the normal ways of dealing with a recalcitrant child, took me under her wing and made me her helper. So I would go with her when she went banking, and I would help her in the office, and when the second-grade teacher was sick, I would take over and teach the second grade. I was fourteen or thirteen. I liked that very much and the children liked it very much. I think I'm a good teacher and I think she was very smart to do that. It was a very good experience. What she did was make me again what I was, which was a responsible human being. These other three schools had treated me as if I was a nerd!

I guess as one gets older, no matter what, one's sense of time is more acute. It's running out! I don't have enough time left to do the things I want to do, whether that's on a daily basis or a lifetime basis. And, particularly with this lawsuit taking up such an enormous hunk of my time, with medicine being such a demanding field, I have to keep reading in order to just barely keep abreast. I feel that when I give up hope, then I will give up life. I will not stay. If I decide, and I've come very close to it on occasions, that there really is no hope, that people are generally bad and not worth saving, then, whether there's another place after death that's better or not, it's no longer tolerable to be here. If the world isn't going to be better because I'm here, then, I don't want to be here. I do not want to be in an environment where people hurt one another. I've had a wonderful life. I've had some wonderful experiences. You've asked about the downer parts of my life, but I've had a lot of joy. I'm known by some of the people that I'm closest to as one of those strange people that can get inordinate joy out of something little. I'm very excited by little things which make me very pleased. Finding good in people. That's not little, but finding that kind of good, that's the best. As a matter of fact, I was talking last night with somebody about how I grew up hearing people say over and over again how exalting and inspiring the mountains and nature's creations are, and I never found that to be true. I find nature's creations beautiful, but I'm inspired by the good things that man does. Inspired to go and try to do something good myself. If I hear Beethoven or see Michelangelo, or read something that really is great, then I say, "Aha! I can aspire to do something on a level like this because I too am a human being!" I cannot aspire to making a mountain. When I was in Colorado in seventy-three and I was driving back at night from Colorado Springs to Denver, the physical environment there was beautiful. The mountains and the clear, blue sky—it's really quite spectacular. Nonetheless, what inspired me was coming back to Denver and finding the city, or a portion of it, spread out in front of me. All these tiny little twinkling lights, this carpet of lights. And I thought about those lights and what they represented. The intelligence and the effort of human beings to invent and build the environment necessary to produce that. That really excited me. What you've just brought out of me, what you've made me realize is that it's the endeavor of one person that excites me.

As I said, I went to school in two different sides of Long Island. The children on the North Shore were a lot more like one another than the children on the South Shore, who were really split. I guess it was maybe two-thirds Jews and a third split between blacks and Italians. And the blacks and Italians were from the wrong side of the tracks. The Jews were quite well brought up, you know, wealthy, well-to-do. Often only second or third generation. I suspect now, looking back, probably there was a great deal of familial experience with concentration camps which I never knew anything about. It was all covered up. I think they wanted to forget. This was the promised land. They were going to make it here and they weren't going to make any waves. I think that whole philosophy—let's not make any waves and the problem will go away—is what allowed Hitler to do away with as many Jews as he did. And I'm terrified of that. People didn't want to make waves. My grandfather used to say, "The cemeteries are full of people who had the right of way." There again, I have that example in front of me of what happens if you don't speak up! If I don't speak up and you don't speak up and Scott doesn't speak up, that's an enormous force to prevent change. I feel that people have an obligation to speak up. Absolutely! It's more than a social duty, it's a human duty. I mean, if you really want this world to survive, if you want to survive, if you care about what happens to the world, I mean—never mind China! And Vietnam! And over there in California, even! If you want your little block to be as good as it can be, you have to do what you can when something wrong shows up. If you walk by somebody on the street who's being mugged and you don't do something to prevent it, to help, you're going to be the next one!*

* As this book goes to press, I have just learned that Chief Judge Constance Baker Motley has set a September 29, 1986 date for *Barrett* v. *U.S.*—the result of Elizabeth's ten years of struggle to bring this case to trial.

Grady Cassidy

"As far as I'm concerned, if you are wrong, you
are wrong, cousin or country."

□ □ □

Common sense is not so common.

VOLTAIRE

*Grady Cassidy is a slender, supple, street-wise middle-aged individualist
who chose to contribute his narrative anonymously. "In this world," he
says, "don't be no more public than you have to be." He agreed to face a
tape recorder with such reluctance that it was plain that his would be one
of the few cases where the mechanical presence would lead to a mechanical,
unnatural conversation. "It would be like talking to some friend in the
presence of somebody I do not know, or being interviewed without my
clothes on."*

*Grady defined principled dissent—"PD," as he likes to call it—as the
"righteous marching under fire." He also defined it as "taking your lumps
for what you really believe in." We renewed an old friendship in a hotel
overlooking Manhattan's Central Park. When I was a young man and
Stringbean, as he is still known, was a youth, I gave him his first piece of
wood and taught him what I know of the carver's art. Now he brought his
latest piece for me to admire. It was an intricately and ornately carved
heavy ebony ceremonial cane.*

*As a youngster, Stringbean's prodigious, discriminating appetite and
slender form were sources of local amazement. Since then he has earned
his living as a cook, a sailor, and a prison guard. He is now employed as a
tollbooth operator, but still dreams of starting a traditional black high
cuisine restaurant. He made me a kingly gift of a mammoth wedge of his
wife Johnetta's sassafras black rum cake, which I suspect was the last course
of his own lunch. Grady's approach to "PD" is very much like his approach
to everything else, not rooted in remote abstractions, but grounded in very
personal, daily experience. He is a truly good man with the wisdom to learn
from both his victories and his failures.*

This is a good question because it is something people should really be talking about, instead of the who-shot-john stuff they do talk about. I'm not into this trivia number. What is the point in being a child or an adult with some smarts if all you are going to do with them is play? Johnnie and I have been forced to get rid of just about anything in the house that plays but the crumb crushers! Seriously, I was being stone misled by my own TV so I junked it. I refused to sell or give it away because if I didn't like it misleading me, what right did I have to contribute to the jiving of some other family? I'm beginning to feel the same way about machines that I do about other people's dogs. I am being bitten by these computers and TVs and robbed and lied to by machines. I was being misled and beginning to like it.

Now you know that every black person living has heard some blackfolks say that "So-and-so done gone from preachin' to medl'n." They'll say it every time. Now that is not a put-down. We say that when somebody has really hit the nail dead on the head! That means that we have finally gotten to the really vital number. It is very important that whoever reads this should understand that for black people, to say that so-and-so has gone from preaching to meddling is not a slip, but a good thing to say about someone. When we say that we mean that so-and-so is talking too much about something that has not been talked about nearly enough. Now that is your PD. Principled dissent is just saying and doing what most people are too afraid to say or do. The most important difference between principled dissent and anything like it is that principled dissent is not just gettin' over. You have to do or say this truth because you really think that it is the right thing to say or do. It is best if you do or say this truth only after you have turned it upside down and front to back in your mind. Now that takes the most courage and that is the hardest thing to do.

This is a very tricky number. Two people might do the very same thing and the first one of these two people might be right and the second one might be wrong. I know from living that this is so. When a certain person we both know was courting this certain young lady—John, never mind about all that. When *I* was courting Johnetta, Roy Clayton liked her too. Now neither one of us was stone serious but we were not just fooling around either. Roy was a better man than I was then. I hate to have to say it, but right is right. He meant better and did better by Johnnie than I did back then. I met Roy when he was in prison. I wanted to hand Roy a hard time because I wanted to beat his time with Johnetta. So I was hot to tell her that he was in there, in the place. Now Roy never did anything to me or got into my business, you understand, but I did not want him to stand high in Johnnie's sight. Half thinking, as I was back then, I never thought that Roy would be, as I would say back then, fool enough to blow his own game. You see that was because I thought I was so damn smart that I was the biggest fool in the whole business. My mother said at the time, this whole business was a parable and a deep one too. That thing taught me more big lessons than any other number I ever had to deal with before or since! We both told the very same truth to the very same person and one of us, me, did wrong to do so and the other one, Roy, did right by telling the same person, Johnetta, the same truth. You know, she never did tell me that Roy had told her that he had been in the place. *He* told me! Right down there at Blake's Bar and used to be Grille, just before he split. Man, talk about feeling like a hole with no penny around it! That was me! The very first thing that came into my mind, sitting in that bar a hard grown man, was a whipping I got down in Bip for looking at Sojourner Coleman's paper back in the fourth grade! I was wrong then too. We were having this test and Miz Suttles had warned me once very nicely to stop peeping and peering in the wrong directions. Now once was all Sister Suttles ever warned anybody, the principal included! She is a principled dissenter if there ever was one. There's a lady you really should talk to. We used to call her Sis Pluck, and there was nothing but respect for her. But anyway, Roy was the kind of man a fool would think was a fool. The way I found out about him telling Johnnie was a kind of an accident. We were talking in Blake's and my beer and my two-cent slickness told me to ask Roy—I remember this as clearly as I remember anything—I said, "Roy, my man, how much lying can you swallow without gagging?" Now when he said, "Not a hell of a lot," I really did rip it. Oh I loud-talked him then and brought my own self right down front. I said, too loud and extra clear, "That's why you figure to tell Johnnie about that time you did in the place, right?" You know, that colored man didn't even put his beer down. He looked dead at me and said, "It would not be right for me to lie to her because I would have no kick coming if she was to lie to me." Now that's how I found out about Roy's principled dissent and how I think I hid my own dirt. I am still not sure what Roy knew, but I do know that he was then a better man than I was and that business taught me more than the war.

I know that a lot of people will not let themselves think like this, but John, looked at on GP, this question of right or wrong is the same whether it shakes up one person out here or a million. All this big action in the world is nothing but these little personal numbers done to death. I mean, an ocean is uku drops of water and a jungle is just the fulfilled prophecy of all its seeds. You see, it breaks down like this, John. Everybody knows that they should do their damndest to get the straightest tale they can before they do anything. Now people are prevented from getting to the truth, which makes them free to do the right thing by three big numbers. Number one, they would rather not know what the real number is. Two, they are afraid to get to the bottom of this business, whatever it might be, and three, they already think they know all there is to know about a particular piece of the truth. Now, of all these things which come between a person and principled dissent, the largest and most common is selfish fear. Most of the time most people know very well what they should do. I do myself. I am a principled dissenter at heart and in enough of my daily actions so that I don't have to lie to myself most of the time to live with myself. I will say this. I am a better man than I used to be and I am glad of that. It is the habit of thinking which has made me a better man. It is a habit and you might learn it all by your lonesome, but blessed is that person who has somebody who really would like him to think for himself.

My mother used to say this thing and I have come to know how true it is. "Son," she would say, "there ain't no sheep like most shepherds." Most of the common sense I learned I learned from what she and people like her tried to teach me through those sayings. She knew what she was talking about.

For a long time I just went along with things. I didn't really think about life or which parts of it were important to me. I just went along. I have a TV so I watched it. Whatever most people ate was food, so I ate it. You are supposed to be with it, so I tried like hell to be with it and talk trash. I was with it and you know I talked trash if anyone did, but the stone fact is that I did not know what I was supposed to be "with" when I was "with it." But I was with it, wherever it was, and all that time I was drunk without drinking much, if you know what I mean. I was wound up by the public and my own greed. I did not know the first things, the seeds and roots of any important matters. I would still probably be among the smart sleepers or maybe dead if people had not kept trying to want me to see around, under and into what is going down out here. My mother is a principled dissenter, not only because of the many times I know she has told folks, white and black, just what was what when they did not want to hear it and could hang her up for it, but because she wanted me to think for myself, not necessarily to agree with her. Now that is the purest form of principled dissent in this world. To help somebody to learn to think is to lose your power to make that person a knife for your will. That power over your mind is what the government wants, but should never have. You hear leaders telling you that you should not ask what your country can do for you and urging you to support your country whether it is right or wrong. Now that is just stone wrong. If you think for yourself you will know that if you help your country to do something, even if it is wrong, to do that thing, then you are doing a triple harm. One, you are prostituting yourself. Two, you are wrongfully harming whosoever your country is wrongfully harming, and three, you are not doing your country any favor by helping it to do something wrong.

My young cousin got too hot to speak to me because I blew the whistle on some of the wrongest action I have ever seen out here. He was wrong and everybody knew it. Now if he had gone ahead with that number which should have had jail written all over both sides of it he might have killed his own fool self and gotten heaps of other people killed or wasted. I think he can almost see that now but I do not give one damn whether he can or not because the only reason he cannot see it is that he is as loyal to his rotten idea as he would like me to be to him.

You know that I was in the Philippines but you also know that we had no business being in the Philippines, and if we had done the right thing way back when, we would not have had to return to Bataan. One time a long time ago, I turned out this bar, or helped some friends of mine to wreck the place. One of us got to drinking and you could not say "Yessir" or "Nosir" to him. He was mild enough when he was sober, but you get a little of that foreign joy juice in him and Marian Anderson couldn't sing for him. So we wrecked this colored man's bar for no reason under the sun. We thought we were cool but this man did not go for us doing up his bar so he got him some help from somewhere and I want to tell you, he made MacArthur's Return look like Bonaparte's Retreat! Now I wouldn't see it then, but the truth is, I deserved every ache and pain I got from that business and if I had died as a result, I would have gotten what I deserved. But that is where supporting some clown or country no matter whether it is right or wrong will land you. That is the seed of Vietnam right there. All of us were dumb as hell and a danger to an honest man because we felt Bret Chambers wrong had more rights than that guy who owned the bar, even though he was stone right. Bret is my friend, but I would not do that now for him or anybody else. As far as I am concerned, if you are wrong, you are wrong, cousin or country. That's why I feel the way that I do about this registering for the draft. He is not a relative of mine, as far as I know, but I give this dude Sasway a lot of credit. I know people who say, "Hell, I went, so why shouldn't everybody else go too?" Before I started thinking for myself, I probably would be saying the same thing. The easiest thing to do is what everybody else is doing, or what you are supposed to do. I mean, like you wear three-piece suits or smoke yourself into an earlier grave or believe in whatever you believe in or vote a certain way or vote at all because of a kind of habit. But you see this draft number is very tricky, like most other numbers. The registration is also a kind of blank check for your very life, which is all you have got in this world. Now everybody should have something to say about what he will risk or give his life for. How about my right to life when I turn eighteen? What happened to it then? You see, it all goes together and that's one of the things that make most people leave their thinking to somebody else. That's what I mean by seeing under and around and through things. Now if you see things that other people do not or will not see, they will call you crazy or evil, depending on how much these things you see blows their game. You can see things that are *not* there too. I mean, sometimes most people see things that are not real just because they are supposed to see these things. That's how most magicians, presidents, and ministers make it in this world, John. But most important ideas and things do not stand alone. Now for instance, this draft number is just the death end of the abortion question. Now you know you can't turn on a TV or a radio for five minutes without some politician telling you about the free world and everybody tells me that it is a free country. Everybody tells me that freedom is what we are spending most of our loot to defend. Now John, I do not feel like I personally am getting what I am supposed to be paying for.

It is a choice between hard knocks down here. But if you choose freedom, then you will have to permit people to be free. Now that takes us right back to how things go together. I don't know all of the ways these things go together but I do know that for a country to be free the *people* in that country must be free. I mean that people would not have to choose between paying their rent or heating their apartments. How damned free can you be if you can't even decide for yourself what you will put your life on the line for? But to go down here and register means that I say, all right, here is my life, spend it in any damned way you see fit. Now, John, suppose my son registers for the draft and they decide that defending the free world means that he has got to risk his life to defend these cracker South Africans against his own color in South Africa? Now what kind of freedom is that for him or me or you? How much freedom can Johnetta or any other woman really have if she has to have a baby she doesn't really want to have?

The most important reason why everything keeps falling apart down here is that nobody puts things together as right as we know how to put them together to begin with. Now we are back to that thing I told you about—the big numbers being the fulfillment of the plain prophecies in their seeds.

I joined Johnetta's church about five years ago and as a new member I expressed my opinion about something I thought was wrong. Now some people didn't like that and some people did. This thing had to do with putting a woman out of the church because she was having this child. Now to me, that seemed very wrong because the fellowship of Christ is supposed to be for those who are in trouble. I thought, and I still think, that if they were not going to help this woman they should have just minded their own business. Now John, I know most of those people and I know that most of us, me included, are no better than this woman. Now we might have been luckier or just plain less fertile, or both, but I thought and still think that we had a hell of a nerve setting ourselves up as her judges. There was a lot of jive connected with this number. One person in there who never did like me said that maybe I was the father of this woman's child. As I told you, some people thought that I should shut up. They didn't say it quite like that. They said something about new members keeping silence in the church. But it came to the same thing. I should not say a word about this wrong deal and by my silence give support to the stupidity and false pride of a few *important* members who had persuaded most other people to go along or pretend to go along with their rotten number. Now the person who should have said what I said because he was being paid to lead all the members in the "Christian" way didn't say or do a damned thing. Now he was a coward because he did not feel like telling that particular pack of jealous sedities who started this jive to begin with, what they already knew in their hearts all the time. John, I know that two of those good sisters had had abortions before they had husbands and I think that that is their business. But I think the lady they got together on had the same right to her private life. She decided to have her child and they decided that they would not and in a free nation or country you cannot in principle deny a woman that right over her own body. Never mind about what will happen if everybody does thus and so, the biggest question before the members of a free church or country or person is what happens if there is no real freedom. I believe that the only freedom you can in principle refuse any person or group of people is the power to destroy people's freedom.

To deal with the questions you asked me, I would let anybody or any-bodies say any damned thing they wanted to say, whosoever they might be; Klansmen, Nazis, Flat Earther, whoever. But I would not allow these people the power to mess up other peoples' lives. If I happened to be in charge of a free nation, by God, it would be free! Not half free! Not free for the rich! Not free for the healthy! Not free for the Christians or the Jews or the Buddhists, but free for everybody in the damned country. Now I know that I would have to give up some things to bring this about. I know that I would have to live in an ordinary house and drive an ordinary car and have an ordinary salary because I have no business asking people who have ordinary houses, cars, and salaries to do any more for the country than the country is doing for them.

John, you know that I had a hard time coming up, like most of us did, but I was raised right. That's why I don't think that people have the right to half-raise human beings in this world. Now Johnetta and I fell out for a while about that. I had been throwing in a little dust, along with some other people, to help my first cousin get to college. She is really Johnnie's cousin, but the girl is young and serious so we helped her. She is also very smart. Now she came up pregnant and she decided that she was not going to have a child at this time and I personally think she was right and that is what I told her when she asked me. Well, you would have thought I had just hit everybody's great-grandmama! Now these same people who were digging down in their pockets to help this girl, I say girl because that's all she really was, anyway, these same people who were willing to part with their hard-earned to help her do something *they* wanted her to do would not help her to do what *she* wanted to do that was her business when they didn't like it. They would not help her to pay for an abortion. I went to one of these armbreakers and borrowed some money, which I gave her. I would have done the same thing, I think, if she had decided to have the baby, but I personally think she did the right thing by not having this child. This girl was sixteen, John, and she didn't have any more business with a child than a hog has with sidepockets. Now she is finishing school just like I think she should. Now that's what you call PD from several angles. I had to put my money where my mouth was and Little Sandra had to know her own mind well enough not to listen to many people she respected. She made up her own mind, but I know that was not an easy thing for her to do. You know, this PD is not and cannot be a pure number. Little Sandra had to lose in one way or another, no matter what. In this world you generally have to choose between principles. You have to compromise. Sandra's mother would not compromise even to help her daughter, her only child, to do something she had got down on her knees and prayed for. You have got to be careful when you compromise. Before this business started, Sandra's mother got down on her knees every day that God sent to pray that Little Sandra should be able to have a college education. She just barely opens her mouth to me now and she tried to scare me by telling me that I would never see my money again. Little Sandra did pay me every cent she owed me. I gave her the money though, and she didn't have to give me anything, but she did repay me and gave me eight books besides!

People do not want to give themselves a hard time, especially when they deserve one. Most things make most people greedy. Look at the way people drive or talk to each other. Most people will fight harder for the wrong than they will for the right! I do not contribute to the jive, John. I keep from contributing to the jive in lots of ways. I want what everybody else wants, but I know that I can't do *at* important things. I can't half-do anything without making it worse. The reason it is always later than you think is that all this half-doing of things means that payback time is breathing down your neck, or your country's collar. All these ways of keeping down the jive add up to not going along with something you really do not think is right.

Al Davidoff

"The toilets get just as dirty in an Ivy League
institution as they do in a factory."

□ □ □

*I wouldn't like to have my people get too wise and
figure out their master's profit.*

KILIAEN VAN RENSSELAER

*Cornell University, the scene of Al Davidoff's principled dissenting, is but
an hour's drive from Syracuse University where I teach. But I first became
aware of Al's existence through his starkly moving verse contribution to a
United Auto Workers anthology of workers' literature that also contained
an article edited by Eva Mack. Mrs. Mack's mother, Margo Koch Ruthe,
had loaned me a copy of the anthology, and I called Al to invite his participation in this inquiry.*

*Al is a personable, confident recent graduate of the institution he helped
unionize. He said he would not mind driving to Syracuse to talk to me as
research was not the only incentive for such journeys. A certain young
woman in whom he had more than a casual interest was also a resident of
that city. So we met a number of times and talked easily in my Syracuse
University office. He talked about his unionizing activity and his service in
the janitorial galleys at his Ivy League alma mater.*

*Immersion in the world of workers' culture is not only a part of Al's
cultural and personal heritage but is also his means of working for a more
perfect social order. In the name and spirit of solidarity he would like to
participate in the forging of a civilization freer of the tragedies of sexism,
racism, and institutionalized avarice and bigotry.*

*Cornell University is now one of approximately twenty universities and
colleges that have UAW locals. In January of 1984, after two years of
preparatory negotiations, these locals consolidated to form a special interest
section of the union called the UAW National Academic Council. The
president of this newly formed group is Al Davidoff. He represents the
labor community on the Tompkins County Planning Board and has just*

been named to the Mayor's Task Force on Economic Development for the city of Ithaca. He tells me that the first issue to be addressed will be that of day care.

═══════

My whole name is Alan Harry Davidoff, but everyone calls me Al Davidoff and that's what I go by. I went to the New York State School of Industrial Labor Relations at Cornell University. By the end of my junior year I'd been involved in a number of labor-oriented projects and programs and was very involved in student politics. I was the president of the student government at my college. At that point there was an employee association beginning to form. It was avowedly not a union drive, it was openly saying this is not going to be a union, we want to work within the channels of the University. And I thought that it wouldn't work and that ultimately people would be interested in turning toward something more serious as an alternative. I saw that association as the best thing happening at Cornell and immediately got involved with the people who were the leaders. Just in a very, you know, helping-hand kind of way, not trying to give them direction or anything so presumptuous, but just trying to offer what I knew and leg work. Then I left that summer to do some organizing and research in Albany, sort of assigned through an organization called Frontlash, which is a youth labor organization, and when I came back I committed myself to getting active in building the organization at Cornell. People realized that they weren't going to be able to deal with Cornell University as a loosely knit group of employees. They were basically incapable of confronting the University with anything other than their own good will and good research on problems that employees faced. So gradually they became interested in considering unions. It was a role then as an adviser that I began to play, knowing something about different unions, which ones to immediately avoid and which to consider. The employee association at this point decided to begin to interview quietly without telling the University. Interviewing unions used to be a rare occurrence. In the past a union came in and just organized. It gets a one-lead call and comes in and does a blitz, but this was a different procedure. A small group of people, including myself, began to interview a handful of unions, looking for a few important criteria. We knew, being part of Cornell, either as employees or as students fighting student battles, that the University was no small outfit and that it would not be beaten easily without a significant financial and resource commitment from the union. So we were looking for that kind of seriousness. We were looking for a sensitivity to certain issues, like women's issues, because we originally started organizing all four thousand, twenty-two hundred of whom are clericals and almost totally female. For instance, one of the unions that came to interview had significant financial resources but was clearly not capable of bringing in any women organizers. They would refer to the clerical workers we were trying to organize as "girls" and you could just sort of tell that they were coming from a very traditional perspective and that they probably weren't for us. Which ended up being proven correct because when we didn't choose them, they tried to sort of butt their way in anyway.

The union drive was really originated by one woman, Kathy Valentino. Her ambition to see some things changed in the University was what kicked things off. She exerted a great deal of influence in the beginning and I was more or less her adviser, her right hand. I wasn't an employee then, I was a student, and there were several other employees involved. The interviewing was a very confidential process. The decision was made in the name of essentially a thousand people, but it is having ramifications for the entire area. I don't want to get grandiose about it, but we are interested in organizing anything and everything. There is very little active, well done, zealous organizing, 1930s style, that is going on in Upstate New York.

There were people in one of the other unions who took a moderately sleazy approach to the whole thing. They attempted really to find out what Kathy wanted out of it, and also what I wanted out of it. They essentially offered me a position upon my graduating from college with the fairly explicit understanding that it would be in return for my persuasion. They also offered me money. They're an outfit that is attempting to rid themselves of a reputation they have from some past experiences allegedly with organized crime. I don't know if it's true, but that's the image they have.

But anyway, we chose District 65 of the United Auto Workers. District 65 was an independent union for many, many years in the New York City area with a very progressive tradition, and just recently merged with the UAW, a much better-known, huge outfit of industrial workers, primarily. They also represent many universities, which was a prime attraction to us because we thought our position was very unique. You know, it wasn't just like a factory. A university is an odd array of constituent groups—students, faculty. Even as the lowest employee in the university's ladder, you can't help but be caught up in the fact that it's a prestigious institution. The toilets get just as dirty in an Ivy League institution as they do in a factory, but the university has a very effective way of being paternalistic, co-opting a lot of sentiment. You couldn't have someone coming in saying "Cornell sucks," you had to play up the fact that most people there think Cornell's what puts the area on the map, and go to the football games and root for the team. Sensitivity to the university setting was important. So we chose the UAW.

I ought to wrap up how I ended up getting to be an employee. I at some point realized that I was faced with a choice. This was getting now to be the end of my college experience. The UAW and District 65 have a fine tradition in most cases of hiring from the ranks, not putting a lot of emphasis on professionalism and degrees and things like that. A philosophy that I agree with. It's a real belief in the abilities of working people to do anything. So, in other words, I wasn't gonna get hired as an organizer— from being a student to being an organizer, no matter how integral I was in the drive. I could have had some kind of bogus internship that they could have arranged for me, which would have been temporary in nature, or I could have gotten a job at the University. Or I could have done something else other than stay with Cornell and the drive. So at that point I decided that this was something very special. It was something that I felt completely a part of and that to remain a part of that I really needed to get a job at the University. Being unskilled in any job sense, I got a job as a custodian. Now why I raised it with you I suppose, is that, first of all, from the beginning I've been sensitive to the fact of my somewhat unusual status as a Cornell employee. Most Cornell employees, the people I'm working with and organizing are local people, and they don't come into Cornell University with a Cornell degree. Although I have come to feel absolutely at home and one with the people I work with, and have more sense of identity with them than any of the people I went to school with, it's a fact that I thought it was well for you to know. Although I have certain perceptions of how I am assimilated, I realize other people don't have them. I face a certain "you're playing proletariat" kind of attitude and that's something that, just for the honesty of your research, I thought it was good to get out in the open. I didn't want you finding out after doing two or three hours of tapes with me that I wasn't quite the person you were looking for.

I have often tried to think about my own background. I don't come from a radical or left-wing or activist family and I've often wondered how I got to the point where I'd be willing to spend years cleaning up after people that I used to go to school with, as opposed to going into a career making twenty, thirty, forty thousand dollars a year as a personnel executive. Just off the top of my head, I'd say it has a lot to do with dissent, I guess. You could just say dissent, but you've made a distinction, you've said principled dissent. I think there are times when people dissent purely when there are other circumstances which are fortuitous for that dissent. It can be an opportunistic thing. I'd say in my own personal limited experience, there've been many times when, within a group, taking the most militant position is also the easiest way to make a name for yourself and gain a sense of leadership in the group when it may not have been the most intelligent decision. You know, biting the bullet for another two weeks, instead of having the demonstration when you wanted to. A decision may be the toughest, but not the most intelligent. As an example. Solidarity Day in Washington, which I attended. In a way, it was a very beautiful event because it really was forced upon the leadership. It was a rank-and-file movement. I think it was a true expression of and was a dissent, whether or not it was a principled dissent. For the ranks who attended maybe it was principled dissent, for the leadership perhaps it was just dissent. Maybe there's a distinction. I don't know. I suppose there are some broader definitions, distinctions. Dissent occasionally gets blurred in with personal opportunism. I've seen people on the other extreme, though, who were into martyrdom and who seem to be willing to—I don't know quite how to put it—there are people that are probably just intentionally self-destructive and take a position that's self-destructive.

But let's see. I'll try to start with what's relevant in my background. My mother's a Protestant German Scot. Her parents' family had been in America for a while. My father's father and mother were Russian Jews who fled the Soviet Union, where there was a certain amount of persecution I understand, and immigrated to the United States. So it's kind of an odd mishmash culturally. My father was raised as an Orthodox Jew, yet he made, I think, looking at it through his eyes, the most radical decision in his life. The decision to marry a Protestant in a sense, in a sort of funny way, was a very principled dissent from the traditions that he was raised in. It was for love, over a whole social-cultural situation that he was in.

In my family situation there was a very keen sense of right and wrong that didn't have much to do with politics. It was just a basic sense of injustice. You know, trivial things, something going on in the neighborhood that didn't translate itself into a larger political question. My mother, who is even less political than my father, is a very stubborn, fiery, Scottish lady with a very strong emotional sense of when something is right or wrong. My father has those feelings but he'd be more likely to give some rationale for why things are the way they are and my mother would feel a greater indignation. I always used to say I inherited all my bad qualities from my mother and all my good ones from my father! My mother's stubborn. She loses her temper. She's very impatient and I guess I've never been quite fair enough to her because one thing that I'm very proud of that I did inherit from her is, I feel, a really keen sense of being able to sense injustice when someone is getting the shaft.

If there's one thing to my father's credit, he raised me with a luxury that he never had—that's the right to respond according to conscience. He may have forfeited this in his insecurity. He respected my opinion even when I was fairly young. He might offer some different opinion about something, but he let me make a lot of my own decisions.

The religious question was always an interesting one. I was raised at least loosely as a sort of Reform Jew. It's not clear to me to this day what my mother's religion is. We would celebrate both Christian and Jewish holidays. They were sort of bastardized in both cases. Reform Judaism is a kind of bastardization of the Orthodox Judaism and my mother's sense of Christianity was certainly far from any kind of orthodox Catholicism. So we'd color Easter eggs three months after we'd lit the Hanukkah candles. I was never very caught up in religion at all. My memories aren't very clear. There were always ceremonies at the temple and we'd cook some of the traditional food, but the point is that my mother and father had made a very important radical decision to marry out of the faith, against his parents' wishes. For some reason I don't understand, there was more tolerance in my mother's family in her marrying a Jew than there was in my father's family of him marrying a Protestant. I'm not sure why. So on the one hand it was a fairly radical, serious decision, but on the other hand, my father borders on being agnostic. He's not a very religious man. He's never pushed us very strongly about it and there's a sort of vagueness about it that seems contradictory in a way. I'm happy I wasn't raised with a very strict religious upbringing. I like the liberalness of it.

But another question along those lines that was crucial, I think, was the economic situation. My father worked since he was twelve, thirteen, fourteen, at odd jobs and really was one of the "success" kinds of stories. He ended up doing reasonably well but he always and deliberately chose to live well within what I've come to understand was his capacity financially. I never had any awareness of it, I just knew that I grew up with working-class people, middle working-class people, blue-collar people who worked in the factories, and teachers. It wasn't a neighborhood full of doctors and lawyers, although my father was a lawyer. I have been accused of being anti-Semitic when I say things like this, but there was a true nouveau riche Jewish community in the neighborhood that was very bent on displays of wealth and status symbols and my father really felt alien from those people, and I still have great respect for that.

I called my father a couple of years ago and tried to tell him I understand, 'cause he's tried hard to stomach the kind of life that I've chosen to lead. That's been very hard for him to do, but to his credit, he has come to some understanding. Anyway, I thanked him when we talked about it. He was making some comments, expressing misgivings about what I'm doing. I said, "Lookit, you know, we're different people. You in a way have provided me with an opportunity that you didn't have. Because of the way you raised me I never feared that I wasn't gonna get a meal. I never worried about starving, I never worried about having clothes, shelter." We didn't live affluently but we always had enough and there was never any fear that we wouldn't, even though my father might have felt that way. And I expressed to him that in a way I've been given an opportunity. It's funny, this may be a simple theory, but I think people who are willing to be principled dissenters have to feel a fairly strong sense of security. That you are going to weather whatever happens and that you are going to survive and that there's a limit to how down and low your own situation will ever get.

I have a firm belief that I have brothers and sisters, even at this young age, that I know will take care of me if the worst times hit. It's certainly not a faith that those I'm dissenting against will comfort me, other than what I suppose you get behind the bars of a jail three times a day. I really feel that. I feel that there are maybe twenty people I know right now that I've fought with and worked with, even in the limited number of struggles that I've been involved with, who I know I can fall on their doorstep one day and that they will take me in till I'm ready to go on. That, to me, is the security. That's something I feel very strongly about. I hadn't been an activist, a political person, very long before I began feeling this way. The flip side to that little theory is that maybe you'll find the other class of principled dissenters, those who feel they have nothing to lose. They are disenfranchised and are not reluctant to do things that are unpopular.

The question of toleration is interesting. For instance, many of the people I'm working with, the thousand service and maintenance workers, voted for Ronald Reagan in 1980. Some of those people are racist, some are sexist, and some, despite being working class, don't have a lot of class consciousness. You have to tolerate certain things to be able to get close enough to people to affect them, and that's hard. I've actually found it hardest to deal with sexism because I find the level of backwardness about the woman question worse than questions of racism or class. I'm in an on-going battle to change some of the ideas that these people have, but I can tolerate those ideas because I understand why they believe these things. I can tolerate that better than I can, for instance, the peers I went to school with, or my fellow activists. People who have made certain conscious choices and decisions about their life to be activist, to fight certain struggles, I expect more from them in terms of acknowledging similar problems. I can't understand how a feminist can be a racist. I understand that exists, but I have a higher standard and have much higher expectations. The labor movement is often accused of being very narrow and self-interested. And I think it's very important for people like me to expect more breadth from people who have class consciousness, to expect them to be able to encompass in their world view battles against other kinds of oppressions. I believe that the union is a way of opening people's minds. That you're hitting on the most basic things you gotta organize people around. Not ephemeral, abstract ideas of social progress. Organizing unions is a key way of radicalizing people. But one of the main goals of having a union is to begin to broaden people's political outlook. To make them more conscious of the similar struggles going on in other parts of our country and the world.

I began when I was fairly young, I think about twelve, for some reason being fascinated by utopian socialists, people who were writing about better worlds. I read the anti-utopian people, Huxley and Orwell, and I was very fascinated. I'm still fascinated by Skinner, despite all the connotations his name carries. I read Marx, Hegel, Robert Owen. It's embarrassing, but I read more serious political philosophy between ages twelve and sixteen than I've probably read since. Which is, in a way, a shame. My parents were absolutely tolerant of anything I read. I was fascinated by questions of social reconstruction, of building society. I firmly believe that mankind is an intelligent enough species to design its own social order, that we don't have to be prey to constructs like "the market," or things like that. It's funny, to me it's so self-evident that man can design his society in a positive way that I have trouble arguing intelligently about it sometimes.

Well, getting back to the tolerance thing, I have more trouble dealing with the incest fellow and trying to understand that and what it can be boiled down to in terms of political meaning, than I do with the Klansman. I think the Klansman is not really a dissenter, and is not principled. I realize that he says he is. He isn't because I think he is serving a function in society that those in positions of power approve of. Maybe not in a day-to-day sense, if he lives up in the North or lives in an area where he feels somewhat less tolerated. I do think that people like that are important to maintaining things the way they are. There is what you and I might consider somewhat a lunatic fringe, the people who believe in things so repugnant and intolerable that they begin to seem fanatically destructive, but who serve a great purpose in making people like Reagan maintain positions of power and appear to be very decent. They serve a necessary function for the powers that be and in essence they are really tacitly approved of. This is maybe not the greatest answer, but I honestly don't think those things ultimately would exist in the ideal state. I think dissent is the catalyst for progress, for change. Obviously we make decisions about what is tolerated and we always will, but in a society that is somewhat sick and has a series of bad traditions and tendencies, you can have someone who will think that being a Klansman is the greatest contribution he can make to society.

Any reduction of civil liberties in America has historically hurt the left more than it's hurt the right, so in the current context—and it's funny because this is a position I differ with many of my friends on—I do believe the Nazis have the right to march. I mean, obviously everyone's torn by that kind of question, but beyond just the immediate emotional feeling about it, in a more objective, philosophical way, I'm afraid that reduction in civil liberties is going to hurt those pressing for the kinds of transformations that I'm interested in more than it hurts the Nazis.

I think there's always been dissent here. Maybe we don't know about it as much, but there's a history out there that's waiting to be heard, that's not in many books. From some of the studying that I've been able to do and some of the people I've been able to learn from, I know that there hasn't been a major war in this country where there wasn't some significant dissent. But from the histories you wouldn't know that.

Well, as for putting together a list of principled dissenters, I've come to distrust so much of what I read that when I think about that kind of question I almost always turn to people I've gotten to know. The current president of the Machinists' Union is a good example. William Winpisinger. Wimpy. His people are heavily employed in military production, but he personally wants to see the defense budget reduced, arms limited, and the military complex transformed into a socially productive force. And that's a brave position, since he's an elected official. He's also an open socialist. He came to the ILR School when I was studying and met with a bunch of labor-oriented students, most of whom were going to go directly into staff positions in unions, and someone asked him, "What's the best thing we can do to get a job with the union?" And he said, "The best thing you can do to get a job with the union is to go get a job!" End of conversation! Which really was a good answer.

I have people I've worked with personally that I have tremendous respect for. There's a woman, a custodian. She's had a very hard life. I think she's had to kick out three different husbands for beating her or alcoholism or whatever. She's had a tremendously hard personal life. She's traveled the whole country doing odd jobs her whole life. She probably single-handedly organized more people in our organizing drive than anyone. She's not in good health, yet she's one of the toughest, most beautiful people I've ever worked with. Yes, I do think of her as a principled dissenter. She's stood up in meetings that management held to convince people that the union was bad—with their slick lawyers and their graphs and charts and all their wisdom and slick talking—and she's put 'em down in front of everybody! Those are the kinds of reasons why we won.

You know, I started out in those meetings trying to argue with these guys and trying to take 'em on in the technical points about what they were saying, and quickly realized that that was their game. I may think I can talk smart and get slick with these guys, but they're gonna beat me at it and none of the people I'm working with *care* whether or not we win that technical point. The way to beat 'em is to not play their game and to just hit 'em with the reasons why we're organizing in the first place. You know, can *you* live on eight thousand dollars a year and raise a family?

Compromising too much comes down, for me, to very concrete instances. For example, one of my people I'm working with, a custodian or someone like that, tells a joke with the word "nigger" in it in front of me. There are a variety of very subtle ways I can handle that. I can laugh. I can deliberately not laugh and leave it at that. I can say, "Hey, you know, we don't use that word anymore!" I can go into a political diatribe about the meaning of all that. It's a subtle choice and it's always a trade-off. You have to have a perspective on that specific instance, like, is this guy gonna talk to me the next time if I give him some kind of lecture, or am I ever gonna have another shot at dealing with this guy and changing some of those attitudes?

It happens in a number of nitty-gritty, day-to-day things like that example. It also happens on a somewhat larger scale in terms of union policy. We get, as I'm sure you can imagine, a number of groups in the community who come to us for support. We've got a group of people from Ithaca and Boston that went to Nicaragua to see first hand what's going on there. They want to do a forum with as many of our people as we can get out to do it. I'm very interested in Central America, I'm very interested in these people who want to share what they've seen with us. I also realize that there's not one in a hundred of our people that would come to that without being pushed and prodded. People just don't have those kinds of interests at this point. Probably a good number of people don't vote or participate in the political process or read a newspaper and are more interested in cutting their wood for the winter and self-preservation. So I'm faced with a sort of series of decisions on this Nicaragua question. Here's a resource that's relatively unusual. There aren't too many people coming in and out of Nicaragua and coming back to talk about it. So what I did was encourage these people to talk to the other unions in town and get a couple other groups interested. I tell them that I'm interested, that I care about the issues and I'm willing to work with them. But there's no bones about it, I'm not gonna let them think that Nicaragua's gonna be a big issue at the next membership meeting.

You know, I took a full-time job at the University while I was still a full-time student, which was a very bizarre arrangement to be in. And I began working in a girls' dorm. Cleaning it. So the sudden transformation from how I was perceived in one part of my day from the other part was absolutely personally devastating for a while. For instance, I'll tell you. The first way I realized it was kind of funny. I had a fairly good personal social life. I'd gone out with a number of different girls and had a nice time and basically positive experiences and was fairly active in a social kind of a way. This was when I was a senior, when you're a little bit better off status wise, and here I was, going into a freshman dorm cleaning it all day as a janitor. A lot of them never knew me as anything other than the janitor and the thing that really struck me was the girls, the young women, the freshmen—I'm there very early so I'm there when they're waking up—they'd run out with like their panties on and a little towel or a T-shirt or something like that, half-naked, totally oblivious to me, 'cause I'm a custodian. I'm like a broom or a mop or a pail and I'm not a person who could conceivably be a sexual being. That's the way they viewed me, I really do think so. On the other hand, these were the same girls who I might be, eight hours later coming back around trying to meet in a social way and they would never have done that, acted so, treated me as an inanimate object, if I had been there eight hours later. They would have made sure they had something on before they ran by me.

I think it's a class problem, or maybe not a problem, I don't know how you'd put it. I've talked to some of the other male custodians about this. It's a depersonalizing and a castrating kind of experience to be with all these young co-eds and to have them being so oblivious to you as anything other than a sort of a deadened person. And you know, for me, being roughly close to them in age and, again, functioning in the other part of my life as a peer, it was a shocking kind of experience for me.

Another kind of depersonalizing experience is being treated as a sort of a servant. There's a specific series of things you're supposed to clean and it doesn't include going into the students' rooms to do any of their cleaning, and occasionally one particularly presumptuous, obnoxious person would sort of give me an order, you know, about doing something a little extra or something like that. For instance, I had a very firm code of what I would clean and what I wouldn't clean. There was a kitchen and if they made an absolute mess, spilled stuff all over, that's a little excessive, and I would try to find out who did it and ask them if they would get it to a reasonable state before I cleaned it. But many of them argued. They'd say, "Hey, it's your job, I pay all this money to come here to go to school and you're paid to do this, what can you do, sucker?" And there were grosser problems along those lines. Students getting drunk and throwing up all over the place and missing the toilet.

I guess there just comes a point where it's a shame thing. It's a personal indignation that cuts too deep and is a personal affront. Everybody draws the line somewhere. Maybe if I did it for the next twenty years, I don't know if I'd still have that code. There's a line I'd say two-thirds of the people I work with won't cross. There's some point that they personally establish that their pride won't stomach. The question of politeness is very important. There's all the world of difference with the people I work with if the student *asks* as opposed to *orders*. If you knew the average Cornell student, they are the masters of our society. Twenty years from now they're the people that are gonna be runnin' the show and that's the way they view themselves. And the truth is, economically, many of 'em are from a fairly well-to-do background. They have servants at home. But working at Cornell there are people whose whole lives have been downtrodden. There are a lot of people who have very little education, have no sense of self-worth, who feel lucky to have a job making minimum wage at Cornell and will do anything to avoid jeopardizing it. These are the people that are, of course, very hard to get oriented toward standing up and fighting. And I'd say we've taken a lot of those people and, through the organizing, trans-formed them. Some of the most miraculous changes have occurred.

The girls in the dorm I cleaned were unaware of who I was. I mean, I wouldn't come back and try and date them per se. I was tempted, when feeling down and downtrodden and, you know, trying during that eight hours of work to find some self-definition that gave me dignity. Oh yeah, I felt down, very much so. It was very depressing. One of the temptations that I am, in a sense, ashamed of is that I would be tempted to let them know who I was. That's something obviously that I could do that none of the people that I was working with could do. Let them know that I was really a student still. It transforms the way they look at you—it's very tempting.

But to get back to the union, during the bargaining—logistically it's really interesting. It's what you'd imagine. You sit face to face. It's you on one side of the table with six or seven of your fellow workers and the fellow from the international union helping us, and four or five or six people from management on the other side. All the differences are so clear—the dress, the style of speech, the general attitude. I've been in meetings on different issues with the leadership of Cornell University and I would have thought I'd be somewhat self-controlled in a situation like this, less easily enraged, but the truth of it was that I ended up being the one who got pissed off all the time. I just started getting into nasty back-and-forths with management. Why? Part of it has to do with getting back to my mother, the gut-level sense of right and wrong. Management themselves are such an affront to what I believe in. I mean, these are people who are full-time out to keep the people that I'm working with in a lousy position. I mean, that's all they *do!* They're not just doing this part-time, occasionally. This is their life! And the people that were on our bargaining committee were a group of high-minded, wonderful individuals who were, for the first time, standing up as workers. The bargaining process is supposed to be one of equals bargaining with each other and yet management consistently adopted a tone of superiority that infuriated me. Part of it was because I was probably less frightened of them and was more willing to get them mad at me than some of the other people, although they were very brave in standing up. They also are probably a little more up-tight with becoming the bitter enemy personally of management. But I swear, the main reason I did it was I was enraged. I think largely because of two reasons. Because of some of my basic background, but I think also because of being so close to the other people on our side of the table. They're just some very precious people to me. People who have lived very hard lives who have finally, in their forties or fifties, blossomed as human beings because of the union drive and the chance to really have a say in their own lives. Seeing the people on the other side of the table, management, so interested in stopping that flowering, I think that's where the rage came from.

When I was very young I remember thinking about, really pondering, religion and God. I think this was the first question of authority I dealt with. I was very antiauthoritarian in school. I remember writing some things when I must have been ten or eleven about the school as an institution, I'm sure in language other than what I'm using now, but in terms of how it works and how unfortunate it was that it was killing whatever natural interests we had in learning and doing things. Now the connection to the bargaining I see is that these people on the other side of the table are, for the most part, much older than me. And a lot of my confrontations have been with people who were at least old enough to be my father. The figures that these people on the management side of the bargaining table represent are consistent with the figures I have been offended by my whole life. I mean, let's face it, the figures in school, a school principal, the religious leaders, are smooth people. They're not people like on the working-class side of that table. They're people who wear suits, who talk a certain way, who have a certain elitist air about them. And there's a consistency there. I've always felt on the other side of the table, even when it wasn't in a working-class situation.

Like I said, I think the first serious question I ever confronted was the question of religion and God. Although I was still at the time going to Hebrew school, intellectually I had trouble with the concept of God. I once went up to the rabbi and said—this was, to me, one of the most profound thoughts I had ever had, and you know it still doesn't seem too bad—"We learn about all the things God created, but who created God?" And he gave me what I thought was an absolutely paltry answer that He sort of, you know, emerged from the cosmos or something like that. Yeah, here we go again, where'd the cosmos come from? But, in general, I didn't really raise these things.

I felt, I think, a certain kind of punky self-confidence. Where it comes from, I don't know. I'm not sure. I feel like I was raised in a very loving family and had a lot of positive reinforcement about myself. I couldn't have asked for a better family. My parents truly love each other and that's not that common, I think, in a lot of families. I had two older sisters who, at least when I was very young, gave me a lot of attention. By the time I started to get into some of the issues we're talking about, my sisters had left for college so I was like an only child from the age of ten or twelve on, which I adored, really. I liked it. I had the best of two situations there. Up to a certain age I got a lot of attention, which undoubtedly gave me some self-confidence, and when they left I sort of had the house to myself and my parents to myself. I had a good childhood, I really can't complain. There was very little to shake my belief that I was a good human being. Yes I had a bar mitzvah and I always joke that the last religious event of my life was cashing my bar mitzvah checks! Which sort of, to me, epitomizes my religious experience. To me, religion itself was, as with school, a kind of oppressive situation. I didn't like it. I thought I had a lot of curiosity. I was oriented toward study and looking at questions and I felt that they systematically pounded out of me what natural interests and curiosities I had.

I think the faculty at the ILR school is very narrow. Not intellectual in any real sense. They're strictly involved in very narrow, narrow specialization. And certainly the irony of it is, it's not just that they're antilabor, antiprogressive, it's that the work they're doing is of no relevance even to conservatives or management! Many of my peers in the school, most of them, are going into management. Some three percent, eight percent, something like that, go into union work. Ninety-five percent go into management or to law school, and even those folks just couldn't stomach these professors who were involved in the most archaic kinds of research projects that no corporation could even use. Out of touch. Oh, things like, "Trends in Benefit Levels for Police Between the 1920s and 1930s" or something like that.

I became very close with a fellow on the faculty who got denied tenure. We talk about it because he also knew the inner workings, being a colleague, and he used to say they have a scab mentality. Stab each other in the back, very conscious of petty status differentials, you know, who landed a grant, who did this. I'm sure you're familiar with this. And I just found them uniformly uninteresting. Not intellectual. A friend of mine came as a visiting professor from the union. He's truly an intellectual in a positive way. He's written a couple of books. Fascinating guy. He worked in an auto plant, was president of the largest local in the auto workers' union, knows the political infighting that can go on in unions, is a real hard-boiled fighter, but he also has a very intellectual side. He's interested in art and culture and really is a renaissance person, and you know, they looked down on him because he didn't have a Ph.D!

I mentioned to you that I worked on the mayoral campaign in Washington with a fairly well-to-do bunch of people. I also worked in a summer camp years ago for over-privileged youth. You know, very well-to-do kids who were very spoiled and bratty, cruel to each other, cruel to the counselors. Oh they were cruel in many ways. Actually physically, they'd hurt each other. I had a kid who had his eye poked out by another kid. They were really messed up. Lots of neurotic kids. I had two kids, these are people that would pull knives on me. I mean, these aren't, you know, urban kids who are used to dealing with knives and stuff, these are kids who've probably sent away for a hundred-dollar Swiss army knife and they're pulling it on me. It was an interesting situation because some of the counselors were people just looking for some kind of job. Like me, they just wanted a job for the summer and some of them were excampers and were pretty wealthy. So it was just an extension of their camping experience to be a counselor. Within the bunk that I was part of, maybe fourteen eleven and twelve year olds, there were like three who were really good kids and maybe five or six who were in the middle and then another five or six were really rotten kids. They terrorized the three good kids, and it was a real nasty set-up. These were wealthy kids. We had one kid who had—this is at camp—his own TV set, chained to his bunk. This camp was a very fancy place. The woods were "something over there" that you didn't need to deal with. It was like a country club. You had your own minibike and go-cart set-up. I was the tennis pro for the whole camp, which was a privileged position that meant that I didn't always have to hang around with kids from the bunk. Oh, I don't think it was designed to teach youngsters anything. It was designed for two things. Well, primarily designed to make money for the owners of the camp. Second of all, if it had any real purpose it was to unburden well-to-do parents of their bratty kids for a few months. The kids came from broken homes largely, well-to-do parents but who were divorced. The parents would take off for Monaco for a couple of months and this is where they could leave the kids. I raise this as a continuing thread that traces back in my life. I think there's a connection between that job and my working as a custodian at Cornell. Many of the people I went to school with come from fairly well-to-do backgrounds. Yeah, it's all very connected. It connects back further even to the gut-level ideas my mother had about right and wrong. You get, you *should* get what you earn, what you as an individual achieve. And here in so many experiences I consistently confronted people who assumed that they had achieved something, that they, by right of their financial position, their economic status, that they *were* something. And I had consistently negative experiences with these people.

There's a quote, I forget who said it, maybe J. P. Morgan in regard to a strike or the building of a union drive, that God in His infinite wisdom has put these certain white Christian gentlemen—this is really a quote too; this is no shit—put certain white Christian gentlemen in the positions of power in our society and this is birthright. Labor relations are sophisticated now in terms of how management thinks, but it really is the idea of who deserves to be in charge, based not on ability, but based on God's will, misusing "God" as a frontman for corporate greed.

I think more than anything the role of a principled dissenter is a matter of persistence and willingness to work. For people who have beliefs, there is a place for them to work to promote those beliefs. There's never gonna be a period where I'm worried about work. It may not be the most remunerative employment, but every town, every community has a hundred little battles going on with people trying to assert their basic dignity and basic right to have a say over their own lives. And in every town there are a hundred people, businesses or conservative forces, that are trying to deny that. And I think that just as much as you need people to blow the whistle, to take the first position, you need people who are willing to man the trenches. That's where it's at. I've kind of lost certain illusions of personally making history. I mean, we all grow up thinking we're gonna make a *hit*, and I just want to be part of the group that makes the *dent* on the side that's denting in the right direction.

Maude DeVictor

"Today's genocide is tomorrow's humanocide."

□   □   □

*If the minds of the people are impure, their land
is also impure.*

NICHIREN

*Affable, clever, wary Maude DeVictor and I were well met long before our
first face-to-face meeting. She had consented to assist me in this inquiry in
the fall of 1980, but it was not until the fall of 1982 that we actually shook
hands at a conference in Chicago. Maude is an articulate improviser. She
not only read her own fine paper but chaired the session when the person
charged with that responsibility failed to appear. Subsequently she delivered
a series of lectures at Syracuse University at my invitation.*

*A number of seemingly contradictory elements are curiously combined
in her personality. Military service and years of conferring and commiserat-
ing with veterans lends a directness just short of abruptness to her manner.
More than occasional exposure to very hard times has made her a keen
relisher of the better things of this life. I have yet to meet anyone who can
extract more pleasure from both the essence and the aura of a champagne
cocktail, a good conversation, or a noble dish than Maude does. She is
inordinately fond of humanity in general and all but the most hidebound
of that species tend to like her. She is an organic initiator of dialogues. She
laughs often and her humor is most often prompted by wry reflection or by
her strong inclination to disarm and teach.*

*Maude's formidable capacity for establishing genuine rapport is essen-
tially being wasted now. Her decision to embark upon what was initially a
one-woman crusade to publicize the dangers of dioxin poisoning has cost
her dearly. After having been relegated to pushing papers at the Veteran's
Administration's Chicago Regional Office and banned from doing what she
does best—person-to-person counseling—Maude was finally fired in January of 1984, after eighteen years of service. At the time of this writing, she
is instituting legal proceedings in an attempt to get her job back.*

Maude has earned the cumbersome accolade of "Mother of Agent Orange." There is far more of commitment and courage in that awkward appellation than triteness. I have spoken to more than one Vietnam veteran who believes that Maude DeVictor should receive the Nobel Prize for her campaign to publicize the connection between exposure to Agent Orange and susceptibility to cancer and birth defects.

However jocularly she makes her points, Maude is serious and unswerving in her determination that the nation, indeed the world, shall know of the myriads of tragedies that spring from the decision to defoliate a sizable portion of the Indo-Chinese rain forest. Getting to know Maude lends appropriateness to the title, "Mother of Agent Orange," for there is a very real aspect of the maternal in the genuine solicitude she feels toward the causes and casualties she champions.

———

What happened was, in June of 1977 I was a VBC—Veterans Benefits Counsellor—and we have two assignments we do. We alternate between answering the phones and sitting at a desk and meeting the public. So I was at that point working in the phone unit doing telephone interviews and this woman called from the pay phone at the VA hospital in Chicago, distraught, saying that they'd just told her that her husband was going to die. He had cancer and there was nothing they could do to reverse his condition, it was just a matter of time. And she said she knew it was service-connected because he'd never been sick. In their marriage he had made two references to this situation. One was that he told her that if his death were ever due to cancer, it was due to the chemicals used in Vietnam. Now the other reference that he made was one time when they were coming into L.A. from the airport. It was the smog season and they could see this crud just hanging like a curtain, and he made a reference to her in the cab that that's just the way it is in Vietnam, only sometimes it's so bad you can't even see your hand in front of your face when they spray. She was always at home, she never traveled with him in his military career, which lasted, you know, for twenty-three or twenty-four years. He was a career air force man who has literally spoken from the grave. Charlie Owens was his name. Yes, he was black and you know, you're the first one who has ever asked me that? That's what I love about you, that's what I love about you! This is one of my themes I always get in, try to get in when the majority interviews me. Your two significant stories of the seventies have been what? Watergate and Agent Orange. Who were they found by? Blacks. Black federal employees. How were they found by blacks? In the course of their "routine" job assignments. And that says something about, you know, maybe if they would activate equal opportunity and let more of us rise to managerial positions, then a lot of this crap and waste and bullshit we have in the government we wouldn't have. And I have spent a lot of my energy so that I wouldn't wind up like that Watergate guard. Ah, where's Mr. Wills now, that's the key question. Where is he? Aha! He couldn't get a job parking cars last time I heard. Yeah, I give speeches, but I don't have a speaker's bureau like Haldeman and Ehrlichman.

So, anyway, at that point in time I had no idea whether they were puttin' saltpeter in his soup or giving him some kind of funny shaving cream. I didn't know anything—just "chemicals," Okay? And so I work with the attitude that the veteran knows, no matter how bad it sounds, even if it's syphilis off the toilet seat, or whatever. If that's what the guy says, that's what it is. I've found that there are two types of reality working at the VA. There is the official reality and the actual reality. And I can tell you best from this because I have interviewed vets who played cornet with John Philip Sousa. I have interviewed guys who were on the sub that brought MacArthur out of the Philippines. I've interviewed guys that were standing guard at the White House when Roosevelt was there. I'm not like a Ph.D. candidate, you know, I've been with the little guys who were bringing in the catsup and whatever, the ones who were putting the luggage aboard the sub, this kind of thing. I've really been at different points in history that are not available to the average person. So this is why I've always dealt with what the veteran says because he was there and he's seen the reality and he was there in the environment. In the setting. Reports are doctored in the wash, you know, depending upon who's contributing to somebody's campaign. I kinda go with the little people.

So what I did, I got in my car and drove to her home and filled out the papers with her because this woman had been doing this, you know, vigilance with the dying husband. Bags under her eyes, shaking. So I filled out the papers and got his discharge. This guy was a finance clerk—like a bank clerk in civilian life. His job at the terminal in Vietnam, when you came in country, was to take your American money and give you Vietnamese money. This man, although he was a finance officer, had gotten numerous awards for suggestions. With his own hands he had built a little thing to make it look like a bank. You might think, well what the hell, in a wartime zone, but he was trying to be efficient and professional, even as a finance officer, because he was an enlisted man. He had all kinds of awards for suggestions, you know. How to do this better, because you can imagine being in a war zone and having your paycheck messed up. This is something not tolerated! He was just a team man. He got all kinds of awards just for being a great finance officer. He got the Air Force Accommodation Medal because he was damn good. So even in his little square of the checkerboard of life, he had professionalism. 'Course he had been in the fighting too. So when I was there, she was crying and showing me these awards and special letters from generals and stuff like that and so I filed it, Okay? I filed a claim for disability compensation. She called me back about a week or ten days later and said he had died.

He had been going to school. He had done his bit in the military, he was a full-time college student and he had a little job on the side. You know how men are, a little job on the side, and then all of a sudden this man died. Between the day that he went to the hospital till the day he died were 110 days. So this is a person who's never been sick. He was about fifty-three years old when he died. He had gotten a ten-thousand-dollar insurance policy from the Supreme Insurance Company. Now quite naturally when the insurance person comes to see a military retiree, there's no questions because they know he's in good health and it wasn't any fraud or anything because he had his discharge physical and all of that and they insured this man. So when it came time to collect, they refused to pay the policy, saying that he had known he had cancer and all this kind of crap. So that leads me to believe—and I heard of this from other insurance companies—that even though the government hasn't recognized or "validated the existence of Agent Orange by action," in terms of what would directly flow to the veteran, the insurance industry has sent up its antenna.

We have a VA reg that if a veteran dies before the claim is adjudicated, the claim dies with the vet. So we have to come back in and file a form for the same benefit, but now for the surviving spouse. It took 'em three months to decide, "No." She just got the basic pension, that any wartime widow of a service veteran would get. It was a hundred and twenty-five bucks a month, substantially less than she would have gotten from the other claim. There were no children so she wasn't entitled to any kind of Social Security. She was a young woman, she wasn't gonna get Social Security for another ten years, something like that. And this was all the money she had because the insurance company hadn't kicked in the ten thousand and she had the funeral bill to pay and they were gonna give her a hundred and twenty-five bucks a month. That was all she had in the world. So, as always, when they deny your claim they give you notice of a right to appeal. And she say, "Well, I have this right to appeal, Maude, and I would like you to represent me on the case." Another one of my duties is to be an attorney-in-fact for a claimant in cases of appeal. So I said "Okay."

Now I said, "What do I know about this man?" Well, this guy was in the air force and he had like a twenty-four-year straight enlistment from World War II up until approximately seventy-three and Vietnam. And I said, "Anything he used, the air force would have, at the bottom line, had to have paid for or stored or transported." So anything that he came in contact with they would have had some kind of knowledge of. That at least started me on what became an odyssey. This man extended his enlistment at least six or seven times, Okay? And when he extended his enlistment he had to sign a document. Now when he signed that document he knew that there was a possibility of him dying, being shot, you know, crashing in a plane, stepping on a land mine, whatever. However, he had no indication of chemical contamination, you see, so consequently, when he signed his enlistment document, it wasn't an informed consent because they hadn't said, "Well, you know, we're using this and that and you might have some problem with it." So in theory, it wasn't informed consent. So I had all this beautiful theory thought out in my mind and I got my rap together, tightened my teeth, and called the JAG, which is the Judge Advocate General's office of the air force, where I was immediately told, "No, you're in the wrong ballpark, this is a health problem." And they transferred my call politely up to the office of the Surgeon General of the air force at the Pentagon. And of course the Surgeon General was out at one of those ever-present meetings and his assistant was there, so I told him what the deal was and he told me he himself was not aware of any kind of problem like this, but that he would alert the proper command element within the air force and have them call me back with complete information. So this guy called whose military rank was captain and whose civilian rank was a Ph.D. in plant physiology. He was also practicing the art of plant physiology in the air force. And before he opened his mouth, I knew immediately I was onto something because my old street rationale said, "What is a plant physiologist doing in the Air Force of the United States?" He himself said that he was the only plant physiologist on staff in the entire U.S. Air Force. I'm a military person myself and I know how you are always being kidded about how you never are able to do what you're trained to do in the military. You never hear of anybody doing that. Now he was a man academically trained, Ph.D. level, I mean, had *published* and was still publishing, pursuing the same occupation within the military. As I said, his military rank was captain, which is kinda low, right? Now since I've met that man, he's a major going up for colonel.

Anyway, that day he called, I thought, "They couldn't have that many potted ferns at the Pentagon to justify the need for a plant physiologist." And then I knew the lady wasn't lying, you know, the widow wasn't lying. So this guy called and he began to tell me the scientific name of the chemical. Want me to spell it for you? It's 2,3,7,8 Tetrachlorodibenzo-paradioxin. Now he spelled that for me and you know what I mean, you don't get that at the A & P, right? He spelled it and he gave me the everyday routine name, Agent Orange. And he also stated that there were other chemicals used in Vietnam. Agent Orange, Agent White, Agent Blue, Agent Purple, all named for the color of the fog they produce. We decided on Agent Orange because it would kill you just as bad as the others, but in terms of the staff handling it, loading it, whatever, it was less toxic and less dangerous to handle for the American troops. But it would all kill you just as good as Agent Blue and White. Agent Purple was a little bit too much, a little bit too wild and so they quickly had to stop using Agent Purple. So Agent Orange was the poison of choice. He told me that it had been used on certain regions of Vietnam and, let me see, he told me that it was a teratogen, which is fetus deforming. He told me that it was a carcinogen, which means cancer producing, and that it was 150,000 times more toxic than—now I don't know my chemistry, I don't know if this is inorganic or organic—but it's more toxic than arsenic. I don't want to say the wrong thing because some chemistry professor would say there's an error in the article, so bullshit to the whole thing.

Okay, so I had to report to my immediate supervisor and he's a fantastic man and he immediately told me, "Hey, document it and call it in." We use a 1946 disability rating book at the VA and because this situation was not in our rating book, that meant it had to go all the way to Congress for approval of this disability. After all, we basically use taxpayers' money to pay disability benefits. The rating board at the VA is made up of trusted servants who have sat there and managed to stay awake for at least twenty years. So Congress has to approve this as an additional disability. We have the same problem with radiation exposure. They didn't have that in the book either. They just got thumbs and toes and ears, you know, the regular stuff, not the exotic stuff. My job was to call in all documented information, scientific papers, and not only scientific papers that said there was something wrong with it, no. *Anything*, every sheet of paper that I could get hold of. So that's what I did. And in the month of October I made 384 phone calls telling 'em that we had a claim and that we were attempting to get to the bottom of it. That's how it all got started. And at that point I was in a state of shock because I was the only one in the world that knew about it. I had to really get myself together. I couldn't sleep because my mind was still running. When the impact of the whole thing hit me, I can't tell you what a hard time I had. There were people who were just dealing with me as if it was business as usual. I had nobody on my job to talk to. All my son knew was that I was bringing all these papers home and my house began to look like a library, and that the phone was ringing constantly.

So I proceeded on with Agent Orange, and of course they denied her claim at the local level. Then they had me write a white paper on it. I've written about two of 'em, two or three. It's been so long, Doc, I'm sorry. In fact, I've lived and died a thousand times since. You know what I mean? Anyway, the regional director asked me to write a white paper, which was totally alien to me, my culture. Here this is a Kentucky colonel telling me to do a white paper and in my mind I'm saying, "What the hell is a white paper?" But I figured it out and just wrote it down verbatim long hand.

People were always coming to my desk, whether they had a change of address, or they'd had a baby and had the birth certificate and I would take care of all that first, then I'd do my own number. I would ask, "Are you tired?" "Do you have numbness in your hands and feet?" "What you might call circulation problems?" "Has your wife or lady been pregnant and then something happened between the second and third month?" And they'd say, "Yeah, yeah, how do you know? I go to the VA hospital and they tell me I'm crazy. They tell me it's nothing to worry about." If they got eruptions on their skin, they'll give 'em something like Pacquins cold cream, which is like a basic dermatology solution. And when you get really bad they give you the kind of stuff that's like cornmeal inside, you know, calamine lotion bullshit. And then also there were the veterans who were having heart attacks, what they themselves thought were heart attacks. The emergency squad would come flying and get him to the emergency room, put him on the EKG machine, do a Code Three, you know, and they get a normal reading. They think, "This son-of-a-bitch, here I was in the middle of lunch." They'll soothe him down and pat him on the head and give him some Librium or something. Then if it happens a second or third time, they send him up to the psychiatric ward, because they think he's just doing it to get attention. But he has the classic symptoms.

The VA has always noticed, especially the old-timers, that there was something funny about the Vietnam veteran. They had worked with returning guys from World War II, from Korea, but these Vietnam guys were a group separate and apart. They used to say, "Something happened over there." I knew that Agent Orange was the cause when the plant physiologist guy talked to me, but it's one thing to know something intellectually, and another to experience it. I guess my blood really ran cold when I began to see these children and these veterans. There was one guy who looked sixty years old, all wizened and bald. The interviewer asked him how old was he and he said, "Twenty-eight." He had cancer and I'll never forget. He died at Great Lakes and I called Great Lakes and asked them had they done a dioxin series on him, and the guy that did the autopsy said no, they didn't tell him to. He said, "You mean this kid had dioxin poisoning?" I said, "Yes." "Well," he said, "there's no mention on his records." So that was like a body that got away. I'm like Dracula, if I can't get 'em alive, I hunt the bodies.

You know, we have a Veterans Benefits Counsellor stationed at each hospital just to take care of the claims. When the regular VBC had a Christmas vacation, they needed somebody to cover the VA hospital. They needed somebody that was familiar with hospital procedure, and I had been a medic in the military, so they said, "Hey, we need somebody, Maude, you go over there." And, I might add, they haven't asked me to do it since! So I had all these people coming in with "DU tumor," "DU lump," which means diagnosis undetermined. I had a couple of World War II vets in there, but most of them were Vietnam veterans, and I had a case that just ripped my heart out. I had a little twenty-eight-year-old guy. His first name was William. He had two children, and his wife was getting ready to file for a divorce. He had fibrosarcoma, which is like a spiderwebby kind of cancer cell. It was growing in his left arm and it was choking off his circulation, Okay? Are you ready? This is a twenty-eight-year-old kid. They had to amputate right here by his breast bone, it came down angular, and all he could think of was, "How'm I gonna have sex?" You know, the old missionary position, right? He lived in the ghetto, on Forty-seventh Street in Chicago, and he said, "They'll kill me. I'll only have one hand." And he tried to commit suicide. And his amputation was so extensive until the prosthesis had to be approved by Central Office in Washington. 'Cause usually when you amputate you go from the shoulder or something, but they had never had a case like that in the VA. He was up on the ledge trying to jump. He had one leg in and one leg out kind of thing, and he just couldn't deal with it. The nurse called me from downstairs. I was in my office and I ran upstairs and I said to him, "Well, it's not that bad." "*You* don't know," he said, "*you* ain't got—" blah blah blah, you know. So what I did, I reached in and pulled out my breast prosthesis—'cause I'm a cancer patient myself—and I said, "Hey, you ain't the only one with the bug, here I got it myself." So that kinda shocked him and he came back in. And I sat there with that man and I what we call talked him down until about nine-thirty, ten o'clock that night. And we had a very deep conversation and I've never forgotten that experience. That made me think about all these guys. They don't know what it's about, why they are suffering the way they are and nothing about Orange is being done. But this is the whole crime of Agent Orange. See, the doctor in Omaha, Nebraska, he's just treating it as a cancer case. He doesn't realize that there's a doctor in Denver, a doctor in Albuquerque that's got the same thing.

When did the worm turn? Okay, well, first of all, you gotta look at the VA in structure. This investigation was occurring because the regional director's attitude was that of the benevolent administrator who says, "One of my staff people found this problem and we're going to help the veteran and give her free rein, and this is gonna look good on my résumé and I'll soon be down there in Washington in the walnut room overlooking the Potomac" kind of thing. So they were encouraging me and telling me, "If you want to do it, fine." But then they sent the stuff into Washington, and it went to a higher level, and it got to the point of, "We can't afford to have this bullshit. Is this woman crazy? All these veterans out here—how many hours of biology does this woman have? Is she a doctor at the VA? No. What does she know? Well, if you want to retain your job, you put the lid on this in Chicago right now."

I guess since then my whole juices have been and my entire expertise has been geared toward survival at the VA. I didn't get in trouble with the VA, they got in trouble with me! I will say this: If it hadn't been for the Vietnam Veterans of America, I wouldn't have my job. If it hadn't been for the Office of Special Counsel of the Merit System Protection Board in Washington, I wouldn't have my job. See, what they did was, they called me into the office and they said I was going to be fired for insubordination. Doesn't that sound militaristic? Insubordination because I had the unmitigated gall to refuse to work in front of the computer terminals. Those things emit radiation and I'm a cancer patient. I had told them this, and submitted a note from my doctor, but the VA told me that my employment was conditional upon me operating the machine.

I wasn't trying to organize the VA in a work stoppage—this is just my own body. So I told my boss, "Well, I've never been fired before from a job, do I leave now or do I work till the end of the day, or what?" And he said, "Oh no-no-no-no, it's just like the military, you have to go and sign out and I'll call personnel and have 'em get your papers ready." So what I did, I ran upstairs to the regional director's office and told him what my boss had said. "Well," he says, "you know everybody is exposed to radiation. Background sunlight, background lights." Then I got pissed off and I said, "Well, let me talk to your wife, because if it was something to do with the testicles and their potency you would never have taken it from the loading dock into the building!" He says—you know what he says? "You're right, Maude." I'm telling ya!

So they didn't fire me. The regional director stopped that and they put me on answering Congressionals. This is where they're pissed off and they write their Congressman. VA people answer those letters, send them back to the Congressman, the Congressman has his gals retype them for his signature. Now they've put me back on it. They asked me to go back to doing that about three weeks ago. They told me in one of those two o'clock Friday afternoon conferences. You know, so it will upset you for the weekend? Anyway, the first time they put me on those Congressionals was back in 1980. It was due to terminate December 31 of eighty. I was down with the flu, came back to work January the 5th and when I went to my little Congressionals desk they said, "That's not your work anymore. You gotta go back upstairs." I went back upstairs and they had put the damn computer thirty-three and a half inches from my desk, facing my bosom, all day long! I said, "I can't sit there, are you kidding? I'm not supposed to be in this area." "Well, it's part of your job, it's part of your job. You gotta—" I said, "I'm not working there." They just knew I was going to say, Take this job and shove it up your ass, but I didn't. I said, "Thanks but no thanks," got up and got my coat on and walked out of the VA. Went home and promptly called the Office of Special Counsel and told them about it. And of course the next day I had a letter from the VA saying, "Notice of Intention to Remove from the Federal Rolls." I sent that in to the Special Counsel. They were going to fire me like February twenty-seventh but the Office of Special Counsel flew an attorney out and all of a sudden the papers for me being fired could not be found. I had the only copy! The day I was due to be fired, that's the day the attorney showed up on their doorstep and they said, "What do you mean, Maude is one of our most qualified, dedicated workers. See how thick her file is?" So they had to stop that. He took a deposition from the people and that immediately halted all firing action. I'm so glad because the following Tuesday I became deathly ill, close to dying in fact. I had gangrene in my gall bladder, plus a stone, and if they had fired me that Friday, I wouldn't have had any insurance that Tuesday and I would have literally died. So, when I became ill, that further cemented the stop-the-firing-of-Maude action, because it wasn't that I was refusing to report for duty, I was medically unable to work. Okay. So we had six weeks of grace. They told me, at the end of six weeks, "You should be back. Report to work such-and-such a date." You know, I had a little bag on me like a little pocketbook that I toddled around with so all this pus and gangrene and crap could drain out. And I told them, "No because I got this pocketbook draining off of me. I've got this crud. I've got to change dressings three and four times a day." And they said, "Oh you can do that right here in the bathroom." I said, "Wait! I'm not changing dressings in my *own* bathroom, what you talking about public-ass toilet?" I'm telling ya! And change dressings, you know. I might get something *else* in there! And I refused to go back to work.

No, they didn't go through with firing me because Special Counsel was there, though I didn't have a settlement, you know, as I should have. Their attorney, who is a fantastic man, is a cancer patient himself. He could understand what I'm talking about. It's a thing of healthy people trying to deal with people who have cancer. They don't understand about sitting in front of that machine. They don't know what it is to be married and you're pulling off your, you know, you go to the motel, you're young, well you can go off to the motel and pull off your wig; you may even can take out your teeth, but to take out your *bosom*? And put it on the dresser? Even your leg you can take off, you know, but the boob . . . ? So I wasn't going to do it. I told 'em, they'll bury me just as deep whether I die as a welfare recipient or as a trusted civil servant. And one thing, I *will* have my one breast. I did, I told 'em. And I said, you can't understand, you're a man. Here's my phone number. Have your wife call me. So now I'm in the Career Development Center, which is one of the few havens at the VA where there's no computer terminal. You see what I'm talking about? Shit. You know what I mean? I'm just trying to tell you. I don't know what it is but I figure I've got the survival streak in me. I think if I hadn't had that I'da just deep-sixed a long time ago.

So anyway, I'm to the point now where two weeks ago Friday, at one of those two o'clock Friday meetings they were telling me that they were going to change my duties again, and I told them, "Well I can't do that because I'm under a signed agreement. Until I confer with the attorneys I don't want to break the agreement and give you cause to not follow it. I'll deal with him and then I'll get back to you. But I tell you this, and I'm just giving you a statement, it's not a threat, that I'm not going to carry on a long campaign with you guys." I said, "I'm forty-two years old and at the point in life when I should be attending the Ebony Fashion Show and attending the Urban League Scholarship Awards Night and going down to Jamaica now and then for a little R and R. I'm Buddhist and I'm always expounding on the dignity of life—and I said, "When I was lying up in that hospital trying to get my health back, I made a decision that it's best for me to be in a federal prison walking around reading law books, writing letters to the editor, whatever, than to be laying somewhere watching blood drip into my body with oxygen going down my nose, or be physically crushed. I have made that determination." And I said, "This is not a threat. I'll tell you who Maude DeVictor is. If you cannot let me enjoy my healthy life on the outside, I will enjoy my healthy life on the inside. I'm not saying I want to kill you or anything like that. I'm saying I'm not going to be pushed anymore." They just kind of gaped. And then they had the Friday two o'clock meeting. It had kind of flipped on 'em and *they* went home shaky. Trying to restrategize and regroup.

I'm an only child and I never realized the value of companionship. Being raised as an only child I've always had an ability to keep myself occupied, but one of the things that was very devastating to me was the situation wherein no one would talk to me for like two or three, well, really for three years I ate lunch by myself. If people talked to me they would be told, "You were seen talking to Maude DeVictor. You realize she's under investigation? This is not going to be too good for you." I knew this because some of those people would call me at night and tell me. On the surface it was like business as usual, but at night they would call and tell me what happened. They would encourage me. They would say, "Maude you're doing a good job, no matter what." It wouldn't be openly. Out of the side of their mouths they would say, "Keep it up kid, we're with you." You know, that kind of thing. Or else they might walk past me and wink. Bottom line, they were afraid of the pressure and the control their supervisors have over them. When there's a job posted the supervisor must evaluate you on a scale A to E, A being the lowest, E being the highest. They evaluated me as being an average writer, average communication skills. And I know that's bullshit. I can make myself understood. I know a little sign language for when the hearing impaired come in. I know a few words of this, a few words of that and there's something about me that I can communicate with people, even people who have psychiatric illnesses. I can tell them, you know, I have done this many times and I wasn't taught this, but I tell them, "You can be crazy just as soon as you get up from my desk, you can resume your whatever. However, it's very important that I get the proper information so I can help you." And I say, "I won't tell that you were here sane as a judge." That might be the wrong analogy, and they come right out of it. They deal with me, they stand up, they go right back into it. So it's like a talent I have for communication. I don't know where I picked it up, I really don't.

What do I think most people think about principled dissent? Not a damn! The current thing is not to rock the boat. But principled dissent is the foundation of this country. Principled dissent is primarily an individualistic thing. If it was mass action, then it would be revolution.

Agent Orange isn't a racial kind of thing. I'm out here speaking for whites, blacks, Hispanics, officers, *and* enlisted men. Even so, it was a black soldier who first mentioned it to his wife, and it was a black Veterans Benefits Counsellor that took the case, and this has come out of the minds and assessments of black people, Agent Orange has. 'Course it'll never be put in the paper of the United States, but *I* know he's a black soldier, I know his *wife* was black. I *know* I'm black. You know, people think niggers don't do nothing but get drunk and get welfare checks.

I think of myself as just a housewife living on the South Side of Chicago. Maybe I have an ability to speak and write the King's English and describe the black situation. That's the only thing that differentiates me from the black housewife who's on public aid and can't do it. Now others say I'm a spokesperson for this, a watchdog for that, a fabulous figure, and, just like Martin King said, a drum major for justice and all that. It's bullshit. I live payday to payday just the same as somebody who was a high school dropout. If I can keep Bell Telephone uptight, and the light company and the landlord, those are still my coordinates. One guy said I'm extraordinary—that has been a definition ascribed to me—but within the bowels of my life, I'm no different from anybody else. Like most blacks, I have never even envisioned a public life—that's for whitefolks and politicians. And those blacks who have been "accorded public life" have always had to cash in their life insurance.

Well, the reason why I participate is that I gave my word to Dad and people who cannot be here, Okay? I think that the beauty of the principled dissenter is that he's like a missionary walking into a house of ill repute, you know, to do recruiting. You know what I mean? He gets swept up in the activities of the evening. We don't start out to say, "I want to be a principled dissenter." I was raised to be an Eastern Star, a Link, a member of the National Black—what's that national black women's association? Maybe a Delta Sigma Theta, and all those other trappings. It's not as though I'm raised to do this. It's that when the situation presents itself something flies up in me and I take action and somewhere, somehow it comes out all right. It's not like my dad was a noted herbicide person, or my mom was a noted teacher, a philosopher, or anything like that. It was like I had all this mixture in me and if it hadn't been Agent Orange, it might have been something as mundane as getting a streetlight placed on the corner. But it's never planned. Just like Rosa Parks. She hadn't left home that morning saying, "Well, this is the last damned day, the hell with the back of the bus." No, she didn't. She was a little churchwoman, pillar of the community, just a little grandmotherly type. She was tired. You know what I mean? And that issue came up and she responded with the statement, "Well, hell, I'm gonna ride this horse till it stops. This is it. I'm through with it." But she didn't say in eighth grade when they asked, "What do you want to be, Rosa Parks?" "Well, forty-five years from now I want to be on a bus in Atlanta and I want to stop sitting in the back of the bus."

I would say all people do what they think is basically right, but they have a kicker. What is right for *them* as opposed to what is right for the population and humankind. I think we all do what is right, it's just that for some people the borders are narrower. Yeah, they know when they're behaving selfishly, but they don't want to know. I don't think it's a question of whether they can distinguish. They feel it's unnecessary to distinguish because, number one, they are dealing out of the self-orientated aspect. I'm just trying to say a lot of people are trying to, shall I say, follow the path of least resistance, so that they don't make waves and they will be able to get promoted, so they will be able to get the finer things in life. Because their universe is the here and now versus the there and then.

When I look back on my life, you know, I was in country clubs at age thirteen or so, and at that time the height of society was playing croquet on the country club lawn. I was doing all that kind of stuff in the fifties. I was playing golf, I was playing tennis. What I'm trying to say is, I had the highest level of living economically—and notice I said economically—and I acquired and became accustomed to that in my father's home. It has been downhill economically for me ever since. I was raised in all that stuff and so I don't pursue it because it's just shallow to me. What is profound to me is to be able—and I know I can say this because I've had experience, and I'm so grateful that you allowed me to have this experience again—to stand up in front of a class and watch the light bulb go on in somebody's mind. For me to be a "bearer of knowledge," to be a resource. What's profound to me is to be able to do that which is right, even though I know I can do wrong and get there quicker, but I can't stay as long. You know what I mean? It's just like check-out time.

I didn't realize I was so different from other people until people started interviewing me. I know I'm not *supposed* to be different from other people. I feel that I was raised very, very right. However, my parents did not realize that the world would go into such an acute level of mediocrity in such a fast time period!

My mother was seventeen years old when I was born. She's had such a hard life. She's not really working for a living now, she's on disability. She's an independent warrior. Not a mercenary. She's an independent warrior and she writes letters. That's where I get my letter-writing abilities from. She will write a letter to the White House, she will write a letter to Sears, she *will* write her letter. I think from my father I get love of people, interest in government and news, ability and desire to help people. My speaking ability, even though I'm trained. Respect for knowledge, love of government and the mystique of government. My daddy was always interested in politics but I couldn't talk to my father because he was behind the counter in the store all the time. I was in such a little world and I felt I had to get away from home, but not far enough away that I couldn't get back, so I went to a school called Ripon College in Ripon, Wisconsin, which is the birthplace of the Republican Party. That's where Lincoln was drafted for his presidency. That's where I first realized that I was black. Before, I thought I was a human being. I was raised in an all-black town named after Elijah P. Lovejoy, the abolitionist, and I've always known black fire chiefs, black principals, black doctors, black wineheads. We had about two white families in town. So I arrived at Ripon on an autumn day in September of fifty-seven. And when we started doing the old sorority rush bit, pledging, I had the nerve to participate. The unmitigated gall to participate. It was a general invitation to the freshman class, but I was supposed to have better sense than to act on this. I was supposed to have read the signs. Now to be part of that whole pledge psychodrama—you have no concept of this—I mean, you're walking around with the little tea and crumpets and you had to have white gloves. The last time I had white gloves on my hand was in Ripon in the spring of fifty-eight. And then people were taking you off to the corner and saying, "Well, Maude, you'd be an excellent pledge, however, we cannot risk having a colored pledge ('cause we were colored in those days) because we have applied to the National for acceptance into their organization and that might be a deterrent to our overall chances of being accepted." Yeah, they got me aside, it was just like going down a receiving line and it would be the president or something like that and they'd look me dead in the eye with those ice-cold blue eyes, you know, and I said, "Well, I'll plant my tree on another shore." So I became president of the Independent Dorm. You know, the cloak of leadership was still on my black shoulders!

And when we would go on the town on Saturday for a movie, you'd stop by the drugstore at bedtime and have a hamburger and a malt or something. Inevitably I was the fifth, the seventh, or the ninth in the group. And it was just hurting me and then that old Sigma Chi—that's another rock in my craw, Sigma Chi. "The girl of my dreams is the sweetest girl of all the girls I know, da dee da dee da." Okay, and they would let the girl out at night and the dorm lights were bathed on the triangle there and she would be pinned and smooched and all that shit. Now this is in fifty-seven. That Sigma Chi was created in the Civil War and I know what time that is, and I would be there with my little black ass just, OH! Just tears. Oh how romantic! And not even relate to the fact that that came from the Confederate battlefield. You know what I mean? That's where Sigma Chi fraternity originated. So I had to go through all that and it was just hell. It was just complete hell.

The only other time I found out I was black was when my grades went caput, you know, and I said the hell with it. But I had had that taste of freedom and I knew I couldn't go back to my daddy's house and be in every night at twelve and this and that and cooking and cleaning and all that, so I went into the navy.

Now I left from Polk Street Station, here in Chicago, and we rode all night and we got off at Baltimore and took a bus. We were going into Bainbridge, Maryland, on the shores of the beautiful Susquehanna. So before you pull into the base at Bainbridge, there's a pit stop because that was before the advent of the toilets on the bus. That was in fifty-eight. September the tenth, in fact. So we pulled into a place called Perryville, Maryland, and that was the day I went from being a house nigger to a field nigger, at approximately 4:30 in the afternoon. What happened was, we come into Perryville, Maryland, and it's like a truck stop, or a bus stop, a way station and I'm the only black, but I don't even notice this, you know. I just wasn't raised that way. So I was the only "colored" girl, and I'm going in with the rest of 'em to go to the bathroom and they stopped me and said, "No, you can't come in this way." They made me go around the back and come in through a basement, stepping over crates. Now all I had to do was go to the bathroom. You know, I'm not trying to buy the place! Or come in there and try to order frog legs. All I wanted to do was go to the bathroom. And I was so gung-ho. Here I am, a representative of the United States Government, going to serve my country and they're doing me like this? And I said, "Well, I'll be damned!"

And there was one incident when I was in the navy, the drill team. I wasn't in the drill team, I was in the band. I said, what the hell, music is universal, I'll go that route. But the drill team went into Baltimore, Maryland, to participate in a parade or something and there was a black member of the drill team and they went into this restaurant to eat and of course they went up to the drill sergeant and said, "We can't serve the black member"; or the "colored" girl. So, the drill sergeant says, "Oh, that's okay." Oh, I guess it must have been eighty or ninety of those girls. The drill sergeant had 'em all to order their food and she told 'em they wanted to be served all at once because everybody had to leave together. So the waitress and the maitre d' said, okay, and brought all that food out there— and of course the poor black gal didn't have no food. The drill sergeant let 'em set it all in front of them and then she called attention and marched 'em straight out of there! And I have always respected that woman! She was a storekeeper, that was her rating in the navy and she was a tiny woman, about four feet ten, but boy she had a voice! I don't know her name. She was white.

Then I'm learning naval etiquette, right? Opposed to social etiquette. And of course one of the main subheadings of naval etiquette is flag etiquette. So one of the naval traditions is that when the flag goes down, if you're outside, they have a five-minute whistle to let you know in five minutes if you're outside and the flag is going down, you've gotta freeze or face the flagpole and salute while the flag is going down. So I was in the middle of what we called the grinder. It was like a huge parking lot and I was in the middle of that and I couldn't get across that damned thing. So, I had gone beyond the flagpole and of course they started the whole taps or whatever and I kept on walking, didn't turn around, kept right on walking and of course when I got to the door I was sent to the sergeant's office and she's like my company commanding officer and she says, "Elmore"—that was my maiden name—"you've committed an infraction. You were seen crossing the grinder when the flag was coming down and you were properly warned and you did not adhere to naval policy." And I made the mistake of saying, "That's not my flag." Now I'm nineteen years old in 1959. I didn't know nothin' about no red, black, and green. All I knew was the red, white, and blue. But I knew those son-of-a-bitches had made me go into the restaurant in the back door in Perryville. I couldn't put the generalities together, but I had the specifics down pat!

What happened when I said it was not my flag? Oh honey! They sent me over to the woman that was the head of the recruiting camp and she said, "How long have you had these views?" And I related to her the Perryville incident and she said she didn't know that had happened. I said, "Well, it did," and she says, "Well, be that as it may—" And when you hear that "Be that as it may" it's like, dee dee da da, the style, the tone is the same the world over. When you get that—"You know that's the flag of the United States of America, you are a member of the United States of America defense forces and that's a heavy responsibility and we must all" —and she didn't say be consistent, but "We must all act accordingly," blah blah blah blah. And she was white and right.

Yes, I've been described as the Mother of Agent Orange and that goes both ways. It's "mother" in the sense of the way we use it in the ghettoese and "mother" in the sense of the dominant culture in that I have been like a universal mother to these guys. I have nurtured, I have listened. It appears to be that I'm a black woman highly visible in a white movement, but that's not it. I'm just a concerned human female that's highly visible in an international movement. There are not too many minorities involved. Minorities many times view it as just another hassle. You know, I can't get no job, I can't get no promotion on the job I've got, and it's just another hassle, the frustration of it all. It's not as if they didn't use the chemicals. It's not as though you bought a raffle ticket and the prize was a year in Vietnam. So the two together, you were using this, this has this side effect, you sent me to this country, I was there, boom. There should be compensation.

This is how I met Paul Reutershan. He's the guy, you know, that founded Agent Orange Victims International. I never actually met him, I just talked to him on the phone for hours and hours. Whenever someone calls and wants me there, Okay, that's the way I am and I just have to trust humanity. April of seventy-eight the phone rang and it was ABC News in New York and they wanted to talk to me and I figured I'd go big time! And they said, "Well, um, Miss DeVictor, we've got this veteran here whose name is Paul Reutershan, are you familiar with him?" I said, "No, never heard of him. Who?" You know. "Says that he's been contaminated by Agent Orange and before he dies everybody's going to know about it and you know our business is the news and we've *never* heard of this before." I said, "Whatever the veteran says is true." "Do you know the vet?" I said, "No, but have him call me tonight and reverse the charges," and I gave ABC my home phone number and Paul called me that night. The only time I saw him was on "20/20." I was on first and he was on behind me. That's how I saw him. And I cried, I was walking around my mother's house and tears were just coming out. My mother thinks I'm crazy. Paul made all of us take oaths, you see, I'm not just doing this. It's hard for people to understand. Paul made us all take oaths, we had to take oaths. Frank McCarthy and I, Roger Pappas, Victor Yannacone, we've all taken oaths that as long as, now I can't say what Victor's oath is, he's the attorney, Okay? About things like, "Don't back off the case," "Don't let 'em buy you off," you know, because Paul was dying. And I'll never forget Paul dying. Paul had his chin on his pillow and he called me and he says, "Maude, I'm dying. My body no longer does what my mind tells it to." And he says, "I don't want to be unconscious, I don't want to be in a coma, 'cause I want to have my wits about me. And I want you to promise me, Maude, you swear, swear to me that you will never let this go, because even though I won't be there, I'll know that you backed out of the deal! I have to depend on you because my body will be elsewhere. You and Frank and the other guys will have to do it 'cause I won't be able to function in this dimension. I won't be able to, so it's up to you guys. I don't care how hard it gets, because we're right."

That's why I look at the politicians and maybe I'm glad I haven't gotten any money out of this. Listen, the VA isn't worth shit. They're not studying the question. They try to romanticize it by having a Vietnam veteran as head of the committee, but they haven't recognized him. You know, why are you going to pay someone sixty thousand dollars a year to head a committee if we don't have an issue here? I mean, what about the guy that's somewhere in an oxygen tent *now* and is trying to file a claim, or some poor soul who's in jail and can't even file a goddamned claim? That's why I have this hidden rage, you know. I get tired of the bullshit because they're all depending on us to die. In fact, they're *banking* on it because we're all kinda sickly and frail. And that's why I don't want no flag, no American flag on me when I go. Paul lives, he lived, in Mohegan Lake, New York. In fact, he's buried in the cemetery at Mohegan Lake. The most beautiful gravestone I've ever seen. Upstate. Peekskill. *Reader's Digest* country. Whatever that is. Mohegan Lake, New York. He died December 14, 1978.

When I think of the veterans who have died, all of that concern, fighting to the last bit, it's something. Agent Orange has changed the law. I mean, they had to videotape these guys' testimony, the ones who had brain tumors. It's just something that you have to experience. Even in a court-room you can just feel it. When you walk into that Agent Orange court-room it's like you're going into an electric field. You think I'm kidding. When you walk into the courtroom your hair stands up on your arm. It's not tension, it's almost like a vibrator chair or foot vibrators, you know. It's a feeling. I'm not lying, I have done it. The hair just stands up on your arm because they are still there. Those guys are there. You can't see 'em, but they're there. People think we're crazy, but we're not. They're dead, but not dead. You can really sense their presence.

The government has already accorded these people special status be-cause they put their bodies between the enemy and the shores of the United States. That alone entitles them to special programs. VA education, home loan insurance, you know, the whole bit. But now the government is taking a new stance, saying that it's too expensive to deal with Agent Orange, but that should be expanded. It's too expensive to be going to war. Something has got to be done. It has to come from the mothers of America. Something happens to you when you go to Washington. It's dangerous for your health. Something happens to human beings when they go to Wash-ington.

You know, it used to be like you had Group A that tried to annihilate Group B and Group A lived to tell about it. And their children are there to tell about it now. Now with the advent of chemical warfare, they who are the perpetrators of genocide are the victims, just as the victims are, 'cause you cannot spray without you yourself being contaminated. So that's what I call humanocide because as South Africa is spraying in Namibia, and Egypt is spraying the Blue Nile for its hibiscus problem, the whole culture goes into the pits for a hibiscus. I mean by under-developed nations trying to increase their agriculture yield to feed their local populations, all of these genetic pools are becoming contaminated. So it's not just one group, it's humanity. That's why I call it humanocide.

No, I haven't done any more research because they haven't acted, the sons-of-bitches, on the research I *have* done. I do not question authority, I support justice. We don't need any more wars, 'cause the fact is, we don't need any more veterans if we're not going to treat them right. You know, they crawl through the rice, they jump out the planes, they eat the K-rations, while somebody in Ashtabula, Ohio, is putting in their roses and their tomato plants or is sleeping at night while somebody is staying awake on a perimeter somewhere, trying to watch for the enemy. And that's the very person who says we can't afford to be paying for this. What you're saying is, you can't afford wars. Don't say you can't afford to pay the vet, say you can't afford to have wars and just leave it at that. 'Cause a veteran is as much an element of war as the cost of the bullets, the gas, the planes, the uniforms. But it's not viewed as that.

I would say I am a typical principled dissenter. The other dissenters I meet are just like sisters and brothers. They are sincere people, they don't have this phonyism of saying what you think a person wants to hear—it's just up and out. And when we get together it's no ego thing. We're not trying to out shout the other or anything like that. It's just like a warmth because it's just like, "Hey, I'm with the ugly ducklings."

Yeah, it was sort of like the Independent Dorm at Ripon. We had our own dorm, and I was the president of that group. These were like the leftovers, this is like the sludge and the dregs. You know, either the ones that kinda had the malfeasance of mind not to even bother with the bullshit or those who did not have affiliations elsewhere. That was a hell of an experience to have at an early age and I'm glad I had it.

My father, not to sound poetic, but my father, his word meant something to him. When you gave your word that meant something. That's the kind of way he lived. He had these little, I call 'em quotable quotes. He used to say, "Peace if possible, justice above all." He sort of lived it. He would just make these comments, you know. First of all, my father only had an eighth-grade education and then it wasn't an eighth-grade education as we would know it today because he lived in Mississippi where they would go to school in conjunction with the harvesting and planting. He lived in a place called Benton County and it's right outside Holly Springs, Mississippi. Our family's sort of entrenched in the soil in that area. My father went to Lovejoy, I guess, because he wanted to get out of that agriculture kind of thing. He didn't go off to war or anything like that because he worked in the stockyards in East St. Louis and he had the common sense to spill a cauldron of hot water on his foot, so therefore he was 4-F in World War II, but he did run one of the local groceries. He had these little quotes I'm thankful for now because the quotes come back, maybe not the situations, but certainly the quotes, because they were so repetitious. "Never forget the bridge that brings you across." I'll never forget that. One day he was sweeping the floor. My daddy had like three grocery stores at one time and he'd employ little cousins and nephews and 'course I had perpetual employment and I said, "Daddy, why are you

sweeping the floor? You know you're the owner. We'll sweep the floors."
He said, "You my little woman?" And I said, "Daddy, you the big man
here." And my daddy said, "No, I purposely sweep the floor, Maude, so I
will never forget the bridge that brought me across. I'll never get up too
high where I'll forget to remember from whence I came." And that stuck
with me. There was another thing. "There's only one right and the rest is
wrong. And you just have to either deal with the right or various grada-
tions of wrong." That's what he used to say.

As I look back, I probably wouldn't have been a principled dissenter
if I had not had my particular religious conviction or persuasion. Why
do I say that? And this is my third religion, Okay? I was born gut bucket
Baptist, you know, the BTU and all that. I switched to Catholicism for a
sophisticated, intellectual, cold, distant religion with the pageantry. Then
I came into Buddhism when my ass was in a corner and I was suffering
from cancer. One thing, I wouldn't have had a sense of mission. I wouldn't
have had a sense of trying to work for world peace. I don't mean by working for world peace that "I-done-beat-the-shit-out-of-you-and-you-too-
weak-to-deal-with-me." I don't mean that kind of peace. I mean a sense
that when I'm happy, then I can work toward making my family happy.
When I can work toward making my family happy, I can work toward
making my community happy. There's a saying in volume ten of *The
Human Revolution*, which is a book on Buddhism, that says, "One man by
changing his destiny can change the destiny of the nation." I love Nichiren!
I love Nichiren. He was a principled dissenter because he remonstrated
with the Kamakura government and he strayed three times with the
government, and when they don't take your advice, you leave the country,
and he left and he stood tall.

I don't have a good method of seeing bullshit and not dealing with it.
It's like the older I get the straighter my back grows. And I cannot bend.
I cannot bend down low enough to kiss ass. I just try to do what's right.
And right is very hard to do because I look up and I see somebody there
that I have trained that is now my supervisor and of course that hurts. It
can't help but hurt. I get tired, I get frustrated.

I could have ignored Agent Orange. I could have ignored the radiation
and not made any waves. I might have survived the radiation from the
computer and been making thirty, thirty-five thousand dollars now. Going
to the Ebony Fashion Show, helping the United Negro College bit, know
what I mean? They're worthy things to do, but the price I've got to pay
to be able to do them!

I think the challenge is to *live* creatively for the issue rather than die
for the issue. But it's still a death. There's nobody riding up with the Lady
Pepperell sheets on 'em and yanking me out and trying to hang me from
the nearest tree physically, but I died a thousand times since seventy-seven
when I first started with Agent Orange. I'm just as far away from the end
tonight as I was the day before Miz Owens called the VA. I don't know
if the bill was signed if it would mean anything. It depends on what it
contains, who sponsors it, and the temper of the country. I know I might
not live to see it.

Well, I go on because, number one, the wheels of the gods grind so slow but they grind so fine. I'm not the only one in this world that can read. I'm not the only one that hasn't been dehumanized as much as some others. I'm not the only one that becames enraged and seeks to contribute toward improving a situation. There will be somebody to pick it up. I've asked my son to pick it up, so there'll always be a DeVictor associated with it and to train his kids to deal with it. I've asked him that for when I'm gone across to the big VA in the sky. But even if he doesn't, I would hope that somebody would. I would hope that people will remember the issue. Since we have Agent Orange today, it'll be agent somethin' else in three years.

Ahmad El-Hindi

"History is a long, long time."

□ □ □

The State of Israel is prepared to make its contribution in a concerted effort for the advancement of the entire Middle East.

ISRAELI DECLARATION OF INDEPENDENCE

Ahmad El-Hindi agreed to talk to me in his office at Filtertech, Inc., the engineering firm he heads in upstate New York. Started in a quonset hut in 1970 and called at first by his friends, "El-Hindi's tent," Filtertech is now a major supplier of filtration equipment for the electronics industry. Mr. El-Hindi also owns an automated bakery that produces some 20,000 loaves of Middle Eastern pocket bread daily. He and his engineers designed the machinery to mass produce this type of bread and his bakery now enjoys what amounts to a local monopoly in the Central New York area.

Mr. El-Hindi is a successful Palestinian Arab-American with the courage of his sometimes visionary convictions. He is a reasonable man sufficiently secure to subject himself, as well as positions and institutions very dear to him, to wry, rigorous scrutiny.

Our conversation was punctuated by phone calls carried on alternately in Arabic and English. As we talked, the impression grew of a resilient, intelligent, practical man. His service on the Middle East Dialogue Group fits that impression. It is what a decisive, reasonable person who has foresworn sectarian zeal would do. The Middle East Dialogue Group is a small group of private individuals striving to facilitate understanding among Arabs and Jews.

As we talked, I remembered other Palestinian Arabs and Jews I have listened to for whom sectarian, nationalist zeal is the very staff of life. I wonder if he dismisses the opposition within his own community too casually. At any rate I left his office with the ultimate impression that if Mr. El-Hindi is a visionary, he is nevertheless a tough-minded utopian whose eyes are fully open.

They call me Al, believe it or not. That's my American nickname. I don't know why, but that's what they do call me, so you can call me Ahmad or Al, whichever you like. In this case, I think Ahmad is more like it. I am, of course, an American. I am from Palestine originally, but I view myself from an ethnic point of view, as an Arab first, Palestinian next, Muslim third, in that order. I believe in Pan-Arabism, although I am an American, but from an ethnic point of view, to solve the Arab problem I am very much an Arab nationalist. In fact, some people thought I was a hard-nosed nationalist. There was a fellow who approached me to be in this Dialogue Group and I said, "Well, what is it all about?" And he said "We're trying to gather a few Palestinians who are from both the Muslim and the Christian following, and some Jews—all these people are American citizens—and some others who are not Arab or Palestinian and non-Jewish. They would be Christian, you know, Irish or what have you. And he said, "We wanted to get together because we honestly believe that the solution to the Middle Eastern problems could be very much influenced by the thinking in America." Of course, needless to say, that is the truth. At the beginning I said, "Now look, you don't want somebody like me because I'm very much nationalist from an Arab point of view, a Palestine point of view, and I certainly couldn't even begin to talk to the Zionist people because I'm really an anti-Zionist. I mean, real, real truly anti-Zionist." He said, "Yes, I want you to sit there because really these people are not so bad and we want to get you guys to talk to each other." Well, after a good deal of persuasion, I said, "Okay." I mean, I liked the individual. I said, "All right, I'll go there a few times." Well, at the first two or three meetings I was quite angry because you're listening totally to the opposite point of view and I even didn't want to go for the third meeting. So I told him, "Look, this is a waste of time as far as I'm concerned." He said to stick with it because we are experiencing the two opposite extreme points of view and maybe there will be other people who will come from the middle point of view and bring the extreme point of view like yourself back. Maybe it is not really as bad as you think it is. So I continued to go to the meetings.

As an American, I honestly believe the interest of the United States is being sacrificed vis à vis the Middle East. Very much so. I mean, taxpayers are paying for it. We're losing credibility and so on. And it's not because the typical American hates the Arab or hates the situation in the Middle East, but because they are very much influenced by the Jewish or the Zionist group within this country. The way I looked at it was, well, these people are Americans. They are American born, they are American raised, and really they must have a sense of responsibility toward America and they must be told that in this phobia of Zionist idealism they are really sacrificing the interests of the United States. So from that point of view I think only they can influence events in the Middle East. If we wanted to give the United States any credibility in the Middle East, only the American Jews in this country can influence the politics of the United States vis à vis the Middle East. Because of that I thought, well, maybe this will give me a chance to talk to these people and see what we can do together.

I did not know any of them. Some of the Jewish people have left and some stayed, and some of the Palestinians left and some stayed. Some of the Palestinians left because they were too sensitive to the situation and somebody might say a word that might upset them or they saw that they just couldn't contribute enough so they figured, well, I can't do very much, so I will leave. I mean statements like, for instance, some of the Jewish fellows would say, "When we went into Palestine the people were under-developed and they were ignorant," and of course, this is very hard to accept because we know differently.

Although I am a Muslim, I don't believe in a so-called Islamic revolution. I think the solution lies in collective thinking within the states of the Arab World. Unfortunately the countries have been subdivided into Palestine, Jordan, Iraq, Syria, and so on, which was a political expediency for the outside world. As far as I'm concerned, we're all Arabs first.

I was born in Palestine in a village by the name of Yazur, outside of Jaffa. I was raised there until I was sixteen years old and I went to high school in Gaza—Gaza College. This school influenced me a good deal, because it was owned by two Christians; yet the only religion that was taught in there was Islam. We were taught to be Arabs, regardless of our religion. It was a boarding school so we lived there really, and I can tell you that I spent two years in the school and some of my really close friends, I did not know whether they were Christians or Muslims or what. I didn't even think of it. That was the last thing to enter into my mind. So that's where my feeling came from that you're an Arab first, Palestinian next and then a Muslim third. You see, this was developed in me, if you wish. And it was a very nationalistic school. After I graduated I taught for one year in a village, and then I wanted to become an engineer, so I came to the United States to study. I came in 1947, and of course in 1948 Palestine got partitioned and everything broke loose and my people became refugees. My family moved from place to place. First into the mountains outside of Nablus and then from there to Jericho and then from there to Jordan into Aman. And of course the family got spread out into the Gulf States, into Saudi Arabia, Kuwait, Abu Dhabi, Lebanon, Syria, Jordan, America, you name it. I was the first one in my family to leave the village; now everybody has left the village. So I came to this country as a foreign student, and when that situation developed in Palestine, we were left penniless. So we set out to work and fortunately the American government gave us permission to work and Syracuse University was very gracious in providing the facilities and the means for us to work. And I appreciated that very much. I think that the American people are extremely generous in helping people. Of course I have been in this country since 1947 so I've been here longer than with my own mother. So I have a great deal of loyalty to the United States, yes. But I am also an Arab.

No, there's no necessary contradiction. Absolutely not. I think if you want to be a good Arab and a good American, they're synonymous because I honestly believe that what is best for the United States happens to be, at this time, also good for the Arab World and vice versa. And because of that, whatever little I can do from the point of view of being a good American, I think this happens to be also good for the Arab World, or the Palestinian cause.

When I was a student in Palestine a lot of my heroes were scientists. I mean, when I was a youngster in high school, I thought Benjamin Franklin was my hero, but I did not think King Farouk was a hero. I did not like him. There were certain times I did not think of King Abdullah as a hero, that's for sure. I mean, my mind was young and I was easily influenced. I thought at one time the King of Iraq, Faisal, could have been a hero, but you see, I did not know enough to develop a hero. I would say I did not develop a superhero, an Arab superhero until Nasser came about. I think he was a hero, he's a fantastic hero. Well, what's an Arab? An Arab is one who speaks Arabic and has the Arabic culture. My ancestors may have come in from the deserts of Saudi Arabia, but I was born in Palestine and my people were in Palestine. For all I know my ancestors may have been Hebrew!

Serving on the Dialogue committee entails some social difficulty for me but I am in a position where I can overcome that type of thing very easily. The rest of the group who are with me in the Dialogue Group are among the most informed and prominent Arab individuals in the community. These people are very active in the Arab community from a political-social point of view and they do not think that what they are doing in the Dialogue Group is socially unacceptable. No. However, there are some people who believe that you just cannot come to any accommodation with the Jews in the Middle East and who think that what we are doing is really a waste of time and we're misguided. Sometimes words are spoken. I mean, they might say you're a traitor to the Arab cause, you know, but I don't think they mean it as such because they know us better. They know that we are more committed to the Arab cause than a person who doesn't do anything, you see. I would say the people who are likely to say that are usually uninformed. Really, it's not that much of a sacrifice on my part. Am I losing credibility among my peers? No, to the contrary. As a matter of fact, my credibility is there because *I* think it's important.

There's no doubt that it's easier to do what I'm doing here than it would be in Palestine. You see, this is one of the great things about the United States of America. You can do what your conscience tells you to do without fear because the law here protects you. Whereas you really couldn't say what I'm saying in the Middle East. For instance, in the Dialogue Group we're saying, well, let's have an accommodation. Let's *talk*, for goodness sake, first. Now some people might say, well the minute you talk to these people you're givin' up on Jaffa. I told some of these people, "I'm *not* givin' up on Jaffa. And I did *not* lose Jaffa. Maybe my *father* lost Jaffa, but if Jaffa's no longer there, I don't want to lose Jerusalem and Gaza at the same time. I would like to have some Palestinian entity in the Middle East and time will change things where we will have back again Jaffa and Haifa and the whole Middle East and the Jews will not lose Tel Aviv and they will not lose Haifa. They will also have the same thing, you see, because as far as I'm concerned, there is enough for everybody provided nobody says, "This is mine and only mine." Yes. We're talking about a secular state. Absolutely. I think the Arab World could be secular and it should be. Religion, as important as it is, is still basically between the individual and his God and the state really cannot be based on religion.

I'm a Pan-Arabist, and as far as I'm concerned, the so-called independent state of Palestine is important, but it's not that important. What's more important to me is to have a United Arab States. I don't want another separate state in the Arab World. We've got too many of 'em as it is. We have a perfect example to copy—the United States of America. Perfect! In fact, I'd even copy the Constitution just as it is. I don't care about a flag! Make a new flag! I mean, it doesn't even have to be called the Arab World. That's secondary. It could be called the United States of the Middle East.

I think this will not come about unless the outside influences which established the State of Israel tell the people within Israel that they *must* cooperate. I think when the Jews outside of Israel just simply tell the Jews within Israel that they must coexist with the rest of the community and we are not gonna support you if you maintain this militarist attitude, then I would say the people within Israel will change. The Jewish mentality outside of Israel has to change. They want the security of their land, and they want to have a motherland that they can go to whenever they want. So, in other words, they have a split personality. On one side they want to be American and on the other side they want to be Israeli. And you just can't have that. No, I cannot be a Palestinian. When I reach a situation where I say, Okay, we need a Palestinian state, or we need a Pan-Arab state or what have you, then I must, at that point, decide within myself as an American, is that good for America? If there's a conflict between the interest of America and the interest of the Arab World and I choose to be part of the Arab World, then I have no business to stay here. Then I should leave America and go and live in the Arab World and be part of that system.

The American Jews here invariably will affect the politics of this country to the detriment of the United States of America for the benefit of Israel. I would say to these people, if that's your intention, then you should not be living in this country. You should go to Israel and live there and fight for Israel because you're really sacrificing the interest of the land that you're deriving your livelihood from for the benefit of other people. No, I am not prepared to do that. I will *not* sacrifice the interest of the United States for the benefit of the Palestinian State, or the Arab World, or what have you.

In my opinion, it just happens to be that the best thing that could happen to the United States of America is to have the United States of the Middle East. Let me just explain the benefits to you. For one thing, we would never have to fear Russian expansionism in that part of the world. A United States of the Middle East is economically feasible. It has the people, it has the natural resources, and ideologically they are very much the same as the American mind. They are very independent people. They are hardworking people, they have many religions, they have many nationalities. The Arab individual, how he feels toward his freedom of thinking, is very much like the American individual. He likes his own personal freedom,

freedom of thought. He is really capitalistic, if you want to call it that, very much like the mainstream of the United States. It would be a very good thing for America to have a partner who is like it in the Mediterranean Basin.

All I can see is a military state supported from the outside. It's an armed camp supported by taxpayers from the outside who are not affected by the consequences of the war. See, that's the big thing. In Israel there's three and a half million people who are fighting, supported by fifteen million Jews all over the world who are *not* sacrificing their children. All they're doing is sacrificing their money and their political support and the interest of their own countries. So that kind of a military camp in the world cannot continue to exist, no more than the bad experiment which we had in Vietnam, when we put our soldiers in the middle of the Vietnamese and we supported them with all kinds of arms and equipment and money to change the situation within the people in Vietnam and then, sooner or later, we had to leave, regardless of how much we supported our own people there. They were fighting a losing cause and I would say that the people in Israel whose ideology is to have a state in that part of the world, based on their own ideology and Zionist experiment, will have to fail too because, you see, they did not go into a vacant land. They went into land that was already populated by people! And either you kick the people out of the land, which they could not do completely, okay? Or wipe 'em all out, which they did not. It was against their teachings as Jewish people to wipe out populations, so they are in a dilemma.

I'm not denying the Jews the right to go back to that land because they are Jewish people, but what I'm trying to say is, just *because* they're Jewish people does not entitle them to all the land. My great, great, great, great grandfather's ancestors were from Palestine. They were there from as far back as we know. There's nobody that knows they came to them from the Maghreb or they came to them from the desert of Arabia or they came to them from Rome. They were always there, you see, and are entitled to be there. So that's why my solution would be, okay, there is an Arab World, Palestine is a state within the Arab World, and there's certainly enough potential for us to absorb whoever among the Jews wants to go back. I mean, after all, half of these Jews were in Morocco and Egypt. They just transported from one area to the other area, that's all they did, really. I mean, maybe one third came from Europe. These are new immigrants to the Arab World, but the rest of 'em were Arab Jews. No different than Arab Christians or Arab Muslims. We have Arab Christians in the Middle East who are very successful. Very nationalistic, and they are just as much Arab as any Arab can be, okay? They're Christian. And somebody else might be agnostic, so what? At the time of the Islamic Empire they did not impose on the Christians to behave like the Muslims. If he wanted to have alcohol, he drank. It was prohibited by the Muslim religion. If he wanted to eat pig meat he ate it and was not put in jail when he ate pork. So they allowed them to exist as individuals and with freedom of thought over a thousand years ago. I eat pork and I consider myself as the best of Muslims.

It's gonna happen. The question is, when? It *has* to happen because societies go forward. This is the only way that it can really survive and prosper. It's no different vis à vis the female and male society. I mean, after all, if we were to adhere to some clergymen's thinking, which is really not so in the Koran, we have to deny half of the population, which is the woman, the freedom of thought. Well if we do that we are *losing* all these people! The woman becomes nothing but an incubator, and yet she has a brain and she has capabilities. Now in Europe they allowed the women to produce and to contribute to the society and they have scientists, they have doctors, they have succeeded. So why can't we do the same thing in the Middle East? We can't continue with our so-called blindfolded mentality. We have to open up a little bit. As far as the Koranic injunction about women, women ought to be covered. The question is, what territory? How far do you cover? I don't think the Koran says that you have to cover her up to the elbow or below the elbow or anything. They don't specify how many inches of the body must be covered. We are in the twentieth century now. The world is too big to be constrained and looked upon from only one point of view. The Moral Majority is just as wrong in their thinking as Khomeini is wrong in his thinking, in my point of view. He wants to impose a certain rigid regimentation upon his own people. The Moral Majority is doing exactly what he is doing. Maybe a little bit different, but it's the same thing. And it's like the same thing that Begin was doing in Israel. So Begin wants Palestine only Jewish like Khomeini wants Iran Islamic.

History is a long, long time. Israel started to exist in 1948, which is a very short period in the span of time. The Crusaders went into Palestine and they stayed there for about a hundred years, and that is a very short period of time compared to the centuries that that part of the world has lived. So in another thirty or forty years, things will change in the Middle East. And I don't mean it's necessarily by the atom bomb or by nuclear fission. I hope it will change because it will develop from within itself and improve within itself, just like what I'm talking about. Rather than have a garrison situation where the only way to remove that situation is by total annihilation, I have a great deal of hope in the people of the Jewish mentality. I think they are more capable of doing the good thing than the bad thing. So far they've been bad bullies and I don't think they're gonna like it too long. Among them there are great minds. Like among the Arabs there are great minds and they can see what's gonna happen if they don't change their attitude, and I don't think they want to have the bad end result. That's why we're talking with people like Richard Schwartz. He's one of the avid supporters of this Dialogue Group because there are many Jews in this country who are really against the mainstream Jewish thinking. But they don't come out and say it openly. They are afraid. I think sooner or later they will have enough courage to say so. I have a great hope that this is gonna exist before it's too late, but time is running out. Israel is promoting so narrow a religious feeling and the beginnings of fundamentalism are happening in the Middle East on the opposite side. When you talk about Zionism, that is really a fundamentalistic society. They want a geographic entity for the Jews and Jews only, and they don't want the airline to fly on the sabbath and they don't want pools to be built in certain areas and they're succeeding in the establishment of their narrow religious thought.

I think there are many many Jews in this country right now who are great thinkers and they realize and they preach and they *say* that the Zionist state as it is in the Middle East is wrong, and their numbers are increasing. These people are starting to realize the situation and more, and more of them are talking about it. They're talking in synagogues and I think ultimately they will succeed in their change of thinking.

Some people say Sadat broke ranks with the Arab cause, he disrupted the Arab unity. I tell these people, what unity are we talkin' about? We don't have an Arab unity! You know, we had a so-called lip service for Arab unity where Egyptian oil was being pumped by Israelis to support their own economy. The Israelis were using this war mentality that we were gonna drive the Jews to the sea to get more and more money out of the United States. So Sadat said, "Hey let's get together in here," so he took some of that money out of the United States, which was smart, and he took the oil wells back and the Arab unity was not there to start with. However, I have to admit, had he not broken ranks with the Arab cause, Israel would not have gone and marched into southern Lebanon because they would have been afraid to tackle such a venture as that. The fact that they went into southern Lebanon and failed in their experiment was a very good thing for the Arabs. The experiment was designed to demolish the PLO idea, the idea of a Palestine in the minds of the people of Palestine. They wanted to kill it, once and for all. They wanted to destroy the infrastructure of Palestinian thinking—the libraries, the books, the idea of having a Palestine—and they did not succeed. Because you cannot change the mentality of a people by killing some of them. Actually they become more enshrined into the idea of *a* Palestine. In that respect, Israel failed.

I think the people in the West Bank will never accept themselves as being a people by themselves without the rest of the mainstream Palestinians who are outside the West Bank proper. The people in the West Bank do not consider themselves as a separate entity by themselves, divorced from the Palestinian people who are not currently living in the West Bank, they consider themselves as one part of that total parcel, because they are cousins, they are relatives, they are brothers. The West Bank is a part of Palestine and a lot of the people outside of the West Bank who are in Jordan and Lebanon are from the villages there, so how can they say my brother doesn't belong to me? So they are part of the Palestine organization.

Some people think, well, come on now, don't give me this. But my honest thinking, the only reason I went into this so-called political thing is because I thought there was only one group in this world that was suffering the consequences in the Middle East more than anybody else, and that's the taxpayers in the United States of America! The Palestinians in time will get their land back and they're being awakened to the twentieth century. Look at the Palestinians today versus the Palestinians when I was a youngster. They are much more awake. They are much more in-

1. Gloria Arsenault at her "easy" job.

2. Joe Bangert speaking at Operation Justice rally.

3. John Bangert with militia members at León, Nicaragua.

2

3

5

4

6

4. Elizabeth Barrett and her late father, Harold Blauer.

5. Maude DeVictor.

6. Morton Fried.

7. Al Davidoff at UAW Local 2300 contract ratification meeting at Cornell.

7

8

8. Simon Geller at his post.

9. Ahmad El-Hindi in his office at Filtertech.

9

10. Margo Koch Ruthe and Clinton at the beach.

11. Andy Mager (center, bearded) at his arraignment in Syracuse.

12. Tim Manley at home in Scranton.

10

11

12

13. Professor Nicklin and the author with the Puerto Rican nationalists at Dwight Correctional Facility. Top left to right: the author, Joan Nicklin; middle row, left to right: Ida Luz, Evelyn, Alicia Rodriguez; bottom left: Dylcia Pagán Morales; bottom right: Carmen Valentín.

14. Pat and Cindy Muñiz.

13

Photo credit: Jim Bartow

14

15. Charlie Sabatier at home.

16. Peace Sunday. Rev. James Robinson and parishioners plant a Russian olive bush on the grounds of the First Parish Church, Brewster.

17. Bob Sampson and his '79 Dodge.

15

16

17

18

18. Sarah's "short caper" in Boston.

19. From left to right: Sisters of Mercy Catherine, Honora, Mary Rita and Justine celebrate their victory in front of Superior Court in Exeter, New Hampshire.

19

20. Mike Yasutake and his granddaughter Cara Miwa Conners.

21. Richard "Red" Schwartz.

22. Carolyn Thorburn.

20

21

22

formed. We have the Palestinian diaspora today and they are very highly educated and they are very productive. All they need is a piece of land to say, "This is my piece of land." The land that they had before. The Palestinian has really suffered. They are refugees and so on and so forth, but mentally speaking, they are more powerful, more capable now. The adversity taught them a lot. Before, you see, my father was very content with what he had and he really didn't care to improve that much. *I* wanted to improve. To my brother now, it is very essential that *every one of his children* goes to college, even his daughters. My father never thought or appreciated the possibility of my sister going beyond a few years of grade school. He didn't want her to do that. He wanted her to stay as an incubator for her husband. But my brother now thinks differently. We awoke. The Palestinians are awakening people and they are the seeds for the Pan-Arab unification through the whole Arab World. If anybody's gonna unite the Arab World and get it together, it's gonna be the Palestinians.

I honestly don't know of anything in my life that makes me think this way. I don't know anything. I think I will say this in Jordan, I will say it in Kuwait, I will say it in Lebanon, and I *did* say it. Now my brother was probably shuddering in his boots when I was talking about this, but I will say it. Because I believe in it! I wrote a letter to Arafat saying what I'm saying. And I sent it to the Palestine National Congress and, fortunately, I think the majority of people who were at the Congress believed what I said. I believe in my idea and I will not be silenced because somebody might say, "You can't talk like that."

The Dialogue Group sits together and talks about different topics and sometimes we disagree, but on those occasions we agree to disagree. Sometimes it's very difficult for all parties. It is difficult to accept a bad situation, regardless of whether you're an Arab (Muslim or Christian) or Jew. What happened at Sabra and Shatila was a very bad thing, and everybody admits it. The only *possible* consolation, if there's any consolation, is that this is the bad fruit of a war that was started offensively by Israel. It's a bad thing. What happened at Sabra and Shatila is no more bad than what happened at Hiroshima, for instance. That's war. But in Hiroshima they were Japanese and they were too distant to me, but in Sabra and Shatila I'm sure some of them are maybe distantly related to me, you know, so they're Arabs. The people in Lebanon, the Falangist group, they sowed the seeds of their own destruction and they are suffering for it. What they did was very bad. When I read about Shatila and Sabra I happened to be at a football game and somebody gave me the newspaper. I did not hear about it until then and I said to myself, "There's only one solution in this world. If God gave me power to push a button by which I will kill every Jew I would do it now." At that moment I meant it. Five minutes later I regretted that I would even *think* about it. No way would I push such a button. Why make all these people suffer for the mistakes of a very few? I mean, after all, we have in this world a lot of people who commit a crime; the English committed crimes, the French committed crimes, the Israelis committed crimes, the Arabs committed crimes, everybody has. You cannot demolish a whole society or a whole race because of a few who have committed crimes. At the moment when the passion was highest, you would probably say so, but later on I hope I'd never have to make that decision because I'd probably shoot myself first. Oh yes, I'm serious. Because when you come to think of it, killing children, wiping out the whole race, no man is capable of making that decision.

It's just like my talking to the Jewish people in this Dialogue Group. Before I thought to myself there's no conceivable way even of sitting at the same table with these people. Now I sit with them. They are really nice people. Good people. They have good intentions. I believe those people that I'm talkin' about would not push the button, no way. They were just as appalled with the Sabra and Shatila massacre as I was. In fact, more so because they actually felt more of the guilt because they thought their actions and their influence were responsible for it.

I think most of the Arabs in the community have some kind of dealing or talking with Jews and I think we look at them as individuals, misguided maybe. They think that these people are doin' the wrong thing, but I don't think they are ready to take a gun and shoot them, no. I think the Arab community, the Palestinian community is very dedicated to the cause. Just because we are not pickin' up the guns and shooting our neighbors, that doesn't mean we are less dedicated to the Arab cause. In fact, if anything, I would say they are doing a good deal more work for the Arab cause than most of the Arabs in the Arab World because we're free to talk about it. We're saying that the American experiment succeeded. Don't forget the American experiment was based on dissent also. What may be in someone's eyes a terrorist, may be somebody else's freedom fighter. I mean, all the PLO members are viewed by the Palestinians and by the Arabs not as terrorists but as dedicated people, freedom fighters who want the independence of the Palestinian state. Now every Israeli thinks it's terrorist. In this country, of course, the mass media is thinking of these people as terrorists. Other countries, like some European countries, don't think of the PLO as terrorists, they think of 'em as freedom fighters. So it all depends. I mean, we thought of the Japanese when they fought the Second World War against the United States as Japs, they were bad, okay? They thought the Americans were bad. But not now today. We don't think of the Japanese as bad people. I mean, these people you were talking about, the Puerto Rican girls, for some Puerto Ricans they're freedom fighters. For other Puerto Ricans and for the established government they're terrorists. I mean, like in the case of Palestine. These people truly were raped out of their territory, they were pushed. And they objected to the thing and when nobody listened to them they finally had to do *something* to bring the cause to the front burner of this whole world; they became terrorists in the eyes of the western world or in America, but in the eyes of the majority of the world population, they're not considered as terrorists. I'm sure that in India they don't think of the PLO as terrorists. And in Red China, if they know about it, they don't think of it as terrorism. And from the major part of this world, they don't think of the Palestinians as being terrorists. This is a political thing. Some people think of it as terrorism, other people think of it as heroic freedom fighters. I'm sure that the kid or the individual who goes and kidnaps the bus or whatever it is, knowing he's gonna give up his life for that cause, is totally dedicated and in his own mind he is not a terrorist. He is a freedom fighter. And his mother thinks so and his brothers think so, but the Jewish kid who died on the bus, he thinks that that is a terrorist and the Jewish kid's mother thinks he's a terrorist because we tell him so, you see. Dissent has degrees of dissension. Sometimes you say it by word, then sometime later on you might have to say it by force, and the dissenter might be considered as a terrorist by some people. If he loses, he is no good, but if he succeeds he's a hero. I mean, we think Hitler is a bad boy because he lost the war. Just imagine had he won the war. Where would Churchill be? He would then be the bad boy, wouldn't he?

Morton Fried

"Courage comes in little cuts along the way."

□   □   □

*I feel no need for any other faith than my faith in
human beings.*

PEARL S. BUCK

---

*Professor Morton H. Fried is a choice and master anthropologist whom I
have had cause to remember with gratitude and respect for more than
twenty years. For me, exposure to fine minds was the excelling benefit of
graduate school and Morton Fried's insightful immersion in Chinese culture still informs his classes and much of his writing. He is a reasonable
iconoclast with a commendable readiness to accord a decent, meticulous
hearing to the unexpected. The following narrative was taped in his New
York apartment in the shadow of the Columbia University Law School.
We finished cubing the ham for the tasteful dinner he had prepared and
as the meat warmed slowly, we talked as people talk who write and phone
one another more often than they meet face to face. We talked through
the evening and well into the night of one day and much of the next morning. Things kept summoning up remembrances and linkages. The basic
cream sauce that accompanied the cubed pork triggered reflections on his
life and service in the Army Cooks and Bakers School. The mighty Chinese
millet liqueur with which we ended the leisurely meal took him back to
China again. As we ate, I remembered the pleasure Mort takes in ordering
a meal in the language and traditional script of China. As we talked, I
remembered acquiring in his classes a tolerance and even affinity for ideas
that were then new to me.*

*Professor Fried suggested that I call him Mort. That insistence upon
informality and a healthy, humane skepticism about what "everybody
knows" are very strong components of his personality and character. I
have never known him to pull professional rank on a student or colleague.
Noted anthropologists often have difficulty remembering that they are
members of the humanity they study. I have never felt in his presence*

*that unwarranted feeling of hyperexclusivity that is so often a lamentable
part of interaction across American caste lines. His reservations about
some main concepts of anthropology flow from this same flexibility and
suspicion of premises graven upon established stone. It was not surprising,
then, to find that he saw principled dissent not only upon the level of the
grander heroisms, but as the daily courage of convictions common and
domestic.*

           ═════

It seems to me that most forms of dissent are probably thought to be principled by the people who are involved in 'em and they would like very
much to defend whatever they're doing on the grounds that it's principled,
it's moral, it's sanctioned. Sanctioned not in the immediate social sense,
but sanctioned in a kind of ultimate judgment that will be made on the
activity by people, by supernaturals, or whatever, so I get confused by
things like the concept of principled dissent. Who's deciding that it's principled? Obviously the person that's involved in doing the dissent would be
more or less skilled in rationalizing the reason that they're doing whatever
they're doing. Anything that is defined by others as dissent will be defined
by the party that's doing it as principled. Not all cases, obviously. There
are individuals who confess to this or that or take the blame or whatever,
but to a substantial extent people doing some very ordinary things think
they're doing them for highly principled reasons. Including taking exorbitant profits or whatnot. It would be hard in this system to see that as
dissent since this system is based on taking exorbitant profits, but that it's
principle is the question. I think that Andrew Carnegie, and indeed, most
of the millionaires of the late nineteenth century were totally unprincipled
in the actions by which they gained their fortunes and yet they were convinced that they were gaining these fortunes in order to give dribbles to
the general populace. Steal ten dollars, give back one, that made you a
noble man. Certainly current politics fits in. If anything, the situation's
worse than it was even in those days. And I say worse because it's bound to
lead to war and war is now the end. It's the end of the world.

    The first name of a principled dissenter in American history that occurs
to me is, of all people, Nathan Hale, who was willing to go to the gallows
for his principles. He was spying on the British. Normally spies are regarded as ready targets for this sort of activity and deserve their hangings
or shootings or whatever they get. Here is one of the great original heroes
of the country who was spying. Practically, he's noted as a principled spy!
In a sense, he is asked by the British to recant and he says no. So he's a
principled dissenter and he hangs for it. And there lies his fame. Well,
whether or not his action was against the majority adds further complexity
to the question. A minority under certain conditions may be the majority
under others. So these are very, very tricky things. Some of the Irish guerrillas, for instance, are dissenters because they want to remain in good
standing in the eyes of their fellows. I'm sure that many of these Irish
Catholics now—and many of them aren't Catholic; their religion doesn't
play any role in their ideologies, but it's easier to talk about them that way,

as opposed to the Protestants—many of them are not in this for particularly deep political reasons I'm sure, but because their friends and everybody they know is doing that and they do it alongside of them. Once again, the lines blur. Many individuals who are undoubtedly famed in history for what has been called principled dissent actually were simply maintaining their images in their countrymen's eyes, their friend's eyes, their lover's eyes, or whatever. To say that principled dissent is nebulous is not to say it doesn't exist, however. Obviously many realities are eclipsed in much, much larger appearances—even our vision of the sun. We rarely see, except with very, very special equipment, the sun itself. During an eclipse, for example, we see this tremendous corona around the sun. So there may be a hard center here, but the hard center is not the whole of the various phenomena that are often identified as principled dissent. I'm convinced that many, to use harsh words, charlatans, cowards, and whatnot hide behind the *appearances* of principled dissent.

I guess my first personal hero was my mother's mother. My grandmother was a mountain of granite. She was never gonna die, she's not gonna get sick. She was a great cook and every time I needed something, really needed it, there she was. And yet she was frequently the source of discipline for me as well. And I could accept that from her with no problem whatsoever, so obviously she was an enormous eminence in my early life.

You've turned another page in my memory. Something happened when I was a sophomore at City College that involved a guy who very, very drastically disappointed me some years later. This goes back to 1939 and the lunchroom at City College. Now the cafeteria was actually in the northeast corner of a very large space that was divided into two levels, the higher level and the mezzanine. The mezzanine was divided up into rooms called alcoves. The first three alcoves were used for political activity and the other alcoves had tables in them and most of them were used for Ping-Pong. One of these alcoves was basically a Stalinist alcove. It was dominated by either Communists or fellow travelers and right next door was a Trotsky alcove. They coexisted, but not peacefully! Here are heroes of my own generation. I was particularly attracted to the Trotskyite alcove. One part of it was this heroic business. I was about sixteen years old at this time. Trotsky, driven out of the Soviet Union, was still sticking to his principled dissent. He was willing to give his life for his ideas and finally he did.

In all of that experience, one of the people in my alcove, another Trotskyite, or guy who was interested in Trotsky, was a man who's now dead. I only discovered that he was dead by somebody talking, quite coincidentally, about him just a week or so ago. This man's name was Boopy Miller. Boopy, that's what he was called. I had never particularly liked this guy, but we talked and joked and played Ping-Pong and pitched pennies and even played some stickball together. Before his death, indeed, going back into the late forties, he was teaching at Yale and he was a specialist on the, I think, governments of Southeast Asia and finally became a very reactionary individual during the Vietnam war. He was totally on the side of the United States government and could see no reason for not jumping in with both feet and taking it over. I didn't see him during any of that time, but I saw some of the articles he wrote about this. Anyway, when I was a sophomore I had taken a particular art course. It was a large lecture course and the most important thing upon which your grade was based was a paper that you did. And I really knocked myself out that semester. I handed in probably one of the most extravagantly worked papers I've ever done in college. It was full of plates that I had bought at the Metropolitan and I don't know where else and all of them relevant to the term's work, and I would discuss the advances of the previous century and the colors used in them, techniques, and this, that, and the other. The paper received an A grade and those were rare at City College. I had really worked hard for it. Apparently the story had gotten around that I had gotten an A on this paper so suddenly in the middle of the next semester, I'm approached by Boopy Miller. Boopy says, "Listen, I'm taking that art course and I have too many things to do. I hear you got a great paper, do you mind if I use the paper?" I said, "I certainly do." Actually, I don't remember what I said, but I know at first I was negative. And he talked me into it. I said, "Look, I'm gonna give you the paper. I don't know what you're gonna do with it, but you'd better give it back to me just as I'm giving it to you." To make a very long story short, Boopy handed in the same paper, but he didn't hand in the identical copy; he retyped every word that I had, but he *tore out all my pictures*, to put in his own. It was different pagination. For a long time I wasn't getting my paper back so I said, "Boopy, how about that paper?" And he was obviously realizing that he had done something and finally he handed it to me—this wreck of torn papers and we had a fight. That was the last time I spoke to him! I must have been about seventeen at that time and, as I say, I've just found out that the man now is dead. And I can't manage much sorrow about it! I see no reason at all for giving him the paper, except very, very bad ones.

I suppose that Boopy was an important man in the alcove, and though I was relatively at the same level, not to have given him that paper would have started a kind of factionalism within this group and I just wasn't up to that. So it was to avoid factionalism over a basically irrelevant issue, because that was a political alcove. I wouldn't be at all surprised if Boopy had, in arguing with me about why he should get the paper, involved socialism in some way or other. You know, "What's this business about individual property? You ought to be damn glad that you have a good paper that you can give away to somebody else!" That would be in the spirit of the alcove. Which made the ultimate betrayal even worse. That's the best reason I can think of, because I didn't like Boopy, I hated him afterward and I really, at this point, think that rather than principled dissent in giving him the paper, it was an act of cowardice. I just didn't know how to say no to him. I *did* say no to him but he argued me out of it. I wouldn't be at all surprised if that was one of the things that made it more difficult for people to argue me out of things later on. Because that paper really was very dear to me and this guy destroyed it for no good reason except that he was lazy. Oh when I got the paper back I immediately hit him. That's how I felt! I felt totally betrayed! I imagine I felt the way a woman feels if she's raped.

I've always been very much interested in art. I'm sure my father was involved in this because he was absolutely negative on sports. I can *never* remember his attending a single sports event. The younger uncles would be taking me to football and baseball and all, and I don't think my father knew which direction people ran around the bases. What he used to do with me was take me to the Metropolitan and to the American Museum of Natural History. I can remember this even now. After we'd spent several hours in the museum, we'd walk down Eighty-sixth Street to a particular German-Hungarian restaurant where we would have a lovely meal, and then we'd go home on the subway and I'd always stand in the front car and look out, you know, to see the traffic and where we were going. They were just glorious days. I knew every room of the Metropolitan Museum, every painting, so finally when I got in college it was lovely. I was really thrilled by the whole thing. I was originally thinking of going into art. I didn't because I wasn't good enough, frankly. I knew.

Yes, I've felt very good about some of the stuff I've written and some of it has to do with principled dissent in a rather different dimension. But in anthropology, for example, I've never readily gone along with ideas simply because they seemed to be in vogue or because they were in books that I was reading, or because professors that I respect had ideas of that sort. As a matter of fact, almost to the contrary, I would look for holes and look for other variations of the material. Difficult to say why I did that. I was never content with the accepted answers that were being given. To be specific, one of the most recent events of this kind has been my work around the concept of "tribe." I know some anthropologists are struck dumb if the word *tribe* is taken away from them. They don't know what the hell to do. I've had phone calls, "If I can't call it a tribe, what the hell can I call it?" For some people it's very important that Marx used the word *tribe*. For anti-Marxists it's very important that the word was used before Marx and is still in use. It's not just a nominal discussion. It affects our entire view of state political organization.

Let me talk about some Chinese examples that might help to put our two systems in comparative light. That might help me anyway, to express some of these complicated views that I realize I'm developing about this problem of principled dissent. I'll give you two sharply differentiated views, and there are plenty of examples of both in Chinese history. Very common is the idea that—it's not put in quite the form that I'll put it in now, but it amounts to the same thing—that principled dissent is basically unfilial. Your body, your life is not thought to be yours. It has been lent to you for a certain time in order to link previous generations with future generations. You should take care of that life because it belongs to your mother and father and your paternal ancestors. So if you become a principled dissenter and should you be executed for your principled dissent, you've only yourself to blame because you're doing an unfilial thing. You shouldn't become a principled dissenter. You should preserve your life and work for your family. Quite opposed to this view is the actual historical example shown by several Chinese court historians. I mean individuals like Ssu-ma Chien. These individuals would carry the concept of principled dissent to great lengths. The notion of principled dissent in these incidents was not so much requests for legislation or particular kinds of actions as they were concerned with truthfulness in reporting history. Ssu-ma Chien is an example of this kind of dissent, which goes back over two thousand years. In describing events in which his own emperor was involved, he was putting it down like it was. Telling it like it is, and he was warned. His version, however, truthful, was not acceptable! Change it! He didn't. Ssu-ma Chien dissented and his balls were cut off. That's one of the most unfilial things that could happen to an individual! The line was being snapped! There are other Chinese historians who were killed or exiled or tortured to death. There's quite a list. One of the main avenues of principled dissent in China was in the field of history. Writing an account of what the hell was actually going on. Incidentally, some of this kind of principled dissent has happened in China under the Communists.

Even at the beginning of the Cultural Revolution, or slightly before, criticism of cadres was virtually unknown. They were setting policy and local people had damned well better carry it out or suffer for not doing it. There was a play called *Hai Rui Speaks to the Emperor.* I won't vouch for that being the identical title, but that's very close. It refers to an earlier historical time, an imperial epoch when a court historian, Hai Rui, taking his life in his hands, more than his life, his whole lineage in his hands because the Red Wrath could destroy many of your relatives and friends, stood his ground and told the emperor what the emperor was doing wrong. It was obvious that this play was not about Hai Rui and not about the emperor. It was about Mao Tse-tung and Chou En-lai, or somebody else who was playing that role at that time. All over China the talk was about that particular play! Principled dissent is very important in China. It was known in imperial days, in nationalist republican days, and in these present days as well. But one of the points I want to make is that principled dissent is morally suspect in Chinese culture. I don't feel that the same thing is true here in the West. I don't find that the opposition to principled dissent has ever involved a moral dimension here. Usually the reprobation of a principled dissenter will be on practical grounds, rather than that such an individual is being dishonorable to his parents or his friends or something of that sort.

Principled dissent can be relatively nonpolitical. You know, Cassandra, a wife, saying something her husband did not want to hear. Or saying something a wife doesn't want to hear. John, courage comes in little cuts along the way. Antigovernment principled dissenting is the largest phenomenon of this kind, but it's not the only kind of principled dissent. Ssu-ma Chien seems to me comparatively more heroic than Isaiah or Jeremiah. Isaiah and Jeremiah had the most powerful force they could think of on their side, you know, their Lord. But Ssu-ma Chien doesn't have anything on his side except the truth! He certainly did know he would pay the penalty of castration. He took his punishment. He could have escaped, he could have shifted, he could have done what he was asked to do. The emperor's whim was the law.

I think one of the parts of the difficulty with this matter that has been bothering me now for some time is that two equally passionate dissenters may be exactly opposite from each other. They may dissent and be passionate about this dissent, despite the fact that they are each presenting totally different ideas, which are antagonistic to each other, and yet both could be principled dissenters.

Frankly, thinking about it now, when I was conducting teach-ins on Vietnam, it was an incomplete dissent. Because, though I was dissenting very definitely from the government position, I was not dissenting from the position that the people I regarded highly and my colleagues upheld, and the same thing is true with the position at Columbia. We had a very distinct dissenting position during the Columbia uprising in sixty-eight. I was chair at that time and I was frequently on the podium here and there giving speeches, and yet I didn't feel myself completely a dissenter. I was rather a person of several, though not identical, very similar ideas. I did not have, quite frankly, the notion that I was in a particular minority political position. It's not that I thought I represented a majority, yet I thought that I represented a pretty damned powerful, or I was involved with a pretty damned large and powerful, segment of the society that was fighting an equally large, a vast, bigger segment. But the differences were not, you know, absolutely tremendous.

I know that that bit I told you before about the mess hall, I damn well knew that I was in a small minority then. But at that time I didn't think about silly things like majorities and minorities! And what it was in Cooks and Bakers School in the army was cuts of beef. Cuts of beef. That was the exam. You know, like the butcher shop charts they have. This part is the rump, and that part is the steak and so forth. It was mostly nonsense because Chinese don't have terms that exactly translate ours anyway, but I knew some Chinese butchery terms and I put them down roughly where the question seemed to call for it. Yeah, in Chinese characters. And the mere fact that I was worried that they should have some reference to the topic that was being discussed was totally mad since nobody there could read it! That was lunacy. Well, it was a protest of sorts, and yet I know damn well it wouldn't have mattered one bit. I wanted to do that and it was important. It was important because I'd had it to six feet over my head! I was in shit, shit, shit. It was impossible. I didn't care what the hell happened to me. Death would have been preferable to life under those circumstances. At least to let them *know* what I thought of this damned situation. And again, to be absolutely honest, on those occasions when I have dissented—whether it's principle or not, that's for somebody else to decide—but in the most extreme cases of dissent I realize that it didn't occur to me or give me a pause for a second as to what would happen. *I had to do* what I was doing.

Well, the mess hall situation was that we were marched over to the mess hall where a large group of soldiers converged for a captain to give us a lecture. Actually it wasn't a lecture; he would read a printed message that had come from Washington. And this one happened to be on race and particularly was in the spirit of, "All races must work together in the United States because that is the only way that we can defeat the Japanese." And the Japanese were very important there because it was on the West Coast and we were going not to Germany, but to fight the Japanese. The captain began to read this thing and it was a very obvious antiracist tract and it was quite interesting. I wouldn't be at all surprised if some anthropologist along the way had been involved, maybe even Gene Welt-fish or Ruth Benedict. At any rate, the captain's face was turning color and he was stumbling over the words and he finally stopped reading and he said, "I want you men to know that I don't believe a word of this. I'm going to read it only because I'm ordered to read it." I think he explicitly objected to the equality of the races that was being exemplified by every line he was reading. He simply didn't believe it! Though I must say, now thinking of it, that captain did not have a Southern accent. I'm sure he was not a Southerner. And I think of that because of a company dayroom I decorated. The officer there was a Southerner, there was no doubt. It was absolutely apparent in his diction, but not this captain that was reading this stuff. At any rate, it was after the captain made that deleterious remark that the men felt encouraged and began to say all sorts of racist things in louder and louder voices. I don't remember the exact content, but he would read some positive statement, and they would contradict it and finally somebody said something like, "Do you think I would let my sister go to bed with a Negro?" "Nigger" was the word used. And I'm not sure exactly what I said in return, but I'm pretty sure it was something like, "Where the hell would *you* get a black girl to go to bed with you?" Or, "Who the hell would want to go to bed with you?" Something of that sort. It was meant to act as a relief to my system and to cause him great em-barrassment and the next thing I knew, the thing blew up like a cheap Hollywood movie scene set in a Western bar. I use that image because that's what it looked like. There was broken glass, there were broken chairs, they were breaking tables, slugging their way around, and the amaz-ing thing was that there were several other soldiers in that room who sud-denly proved to have the same ideology that I did and we gathered together in a corner of the room and we were holding on. It couldn't have lasted very long, but we were holding on through this wild attack and suddenly the MPs broke in and fortunately, I realize now, no arrests were made. And one of the most interesting things about this whole thing was that by the time I picked up my wife, less than an hour later, she had heard the entire story about this. And I suddenly remember another point, John. She was, what's that word when people will not approach you, in coventry. She was put in coventry for that. Yup. People in her office wouldn't asso-ciate with her because a woman bad enough to marry the type of man that I obviously was, she must be a Red, to say the very least. And she was made really to suffer for it. Not only by this coventry, but she was given every shit detail that came along in her office, other people would get time off for coffee breaks or this, that, or the other and a paycheck was delayed or something and it was pretty obvious that the guy in charge was trying to make her feel exactly how upset he was by all of this.

Then another time I decorated a dayroom. The only time officers would be in there would be to make inspections and at payday. Pay was paid for that particular outfit in that room, but soldiers when they were not on duty would congregate in that room, particularly on colder days, and there were card tables there. There would also be a couple of unread books. Soldiers *rarely* read books. And since I was the post artist, I was sent over to this guy who wanted some kind of a mural painted in the dayroom. And the only thing I asked him, and he was very pleasant about it, I said, "Please don't come in until I have it all done." So he thought that was reasonable and so I painted this great, big picture—which I think is one of the best things I ever did. It was the first and only mural I ever painted in my whole life—of three guys going over the top. A black guy, a yellow guy, and a white guy, and there were bombs bursting and it was a really rough scene, as rough as I could draw, except that the guys were unusually handsome! It probably looked more like a comic book, on second thought, but still it was a work that I was proud of and I ran out and got this guy. And as I said to you, I had known before he had a Southern accent but it never penetrated my consciousness and he comes in and doesn't say a word! Minutes pass. He was silent. I'm looking at him and he's changing colors. And suddenly he notices that these three guys going over the top to their deaths or whatever, are not wearing ties! So he points at it and he says, "Those men are out of uniform! I want you to whitewash that wall!" And that's what I did. Next day, whitewashed the wall, maybe the same day, as a matter of fact. He objected to the idea that the races would work harmoniously. The idea of having a picture of a black man in his dayroom? I'm sure that both of these ideas were terribly upsetting to him. But I think basically the main thing was that ideologically he didn't want his soldiers subjected to a subtle picture of three guys who didn't care what their racial status was at all, because he did, and he thought it was very important. I must have known that that guy was a Southerner because he had a Southern accent. I suppose I didn't put those things together because, well, I'm not really sure. I think I can say honestly I did not expect that negative reaction until that last moment when I saw him changing colors. Getting redder and redder and redder. I thought he was gonna praise me. Yeah, I did. This was my best painting!

But getting back to what I was referring to before when talking about absolute differences between principled dissenters. The principles are not necessarily yours or mine, yet it's principle. Principled is simply adhering to a stated platform, I suppose, or even an unstated platform. That word *principled* is a *very* sticky word. It would be so easy if we could define our principles and the other guy's principles would simply be rotten nonsense! And yet, the world doesn't come in packages quite that simple.

You know, John, I have no clear recollection of my growing awareness of all this, but the central thing that I was heading at before, and it's relevant to the question you're asking now, is that my first act of principled dissent was heavily dependent upon my father's atheistic attitudes. As I approached thirteen, all of a sudden, out of a clear, blue sky, I remember my mother became concerned that I should be bar mitzvahed. To me bar mitzvahed meant that I would have to learn Hebrew so I could read the prayers. And I remember they got some very old, very fat man who came regularly to instruct me, and it couldn't have gone on for more than a couple of weeks when I remember drawing myself up in front of my mother and father saying that today was the last time and I do not want to and will not be bar mitzvahed. And I was not. And of course, I don't know what would have happened if my grandmother had been alive 'cause

I'm not so sure I could have resisted so bravely and contradicted her. She would have been afraid for me. The best thing about it was that it was easier than I had expected it to be. I had expected far more struggle and there was no struggle to speak of. I didn't expect it from my father, but I expected my mother to carry on and that didn't happen. It turned out not to be an act of principled dissent in the struggle sense, but I can say absolutely and flatly that I never saw that Hebrew teacher again and I was not bar mitzvahed. It was simply passed over. I didn't see it as a moral act, it was to protect my sanity! I just didn't like this instruction! I was an atheist at that time so that's why I raise it as a principle. I was a declared atheist. I had declared it to my father and I remember arguing with my father, but I don't remember any reaction. I used to argue, before I was even thirteen years old, with the other kids about atheism. And the kids had me tabbed as an atheist and it didn't really matter because I was a pretty good batter anyway, and they never expected me to get bar mitzvahed.

When I announced to my mother and father that I was going to become an anthropologist, there was another, and in a sense, more interesting confrontation with the elders of the family. When I was about nineteen years old I had graduated from City College—at night, incidentally, because my father had gone blind. At any rate, when I announced that I was going to become an anthropologist, the family was in an uproar! They said "What are you going to do for a living?" They were absolutely outraged. They wanted me to do *anything* else. One of my mother's sisters was married to a man who was the owner of a trucking corporation with rather shady connections. I mean, this guy was really a rough guy. That guy could take on any two of his drivers at the same time with bare hands! He was the toughest man that I think I've ever seen, in the army or out of the army! He wanted me to work for him. "Doing what? What the hell do you care? You'll get paid and I'll tell you what to do and it'll be a lot more than you can earn as a—what didcha call it?" And that's what the family thought I'd do, that I'd work for this uncle.

After my father went blind he continued to work as a customs inspector. It's very interesting. He had the support of his fellow workers. It was a sub-rosa kind of thing. He could no longer work inspecting baggage, of course, but he had sufficient friends in the force at that time so that, as it turned out, the other men were perfectly willing to cover for him. But what he would do—I went down several times and saw this actually happening —the phone would be constantly ringing, from all over the metropolitan area. Newark, Brooklyn, Manhattan, and they even would get long distance calls. Other customs men working elsewhere would run into problems. My father never got beyond the sixth grade in school because his father made him get a job at that point, but he was a very intelligent guy, and he was regarded as an expert on customs law and procedure, and the phone was constantly ringing from customs men all over, up and down the East Coast who had run into weird things and they weren't quite sure what the hell to do and my father would tell 'em what to do. And that's what he did the last several years of his life. Utterly blind, answering the phone, advising other customs men about procedure. At any rate, it was largely through him that I conceived first the atheism, and I'm sure, in general, many of my other attitudes. Among the other things that I remember well was that business of his being in the American Legion. Even though he enjoyed their activities and used to go to the meetings and so forth, he used to argue with those guys endlessly. He was invariably on the other side of every topic, and he loved it! I'm sure that that's a lot of what was in it for him. He would be able to find those patsies and see he was smarter than all of them. He would take them on and have this glorious time! And there I was, this little kid, seeing this and never even dreaming that it was going to affect me.

Simon Geller

"I've got myself an attorney and I don't count on getting out of the radio business."

□　□　□

This case is . . . another regulatory example of justice delayed being justice denied.

SENATOR BOB PACKWOOD

Simon Geller is the sole owner and total staff of WVCA-FM in Gloucester, Massachusetts. His programming is nothing if not personal. This low-watt purveyor of serious music is almost exclusively undimmed by canned news and other uniform network fillers. For over ten years now, Geller, a spirited, chronically ill individualist, has been fighting to keep his FCC license against a much wealthier competitor. That protracted struggle has neither daunted Mr. Geller nor diminished the persistence of a strong local support group that calls itself Save Our Station.

Mr. Geller worked his archaic board at intervals as we talked in his kitchen/bedroom/broadcasting studio. A succession of dedicated young women visited him as we talked, bearing assurances of support and a gift of lilies of the valley. His devoted listeners have contributed thousands of dollars to assist him, and for twenty years he has given them what he has reason to believe they wish to hear. Gloucester is served by no fewer than twenty-seven AM and twenty other FM carriers. Simon Geller is now broadcasting one hundred hours of serious music per week. He presents lengthy works in their entirety and his programming represents a welcome alternative for significant numbers of people in his listening area. If his equipment is antiquated and his library limited, his programming is judged tasteful by many and his independence and tenacity command respect.

Simon Geller's struggle to keep his spot on the dial is the leading edge of a campaign to increase quality and variety in broadcasting. In recognition of the fact that the tyranny of what are supposed to be majority interests should not overwhelm alternatives like those offered by people like Simon Geller, the U.S. Congress is deliberating this question. The

Senate has passed broadcast deregulation measures and a bill currently before a House subcommittee would, if passed, resolve most of Mr. Geller's difficulties. Needless to say, the resolution of this question is of relevance to far more than the forty thousand or so listeners served by WVCA-FM.

———

There's no problem with what I tell you because this is public information anyway. I filed an application for renewal of my license in 1975. The Republican State Chairman and another man were parties in an application for the same license. That's all there is as far as that goes. They're still fighting to get it. That's right, the Grandbanke Corporation. One of the principals has a license up in Vermont, the other one has a license in Massachusetts. The FCC said my license wouldn't be renewed after May 20. They said I didn't broadcast enough news. What they called it was informational programming. Yes, in this area there is a great abundance of that. My station, WVCA-FM, does strictly symphonic music. People make contributions. I don't publish a program guide. It's strictly symphonic. I play full symphonies, chamber works, ballet, and anything else that's symphonic that most of the other stations won't play because they feel that they're too long or they feel that they may not get a big enough audience. About once every six weeks I play the full *Swan Lake* ballet, which runs about two and a half hours, without interruption. And I'll play with the same frequency the other Tchaikovsky ballets—*The Nutcracker* and the *Sleeping Beauty*. In their entirety. During prime time. I do some grand opera highlights, but I found that my audience resists vocal music. My reasoning behind it is the less experience you have with music, the less likely you are to like the vocals. It takes time. You have to expose yourself a longer period to the music to learn to enjoy the vocals and many of them are just new to the music so they like the orchestral. I have enough music to take care of thirty-some days of programming. I rotate it. The way I arrived at this programming was from letters from my audience. They say they like it exactly the way it is with no interruptions for talk. So I give them no talk! If that's what they want, that's what they get. The output of the station is 3,000 watts at 260 feet antenna height at 104.9 on the dial. I have some advertising, it's a commercial station, and I get the balance by contributions from the audience. Thus far, I've got copies of more than a hundred forty letters that were mailed to the FCC by my audience. And I'm sure that not everyone who wrote a letter to the FCC sent me a copy. All favorable! There hasn't been one unfavorable letter!

My audience is mostly professional, business people. I have a large number of doctors, lawyers. In fact, I had some letters, I think two or three letters, from doctors at Harvard Medical School. I had a couple of letters from college professors in support and then I have letters from retired people in support. Quite a good number of retired people. You don't know what they did before they retired. It seems that the attitude today is to supply programming for the group eighteen to thirty-four and to heck with everybody else.

The struggle has been going on since 1975. Chronologically, this is what happened. In 1975 Grandbanke filed the application against me. In 1977 the FCC held a hearing in Gloucester. In 1978 the judge ruled in my favor, that my license should be renewed. Immediately Grandbanke filed an appeal, but it took them four years to get the case to the full commission. I don't know why, except that I feel they were waiting for the balance of membership in the commission to change so that it would be favorable to them. You know, one of the partners who was trying to get my license said I was killing myself with all this programming. "He can't last long," he said. Well, in March of 1983 *he* died! He was sixty years old. I'm sixty-four! And the other partner is being investigated by the Attorney General so I figure if I can just hold on long enough—I never did believe in God, but maybe somebody up there does like me! I've got myself an attorney and I don't count on getting out of the radio business.

There is a local group that's supporting me. I know the person that's handling it, but I don't know if they've taken any name yet. Then there's a group in Ipswich, the Save Our Station Group, they call themselves. There was one woman in the Magnolia section of Gloucester that collected over three hundred signatures on a petition. If I have to go to Washington for a hearing I'm not worried about the manning of the station. I'd just as soon go off. The audience is more conscious of a sense of losing. If it's continuously on, there's less sensitivity in the audience that it could go. It isn't a profitable thing. All I can do is get food money out of it and in five or six years, get a pair of shoes and a suit. That's about all I can do.

Why am I doing it? Because I became unemployable in 1948! Overqualified, as they put it. I went to CBS in New York to look for work. In the interview I was told, "You won't be happy here. You know too much." That's typical of American capitalistic business. What do you expect! I'm not a trained broadcaster. No, if I were trained I wouldn't have the audience I have. One thing training does is tell you what you can't do. When I started this, I made up my mind that there was nothing that I couldn't do. I'll give you an idea what I do. Today I had Symphony no. 3 by Glière, a sonata for violin and piano by Mendelssohn, Piano Sonata by Schubert, a symphony by Cherubini, a sonata for cello and piano by Grieg, piano concerto by MacDowell, the Symphony no. 92 by Haydn, the Concerto for Violin and Orchestra by Mozart, My Fatherland by Smetana, music for harpsichord by Claude Balbustre, and the Hungarian Dances by Brahms. That's one six-hour segment. I try to appeal to everyone. I have the peculiar idea that everyone is entitled to radio service, regardless of who they are.

I've been interested in serious music, oh, let's see, since 1935. I became interested in it during the WPA period under Roosevelt. When he had these WPA orchestras that were giving these free concerts I would go and I became interested. My father used to like symphonic music and I wanted to find out why. He died in 1933. So I started listening and I began to enjoy it slowly. It took a long while, but I did. I studied violin for five years but I don't play it now.

Well, in broadcasting there never was any principled dissent! I don't know how to put it. There never was anything in broadcasting except the chasing of the almighty dollar. We have a lot of people doing not what they think is right, but what they think is profitable. There's a big difference. I started this as a service. I knew that there were other stations doing it and that they had more power. They had stereo so they might be able to hold the audience. But it turned out that, in the area I'm reaching, I'm the primary service and they've become the alternative service. They don't like that! Particularly CRB and GBH. That's right! Some of my people were foolish enough to call the GBH morning man and ask him to help out, to mention it on his program. So he went into a tirade that I should lose my license because I'm doing everything wrong. I don't play news and I play old records. By old records, what he means, for example, is that I concentrate on records that were recorded by Heifetz. The reason I do that is that a professor was interviewed about two years ago on WGBH. He said that Heifetz was the greatest violinist who ever lived. So I figured I could give my audience the greatest, so why do anything less? No, the GBH guy wouldn't support me. Also I'm in competition with him. Now that I realize how he feels, as soon as I get around to it, as soon as I get this problem solved, I'll probably go on at seven in the morning and take away his whole audience! I don't believe in getting anybody like that, but of course, if he's after me, I'll have to fight back.

The profit motive. That's what's causing most of our problems. I don't feel that I'm doing anything substandard here. My main motive isn't profit. Of course, I'd like to have some money coming in, but it isn't to get rich. I don't think I would become a great profit-making venture, because of the way I've set up my operation here. I set a maximum for the amount of commercial time I'll put on and at that maximum, I can never become rich. Four minutes an hour. I figured out the length of the pieces I play and I figured that's all it could support. If I did more than that, they would start tuning out. Most stations figure it the other way. They say, how many commercials can I get in this area in this town and then they select a record to fit in, to fit the commercial. That's what they all do.

Well, I think there is some tradition of principled dissent in this country, but it's slowly disappeared. First of all because life has been made too easy over the past forty or fifty years. Most people have not had to sacrifice the way they did during the Depression. I think sacrifice makes us stronger as individuals. If you're used to sacrificing material things, you would be more likely to stand up for what you think is right. I think the reason that two commissioners on the FCC board voted in my favor was that they went through the Depression and they knew the meaning of sacrifice. The oldest one of the others is fifty-one.

Yeh, I know my image of eccentricity is growing. It's growing but I had nothing to do with it. I can't change that! If they think I'm a nut I would want to change that! New England is not a region of rampant eccentricity, it's a region of rampant conformity! I don't think dissent is troublesome, I think it's good. Anything should be tolerated if it doesn't infringe on anyone's rights. I question the Nazis' right to march because they were trying to inflame public opinion. I wouldn't question their right to publish their material if they sent it only to people that asked for it. They have the right to use the mail to disseminate any ideas that are considered legal. If you're preaching violation of law, no! Change the law first. There should be changes, but they should come by evolution rather than revolution. I think they are coming by evolution, slowly but surely.

Well, if somebody passed a law saying I couldn't play glass harmonica music, I'd disregard it. Oh definitely! That's not a reasonable law! I'd have to justify playing that music, breaking that law, to others, but I wouldn't have any trouble justifying it to myself. Normally I don't agonize about decisions. How do I manage that? I just shut my mind!

Well, going back to the Depression, I was living in Roxbury at the time. It was a reasonably good section in those days and I was beginning to get interested in serious music. And I was sick and tired that except for one, WCOP, which has changed call letters now, they had an hour in the afternoon and then two of the big stations had an hour between twelve and one in the morning! And that's all you had! So that was the time I decided that if I ever got to the point where I had my own station, that I would program for minority taste. They gave it at an hour when very few people could listen. At least the big stations did it that way. Because I was in the minority, I figured that minority tastes should be served. First of all I was Jewish. I had hopes of going to college, which I never did make. I went to Northeastern University to investigate and was told by an admissions officer, "We can't place Jews, Catholics, or blacks." My father came from a part of Poland that was under Russian domination at the time. They had no rights at all. The only right they had was to serve in the army. He was a dissenter, but he was a rabid right-winger too. For one thing he hated with a poisonous hate the Communists. Now maybe he had had some experience with them, I don't know. I don't hate anybody! I feel that if they have something, try to get them to use it to your advantage rather than not having anything to do with them. I believe in a positive attitude. Be pro something rather than anti.

I would be a socialist if you could generate pure socialism, but there's no such thing as pure socialism. When you have a socialist state it disintegrates into communism. I think I'm practicing pure socialism right here. The socialists say "To each according to his needs, from each according to his ability." That's exactly what I'm doing! There are more people that actually believe in socialism than you would think. I'm doing what the Congress and the FCC have been saying should be done since 1934, serving the public! That's what I'm trying to do! But I don't think they have the right to determine *how* I serve the public.*

* On December 10, 1985, in a rare public vote, the FCC renewed Simon Geller's license. He also tells me that his 29-year courtship of Miss Carol Hill is rapidly approaching the critical stage and a marriage may very well be in the offing.

Margo Koch Ruthe

"If you believe in something and you don't say it,
then it's just as good as if you don't believe it."

□ □ □

*Civil disobedience based on ethical considerations
is one of the strongest weapons in the arsenal of
justice.*

MARGARET MEAD

*In the summer of 1982 the Selectmen of her small New England town
attempted to deny Margo Koch Ruthe the right to dispense literature about
alternatives to military service from the Town Hall public parking lot.*

*Hours of pleasant, often profound conversation with her revealed that
her insistence that the Town Fathers respect her rights was of a piece with
much of the rest of her life. Margo is a young-looking, young-sounding
grandmother in her sixties who has been politically active for decades. She
has invested heavily in her Quaker commitments. The Poor People's Campaign, disarmament, and the facilitation of dialogue among deadly enemies
have all claimed her whole-hearted allegiance. She is not an especially
confrontational person, but she participated in the blocking of the Pentagon
in 1971 as a protest against the Vietnam war and refused to permit her
daughters, Faith and Eva, to take part in what she felt were futile and
jingoistic school civil defense exercises.*

*A quiet woman with active hands and a well-modulated, slightly ac-
cented voice, Margo's German origin lends a touch of charm to her excellent English. She is a vegetarian who bakes her own bread. She regrets the
necessity of life to feed on life, but her vegetarianism is rooted also in her
fear of chemical pollution. Although Eva and Faith now live in widely
separated parts of the country, she maintains close ties with them and her
three grandchildren. They are a trio of political activists bound together
by a firm conviction that life is sacred and that femaleness carries with it
a special responsibility to guard and sustain it.*

*Margo rescued her admiring canine companion, Clinton, from the sadism
and privation of the street stray's existence many years ago, and they have*

lived companionably ever since. He accompanies her on long walks by the sea, even in storms, goes to Town Meetings and the Friday evening movies, and sits quietly alert to her moods and suggestions.

Painting and choir membership exemplify the strong elements of solitariness and sociability in Margo's personality. Her love of nature and the organic existence and her respect for the unity of living things owes much to Schiller and Goethe, but she lives in this decade of this century. She has borne everything from ostracism to imprisonment to oppose whatsoever things that are, in her view, life threatening and injurious to untrammeled exchange of opinion and respect for diversity.

I was born in Wiesbaden, Germany. It is a well-known, internationally known, spa. As a matter of fact, at one given time, it was called the town of a hundred twenty millionaires. They came for the derby, for the races, for the cultural events, for concerts. So mine was anything but a poor and deprived childhood, in terms of material things.

At home we were surrounded by servants. The families that we dealt with had servants. The families were very good to them. It was never thought that they were not people, but it was never thought that they could be something else except servants. And I didn't know any better. I didn't know any different, except that I usually sat in the kitchen with the servants. I don't know why. As a child, I cannot say that I identified with them, but it felt very natural to be with them. By natural, I mean, I don't want to appear what I'm not. I'm not interested in impressing people. And what people really need—love, respect, recognition, encouragement—I believe, in my way as a child, I received that from servants. It was a mutual empathy.

You know, in our first conversation you asked me where was the turning point, or what made me what I am, and I kept saying, "I don't know." I guess I said to you that I feel I have—though I don't know where I got it—this very pronounced sense of justice. Then you said that it is a very intellectualized concept. I thought about that and I cannot really see that. Because, to me, it's an emotional thing. If you have a cat here and somebody comes and puts a match on the cat's tail, I mean, I can't stand it! But that has nothing to do with logic. I would protect the cat and I would challenge this person. I don't like spiders but I cannot really—perhaps it is crazy—but I cannot really kill them. So I have a technique. I have a glass and a postcard and I lure them into this glass and cover it with the postcard. Then I shake them outside, knowing full well that if it's very cold, they will die within minutes. I know that, but I cannot kill the spider in my house. I close my eyes, that's all I can do. Oh, my friend had a mouse in the house. I wanted to take the mouse out. Well, it ended up in a trap. I guess I identify with pain or something. I mean, a fly! I don't know, not having been a fly, I don't know what a fly feels. But I believe a fly, I believe a stone feels! I believe that. It is part of the universe and there is a universal sensory capacity of everything that is around. I hate jellyfish but I take them back to the water if they are stranded on the beach. I mean, they sting me, but I cannot destroy them. What is alive needs to be alive, I think.

I really have been thinking about this. And then by and by I made notes. There were incidents that really give you an idea that I was not a very compliant spirit. Perhaps that's it, I don't know.

Now, I tell you one thing that I can remember in my early school days. In a shoestore in my hometown, I saw a pair of bright red shoes. There was only one pair and I really really wanted them and I got them. And then people said, "Oh, you look like a bird! You look like a duck!" And they said, "Why do you want these shoes?" And I can remember saying, "Because I want to be different." I don't know how that fits into this whole thing. Another thing from school I remember is that I invented my own handwriting. You know in German schools you have to write German script, which is very pointed. When you have other languages like Latin and French, you have to learn another, rounded script, which is called Latin. That set much better with me, that round script. So I started to use that Latin script for writing German. Ah, hah! That was a "No no." So they decided that I should sit back after school and rewrite everything in German script. I became so incensed about this that then I decided that I should combine the two scripts, Latin and German, and there was great upheaval in the school. But we had a very interesting director of this school. It was an all girls' school. He neither chastized me nor did he endorse the punishment that the teachers were giving me. He was very broad-minded, very avant-garde. He said, "If that is really what she wants to do, the teacher's job is not to punish, the teacher's job is to advance." Perhaps I'm saying this now in my more adult way, but that's what I recall. Verbatim I don't recall, but he protected me from the teachers' punishment and then they couldn't punish me anymore.

Ya, ya, I didn't want to be like everybody else. But that's interesting too, because perhaps it's really a kind of vanity. That's what I think sometimes; when I'm thinking about it now, I don't know. Wanting to be like everybody else is weakness because you conform, take solace in each other, and you all march to the same tune and you have the same clothes and the same uniform and same whatever.

I thought about something else. You see, my grandfather was a very independent man! Oh, he was extraordinary. He came from a humble family in the eastern part of Germany near the Polish Corridor, and he was one of twelve children. He married my grandmother when she was twenty and he was twenty-one. And they celebrated their sixty-seventh or sixty-eighth wedding anniversary together. They made an unbelievable life really. My grandfather was thought by many people to be a tyrant. But I really adored him and I guess it was mutual. There are many stories about him. And one of them was that when he had this restaurant in Wiesbaden, people from all strata of life and many celebrities would come to his restaurant. He had developed great social facility and knew how to cater to people. At one point my grandfather was offered a title. This was before World War I. By the late Kaiser. Imagine! And my grandfather said, "My name was good enough for my father and it's good enough for me. Thank you very much, but no." This is my mother's side, right? And then on my father's side, you see, there is really nobility in the family. I did not know this grandmother who was of blue blood, or whatever, because she died when my father was a little boy, but I have seen writings of hers. She was a poet, and I had two volumes of her poems, which burned with the rest of it when the house was bombed in Wiesbaden. So many treasures were lost and that was one of them. So, when you talk about what makes you, I really think you come with a certain something. We are not just a blob of nothing when we are born. I'm so convinced of that. Environment does its part, but there are things that are really there from the beginning.

Your question came back to me time and time again. Where did I start? Why am I this way? I thought about this and then I thought about my school days. And I thought about this one friend. I have never heard of her since. She was Jewish. What grade was I? Eight, nine, I don't remember. I used to go to her house very often. I didn't like her particularly, but they had these marvelous parties. They would hire clowns for the kids and puppet theaters, I mean, they were very wealthy. Giesela was an only child. I remember she always had polished fingernails, and I couldn't believe that because I always dug in the ground. I didn't like her particularly, but I felt she was very lonely. So one day one of my uncles called me and he said, "I understand that you are friends with Giesela Metzler." And that was in the beginning of this whole Hitler thing. And my uncle said, "I really think that you should not—" You know, I'm telling you in my own words now. There was a confrontation between this uncle and myself. I said something like, "She's my friend and not your friend, and you cannot tell me what to do with my friends," and I kept on going. And from that day on I never talked to this uncle. How old was I? I don't remember. Ya, I understood the political implications. I knew the reason why I shouldn't see her was that she was Jewish. My uncle had a restaurant and he couldn't deal with a niece who goes to Jewish homes.

My stepfather sent me to Switzerland to learn the French language during World War II. The war was going to be over in six months anyway, he thought. Well, the war lasted and I was asked to return to Germany in order to work in a munitions factory. I chose to remain in Switzerland because I didn't want to support this whole war machine! There was nothing that I could do otherwise in good conscience. I don't know, perhaps it was selfishness. I had no way of knowing what the eventual outcome would be and if the Axis had won, I would have been in trouble. I was perhaps twenty. My mother was in Italy and there was very little connection. But my grandparents were in Germany and that was really very hard. I think they thought that I was safer in Switzerland, no matter what. And then they could not send any more money. Up till that time my grandfather had sent me monthly stipends for school, but that ceased at that point and I guess he said, "You can make it one way or another." That was really very courageous of my grandfather because his whole belief was, he said, "Whatever money you can inherit can go overnight, but education will never leave you. The best education is just good enough." And that's something that stuck in my head. "The best education is just good enough." It never occurred to me that it was difficult. I mean, you just do what you feel you have to do. I didn't measure it against anyone else who did more or less. I just did what I felt I should do.

I really think that throughout my life I do what I feel I have to do. I don't consider myself a leader but perhaps I'm not a follower either, except to my own conscience. I have a hard time telling people what to do and for that reason, I couldn't be a leader. There are not too many people —perhaps this sounds arrogant—but there are not too many people that interest me. I don't like small talk, I guess. I avoid coffee klatch situations and things like that. It's not my life-style. I'm very good company to myself. I live alone and I do many things on my own. I like to walk, as trivial as it sounds, I bake my own bread. I guess I'm a loner or whatever. You find people. I have always found and increasingly so, groups who think the way I do. That's where you get strength, with people who think like you do. Many Quakers support what I do. Many do the same kinds of things. For instance, there is a very strong movement for tax resistance. I understand that there are Quakers who support militarism. I have never come across them. I wouldn't know what to say to them.

At the Pentagon in 1971 there were seven of us—one Methodist, one Church of Christ, one Episcopalian, three Catholics, and one Quaker, me. Our action consisted of sitting in silence in front of the five doors of the Pentagon, blocking entrance and thus symbolically asking for the end of the war in Vietnam. Arrest, short imprisonment, and trial followed. I'd like to read to you my statement explaining to the judge, to my family and my friends why I had taken this step. Here it is.

Over the last eleven years I have signed petitions and written letters to three different presidents of this nation. I have distributed antiwar literature and collected signatures. I have visited Congressman Murphy in his local office in Staten Island and in his Washington, D.C., office. I have walked with individuals and groups across the country. I have participated in countless vigils, some held by candlelight, some held under scorching sun, some in midwinter blizzards. In silent protest I stood in my home community. I stood in front of induction centers, in front of the American Mission to the United Nations, in front of the laboratory for chemical warfare at Fort Detrick, Maryland, in front of the United States Treasury Department in Washington, D.C., and finally I stood on many occasions in Lafayette Park opposite the White House. And all of this energy for one cause and one cause only—for my belief in peace. But it seems as though the hope for peace is moving further and further away. The hardly perceptible abyss between the people who seek peace and the government who is unable to realize it widens every day more. The government, in pursuing its own economic and military interests, has overextended itself and has failed. Tens of thousands have died for a still unjustifiable war in Southeast Asia and people here at home are getting appeasement but not peace.

I have lived about half of my life. At this point I have little to lose except for the future of my children and the generation of which they are a part. As a mother I have perpetuated life and as a mother I have the holy obligation to maintain, foster, and protect life, be it the life of my own young, or that of all young people struggling for identity and survival. It is indeed my job to help and bring youngsters to the threshold of adulthood where they can and will want to decide what to do with their lives. But there the government has already stepped in and decided for them how to best spend a part of their young lives, or, for that matter, their premature deaths. The high school slogan, "From graduation to the battlefield" has become quite unpopular. Yet, over 55,000 coffins have been sealed forever, holding over 55,000 young bodies, causing over 55,000 wasted lives and wasted deaths—not to mention the unbearable pain inflicted upon those who make it home with shattered limbs, minds, and souls. Will they ever be able to make it really home? And with this we have not even touched on the wounds, sorrow, total despair, and death toll bestowed onto a tiny nation thousands of miles away from these shores. How much have we already hardened to the violence in our intellects, in our hearts? How apathetically do we listen to the daily scores of American soldiers and enemy troops that have been killed or lost in action? How do we manage to constantly and consciously block out the incredible sum of two million, eight hundred eighty thousand American dollars spent every single hour when we know that over twenty million American citizens are every day hungry? Again, over two million dollars per hour spent, in sharp contrast with the yearly income of three hundred dollars for families who subexist on far less than the minimum. How do we account for the slow starvation of several millions of Americans who, according to reports, are too poor to be helped by the federal government? They just starve away while the money owed to them is being used for invasions into Vietnam, Laos, and Cambodia.

I only mentioned an infinitesimal number of problems. There are many, many more. Yet, people who in deepest anguish, outrage, and frustration are trying to bring some of these very problems to the conscience of the government are being seized, convicted, and labeled as nonpatriots. Yet, to lend our bodies, to silently sit in front of five entrance doors to the Pentagon was the only language of protest left to us. A nonviolent, wordless outreach for peace. We wanted to be seen and heard. We wanted the people at the Pentagon to pay attention to our pleas, to read our requests and acknowledge our presence. We are fully aware of the fact that seven people can do no other than bring to bear symbolically what we feel is our commitment. It was our fervent desire to sensitize all those directly involved in daily governmental proceedings at the Pentagon and to hold up to their compassion only small parts of unspeakable sufferings. Sufferings which this war is producing and multiplying endlessly. Every day, every hour, every minute.

In the eyes of the law I realize I have trespassed. Yet, these laws, as complex or inadequate as they may be, are manmade laws. In the eyes of my conscience I have acted upon a higher law and my allegiance belongs to it. In a conflict between a law made by man and a law formed by conscience, Sir, I had no choice. As a Quaker and a pacifist, I have to do everything in my power to do away with war and all outward weapons leading to war. We all have convictions and we live with them for a while. Then we either discard them and find new ones or we keep the old ones and feel them grow. A conviction slowly solidifies and becomes part of us. To reach this stage it takes time. To hold on to it, live with it, and stand up for one's convictions is, in the end, fulfillment of the self and reason for being.

This was signed May 24th, 1971.

Professionally I went into the mental health field. It's compassion and it's being incapable of watching suffering, no matter on what level. By incapable, I mean feeling that you have to do something to diminish the suffering. No matter who it is, no matter what it is! Diminish pain. There are so many forms of suffering. Where does it come from, I don't know. I really don't know. I guess perhaps that one compensates for what one would have liked to have but didn't have?

I think of my mother as a totally self-centered person. She was truly a very beautiful woman and her life's occupation was to keep herself so. She wanted to be seen as the benefactor of the world, right? And I remember one thing, perhaps, that illustrates that. She came to see me one time in Switzerland during the war and everything was on coupons. She took me to a restaurant and we had tea or something and she asked for sugar. The waitress said, "There is saccharin." And my mother said, "I can't take that." So the waitress produced some sugar for her. And then she took the saccharin in her purse and said, "I'll bring that to the poor people who don't have any sugar." The truth of it is she never gives anything away! She does not give of herself as a person. She's not a compassionate person. Her self-image is that she is the saint of the world. That's how she sees herself. She probably gave the saccharin to people from whom she expected a service. You know, people she expected to be totally grateful for this little "treasure" that she brought back from Switzerland. She expects them to be grateful. I know, because that's the way she is. I guess she had no compassion, but she did not know that. Surely she did not intend to be so.

You know, many years back, my mother would give me her clothes that didn't fit her and she would say, "This is very expensive material." And I would say, "This is the truth, but they don't fit me and the style is too old for me!" Then she said, "Well, if you cannot be thankful for them, I'll give them to other people who will be very thankful and who will kiss my feet." Because I said I really couldn't wear them she repeated, "But it is really very expensive material!" I said, "It doesn't fit me!" And I didn't want this style. I mean, her style is not my style. But she would not buy me something new! That would really cost money. Oh, the "mother thing" is a very heartaching thing. Instinctively, as a child, I must have felt how cold she was and really how artificial. Perhaps that may have something to do with how I grew up to be, I don't know, John.

I believe that dissent comes from where the shoe hurts. I think that basically dissent comes from situations of discontent. The people who have the most discontent are those who have no food or cannot warm themselves in the winter, who have no work. If they find intellectuals who support their dissent, then you got it made. See, dissenters come from all walks of life. It depends how sensitive you are to your brothers and sisters. How sensitive you are to the people who don't have what they should have.

Caring, I guess, it's the caring. That's it. Taking care of, providing, giving comfort, rest your head on my shoulder. Things like that. Perhaps out of that also comes the sense of protecting and beyond protection, helping people to get what they want. That was the major theme—we're going back now in my career—to my time in the mental health hospital. I believed that it was my obligation to myself to help these poor people not to be shoved around and not to be medicated and not to be guinea pigs for research people. To let them know that they had rights and stand up and help them to advocate their rights. It was a good job! There were some staff who sided with me and when it became very hot, they shifted. Well, I tell you. There was this one man and he was a wizard, very bright. He came new to the staff. It was toward the end. At that time, I didn't know it was the end, but it was. Seven years of employment at that hospital. Well, he was bright and ambitious. So he would study and very soon he was close to his Ph.D. When he first came he was just my peer and with my little issues that I brought up he said once to me, "Margo, you are the conscience of the staff. You say things that other people don't say." And I always valued that. This man got his Ph.D. and subsequently was very rapidly advanced. He became my superior, and from that time on he disciplined me very sharply for the things which he had valued a year and a half before. That's what I mean by shifting. You know, you don't find many allies if you step out of the regular line.

When I was going through my papers I found this one letter here. It is dated June 1961 and it is to the principal of my daughter Eva's grade school. I say,

Dear Mrs. Keegan: Again we ask you to please excuse Eva from participation in the shelter dispersal. As I stated in my previous conversation with you, we believe that civil defense drills in our schools offer no protection whatsoever since in the event of an atomic attack on the city of New York, none of us would survive, ever. We believe that these drills lead to an acceptance of the concept that war is inevitable and therefore, by encouraging this concept, they bring war closer to reality. We further believe that the Board of Education, apart from basic knowledge, should teach our young the science of living together harmoniously. The approach should be directed toward the positive aspects of life rather than the negative resignation to the acceptance of possible annihilation. We believe that all their efforts should go toward constructive and peaceful thinking, rather than into fearful apathy. The Board of Education's physical and material potential should tend to enrich the child's world of experience instead of fostering senseless and psychologically damaging defense drills. With our trust in peace and in the spirit of love for our children and mankind, we ask you to dismiss Eva from any further defense drills and hope at the same time that other parents will come to share our viewpoint. Sincerely,

Well, Mrs. Keegan and I, we had a telephone conversation. I don't remember at what point I wrote this letter, but I used to call her up and I would say to her, "Mrs. Keegan, Eva cannot come to school today, but she's playing in the garden, don't worry about her. She's in good health." And she'd say, "But she has to come to school." "But you have a drill today and remember that she can't come to school when you have these drills." And she'd say, "But if you only would tell me that she is ill. Don't tell me that she is playing in the garden. I have to report that." I said, "I'm so grateful for this. It is exactly what I want you to do, report. Otherwise, how would it be known that I disagree with your policy of conducting defense drills?" She could not conceptualize that.

Oh the Selectmen. I don't know how they think. I don't know how their brain waves function, but they can intimidate and make townspeople believe that the parking lot belongs really to the grounds of Town Hall. I had requested, as I had the previous years, a small place on the Town Hall parking lot for every Saturday morning from ten to twelve from July to Labor Day. They denied my request. But they could never in a hundred years say that the sidewalk belongs to Town Hall, never! I know it seems strange, but you must realize that their whole thinking is strange! That was one of my points. I mean, I said, "I feel that you are hampering with your own opinions the job that you are elected to do. You are in this position because you have been elected by us." I say it now in shorter terms. "We did not ask that you run the town government on your opinions." That is not done, right? Town government has to be run on town government rules and regulations, and not on the Selectmen's opinions. They brushed it off. They didn't hear it. In a small town you know each other. I felt that they were in a one-way street and couldn't get out. I wanted them to understand that I'm not asking the impossible. I'm asking for my rights and I'm not a monster. I was acting in accordance with my belief and I wanted them to hear that! You know, one of them said he had been in Vietnam and that if he had not fought the war, everybody in America would grow up today in a rice paddy! I mean, you see the constipated way of thinking these people have.

You see, they denied my right to be there. I just wanted that little piece of ground that takes a sizable card table outside Town Hall on the parking lot. The spot I had last year and the year before and the year before that. I sit there quietly; I have always a pot of fresh flowers and I just sit there and have the literature on draft information and if people come to ask, I give them answers. I did not especially peddle it, but people knew what I was sitting there for. I had made a huge peace sign that was draped around the table and all I wanted was Town Hall's consent. The Town Hall parking lot is, in my view, public property. Paid for by my town and state taxes. Now, the people in Town Hall believed that they had jurisdiction over it. They said, "No, no, this does not really coincide with our policies and thinking." I said to them, "Well, you have your thinking and nobody challenges that, so I don't want you to challenge my thinking. There is nothing that I do that is unlawful." I went twice to a Selectmen's meeting. The last time I went, I requested a special private hearing in their office because I felt it was difficult for them to back down in public. But they just would not budge. Was it a matter of conviction? I'm trying to figure that out. I think it is a matter of stubbornness. Is stubbornness conviction? Perhaps so. Legally, as I learned from many supportive newspaper articles, they knew that they were wrong in saying that I couldn't be there. Since they would not give in, I went home. And the next Saturday came. I sat at home and ten o'clock came and I said to myself, I should be there right now at the parking lot, but I don't want to make an issue. What could they have done? They could have jailed me but they didn't want to do that. I live in this community, I didn't want to antagonize them to the point where they would have to take a public stand. So, a thought came to me. I had this basket and I put all the literature in the basket and I called my friend and stood on the sidewalk because the sidewalk belongs to everyone. So, from then on, I stood on the sidewalk every Saturday with my basket and my antiwar buttons and antidraft buttons and I just stood there. People knew why I was standing there. I just stood there. The Selectmen would drive by in their cars and either look the other way or look straight forward.

It was very interesting. There was a young policeman. During the summer there is a little circle in the middle of Main Street where the policeman stands and directs traffic. When traffic was not heavy, he would come up and he would sort of talk from the corner of his mouth so it would not be seen that he was talking to me. And he said, "I just want you to know that the Department is really behind you. The Selectmen are absolutely stupid!" And I said, "Do you know what you're saying? You are in uniform!" He said, "Yes." Then I said, "Would you be interested in reading some literature?" He said, "I cannot take it now, I'll pick it up later," and he did. I thought that he was courageous to do that because he did not have to come over and sort of stand two feet away from me. I was very moved by that. He was a young officer so perhaps what he said was said with enthusiasm. But he had the courage to tell me that and that was very gratifying.

Perhaps forty percent of the people walked by and just didn't do anything. Some people would slow down their cars and make with two fingers the V sign. Other cars would go by and honk, people who had never said a word would say hello. That was all they could do! I was grateful for any kind of acknowledgment. There were many letters and some of them were most substantial and supportive and I believe they must have been written by people who know the law. That went on for four or five weeks during the summer. There were letters to the editor of the local newspaper, editorials in my defense, that were really quite remarkable. And I guess the Selectmen became increasingly more uncomfortable. The way out of the whole situation for both parties came when I had to leave for the West Coast. I have already applied for next year! And this time I will contact the ACLU. The Selectmen won't want to run into a case with the ACLU. Yes, I believe they acted on their own and that was exactly what I was trying to tell them when I was in their little chamber. I tried to tell them that we all have opinions and no one wants to be deprived of their opinions. I might not share your opinions, you have the right to have them, but you have no right to mix your opinions with your town government job. They have nothing to do with each other. Then they said, "We cannot allow this kind of activity. It is our privilege as Town Fathers," blah, blah, blah. But they really did not hear. They couldn't afford to hear. They were too small in spirit to acknowledge me. I thought that when I went to their office it would have been so easy for them to say, "There was a misunderstanding, we didn't really mean that." Especially since last year and before permission was granted without question. They had a different Selectman, a more liberal person. I reminded one of the Selectmen of how he had sided with him last year and I asked him, "How come your opinion changes?" He said, "That was last year." That was all he could say. He was not strong enough to have his own stand.

Well, as for the alternative draft literature, if you believe in something and you don't say it, then it's just as good as if you don't believe it. Absolutely I feel an obligation. It is based on helping to make people see that they have a choice in life and that they cannot be pushed around by a government or by a dictator. If they decide that they want to go to the military, that's fine. I cannot tell people what to do. It's not my intent. But I can say what I stand for and I can say here are the alternatives. Now it's up to you to choose. Well, if the government doesn't permit that, then it's a fascist government. Free speech, up till now, is one of the great things of this country. Let's hope we can maintain it.

Every person has the same needs and rights. Why should some be deprived? Why should people be categorized for, I don't know, looking differently, for being born in a different country? How can I want something for myself and assume that the other person doesn't want it? It's a basic respect that I have to give each human being.

Wars are being made by people who sit around a green table. And then they sort of have the talent to instigate and fire enthusiasm and all these young people go! But they have better things to do than risking their lives by being cannon fodder. And there's all this propaganda! Yesterday on the radio they talked about the new tank and the tank is called the M-1 something or other. The objectivity and callousness with which they can talk about that tank! It is speedier, it has a greater killing capacity. It seems that the drivers, the soldiers who manage the tanks, have less possibility to escape because it doesn't open as quickly, but that doesn't really matter. Then somebody said it's really impractical because it runs on one—how is this now? It runs thirty-five miles on four gallons and that's really impractical. And then somebody else said it takes an hour to repair, whereas somebody else said, no, this is misinformation, it takes two hours to repair. All this talk about a machine that inflicts *death*.

What I was so appalled by is that this is the same callousness with which people during the Vietnam war would every morning on the radio say how many people they had found dead and then go on with the cereal ads! I mean, it's that total disregard for human life, for human capacity to suffer which appalls me. War is not a normal way of life! It's a wrong way of life. There are many things we have against each other, but there are things that we have in common. Yes, we have hatred, but we have also love, and we need *respect*! If you want to be respected, then you have to give me the same in return. I will never try to convert people. It doesn't work. I can only say what I believe. But what I say, I say with my total conviction. My total sincerity.

If I sit around with my opponent and I tell him what I need from him, he has the same right to tell me what he needs from me. What we have in common is humanity. What we disagree on are our opinions, which come about through the circumstances, through upbringing, through education, through ethnic backgrounds, whatever. But these are things that can be overcome. Our basic humanity is not to be overcome because we come from a female womb, all of us. Can we not make this a basis to construct rather than destruct?

Andy Mager

"I will not kill other people."

□ □ □

You can no more win a war than you can win an earthquake.

JEANNETTE RANKIN

Andy Mager is a dedicated advocate of pacifism and a more organic future. When mandatory registration for the draft was implemented by President Jimmy Carter in 1980, Andy was among the first group required to register. Keeping faith with his convictions obliged him to refuse. When fellow draft resister, Ben Sasway, was indicted, Andy wrote the Selective Service System informing that agency that he had not and would not register for the draft. His decision to stand publicly for his convictions has greatly accelerated his activism. Lecturing, demonstrating, and participating in his region's antiwar and antinuclear dissenting activities are a substantial part of his life now.

Andy is a vegetarian because he regards as criminal waste the massive investment of vegetable protein in livestock for a minimal return of edible flesh. When it comes to his dissenting values, Andy is that least common of principled dissenters, the individualist team player. He expressed that position in a letter to me.

Dear John: Something which we never got into in the interviews, which I think is at least as important as any discussion of personal history, is the role of support from other people in enabling someone to take risks. I don't know if it is fair to generalize from my experience, but I know how crucial the support of other people was in my own decision to become public about my refusal to register. It was over a year after I decided not to register that I decided I wanted to speak with the media about it. The primary change during that year was that I felt really supported in my decision to go public. I knew other people who had made that choice, and I recognized that there were thousands of people around the country who would come to my aid if I were prosecuted.

Less than a year after Andy wrote this letter, he was sentenced to three years in a federal penitentiary for refusing to register for the draft. All but six months of this sentence were suspended. On the eve of his trial, in a letter to the New York Times, *Andy wrote:*

I have been inspired by the struggles of people of similar views around the world: Israeli soldiers refusing to fight in Lebanon, East German antinuclear activists, South Africans struggling against apartheid. As a responsible citizen of the United States and the world, I feel I have a duty to speak out and to act in a manner that will promote peace and justice. Refusing to register for the draft is one way to fulfill that responsibility.

Andy and I had the following conversation some two years before his arrest. Since that time I have noticed no appreciable diminution in the strength of his convictions.

———

A little over two and a half years ago I was, along with several million other young men, called to register for the draft. And before that I had decided that it wasn't something I would do. That for me to register for the draft would be to be complicit with and to support the efforts at war making that were going on and also to show support for what the U.S. Government was doing around the world. And I wasn't about to do that. I guess it was a little over a year after I'd refused to register that I went public and began talking to people and talking to the media, putting my name out there more. It's only recently that I've come to consider myself a pacifist, but I do. At this point in time I see it as almost necessary for the survival of the species for us to find other ways to resolve conflicts, other than force or violence on an individual level and other than through war on an international level.

I'm twenty-two years old and grew up outside of New York City in a suburban area in an upper-middle-class Jewish family. One of the things I gained from that, I guess, was a sense that what I thought was important and that I had some power as a person. And I think that certainly related to my class upbringing. I think that everyone has power. I think it's not a coincidence that we're taught we don't have power and we're taught that it doesn't make sense to do anything besides what we're told. Part of it was that my parents listened to what I had to say. I have an older brother and two younger sisters and I think that we were all encouraged to think on our own a certain amount.

I always excelled in school. I was also pretty active in sports. The regular curriculum for school wasn't at all challenging. I was encouraged to kind of explore on my own more and to think for myself. I think at that point I still had a real interest in learning. I think children, when they're very young, are very curious and have a lot of interest in learning, and I think that our educational system tends to destroy that curiosity. I'm not sure why, but I think I retained that curiosity at least probably to early in high school. But I'm not interested in learning through school anymore. From talking to children, it's very clear to me that when children begin going to school they really want to go to school. They really want to learn how to read, but generally, within a couple of years, they no longer enjoy school. They find it boring and they'd rather be in the play-ground. One of the other things that I think is very strong in my up-bringing, that I don't think everyone in my family got, was that I've always wanted to please people, which in some ways doesn't make sense with where my life is going.

I think my parents respect what I'm doing and they're trying, within the limits of their world view, to support what I'm doing. It's very clear to me that they would prefer that I didn't talk very much about what I'm doing. I think that they would prefer that I didn't register, but they would much prefer that I didn't register and didn't tell anyone about it. One of the reasons that I'm interested in this project is that I don't feel like I have ever traced my personal evolution and figured out where some of my ideas have come from, so it's something that's of interest to me to try and work through with you to hopefully gain some insight.

A number of my teachers early on urged me to take initiative. I think partially they saw that I was frustrated with what was going on in the classroom, feeling like most of the stuff, most of what was being taught in the classroom was information that I'd already learned. When I was in eighth grade there was a teacher who had been my math teacher and I believe he was arrested for pulling a gun on some people during a pool game in a bar or something. He tended toward being a violent person, although he was a pretty good teacher when he wasn't out of control. There was talk about trying to get him thrown out of teaching for this. I guess it was parents mostly and some other teachers and the school board. I grew up in a real small town. It was small enough so that you could tell who was doing things, even if they were being done behind the scenes. And I, along with a number of other students, tried to petition to allow him to keep teaching. Basically I think we made up petitions and passed them around and tried to get any students who felt like he was a good teacher to say that they thought he should stay. I felt that he was a good teacher and that it would be a shame for him to be kicked out of the school, given that there were few good teachers, or few teachers who really communicated information to people. There were times when he was somewhat violent with students in the classroom, so this single incident wasn't completely out of character. I think our supporting him was unpopular, but I don't think that I was in touch with its unpopularity. I mean, I knew that there were other students who didn't like him, but I don't ever remember having any teachers come up and say, "Now, why are you doing this? This is a bad thing." I think my mother was the person that I talked with about it most and I think she had mixed feelings about the teacher but felt good that I was doing what I thought I should do, you know, and that I was acting on my beliefs. No, there was no opposition to my doing it, not particularly, and it certainly wasn't expressed to me in that kind of way.

At that point I was very caught up in being, and in some ways was, the good child who didn't have any problems, you know, got along with everyone. Looking back on it, I think that my parents kind of put me in that role and I stayed in it. I got out of it toward the end of ninth grade, I guess. I started to smoke pot. I think that was my first major breaking out of what I was supposed to do. My best friend from childhood and I would go and smoke pot and then play basketball after school. And then the next year I started smoking in school a lot of the time. I think a lot of the reason why I began smoking pot a whole lot was that I was feeling very bored by school. I remember specifically smoking pot before I would take a test because it would make it more interesting, because I had to concentrate a little. I remember one time we were going on this field trip to a laboratory and some of us had decided to turn it into a party, so people brought along pot and beer and screwdrivers and various other things and we had a grand old time on the way out to the lab. When we got there the school official who was on the bus had us stay on the bus and closed the doors and called the school and told them what had gone on. I guess the assistant principal told her that she should just turn the bus right back around and bring us home. And so we came back to the school and were herded into a classroom. In the classroom they basically told us that they were assuming that we were all guilty unless we were proven innocent. After probably a couple of hours of squabbling, one woman stepped forward and admitted that she smoked pot and two people admitted that they drank beer and then they let the rest of us off.

I started having to go to religious school, being forced to go, and I didn't want to go. I had begun to have questions about school and religion wasn't something that was interesting to me at that point. We started out in religious school learning about Jewish culture and history and stuff. In sixth grade we were dealing more with what led up to the establishment of the State of Israel. I remember being extremely captivated by this tremendously long report that I ended up doing about a number of the people who were instrumental in establishing Israel. It was short biographies, about ten pages on each of the people, about their lives and their relation to the establishment of the State of Israel. I don't think that I tried to tie it together in any way. I certainly was not at all critical at that point. I guess I wasn't exposed to much information about the fact that Israel was established where there were Palestinian people living. I didn't bother to ask what happened to those people and all those kinds of questions.

My family vacationed in Puerto Rico maybe three or four times. The first couple of years we went to Luquillo Beach. We stayed in these small apartment complexes. I guess only during the last year I've begun to see the plight of Puerto Ricans as a political struggle. There's a press at the Peace Council and one of the people who used to work there is a Puerto Rican woman. As far as I know, she isn't particularly involved in the violent things that are going on, but she is involved in agitation.

I went to Europe after I'd finished high school, the summer afterward, and I guess I wanted to see what more of the world was like and see the great sights of Europe we were all supposed to marvel at. In retrospect, I feel somewhat like I wasted the time because I spent so much time worrying about tourist sights and didn't really get to understand the cultures particularly. If I had gone even a year later, I would have tried to hook up with people who were involved in political organizing and I think I would have gained a lot more insight into the cultures.

The one memory from the time I spent in Puerto Rico most meaningful to me is this: I got my finger caught in a door when I was there during one trip so I couldn't go swimming for a while. So my father took me to get this toy that I really wanted, and on the way back from getting the toy, we took a short-cut because we were in the midst of a traffic jam, and we ended up in the midst of a real ghetto. I remember just being really struck by the tremendous poverty. You know, naked children crawling in and out of garbage cans and stuff like that, and I think that that is an image that I still have with me. It didn't spoil the vacation, I think partially because my father's response was kind of like, "Oh yeah, that's a bad thing, isn't it?" And not trying to deal with it. I think a lot of that has to do with where he came from in terms of money. His parents were basically pretty poor. They ran kind of a TV, radio, fix-it shop and lived above the shop. The last time I saw my father and spent any time with him we talked a fair amount about our views of the world in terms of money. When he was young he felt embarrassed when friends came over because they lived over the movie theater. We grew up in very different surroundings, but I still think that he isn't very conscious of what being rich means to people who are poor. Given that we have a finite amount of resources, to me the fact that we have very rich people means that other people are starving. I think that's true within the United States, but I think it's even more true when comparing the United States to other countries.

I think that the way I was taught history was that the American colonists were people who fought against oppression. So I would say that this was probably my first model for principled dissent. I was probably a little captivated by Paul Revere. Also Thomas Paine sticks out a little bit. Although I was never really taught the truth about Thomas Paine in school in terms of his further ideas about the structure of society. I remember my brother doing some reading about the Berrigan brothers but I think that I didn't really understand who they were or what they were doing. I was probably six or seven at that point.

I feel like I've internalized a fair amount of anti-Semitism. I think I've begun to get more objective about that. I guess I kind of rebelled against identifying myself as Jewish. I grew up where there's a large upper-middle-class Jewish population and I have kind of not wanted to identify myself with that culture. Probably more because of its middle classness than because of its Jewishness. I felt that there was a real falseness about the culture, that what was important to people were things that weren't vital issues. Oh, you know, who's wearing the nicest clothes and shopping in the right stores, living in a real consumers' society. Yet I think there's also a certain amount of cultural stereotyping about Jews being, you know, successful, middle-class people wherever they are, and also the whole imagery of Jews being so concerned with money, which I think is certainly part of American mainstream culture. I guess I heard other people talking in those terms and absorbed it myself and didn't for a long time look at the progressive roots in Judaism. You know, some of the Jewish people who put their lives on the line for what they really believed in. It's only recently that I've begun to see that and to be able to celebrate positive aspects of Judaism.

I guess I tend not to think of things in terms of the truth, or try not to, because it really sets up a "we have the truth, they don't have the truth," situation. I guess thinking of it in terms of Gandhi helps me to clarify it. I think that he had a good grasp on the way people could and should be interacting. He thought it was important that we should confront oppression wherever it existed and that we should try to confront it in nonviolent ways that allow people to change, and not to attribute a person's ideas to the core of that person. Not to say, for example, "Richard Nixon was a horrible person," but say, "Richard Nixon had some ideas that led to bad consequences." That's something that I certainly find difficult to put into practice in my daily life, but I do think it's something to be striving for.

I think people and their ideas can be separated, in that people can always change their ideas. I have a great faith that people can change. Maybe I'm not being real clear on it, but there's a difference between confronting Nixon and saying he's wrong, and saying, "Well, what we've got to do is shoot Nixon because he's a bad person who's never going to come around." It's done already, whether you shoot him or whether you convert him. I think people can be motivated by higher things. Things that I consider more important than personal gain. I guess that people ought to be able to satisfy their material needs on a basic level and then have time and energy and help to fulfill their spiritual and intellectual needs. One of the things that is happening with the disarmament movement is that people are saying, "What we've got to do is do everything we can to survive." There's another saying that I think makes a lot of sense, "Survival is not enough." You know, we've got to be moving toward more than just surviving.

I think that we need to remember that most of the U.S. military is for offensive, not defensive purposes, unless you believe that Vietnam was a defensive war. We could get rid of most of the military, well over fifty percent, and still have a focus on defending the continental United States. We would need to reduce our need to be importing all that we are importing from all around the world—food, our energy needs, natural resources —because what the U.S. military is designed for is to maintain that open access. I guess I eventually see us moving toward getting rid of the United States as a concept and having a more community-based way of living. I think that an economic and/or political unit the size of the United States is larger than makes sense in terms of administering it. Also it is not necessary. This is assuming that we've managed to achieve a lot more international harmony. I would like to see a kind of world harmony and a recognition that all people have very common interests based on living in harmony with the earth. Which basically would mean that we don't see positive value in exploiting each other, economically, socially, or politically, but see the value of each human being as a unique, important person. I guess I think that it's not natural for people to want to hurt each other and oppress each other and treat each other badly. A lot of what I believe is based on an idea that people want to work things out. That we want to settle conflicts in nonviolent ways. Yeah, there's a number of people whom I feel that kind of agreement with. I certainly don't think that I or anyone else has gotten rid of all the racism and sexism we've been taught, but I guess I see it as a process. For me, one of the things that allows me to be public and open about not registering for the draft and to be involved in a daily struggle to try to create a new society, is to have a vision of where we're going and to see that people could relate in very different ways.

My order doesn't have anyone presiding over it. I see people making decisions in much smaller groups than a nation-state. And I also see that if we've gotten rid of war, if people have learned skills of relating to each other and solving conflicts, I don't think we'd have the kind of disagreements that we have. I don't have a blueprint, by any means, but I think that people in general don't get real, genuine satisfaction out of hurting other people, out of killing other people. What makes me think that is my own personal experience. My experience in dealing with other people. I think that it's taken thousands and thousands of years and all sorts of problems to bring us to where we are.

Sometimes I have a real hard time, and I think that one of the challenges for me, and other people who see a real need to radically alter society, is to learn to express our ideas so that they can be heard by people who are very far away from those ideas. I think that there are common experiences which can be built upon. I guess in thinking about my own radicalization, or politicization, the issue which really changed my life was draft registration. From there, slowly, lots of doors and new ideas began to open up. But that happened with a lot of people. Finding the issues that connect peoples' lives—whether it's someone who's a Vietnam veteran who came back emotionally crippled as a result of that war, who came back to find out that what they were supposedly fighting for was a sham, or some other person—or people who are really disenfranchised by American society—black people, Hispanic people, poor white people, people like those you were talking of who don't have much of a stake in what's going on, I think that's fertile ground for this sort of thing. I think that somehow we need to make connections about what it is that's causing their lack of power.

I don't think that my home situation was typical of middle-class America. I mean, there're numerous instances of people being upper class and trying to work to change things, and I think that part of what needs to happen is that people, particularly upper-class people in the United States, need to be confronted with what's going on. I think the problem is caused partially by misinformation and indoctrination. People need to be open to hearing and thinking about alternate views. I think that we're taught that we should do what we're told and that the law is the ultimate thing. I mean, certainly in the work that I do, I talk with a lot of people about why I break the law and why I advocate that other people break the law.

My point about Nixon was that the essence of Richard Nixon isn't the policies that he carried out. It's feeling that he did what he did out of ignorance and out of his position in a society where we're all hurt and we're all stepped on in various ways. Some of us stepped on a lot more people than step on us. I'm not saying that he isn't responsible for what he's done. What I'm saying is that we can approach it in ways that make it impossible for him to change, or we can approach it in ways that try to give him room to change.

I think we need a sense of common humanity. I think that what happens when we punish and repress people who've done wrong is that they continue to have reasons to try to overturn any changes that we've made. I'm not saying that by being nice to them and saying, "Oh, we excuse you," that they're necessarily going to come around, but I think we're giving them the opportunity. I think of it in terms of the idea of what does "revolutionary" society do about counterrevolutionaries after the revolution.

I don't see social change as divisible from individual change. Society's made up of individuals, and a government can't impose changes on that society if the people haven't changed. I guess in this specific case, I see that what makes the most sense for me is to continue to advocate publicly my opposition to the draft, and if that means that they're going to try to take me to court and put me in jail and that kind of thing, then that's what I'll do. Draft resistance is a good case to deal with because at this point there have been at least a half million people who still haven't registered, and the federal prison system can handle about 27,000 people at once and the federal court system can handle about 40,000 cases a year. So that, in effect, if all half million of those people were to be open about what they're doing, there's nothing the government could do. They could single out a few individuals or they could try to go outside of their own processes. They could shoot the lot, but that would be going outside their own processes. I see a real problem with this kind of big government, and I think that what I'm doing opposes it. The kind of educational work that I'm trying to do opposes it. The level of violence with which the government can respond, I think, is related to public opinion. I mean, I don't think there's a direct correlation there, but I think that they're related.

I see things on an ongoing basis, that allow me to feel hopeful about people's ability to change. There are times when I feel hopeful, there are times when I feel very despairing, but I'm generally hopeful. I've been working some on the Dennis Banks case, on trying to educate people, and the response that we've been getting in general has been very positive. Most people have been able to see that there is a tremendous racism toward Native American people and to understand that maybe this case was developed in a climate of that kind of racism. Banks was never given a fair trial and he should be granted sanctuary, even though it is in violation of the laws. Things like that allow me to see that there are people who are breaking through some of those negative positions.

I clearly see the law as something established by people in power as a justification for their position and something that they try to erect a mythology around to try and convince everyone that it's the natural course of events that they're in power and that things are the way they are. But I don't have any great respect for the law. The kind of activity that I particularly have questions about is activity that encourages violence against other people. The Ku Klux Klan is a good example. I think that the Klan is going to continue to exist until that ignorance which leads to it is gotten rid of or corrected, or however you want to look at it.

I see a real danger in institutionalizing repression against anyone. On the other hand, I'm going to do whatever I can to stop the carrying out of violence. You know, I feel fine about sitting in front of Selective Service with other people and trying to, by my presence, stop them from carrying out that business. In some ways, some people would consider that I am violating their right to do what they think they need to do. And likewise, I would do that at a nuclear weapons facility or a number of other places. A group of us went from here to Selective Service in Washington in October and because of a large police presence, we weren't able to get real close to the building, but the group that I was part of did manage to get in front of the flow of people who were walking to the building and did manage to communicate on some level with them. Also, I think, just our presence there communicated our moral opposition to the existence of that institution.

I think that what needs to happen is that the way people live their lives in the United States has to be changed. There would be a changeover, for example, in the way we produce food. We would produce for human consumption as a main priority. One of the reasons I'm a vegetarian is that we produce thirteen pounds of protein in soybeans or other animal feed for every one pound of protein we get out of these animals. And that's true world wide. Part of the need for us to change is that the way we live our lives here now inflicts pain on people all over the world. As a result of that they have legitimate anger at us. The kind of anti-Americanism that's talked about in Iran or other places, that's legitimate. I mean, we imposed the Shah on them for over twenty years. That's certainly not an isolated incident. What we need to do is to take the steps here in the United States to ease that burden that we're putting on people around the world. So that the legitimate reasons that they now have for hating the United States would be lessened if not eliminated. I think that it's important to look at how things feed into other things. For example, if the Soviet Union couldn't always be telling its people that the reason they need to live on limited rations and all be in an army is that the United States is out there trying to get them, if they didn't have that kind of a justification, I don't think people would put up with what they have to put up with. People would refuse to serve in the military. I'm sure that's happening as it is now, although I don't know what the consequences are for people who do that. People basically wouldn't allow their labor and energy to be used to support a system that they didn't feel they were benefiting from. And it's certainly important to consider that the level of U.S. threat to the Soviet Union is exaggerated in the Soviet Union, just as the level of threat that the Soviet Union represents to the United States is exaggerated here.

My idea of it is that we are part of the saber tooth tiger and that each of us is one of those teeth. Each one of us who refuses to pay the part of our tax that's going to build nuclear weapons, who refuses to participate in the military, you know, every person who's taken a step in their own life to not be part of that is in some way disarming that tiger. That tiger has some existence outside of us but its *entire* existence is not outside of us.

Tim Manley

"My motto is . . . Stand for something or you'll
fall for anything."

□ □ □

*A man's mind plans his road, but the Lord directs
his steps.*

PROVERBS 16:9

*Tim Manley's Irish-American good looks, natural good manners and
general intelligence are powerful assets in his own Roman Catholic world
of social service and beyond, but I have great difficulty imagining him as
any organization's man. When I first met him he was a senior at the university in his hometown of Scranton, Pennsylvania. After reading an oral
history work I had written on black culture, he had invited me to come to
the campus to address the Social Science Club. Tall, slender, civil but
persistent, he longs for the wider waters of urbanity and the diversity of
the great world. Since I met him the currents of his career have borne him
from the confinement of his hometown to the nation's capital, where he is
now a deep water sailor upon those seas that summoned his youthful
imaginings and hopes of service. He was reveling in the richness and
strangeness of the voyage when I last heard from him, but it is difficult for
me to think of him as being fundamentally altered by it. We still write and
talk to one another occasionally and I follow his fortunes with more than
casual interest. Principled dissent will probably remain a fixed star in his
life course, even if his chances of advancement are marred by his persistence in asking fundamental questions and acting upon the truth as he
understands it.*

———

I guess the first kind of pressure that I came in contact with outside my
own family, where I think that I was a principled dissenter, was peer
pressure. Sure I can tell you how it worked. I have no problem with that.
When I was in high school, friends around me were drinking. It was like

beer parties were the thing and for some reason I didn't go for the whole idea. I think it wasn't totally a question of principle. Part of it was that my parents had told me that if I was caught drinking I wouldn't be allowed to drive the car! I like to think it went beyond that! When these people would always say, "Aw, just take a sip, just have a few beers," I would end up a lot of nights just going home. I think in the beginning it was just, "Come on, why not have a few beers with us," but after a while it was, "This guy is really going against this, he's really giving us a hard time." And it became almost like a game. A couple kids would say, "Hey, if you don't come drink with us we're gonna come and throw beer cans on your front lawn." And they did it. One night they drove by and you heard, Smash! Those weren't my friends, my friends would be the ones who just said, "You're a baby" or whatever, and call me some names, but they wouldn't cause real problems for me. But it was like the more I resisted, the more of a challenge it was to "Get Manley to drink."

There was pressure in elementary school too. There was a need to conform to the "in" crowd. Growing up, I was somewhat obese, so right away I had something against me. And I think part of that was my own doing because, realizing that I wasn't readily accepted, I would try to over-compensate by becoming the clown. At times I challenged certain individuals, which caused me to be noticed, and in turn they'd notice me by challenging me back, and before I knew it I would be in for it. I always wanted to be the loud person in the group. If there was something I didn't agree with they heard about it. I have to look into my own negative side. Because I was obese, I wasn't very physically coordinated, Okay? So I wasn't the first one to be picked for athletic things and I would let them know that I thought that was pretty crummy. Well, they would, in turn, let me know that I was lousy and whatnot. And from that, usually a physical fight enused.

I was always the big joker. I would do outlandish things. I would remember all the commercials and riddles and jokes and stuff and put them on for my classmates. I wasn't always the funniest one around, but I would push the point sometimes and tackle things where I shouldn't have. I pushed my humor a little bit too much. The clown of the class is usually accepted as being that. Well, I wasn't totally accepted as the clown. I was somewhat of a fool at times.

I remember one time a friend of mine who was very short and, as I think back now, probably had a lousy self-image, was always challenging me, and was always ready to fight me. I was big and round and he was very short and small and the big joke was he'd probably knock me out. And that wasn't the truth at all. But he wouldn't think twice. If he even thought that I was giving him a hard time he'd give me his fist. And the funny thing about it is we were friends. It would be very heated and then it would be a very cold friendship. Once about seven or eight other boys were running after him and I can remember stepping in and—I'm not sure what I exactly did—but I know that I got those other guys off his back. And the joke behind this all is that those guys weren't really thrilled with me either, but for some reason they *listened* that day! I don't know why. They could have beat me to a pulp, but for some reason they listened to me and I protected that other kid from getting beat. I just didn't feel right about it, you know, and this kid was really scared for one time in his life. And well, I guess there was a little bit of me that was kind of *glad* to see this turkey get what he was due, but at the time I felt bad for him. He was goin' to get his block knocked off. I guess I wasn't thinking of them turning on me.

I think everyone is called upon at one time or another to dissent. My motto, you know, which I picked up along the way, is, "Stand for something or you'll fall for anything." So I think somewhere along the line everyone should make that decision. I'm not saying they all do. Some people just kind of fall in with the status quo. They go along with the tide. They are the people I would consider boring. I think I would get a lot of flak if I were to say that openly. You know, it's easy to become very comfortable with not fighting city hall. Oh yes, I believe we can fight city hall.

No, I wouldn't let the Nazis parade. Because it's just the whole idea of what the Nazi flag stands for in our minds. It stands for brutality, it stands for the loss of life, you know, at the hands of these criminals. Governments are still trying these war criminals who killed people. No, I think I'd say the Nazis, the Third Reich were a black mark on the history of mankind and I think it's something that should not be brought up and celebrated. Well, as for disseminating literature, you don't know whose hands that sort of material will reach. I would hope the majority of people who would see that would throw it away. Well, would I permit it? No, I probably would look at it with the idea that someone might get it that's so impressionable they might take it to heart. Would I make the Nazi party illegal? Seems that's the direction I'm going, isn't it? The alternatives are becoming very narrow. You know, it's good to have rights, but when there's a possibility that the use of their rights could hurt the rights of others, namely the rights of the Jewish population, then I think we have to go for the good in the situation, which is the right of *all* to have life, liberty, and the pursuit of happiness. Yeah, what about the Nazis. I kinda feared that was coming! Yeah, what about *their* rights to life, liberty, and the pursuit of happiness. Hmmm. Does one man have the right to shoot another because it satisfies him? Does he have a right to satisfy himself by hurting another person? I would say no. So in the same vein, could we possibly allow the Nazi Party to operate? I see that same kind of principle there. I wouldn't let the KKK have those rights either. I've seen on film and I've heard a gentleman tell me a story of how his cousin was castrated by a member of the Ku Klux Klan. I think what you're letting loose there is negative, animalistic attitudes and you're allowing them to run loose. As for advocating incest, the first thing that comes to mind is the youngsters that I presently work with. I'm a counselor and I've come in contact with some youngsters who have been victims of incest. I have seen firsthand what it has done, so already I have a bad taste in my mouth for this general idea. Yeah, this goes back to the whole thing of, how much rights do we give before there's no wrongs at all?

Sincerity of belief and suffering are not enough to make it principled. Not necessarily, 'cause you have to look at the individual situation and see what this person is sincerely believing in. It could be a lot of bunk. A member of the Nazi Party could be a principled dissenter for what he believes, but also at the same time it could be something that would be hurting someone else. I guess the bottom line is, the most precious thing to me is, the human being's right to exist, to be, without having that interfered with.

I don't think that you can totally remove any principled dissenter from being somewhat self-seeking. There's definitely a part of the person's ego involved in the whole process. I would look at the person and try to see what they were getting out of it. If after watching them and examining the situation it seemed they were in it for their own jollies, so to speak, if there was no long-range, or very limited-range, good for others, or for the issue they were standing on, then I would begin to really question what that person was all about. To do nothing is to do something. It's being lukewarm. In the Bible somewhere I know it says that God will vomit the lukewarm from His mouth. I see a person who does nothing, who goes along with peer pressure, as being somewhat lukewarm. He's not standing up; there's a man who's trapped. He doesn't totally agree with these people that he's going along with, and at the same time he's giving up the only thing he has, and that's his own idea of what's important. He's a hypocrite to himself it seems. In this society we're always looking for results, for the outcome. We're trained to look for results and when I don't see any results, when I don't see an outcome one way or the other, I become somewhat confused. I guess I'm somewhat of a pragmatist. I've gotta have something I can put my hand on to make my decision.

This is where I guess it begins to sound a little weird. When I pray, I find that God will not only talk to me in what some people call "the inner voice," but He will even direct me to writing. Like I said, it sounds weird. This experience has happened to others. I'll have the Bible nearby, and I'm not a scholar of the Bible—I haven't even read the whole Bible. In any case, though, I will find that at times a certain section of the Bible, chapter, verse, will come into my head and when I go to that with the question that I have in mind, the question is answered, almost to the point of it being a written down answer. It's not something that I take and interpret, or that I have to. Sure I can give you an example. This happened not with the Bible, but with another book, a book I wasn't familiar with. It was written by a Passionist priest—*Pardon and Peace* or something of that nature. I can't think of the name of it right offhand. In any case though, it was a question that many Catholics go through at times, "When do I go to Confession? When do I have to go to Confession before I can go to communion?" I had been struggling with this for a few days 'cause something I felt I had done wrong was on my mind and was wondering if I had to go to Confession before I went to Communion again. And in prayer I was directed to this book on my bookshelf, which I don't recall ever opening. I was standing up looking at the bookshelf and my hand went over and picked it up. And then it told me to go to a certain page. The inner voice. When I turned that page I began to read *in italics*, in italics, on that page it said something like, "Confession is *not* a requirement for Communion, but it's something that you should do." Then it went on to say that you should do that, but it's not a necessary preparation for

Communion and that literally blew my mind! Here was my question answered in italics! Like I said, I might have picked this book up before but I'd never read the book and I don't have a photographic memory so it wasn't some conscious place where I had placed this answer and then, you know, pulled it out when I needed it.

I haven't made a lot of important decisions on this basis. I still insist on doing things on my own when I should put more trust in God. I still, you know, in my human condition, want to run the show. I need to be in control. That's when I feel the most comfortable. It's hard turning over control to God. I can't help but think about what a friend of mine, a psychiatrist, jokingly said to me recently. He said, "You know, if a man talks to God, we send him to a monastery, if God supposedly talks to man, we send him to a mental institution!"

Usually God doesn't put me on the spot too much. I'll give you an example. In counseling a youngster one day I was having a heck of a time getting this youngster to talk. He was very resistant, very passive in therapy and before he came in I prayed a little bit to God that He would— because this youngster was God's first, before he came under my care—I prayed that He would guide me and I really threw the control of the session into God's hands as opposed to the times where I would want to control it and take it where I wanted it to go. During the session, in the midst of all our small talk, I was quiet for a second and then something popped into my mind. God, that voice inside of me, said, "Don't say a word. Be quiet." Really called me to silence. I mean, and I've used silence in therapy before and it's very productive, but this time I felt it was different. I wasn't making the decision on my own. A voice inside my head said, "Be quiet. Don't say a word." And I didn't. I didn't say a word and the kid started to reveal some really important information that I was really able to go with and we had an excellent session and you know, worked from that session to the time of the youngster's discharge. It wasn't a thing of, God didn't say to me, say this and it'll all be better. He just said, "Be quiet, be still. It's okay." And then that kid spoke. Oh yeah, I was going to open my mouth and talk again and the voice said, "Be still." It was against what I was naturally going to do, so that's why I would say it's not necessarily me, but some greater Being.

I have been considering entering the priesthood off and on since I was in high school. It's a thing of gut feeling and my own desires and passions. It wasn't until last October or so that I really sat myself down to have a direct talk with God and I told God, "I'm also gonna listen to what you say." I think that God had probably talked to me before but I was, again, trying to pursue my own ideas of what I thought. I think at one point I wanted to be a priest to give me an identity. One that I needed. I guess I didn't feel I had one. As a person, I guess if you put a "Father" before my name and popped me in black clothes, I guess I could then feel good about myself. Possibly because I didn't feel good about myself before. I think a large part of that was the wear and tear on me from growing up where I wasn't totally accepted by my peers because of stuff I talked about earlier. Being a loudmouth, being obese, not used to being razzed. I think I took things too seriously when I was a youngster.

How would I describe myself? This is probably one of the hardest of all the questions you've asked me! I see myself as a sensitive person, sometimes oversensitive to other people's feelings at the cost of my own self. I've been in situations where I worried so much about a person being hurt, and I think part of it is also worrying about my own reaction to their hurt, so it was kind of selfish, that it's gotten me to the point where I've gotten physically ill. So, being ultrasensitive, I'm a dreamer. I like to think that I would follow the saying of Senator Robert Kennedy. You know, "Some men see things as they are and say, 'Why?' I dream of things that never were and say, 'Why not?' " You know, ask why not?

I dream about people getting along with one another when I hear of people cutting down others. Usually the higher the intensity or the larger the amount of ignorance on the part of the person who's doing the cutting, the more I come to aid. I guess I'm also, in that sense, a lover of the underdog. I think part of my respect and love for Dr. Martin Luther King comes out of the whole attitude that here was a man sticking up for some people who had been violated.

When I was a senior in high school a group came in and gave a talk in my religion class. What they were all about basically was going out and serving others. They were lay people probably in their early twenties and I was so caught up in what they had to say I went right back to them when it was over and said, "How can I join you? How can I become a part of what you're all about? You're something I've thought about and I didn't know you existed." They said, "Well, would you like to come with us on Wednesdays and go up to the low-income area and play with the kids and do arts and crafts and stuff like that?" And so I did that in my senior year of high school. I would go up there for a couple of hours and just be with the kids and play a little basketball, and you know, I felt good about it. I guess because I was doing something that should be done. I don't think it was guilt on my own part. That I was hogging so much that I had to pay back, you know like Gatsby, who was teaching catechism or something to make up for what-all he had done. But at the same time I can remember thinking I was making up for somebody who was doing something wrong. These kids shouldn't be violated the way they are.

I guess it was making up for the guilt of the society as a whole. That's what we're all about as Christians. And I guess that's where I come from. The whole idea of what Jesus Christ—whether he was the son of God, which I believe, or whether he was just a great teacher—spoke of. He really touched on the importance of what life was all about and that's making sure that the people get something to eat and know to love one another.

Yeah, I know my interest in *Drylongso* is a minority position. Especially in my area where I couldn't even buy the book! I had to write it down on a pad of paper. I was in the midst of taking a course in sociology and minority groups and because I knew so little of the minority that lived around me, I thought, "My God, if there's any place to start, it's right in my own backyard." I wanted to know about these people because, well, there was a curiosity there. I knew there was a difference and as long as I could recognize that there was a difference, I wanted to know what the differences were. I never knew a black person till I went to seminary. I got to be friends with him. Not intimate friends, but friends where we could go downtown together. I also remember walking downtown with him and getting stares from some people. That kind of irked me a little bit. It was fun to look back at them, you know, "What are you lookin' at?" I didn't like the idea that they would do that. I thought, what's the big deal? So that, I guess, pushed me to find out what the big deal was. And then when I dated one girl from the university, her roommate was black and we became good friends. We'd go downtown together or she would see me on the street and throw her arms around me in the middle of town and that *really* drew a panic from the people! And she knew it and I used to get a charge out of her, 'cause she'd do it just to get that goin' and I'd have to laugh because there was something in her attitude, I guess kind of a brassy, sassy defiance that kinda caught my attention. I liked that about her. In any case though, I elected this course, and again, like I say, knowing very little about the black people all around me, having gone to an all-white school through twelfth grade, I just decided to do some investigating. I was listening to "All Things Considered" one night on National Public Radio and they had this special on the Saturday night show. "Drylongso: A Self-Portrait of Black America" and I sat and listened to it. Wow! What a great idea. It sounded really interesting and I said, "I wonder if I could do that?" Go around and talk to the people and get them to tell me about themselves in that way. So that was also a kind of a challenge. I had to pick up your book in New York City. That was the place where I bought my own copy.

Then things along the way, like when I was doing the tape, added fuel to the fire. My interest was in just learning about someone's life and having them tell me their story. What I was out to do was prove that there was prejudice still around and boy, I'll tell ya, the biggest thing was when I started to get harassed by students in the dorm. Getting letters with jokes about black people in them. And the point is, they didn't stay around to listen to my laughter or get my response. They knew I didn't care for it so they would just slip it under the door and go. It was just done to be malicious. Having black students and people from the community come into my room to be interviewed—that was terrible. The jokes were things you've heard before, I'm sure. God, I'm trying to think of some of the jokes now. I forgot them. I only saved them long enough to give them to my professor with my tape, as part of the presentation. I'm trying to think. Oh, "What's black and yellow and screams? A school bus full of black children going over a cliff." That was one of them. Yeah, subtle humor. I think that gives you the basic idea.

Well, what my mother thought of this was, she was panicked. My dad doesn't say a heck of a lot. He's kind of quiet. Mom just panics. And I don't know, maybe I'm on this road to self-destruction, but that'll only make me work the harder because of the feeling of, all right, maybe I like to cause a little stirring up among the crowd.

Some students reacted, more than a few, but I wouldn't say a lot. But the reaction could have been there if enough found out about me. I didn't know these people well. The people that I did know well said, "I know why you are doing this, but you'd better watch out." They thought I should watch out for the people who were sending the jokes. To be honest, I didn't expect them to do anything other than what they did. And I don't think they did either. But I guess there was always the possibility that someone would become really crazy about the whole thing and start something. The potential is always there. In the hall they would pass comments. They would tell me a joke and then laugh and walk away. But I didn't worry about those because they confronted me head on with the joke. Oh also, what else they did besides jokes, they would pass comments saying, "What are you, part nigger? Well you've got the hair for it at least." That sort of thing, because my hair is curly.

The other students didn't get involved. A close friend might say, "They're acting like jerks, don't listen to them." Not publicly, to them, no. Peer pressure was opposed to what I was doing to some extent. Let's put it this way. The ones who were supporting me weren't saying anything! It was only the ones that had something negative to say that would open their mouths. Well it's obvious that the ones who were silent were the majority. But then, the silent majority doesn't really add up to a whole heck of a lot. The vocal group had set the pace, the tone. Had someone first come out and said, we think what you're doing is a great idea, we really need something like that to happen on this campus, to really start to bring people together, had someone set the tone to start with that way maybe there would have been more people to come to my support. I didn't get anything from the professors at all. I kept the one professor who I had the class with abreast of what was happening. He would just shake his head and mutter a little bit. I never thought of doing it anywhere else. I felt that my room was where I wanted to do it and I had that right to it. I was paying for my room. I had no thoughts or fears beforehand that this would happen. Not really, no. I was out to prove there was prejudice, but I didn't think I was gonna be able to prove it the way I *was* able to prove it! With letters. I thought I was just going to get the black opinion, the black view, and not get too much mouth from the whites. None of the black kids gave me grief. Two blacks, I think they were both ball players on the college team, would not allow me to tape them, but they were both open to giving me interviews after talking to me for a while. These guys didn't know me as well as the other black people I interviewed. For some reason I was able to get their trust after talking with them for a while, but they wouldn't agree to be taped.

The white students who verbalized their thoughts were, I guess, what would be considered the rowdies. If they weren't educated you might call them the rednecks, the roughies. The sad part about it was, I thought that that group would not exist on a college campus. I was surprised and kind of felt bad to find out that that was a pipe dream. But, sure enough, I guess you have turkeys everywhere.

It wasn't a continuous harassment. Roughly on and off over a period of a month. My bringing the people into my room brought it to their attention and they asked, "What's Manley doing? What's he up to? What is this

business of having black people in his room?" They might have been looking for something to complain about. Or someone to jostle and I kind of
walked into their prejudice, into their trap, into their hang-up.

Some of the black students knew what was happening 'cause they were
friends of mine. They weren't surprised. They had had experiences of their
own. I guess what they were basically saying was, "Well, now you're getting
a taste of what we get." They didn't come out and say that but they didn't
have to. I just didn't go along with what other people believed was the
"in" thing at the time. I don't know how people know what the "in" thing
is. Some turkey must set the standards.

My interest in minority groups got started in college. I realized that
there were other races around and my God, here's a culture right next to
me that I've never investigated. And they were forming a Black Culture
Club so I decided to join. I believe that there were one or two other white
people that started with them but I was the only one that stayed in the
club. I might have been teased occasionally by other guys in the dorms.
The black people didn't tease me, no, no. They were very big in helping
me. I think they could see that I wasn't just being phony. I was really, truly
interested. We would get together and have meetings. A black opera singer
performed for us once, we had a Black Culture dinner. See for me, I was
still on the basics, I wasn't even really into the deep culture. The one thing
I had to be careful of was at times I would have a tendency to ask so
many questions I would begin to weary them. Some nights we'd be going
for two, three hours. I remember one guy, Jay, was showing me how one
would walk the different walks you'd find in different neighborhoods. And
then the girls would tell me stories of being in stores and the white clerks
acting a certain way. What they did was basically make me aware of
prejudice. If any members resented my presence, they didn't make it
known. At times I would worry about that and that was where I said I
would have to be careful not to ask too many questions, not to weary them.

My true friends, my roommate and my other best friend, both backed
me in what I did. I remember my best friend, Bob, saying "It's great. I
think whatever you're doing is fine." I'd get teased by my roommate occasionally. He'd say, "Where you going?" "I'm going to Black Culture
meeting" and he'd go, "Aw, Black Culture meeting."

I think my parents wondered why I wasn't interviewing Irish people. I
can see a progression there, a progress of some sort. I like to think of
myself as a liberal. However, even though I hold myself in this light, I
think there's some societal prejudices in me that I can't shake. I didn't
realize this until recently and it's something I'm still working on, working
through. A girl I was dating said to me in passing one day, that she had
dated a black guy. Now, being a person who had done all this research
and all this study, I thought, "That's gonna be like water off a duck's back."
And it stayed with me. I said, "Holy God! I don't believe this!" Yeah, it
bothered me. No, no, I don't feel differently about her. I'm crazy about
her. Because at the same time I had enough common sense in my head to
know that it's not her hang-up, it's mine, and I've got to deal with this.
And I had to tell her, I said, "You know, I never realized this, but I think

I'm prejudiced in that vein." It was a prejudice that was never challenged and she brought it to the surface.

The last part of my senior year in high school when I had decided to go into the seminary, in a sense, while I wasn't literally standing alone as I was the nights I told 'em I wasn't gonna go drinking and ended up walking home, I was standing apart from the crowd because I was the only one with that interest at that time.

In the seminary it wasn't a question of blacks or drinking particularly. In the seminary I can recall a very intelligent seminarian who had entered with me who had become a Roman Catholic shortly before entering. I can remember driving him home. He lived in a very rough neighborhood in a town south of Scranton. He wasn't accepted because he was very different. He had shoulder-length hair and he wasn't what you'd consider good-looking. He was harassed at times. By peer seminarians. He didn't want a bed in his room. He used to put the mattress on the floor. He had only a few things: his stereo, and his mattress and his crucifix and his Bible and that was it. Very super intelligent. We had carpets and chairs and all the niceties of life and he went for the bare existence and he was making this change in his life. Oh he was the campus weirdo, the oddball. Not too much said, they just shunned him. I didn't. Possibly they stared at him, I don't recall that. They didn't stare at me when I was with him but I knew that I was going against the current. Now this young man also helped me because he was very, very intelligent. If it wasn't for Jim I might not have passed Introduction to Philosophy in college. I think occasionally someone would say that he was an oddball. They didn't say I was an oddball for hanging out with him. Not to my knowledge. They might have thought that at times.

It's also interesting to add that a few nights before I left the seminary I left my cassock and surplice and collar out. I had forgotten it and it was out for a couple of days in another room and you would think a seminary would be the safest place to leave things. I went to get it and it was stolen. It was gone. In the seminary!

I reported it and I also attempted to make an announcement at community dinner, one of the last meals I was to have there. I even attempted to say everything but "stealing," so I said "appropriated." I think I might have used the word *appropriated*, or *borrowed, misplaced*, trying to leave there without saying someone stole my cassock and collar. I guess I was unsure of myself and I didn't want to make too many waves and I thought, if someone did not steal it, if someone did misplace it, I would feel like a jerk. We didn't have names in 'em, but everyone had one and I had a special, what was called a Jesi Year-rounder. A Jesuit cassock, which was a little bit heavier than the summer cassock, and it came down to my sox. It was in a blue traveling bag like you put suits in that my parents bought me to carry it in and the bag was still there so it wasn't a thing of mistaken identity. It was close to a hundred-dollar investment. My parents bought it for me and they felt very bad because they wanted to give it to somebody and instead it was *taken* by somebody!

Now I could have left that seminary feeling very bitter toward the church and toward the men and toward the priesthood as such, but for some reason I even thought of going back some years later. And I don't feel bitter toward those people. All I can hope is that the guy that got it is about my height!

Well, I agreed to be taped because I'm not afraid of what I feel and what I feel is important. I know not everyone would agree with me and at the same time, I'm not out to have people agree with me. No matter what I believe or feel, I'm not gonna always have everyone agreeing with me. So the only choice I have is to either remain silent and keep my attitude and ideas to myself or speak out, and I guess I just choose to speak up because I'm not afraid of what I have to say. If I were anonymous where would my ideas go then? They would belong to an anonymous person who, in wanting anonymity, is saying, "I'm not too sure about how I feel. I don't think what I feel is right. Or if I do feel I'm right, I don't feel I'm right enough to stand up for it and face the consequences for what I believe." And that says something about what you believe.

I guess the whole thing is, angels avoid where fools are treading. It could be seen as one of the two. I have great courage or I'm a fool. Plus what I'm saying is that people are basically good and we should be willing to serve one another. That's where it all comes from. That's where it all originates. And I'm in good company in that. I mean, the Son of God said the same thing and was willing to pick up his cross for that, so I'm comfortable with that thought. I'd rather go with someone like that as a guide than anyone else.

Pat Muñiz

"I'm very glad I didn't read the sociology books or else I would have put myself in an institution!"

□ □ □

I have spent many years of my life in opposition and I rather like the role.

ELEANOR ROOSEVELT

Almost two decades have passed since Pat Muñiz and I were graduate students at Columbia University. Blind since her teens, even then she enjoyed and earned the reputation of a clever, good-humored gadfly. Time and the press of our respective lives have never completely separated us, so I was only mildly surprised to hear her slightly nasal voice wishing me a happy Chinese New Year a couple of years ago. The description of my inquiry into principled dissent was a small part of the ensuing conversation. She asked if she could help me, another response you can count on from Pat. Some time later she and her cynical, gifted thirteen-year-old daughter Cindy and I met for lunch and conversation. Some of Cindy's mordant parenthetical observations are included in this narrative. Before Cindy was born her mother made jokes about keeping the prospective baby as a captive reader. Now they are a tight team of good companions who watch out for each other.

When I first met Pat she was weighing two career possibilities, stand-up comedy and the teaching of mathematics. In her case these vocations are not mutually exclusive for her humor is essentially didactic. She illustrates her own personal foibles and her social and political observations with the same jocularity. Her femaleness, her Hispanicness, her blindness all receive the same wry, whimsical scrutiny she reserves for the general human condition. She is keenly interested in the political process and basically well informed. Since I last saw her she has become a vice president of the New York County Republican County Committee.

To some, Pat is a kind of indefatigable Doña Quixote tilting at immovable Upper West Side Manhattan windmills. Others see her as a persistent, reasonable crusader in the struggle for excellence and equity.

It seems that everybody talks about the poor except the poor. Everybody is telling me, you know, they're talking about disabled people and Puerto Ricans and all of these protected groups and nobody ever asks us! That's the reason I wanted to become a member of the school board. You know, if I tell you this, you're going to think it's the Latin temperament. You're going to think it's the wild Latin again, but I tell you, it started hurting me. I actually felt physical pain! Going in there caused me pain. I tell the school principal, the drug! The marijuana! You know, the smoke! These are eleven, twelve-year-old children. We're not talking about eighteen- or seventeen-year-olds. Eleven- and twelve-year-old children in junior high school. Some of them actually being forced to smoke. Right there! "What's the matter with you? You haven't learned to smoke yet?" All right. So I went in and I told the principal that they were smoking marijuana in front of the school. He said, "Oh no! Not in my school!" I said, "Sir, I realize it's a big school and you can't possibly see everything. I'm blind and I can see it, but maybe you can't." And one day I went to the trouble of bringing him the joints. What they call roaches. I got all the kinds. Half of the kids in there, especially the seventh graders, the ones who had just come in, were unhappy about this. They didn't want to be forced into taking drugs and some of them were even allergic to it! They were the ones giving me the information as to where it was, why they couldn't even go into the lunchroom because you can't breathe! Anyway, I got a list, a long list of every nook and cranny in that school where they would smoke! And, by the way, marijuana was the least of the problem. There was white powder and all kinds of little pills. As for heroin, that was passé. I forgot the name of that new white stuff. I went to the principal and I told him and he said, "No, there's nothing in my school. Nothing." No, he was not a member of a minority group. As a matter of fact, the only member of a minority I saw in that school is the one working in the lunchroom. And the jazz teacher. That drug number, and what I found was happening to the intellectually gifted hurt me. They were not being taught anything at all! They had an English teacher trying to teach them math.

Anyway, I found that Cindy wasn't going to the lunchroom and that the reason that she and a lot of other kids were not having lunch and were not telling me or their parents about it was that they were afraid. They were afraid to blow the whistle. Cindy knows that the minute she tells me, I'm going to be in there! In the lunchroom! Talking to the principal! The superintendent! Do you know what I mean? So I started going there at ten o'clock in the morning. I'd wait outside and believe me there were more kids outside than inside! And after a while they want to know who is this strange woman who sits there reading pimples on a piece of paper. And they started getting to know me. I'd say, "What are you doing out here?" They'd say, "Oh the teacher didn't want to teach today so he told us we had to wait outside!" I mean, this was last year! I'm not talking about 1942. About the other thing that bothered me, the neglect of gifted kids, they call the math class "high gym" because there's nothing to do. They just go down to the gym or get high because there's nothing else to do! One of them said, "I want to learn math," but, you see, they have math once a week because the gym teacher, who taught them the math, naturally, only taught once a week. Meanwhile, they're supposed to be getting a five-point class. I'm telling you the absolute truth. The gym teacher was teaching math. Oh well, he was one of the better qualified. The *math* teacher was teaching math and he was telling the kids that one-third was thirty percent! Well, it's thirty-three and a third percent, but he said, "Ah, that's close enough." He didn't care, you know. Needless to say, they don't teach them one-tenth of what's in the city-wide test. If you don't know the answer to a question on the city-wide test because it was never taught, they call it a crazy. Of course I wanted to see the city-wide test. I would try to get a copy of the city-wide test but the teachers wouldn't give it to me. I would finally prevail and they would cut the bottom of the test off. Because on the bottom was the half of the test which had never been discussed in class. There was no way that I wouldn't know what they had been taught because I did the homework with the kids. I knew exactly what they had been taught.

Let me tell you something. The school was indicted for spending more money on its employees than on the education of its students. This came out of a report called "All Schools Created Unequal" by Abrams in City College. I would tell the principal, he'd do nothing. I'd go to the school board, one member of the school board would tell another and another, and it would go right back down to the principal! Then it would come back to me. So one day, out of sheer frustration, in a public hearing, in a community school board—they have a hearing once a month where the members of the public can get up and they get three minutes—I let it all out! I said, "You know, you gotta be blind not to see it!" I said, "I'm blind and I see it!" Believe me, if this doesn't appear in your book, *I'll* write it! I never mentioned the name of the school in the public hearing because everybody knew the school my daughter went to, right? But the next morning I got a telephone call at eight-thirty in the morning from three principals in the district! There were three guilty principals. They all said, "How dare you talk about my school like that!"

In my district, they call schools either white schools or Harlem schools. The white schools are very good because they use all the money that's supposed to be used for the poor—the Title I money. They're very good. As a matter of fact, they're little private schools. They even have fund-raisings. They actually get the private sector to contribute matching funds whenever they want new books, new library, new this, new that. On the other hand, all you have to do is look at the reading results of the Harlem schools that come out in the newspapers once a year and you'll see that they are sixty or seventy percent below reading level.

I ran for City Council. A lot of people thought I had been elected. That's how active, or inactive, the incumbent is. They thought I was the council member. And so I found myself getting involved in all kinds of things. They would say, Council Member Muñiz, would you help me to do this, would you help me do that? So I finally told my sister and she said, "Look, don't tell them, just say, How can I help you?" So I found myself getting involved in every little thing. I found out that some of the principals thought that I had been elected because they didn't know who the incumbents were either! You know, when you walk in there with shabby-looking clothes, no makeup, hair a wreck, a white cane, they say, "She has to be somebody or else she wouldn't dare to go around like that." You know, people like that are usually put in institutions! So I actually had this reputation of being the eccentric councilwoman. A blind one at that, and here I am, not even involved with the Democratic Party. You know, for Manhattan there isn't one Republican elected to the City Council or anywhere. Here I am with the opposition party! They even thought I had an "in" with Reagan! You know, I was the only Republican.

Now I wanted to find out why the kids of illegal aliens were being pressured to sign up for free lunch. They don't want to sign anything, right? They would come to me and tell me about this. Now you say, why should they come to me? Well, I speak Spanish and I can't see them, which is perfect! Also, I don't wear ermine and pearls in Harlem. I had been standing out there, sometimes in zero-degree weather, in front of that school with all the drug addicts and the drug pushers. These children of illegal aliens and some of their parents came to me and said, "We don't want to put anything in writing and we don't want free lunch. I don't even like the lunch in there." "My daughter has asthma and emphysema and all kinds of diseases from the smoke in there. But they told me that if I didn't sign for the free lunch that I would have to bring in my green card." Meanwhile, I read in the *New York Times*, right? How this was a model school in Manhattan! Cindy, what did the principal call it in the paper? (Educationally sound.) And he said it was orderly, functional and educationally sound. Cindy, what did you say the kids call the school? (Perdition School.) Okay. So I wanted to find out why they are forcing these people to sign lunch slips. I mean, am I going to go over and intimidate you so that you will sign for a free lunch? So I started to go to all the meetings. Whenever there was a meeting, I was there. Well. I found out they have to have forty-two percent of the kids having free lunch or they lose federal money. That's the reason! They get paid by the child.

I brought three kids into the principal who wanted to stand up and be counted. They wanted to complain about the school, about the drugs, and he wouldn't even hear them. A lot of people were saying that the kids had to be afraid because there were gangs and if you told on them they'd kill you. Well, I don't know if there are gangs, but I know that there are young men—by young I mean maybe eighteen or nineteen—in a junior high school where children are maybe eleven, twelve, thirteen, who just go in there and sell drugs. I spent eight months of my life standing there from eleven o'clock in the morning till three o'clock in the afternoon. Every kid I knew, and I got to know and meet a lot of them, says the same thing. I stood out there. Then I'd go into the anteroom. Then I'd walk around to the park. There are so many other problems! Look at this pregnancy. You know, they give the kids these birth control pills without telling the mothers. There are abortion clinics that get paid by the abortion. So they'd better get as many as they can, right? I met one little girl who was one of Cindy's friends. She was thirteen years old and she had a two-year-old baby. She was in a mentally retarded class, which meant the school got more money for her. I don't think she was mentally retarded, but I could tell that she had had a very inferior education. I said to her, "How did you get pregnant?" And she said, "Oh my boyfriend is a forty-year-old man." (She's one of them that get with the oldies.) Didn't you see her with that old man, Cindy? (Everybody saw her with that old man!) But you see, John, what I'm trying to tell you is that every day it was a new problem. Suddenly I said to myself, "How many of them are there?" I said to this girl, "How did it happen?" And she said, "Well, you know that park right next to school where the teacher throws the kids out when he doesn't want to teach." There are men who loiter in this public park. This park is contiguous to the school and this is where those teachers are throwing these eleven- and twelve-year-old girls! These men entice them with candies and silk blouses. I know one who got pregnant for a silk blouse! When I told the principal that these children were being thrown out into a dangerous park, he said, "Well, I can't tell them what to do. That doesn't belong to the school." I said, "Well, why are they throwing these children out there?" And he said, "Oh, no, that was the first time." I said, "I want to tell you that I have been here for eight months of my life!" One more month and *I* would have had a baby! You know, I have been here in this school, out here in this street. I've talked to so many kids. Every time I tried to report something, nobody would listen.

I spoke to most of the school board members. They knew what was going on. But they weren't going to do anything about it. I was going to run for City Council again because I thought that what you needed was an expert. A person with firsthand knowledge of poverty, disability, racial minorities, and single parenthood, and I was the only one! But I suddenly realized that all I had was raw courage. Raw courage isn't enough without a little finance. You really have to have economic independence because, for example, one of the lunchroom staff at the school said, "Please don't tell anybody that the kids aren't eating lunch because then I'll lose my job." And she gave me a big long sob story. No, I shouldn't really say that. A really true story. If she didn't have that job serving lunch to phantoms she really would be in trouble. One of the people who worked in the school told me that a school board member used to take the food for the free lunch program home by the crate! It was in all the papers and on the radio stations. He was indicted, though he hasn't been convicted yet. But he did resign and now they're trying to fill the vacancy on the school board. Somebody put my name in, so I started talking to all these parents. Yesterday they had to give their approval, and naturally they approved of somebody else. You see, I am a Republican and I am not forgiven for that, by the poor. Well, I'm a Republican because there is no room for dissent in the Democratic Party of the Upper West Side. The middle class doesn't like me because I am a Puerto Rican. I'm not supposed to be educated but I'm more educated than some of those teachers in there. They hate me, okay. So I speak Spanish and English. That's expected of Puerto Ricans, but I also know French and German. I studied Latin. That's just too much for them.

The trouble with the Puerto Ricans is that we are supposed to be lacking
in culture! I can't tell you how many times I've sat and listened to people
telling me that Hispanics and blacks don't intellectually stroke their
children. It is something *cultural* and no amount of money will change it.
I'm very glad I didn't read the sociology books or else I would have put
myself in an institution! I wasn't privy to this information which classified
me as inferior. These people who write the Ph.D.'s on minorities, and disabled people and single parents and poor people, you know, and maintain
that there's something wrong with us, they can't possibly give up all that
work! The truth would destroy their whole thesis, right? For a lot of them,
it is convenient and expedient to believe that because that means jobs. If I
pay you good money to help the poor, it's in your interest to keep them
poor.

Okay, so I decided I wanted to do something with my life to fill up my
free time. But believe me, every time I went to volunteer they thought I
wanted a handout! So then, somebody said to me, "There's one person who
will never refuse volunteer work." I said, "Who is that?" And they said,
"A politician." They told me politicians don't care what you look like, who
you are. If you're willing to sit there and stuff envelopes and vote for them,
they'll accept you! So I went to my local Democratic Party. Let's face it,
I'd been a Democrat all my life. The minute the woman there saw me she
said, "What more do you people want? We give you food stamps! Welfare!
Free hospitals! Free housing! Free schools! If you want any more, go to
the Republicans!" I'm telling you, she was converting Democrats into
Republicans. She had no qualms about saying these things, definitely not.
She said these things in front of me and in front of Cindy. And of course
at that time I was melodramatic enough to think that you don't wound my
daughter, you don't attack her pride. I said, "Look, all I want to do is
volunteer." You know, all you want to do is give of your time and they
don't want to take it. So I went over to the Republicans and I got on my
high horse and I said, "Look, I'm a Puerto Rican born, Puerto Rican bred,
and when I die, I'll be a Puerto Rican dead! And I'm proud of it! I don't
want any more welfare! I don't want to take a check! This is the land of
opportunity and if you want my help in bringing opportunity to those who
have been denied, here I am!" And a whole bunch of Puerto Ricans came
in from the back room. I said, "¿Como 'stamos?" There's this nice little
Republican Hispanic assembly! That woman had been insulting all these
Puerto Ricans for years! Driving us away.

I was in a meeting of Democrats and the man said—that day I was wearing my sister's clothes, I looked a wreck—he said, "Don't worry about the
poor, they're going to vote for us no matter what." And they didn't worry
about the poor. Or they don't vote at all, which is much better. When they
don't vote the politicians are happier. If all you have is a hundred voters,
all you need are fifty-one, but if you have a thousand voters, you need five
hundred and one. So public apathy is a politician's dream. I know this is a
matter of fact. First of all, I've worked on a lot of campaigns. Look, if you
have to hand out a hundred thousand pieces of literature, that's a lot of
people you need to volunteer. You have to persuade that many people,
right? But what if only ten percent of the electorate votes? Why should

you encourage more? You know, isn't it common sense? The only time they're out there at voter registration, really, trying to get you to vote is when they're losing. They like to get voter registration, but not voter participation because, you see, they can collect according to how many people are registered in the party. There's a formula, I've forgotten what it is, but the greater the number of people in a particular political party, the more money. You see it's in their interest that there be a lot of people registered but it's not in their interest that these people vote. Let's face it. I mean, if it were really vital, by now you would think they would have ninety percent of the people voting. Participatory democracy sounds good, but if you move, you have to reregister. You can't vote that year. They have certain dates, if you haven't registered by that time you can't vote and they don't make the dates too public. And then all these primary nonsense things, then you have to vote every two years.

I was denied the vote once right here in Manhattan, at the 70th Assembly District. I went in there and I couldn't push any of the little things because they wouldn't move! They were jammed. I don't know if it was deliberate. All I know is, when I left there, one man was telling me that five people had walked out because they weren't allowed to vote. And then they wondered why the 70th was the lowest voting assembly district in the city practically! They told me, "That's it. Once you go in there and you come out, that's it." I said, "All right. Cindy let's get out of here." You see, then I didn't know what to do. I felt terrible. I wasn't going to go in there and not even vote. I thought, "How dare you?" So then I called up the Board of Elections and I told them, I have been denied my right and I'm going to, blah, blah, blah, go to the *New York Times*. Too many people were coming out of there not allowed to vote. The man said, "Well come down to the Supreme Court and tell it to the judge." So that's when I went down and they asked me the impossible question, did I know where my election district was? Of course, Cindy knows everything and then I told this story to a woman. I was sworn and I testified and then they gave me a subpoena?, or something, a nice official piece of paper and I took it right back there. And I said, "I'm voting." And he said, "I knew you'd be back." And that time the machine worked. When I walk in that machine works now. But even last time I got the same report. So I said, "Look, let me go in there with you," but they said, "No, I don't want to start anything because you know, I have a job in the school district or I have a job in the city hospital." They're afraid. Yes, I think there's a possibility that the machine is interfered with. You know, I've lived around here for about twenty years. I've voted in the same place too many times. Too many people tell me, "I go in there, the darn thing doesn't move, I come out to report it and they tell me, I can't go back in." You don't believe it and then after a while it happens to you. You see, if anything goes on long enough it happens to you! Yes, that's Muñiz's law. If something can happen and it goes on long enough, sooner or later it will happen to you.

I can actually tell you that Cindy was penalized by two teachers because of my participation in the school. She was humiliated in the class. Of course, Cindy is beyond that. Oh, they take off grades. The teacher told me, I took five points off of your daughter's this or that or the other. And she says, "I *hate* parents who get involved in schools instead of leaving it to the faculty!" You have to remember that Cindy was eleven years old. And it got to the point where she wouldn't tell me anything. I had to get it from the other friends. She was afraid that I would go in and tell another teacher off because of what they were doing. Listen to this. It was so petty, it's really a shame to talk about it. They gave her homework, tested her on it, her grade depended on these tests, from a book that was out of print! That was available in the New York City library in Staten Island! I spoke to the English director and this one and that one and they said, "Well, we have a limited number of books and we lend them out arbitrarily." And needless to say, that teacher wanted to punish Cindy and she made absolutely sure that Cindy very rarely got the book.

And they had a spelling bee. You know this national spelling bee? They made sure that only the two white kids in Cindy's class and two isolated white kids in another class got to be in the run-off, which they did privately. Nobody knew there was a spelling bee. And then one of the kids came over to me and said, "You know, I won the spelling bee last year in Spanish and English and they wouldn't even let me into the run-off." I said, "What spelling bee? What run-off?" I didn't believe that anyone could be so petty. So then I spoke to the principal about it and he said, "Oh, look, a spelling bee! That should be the worst of your problems." So then, one of the women said, "I know this is too small, but my daughter is thoroughly demoralized." I said, "I can't believe this!" I went to the superintendent's office and he couldn't believe it either! He said, "You mean a spelling bee is rigged?" I called up the *Daily News* and the reporter said, "No, I don't believe this." It was a run-off. I think they made sure that any black or Hispanic kid who could spell was not allowed to participate and they did all this in secret.

Well, after that the principal knew that he and I were at war. I mean, you had to be blind not to see it, and I saw it. The drugs and everything that was going on, and the kids being thrown out into the street. And sometimes, John, it was really cold. Then I find out that this principal, this beautiful principal and his school have been written up in the *New York Times*. The writer must have been his cousin. I'm sure she was a relative. She wrote this school up as one of the best! I called up the *New York Times* and I said, "How could you write this? Quoting only the principal. You never interviewed the parents, you never interviewed the school board, you never interviewed the kids. All you did was interview the principal." You see how this is bigger than life? Don't believe everything you read in the papers. I told the principal what I thought about that "educationally sound" school of his. Some time after that I was asked to join a screening board to read résumés for a sixty-thousand-dollar job in the community as district superintendent. And guess who was applying for the job? The principal! The same principal who allowed all the drugs and threw the kids out into the street, who rigged the spelling bee! And who should be representing the Hispanic parents on the screening board? Me. We looked at his résumé and his credentials were all wrong! This guy wasn't even certified. I don't think he's even qualified to be a principal, much less to be a supervisor! Every parent on the screening board asked the same question. Mr.

So-and-so, why haven't you given us a picture of your certificate? He said, "I didn't finish it. I only had nine more credits to do and I don't need them." So you see what a tangled web you weave? You catch them rigging the spelling bee, they're also going to rig the supervisor's certificate. And so he was disqualified. This principal put bilingual education on his résumé. He can't even speak Spanish. I think that screening board meeting is on record. I think it was taped. Anyway, I can definitely prove that he wasn't certified. That can be checked. What I'm telling you is absolutely true. This is, to me, divine retribution.

While none of these parents will go as far as to elect me to the school board, or to vote for me for the City Council—they won't go that far because they mistrust that Republican label—at least when I gave them the facts they followed it through. So that we disqualified the spelling bee rigger. You see, to me, this man is criminal. I hate to get serious on you, John, but to me, what this principal is doing is criminal, absolutely criminal. I'm trying to interest the Puerto Rican Legal Defense's Educational Fund, somebody I know there, to take this to court. They are suing in Chicago, I think, where the children are the plaintiffs. I would like to make the children at Cindy's school plaintiffs with the Puerto Rican Legal Defense Fund.

This is another reason why I stick to principled dissent. Another truism is that, one thing about a diehard, sooner or later somebody will listen to you. Sooner or later you'll get results. I got up there in the school board and said, "Here is a principal who says he can't see the drugs in his school. He can't handle his own school and now he wants to handle the whole district. Twenty-two schools would be under this man. This man's a criminal. To throw out kids in the middle of the winter. I told him about it so he can't say that he didn't know it was happening." So I stay with it because, sooner or later, I prevail. Maybe not in the ways I have it planned, you know, running for City Council or Congress. I may eventually have to run for something big. But I do have these minor victories.

You know, things happen sometimes because you're not paying attention, because you're not organized. I thought, there's nothing deliberate, there is no conspiracy, there's no plot. But now, I think there is. First of all, you see that the minority kids can't read. And fifty percent of the Puerto Rican population, according to the statistics, are at or below the poverty level. You know what I'm saying. That makes you wonder.

I remember a million years ago when I was going into high school. I can remember the principal of P.S. 60 in the Bronx forbidding me to take the Hunter College entrance test. Forbidding me! She said I would be lonely, and then finally she said I would disgrace the school! These were my teachers, none of whom were black or Hispanic. Yeah, it would disgrace a little Harlem school. First of all, I brought in my grandmother. She couldn't speak English but she looked mean. And she brought in a priest. My mother used to say, "If you have to be Hispanic or black, the only way people will accept that you're educated is that you have to be a priest." Right, because nobody would ever accuse a priest of being uneducated. But anything else, no! You could be a Nobel Prize shaker or maker or whatever, and you'd still be considered stupid. Anyway, so I brought in this priest and he told the principal that he was going to bring in the Pope! Anyway, I got the highest grade in the school. I was the only Puerto Rican in my whole class! Then, ten years later, it's time for my brother to take the test. The same thing. "You're going to be lonely." My grandmother was still alive, she couldn't speak English but she still looked mean and the same priest comes in. My brother took the test and he passed. And just about ten years after that, one of my father's relatives is telling me that *his* child is not allowed to take the test. Then! You see? I told you, sooner or later it happens to you. You might think that you are an exception when it happens to you first. Then, along comes Cindy Liza Muñiz, my daughter. They were putting her in the slow classes, so I had her tested and I found out that at eleven years old she could do ninth grade work. (I was ten.) Oh ten, right. But her reading level was twelfth grade then. The psychologist from the Children's Consultation Service of N.Y.U. recommended Cindy for Hunter, but the principal of Hunter would not allow it. He said you can't do it that way, we can't get recommendations from psychologists. That doesn't count. The only way we will accept it is if the principal from her school recommends her. Well, I had already had so much trouble with the principal of her school that the only thing he would recommend her for would be Alcatraz or the Tombs!

By the time I called all the politicians the deadline had passed. And then I said to her, "Cindy, you're better off in a Catholic school where I can at least go and talk to the people on moral grounds. You know, I might find a few black and Hispanic priests or somebody. You won't be so lonely!" You're asking me why I think there's a conspiracy. Every day you find out how the system works. It's insidious. The fact that the principal has to recommend you is bad in itself.

You know, maybe we should write a book called "Perdition School," Cindy, John, and Pat, and just not mention the name of it. Because you know I can't prove any of this, you're just taking my word for it. I can't prove anything because the children are too young to testify, the parents are too afraid to testify and the others are intimidated. But let me tell you something, John. I can't live my life according to what I can prove in a court of law. I can live it only by what I know to be true.*

---

* Pat died suddenly and inexplicably in April of 1985 while hospitalized for an asthma attack.

Puerto Rican Patriots Alicia, Carmen, Dylcia, and Ida Luz

"We are not terrorists. We are captured combatants in a decolonization war."

□   □   □

I have acted from a sense of duty and am content to await my fate.

JOHN BROWN

At a time when John Hinckley was freely informing the media about his attempt upon the life of the President of the United States, the four Puerto Rican nationalist women prisoners I visited in Illinois were refused the right to participate fully in this inquiry. I was not permitted to carry a tape recorder into the Dwight Correctional Facility where they were then being detained. Nevertheless, we met and talked over impromptu lunches of raisins and nuts and fruit juice obtained from the prison store and these young women spoke at length of their dedication to an independent, socialist Puerto Rico.

As these Puerto Ricans represent the most extreme and probably the most unpopular and least understood example of principled dissent in this book, it is especially unfortunate that a personal account of themselves and what they believe and why they believe it cannot be included here. What follows is my presentation of their position based on my meetings with them and their supporters and their letters and published writing.

Charged with "seditious conspiracy," Alicia Rodriguez, Carmen Valentín, Dylcia Pagán Morales, and Ida Luz Rodriguez were arrested in 1980 with seven other Puerto Rican nationalists. The subsequent legal proceedings did very little to clarify their position as, consistent with their claims of Prisoner of War status under the provisions of the Geneva Convention, they refused to cooperate with those juridical proceedings. These talented, dedicated young women have abandoned promising careers and are suffering the rigors of what amounts to life imprisonment for what they believe. They are sustained by a devoted Puerto Rican nationalist constituency and by the conviction that they will ultimately be vindicated as soldiers in a colonial war. Their rigorous detention for their cause—armed struggle for the establishment of an independent, socialist Puerto Rican Republic—is undeniable proof of Andrew Young's unpopular but incontrovertible assertion that there are political prisoners in this country.

The conditions under which these prisoners are being detained and the cause for which they are imprisoned are magnet issues in civil libertarian circles. The case of the Eleven Puerto Rican Prisoners of War, "Los Once," has generated everything from debate in the halls of the United Nations to supportive community festivals, church suppers, and garage sales. A great quantity of supportive literature has been produced, as well as a recording of a musical tribute to them entitled, "Los Once."

John Brown was hanged because he advocated armed opposition to a repressive government. His soul goes marching on, of course, because the alchemy of time has transmuted his premature heroism into the proud heritage of principled dissent. It might be well to remember that in his none-too-distant day, he was regarded as a demonic terrorist also, and was certainly no less unpopular than these Puerto Rican nationalist prisoners. Of the four extremely controversial issues of unpopular dissenting that frequently generated pronounced responses in this work, the dissenting of these four political prisoners, though by no means universally opposed by all the people I discussed it with, was certainly the most difficult for most people to square with principled advocacy and action.

Historian Joan Nicklin was instrumental in creating my opportunity to talk with Dylcia Pagán Morales, Carmen Valentín, and the Rodriguez sisters, Alicia and Ida Luz. Carmen was a friend and professional colleague of Joan's at the Central YMCA Community College where they both taught. When Carmen was arrested, Joan was moved to educate herself on the subject of Puerto Rican independence. Her studies led to the production of a very reasoned position paper and the conclusion that, "Just to see them as terrorists is to avoid the whole history of Puerto Rico." Joan helped found and is an active member of the Civic-Religious Committee in Support of the Puerto Rican Prisoners of War. The Committee sponsors educational symposia, raises funds and generally acts in aid of the human rights of the detained political prisoners.

The depth and ambivalence of sentiment surrounding Carmen's popular press image is evident in this portion of a letter to the *Chicago Tribune* signed by twenty-five of her colleagues at the Community College.

We, faculty of Central YMCA Community College, who have worked closely with Ms. Valentín for many years, wish to express our sense of outrage at the article entitled "Ex-Chicago teacher called godmother of FALN here." The term "godmother" was chosen because it suggests mafia-type violence. . . .

Ms. Valentín is a patriot and has never concealed her concern about conditions in Puerto Rico and the conditions of Puerto Ricans in the United States. The article indicates that wherever Ms. Valentín went there was "student unrest" and "bloody riots." Sooner or later oppressed people will rebel. This rebellion is caused by conditions and not by a sinister "godmother."

All four women have been unequivocal in their endorsement of the goal of Puerto Rican liberty. Carmen's verse, her teaching and counseling, her street mural projects; Dylcia's poetry, drawings, and television productions; and the essays and public statements of Alicia and Ida Luz all celebrate the attainment of independence and socialism for Puerto Rico. Alicia, younger of the two Rodriguez sisters, declared at the juridical proceedings where she was sentenced to a lengthy prison term,

What happens to us does not matter. What matters is that independence and socialism for Puerto Rico are inevitable. . . . The conditions of my people (both in Puerto Rico and in the United States) have forced us to move against subsistence wages, extremely high inflation, mass unemployment (which forced the migration of almost half of the population of Puerto Rico), genocide (40 percent of Puerto Rican women of child-bearing age have been sterilized), and the perpetual effort of United States colonialism to destroy our language and culture through forced assimilation and annexation.

Dylcia voices the same opposition to colonial exploitation as manifest in continued industrial and technological overdevelopment when she denounces a projected scheme for the accelerated construction of petrochemical and ore-processing facilities and a massive increase in both strip and deep mining of a large portion of Puerto Rico. Completion of these projects is projected for the year 2020.

Plan 2020 is the United States' strategy to continue its genocidal policy for the people of Puerto Rico. It will displace thousands while at the same time pollute the environment and convert our beautiful homeland into an industrial/military complex to further the aggression in Central America and elsewhere.

Perceived of as extremely dangerous, with bail set at two million dollars each, the prisoners' self-perception is reflected in Carmen's response to the charge of terrorism.

Your press, your justice system, your repressive forces, your government has branded us as terrorists. But the word terrorist no longer means to the Puerto Rican nation what it used to. Instead of arousing fear or censure, terrorism is a call to action. To be called a terrorist by our enemy is an honor to any citizen, for this means that he is fighting with a gun in his hand, against the monstrosity of the present government, and the suffering it causes.

Ida Luz affirmed the same general aims in a letter to me.

Our movement moves beyond the sphere of principled dissent and enters the realm of revolutionary struggle. We are more than dissenters—we are revolutionaries who strive to dismantle a corrupt, inhuman system which seeks to destroy life. . . . It is very important to remember that our thoughts and actions are just a continuation of the struggle that our people have waged since the nineteenth century; a struggle for national liberation.

The demonic masks with which much popular press and media attention has fitted these women are in total contrast to their view of themselves. In

1982, on the occasion of International Women's Day, Carmen and Dylcia, in a jointly authored essay from prison that appeared in *Puerto Rican Women: A History of Oppression and Resistance* wrote:

Many who have visited with us [the Eleven Prisoners of War] have inquired as to the circumstances that led to our decision in becoming combatants in our war of national liberation. To best answer one can say that as individuals, specific experiences in our lives aided us in making a decision, but the essence of all of us is a strong sense of love of our fellow man, a strong sense of justice, and a continual commitment to our principles. It is true that most of us have children just beginning to talk and at crucial ages. We have husbands and wives from whom we must be separated as part of the sacrifice for creating a new life for our people. We, as combatants in the war for national liberation, chose to commit ourselves to struggle no matter what the consequences.

Quite apart from the disinterested civil libertarian support groups that have assisted these prisoners to secure the general human rights of incarcerated persons, there is a strong support group of kin, friends, and ideological partisans who are devoted to the prisoners' well-being. For this nationalist segment of the Puerto Rican community, these four women are captured prisoners of a war that has its origin in the United States occupation of Puerto Rico during the Spanish-American War. This position was taken in court by all four women in statements very similar to this one made by Alicia Rodriguez.

It is a historical fact that in 1898 my country was militarily intervened by the U.S. armed forces. Since that time, our nation has been in a continuous state of war against the United States. . . . I must interject at this time that our actions were not dictated by whims, but by a clear understanding of the colonial situation in Puerto Rico. . . . The General Assembly of the United Nations explicitly points out that we as a colonized people have the unquestionable right to fight for our independence through armed and violent means, and they also state that to continue the process of colonialization is a crime. It also reaffirms that I as a captured anticolonial freedom fighter should be treated as a prisoner of war.

The case for Puerto Rican national independence and the recognition of Prisoner of War status for these prisoners has been formally made before the Special Committee on Decolonization of the United Nations. I visited the Puerto Rican Cultural Center in Chicago through the courtesy of its Director, Northeastern University professor and historian José López, who was instrumental in the drafting of that United Nations Petition. The Center provides a variety of community services, ranging from child care to alternate secondary school education, and Puerto Rican nationalism is a key element in its varied cultural offerings. Largely devoted to the restoration and preservation of traditional Puerto Rican culture, the Center's efforts are reflected in the home life of people who are not directly involved in its operation. Evelyn Rodriguez, eldest of the Rodriguez sisters, described this feedback with some chagrin in a taped interview she granted me one November evening in my Chicago hotel room.

It wasn't fair, you know, to celebrate Christmas at my home on December 25th when they were teaching my son about Three Kings Day at the Puerto Rican Center Child Care Program. Somewhere along the line you have to start establishing some sort of a consistency.

Children in the Puerto Rican Cultural Center write letters of gratitude and exhortatory encouragement to the "Prisoners of War," and the regard for the children as harbingers and seeds of the revolutionary future is apparent in the verse published by some of the prisoners in *Have You Seen "La Nueva Mujer Puertorriqueña? The Poetry and Lives of Revolutionary Puerto Rican Women.*

> Listen Borinqueño child,
> the soul of our country.
> In you we see the future
> of our struggle for independence.
> Our homeland is courage and sacrifice,
> as Dr. Albizu taught us.
> Walk with your heads held high,
> because your parents are freedom fighters. . . .
>
> DYLCIA PAGÁN MORALES

> Children of our country,
> Children of armed struggle,
> Always ready, always strong,
> Soon your moment will come. . . .

> Arise Borinqueñitos,
> We have given the sign.
>
> CARMEN VALENTÍN

The draconian duress that characterizes official treatment of the political prisoners has its reflection in the lives of their kin and known sympathizers. The FBI staged a predawn raid on the Puerto Rican Cultural Center, an action justified by the unfounded premise that it was doubling as a "safe house" and arsenal, as well as a child care center. Most of the people I talked with in connection with this aspect of this inquiry into principled dissent proceeded routinely upon the assumption that their phones were being monitored, and phone conversation with them certainly displayed a degree of technical difficulty far beyond anything that might be reasonably expected. The prisoners are frequently transferred, thus imposing a heavy burden upon the time and resources of their families, friends, and partisans who wish to visit them. Evelyn's situation is not uncommon.

We've developed a very special closeness which we didn't have before and which will be severed soon when they take Lucy away. It's going to put an economical strain on the family. We're not people who can come and go as we please. I have a job; I can't just say I want the afternoon off.

I met the Puerto Rican nationalists during a late autumn hiatus in my teaching. I was then giving classes in the Contemporary Caribbean and Minority-Majority Relations and I discussed this research with both classes as it was relevant to both contexts. Some students were appalled at the idea and warned me that my life would be at risk as these "wild-eyed fanatics" would doubtless set upon me with murderous intent if I were to disagree with them in the slightest degree. Some other students, most of them members of black, Hispanic, or other Third-World-oriented American ethnic constituencies, stressed the perils, real and imagined, of dealing with prison authorities and envied me the opportunity to speak with "real revolutionaries." I have had an opportunity to talk with scores of Americans about this issue. The same two diametrically opposed views keep surfacing and the absence of the middle ground is conspicuous.

Particular to every variety of dissent is its vocabulary and style. Convictions are couched in those styles and it is often difficult to get beyond the rhetorical dialects to the dissenting person. These four women are sacrificing much for what they believe. Dylcia Pagán Morales, Carmen Valentín, and Ida Luz Rodriguez are separated from their young children. They have all given up promising careers; Alicia in the natural sciences, Carmen as a teacher, counselor, and doctoral candidate, Ida Luz in the social sciences and Dylcia in television programing, editing, and investigative journalism. They have been deprived of those myriads of little freedoms that are the savor of civil existence. The right to uncensored correspondence, the right to read what one pleases, the freedom to indulge personal preference in matters of food, dress, music, travel, waking, and sleeping: the simple, invaluable right to be where one chooses to be. Dylcia misses New York, "filth and all." She has an intense, parochial passion for the little particularities of that city—the doughy, salt-spattered monstrosities that true New Yorkers insist are pretzels and the bloated, superannuated cucumbers that they consider the best of all possible pickles. Diminutive Carmen nurtures as best she can her delicate beauty and worries about her thirteen-year-old son, Tony, even though she knows he is "well taken care of" and that she was "an excellent mother."

In a very literal sense, these women are living flags: symbols of a persistent movement. As such, a great deal is expected of them, as Evelyn Rodriguez indicates.

The Prisoners of War know that they have to maintain the highest of standards and the highest of principles. Their lives no longer belong to them; they represent the Puerto Rican nation's struggle. They can't live for themselves anymore, they have to live for the struggle.

To their nationalist constituency, these prisoners are the focus of inspiration and aspiration. They are the centers of almost holy regard. On the anniversary of the death of Angel Rodriguez Cristobal, a Puerto Rican nationalist political prisoner who died under dubious circumstances in a Tallahassee prison, a large group of Puerto Rican nationalists met at the Lakeview Presbyterian Church in Chicago. People paid two dollars and got a good traditional Puerto Rican dinner and a feast of exhortation and dedication from people facing imminent imprisonment for their cause. Julio Rosado, who was subsequently sentenced, with four others, to a three-year prison term for noncooperation with a Grand Jury investigation spoke that evening. "North American" Shelley Miller, member of the New Movement in Solidarity with Puerto Rican Independence and Socialism spoke also. She too has been sent to prison for refusal to testify before a Grand Jury. Jaime Delgado, of the National Committee to Free Puerto Rican Prisoners of War spoke and Professor José López synthesized the sense of the meeting and summarized the current state of the nationalist movement in the reasoned, measured style that is his customary manner. All the speakers received the kind of deferential attention normally encountered in the most solemn assemblies of the extremely dedicated. Marta Rodriguez, a fine guitarist and composer of elegantly crafted satirical songs, played and sang in both Spanish and English. Throughout that long "Evening of Resistance," a sustained atmosphere of intense solidarity and tenacity was manifest in everything from the quietness of normally noisy children, to the rapt attention and thunderous applause that greeted every speaker and every song. The plain message of that and countless other feasts of solidarity and perseverance is the same as that carried by so much of the verse of the prisoners.

> While there is a breath still left in me,
>   I will engage in conspiracy.
> While my spirit still can run,
> While my arm can raise a gun,
> Or my hand a pen still lift,
>   I will be secret, subtle, swift.
>
> As long as you can hear the "le-lo-lai"
> As long as palm trees and the flamboyant still survive
> So long as my people answer the call—
> Count on me, at the front, with you all.
> As long as I can breathe,
>   I will conspire.
>   CARMEN VALENTÍN

The impact that these women exert is by no means narrowly political. Evelyn Rodriguez reflects on this complex metamorphosis.

You have to start thinking of the Eleven as the new men and the new women. We draw strength from each other, which is what keeps us going. I learned from my sisters that a woman can be strong because living in a prison system is not easy. What my sisters are doing has made me see to what level a person can rise as far as the development of their own selves and character is concerned. You're so used to seeing your sisters in a certain way and all of a sudden, you see them as Prisoners of War, fighting for the independence of Puerto Rico. You see a side to them that you never, never saw before! And from that side of them they give you strength because you feel that what they have gone through is something you have not gone through, and look at how much they have accomplished as women! When you begin to see underneath the surface and once you really know what is happening, it's kind of hard to go back. You say, "Hey! There's a little bit more to life than going to work and taking care of your babies and paying your mortgage and your car loan." There's a cause out there! Fighting for your own identity. And I think, as a Puerto Rican, it's your right to know what makes you different from a black or white or Japanese.

Psychologist Gordon Alport once observed that in the realm of social science it was the unexpected that should be listened for. A proper regard for the integrity of the marketplace of ideas means that even—and especially—unpopular ideas should be heard, and I deeply regret that I was not permitted to present here the personal narratives of these four Puerto Rican nationalists. Professor Nicklin's statement of the case is, I believe, very germane in a society with plural democratic pretensions.

I'm not saying that the Puerto Rican nationalist way is the only way or the correct way. I'm not saying that Puerto Rican nationalists should or should not engage in armed struggle. I'm not a Puerto Rican, so I have no right to make that decision for them. What I'm doing is trying to talk to you and hope their point of view is looked at. What Mike Yasutake is doing is getting all these Christians together to support these prisoners' right to humane treatment as best he can. I respect all these people and I respect myself. I don't really believe in principles for the sake of principles. I mean, principles are something you live.

James Robinson

"I believe there's a moral law in the universe, and
if there's a state law that significantly denies that
moral law, then I have to choose the moral law."

□ □ □

*I am thankful to God that some noble souls from
the ranks of organized religion have broken loose
from the paralyzing chains of conformity.*

MARTIN LUTHER KING, JR.

*The First Parish Unitarian Universalist Church of Brewster is a comfort-
able congregation in a generally comfortable little Massachusetts town
with a keen sense of the appropriateness of its past. The owner of the
historic general store had to argue long and hard for the right to cover his
traditional clapboards with vinyl siding. The Reverend James A. Robinson
now serves the same congregation that was served during the Civil War by
that apostle of American positiveness, the Reverend Horatio Alger. This
congregation's endorsement of Sanctuary for Central American refugees
was the product of much debate and conscience wrestling. The heirs of
those who could not find it in their consciences to obey the fugitive slave
laws are now prepared to defy the United States Immigration and Naturalization Service.*

*The Reverend Robinson is by preference primarily a vegetarian but I
didn't know that when he came to my house. We ate grilled cheddar and
bacon sandwiches, raw carrots and celery, and drank cider and coffee. Our
conversation had much to do with alternatives—mystical alternatives and
social alternatives. The dialogue returned often to India. Jim plays the
sitar and says his sister is the best sitar player he knows. The Robinsons
have given their only child, nine-year-old Ananda, an Indian name. It is
more than a truism to say that Jim is a spiritual seeker. I sensed in him an
aspect of a certain discontent with the current religious dispensations: a
basic unhappiness with patriarchy and the dead letter of stilted decorum.
He is an advocate of Liberation Theology, that doctrine which maintains
that both clergy and laity have the right and the duty to struggle against
oppression in all its forms. Taken in its broadest sense, Liberation Theology*

frees more than oppressed Central American peasantry, and I think the Reverend Robinson's fidelity to his higher moral law is his way of being a responsible instrument of that wider freedom.

═════

The members of the church which I have the honor of serving have become increasingly aware of the situation in Central America. Particularly as the civil war is raging in Guatemala and El Salvador, the people in the church became aware of the large number of massacres and death squads and simply the turmoil of being in a civil war and decided that they'd like our church to do something to help the victims of this situation. And then we became aware of the large number of refugees in the United States, particularly Salvadorans. People have different estimates of how many there are, but there could be half a million, and the fact is that these people are illegal aliens and not allowed any legal status in the United States. We became aware through church studies we had read that a large number of these people are deported back to El Salvador. In the studies following up these people, once they've been deported, it appeared that a significant number of them, maybe up to a quarter or a third of them, end up dead within several months. There are even some shoot-outs at the airport and this, according to our expert at the Unitarian Headquarters, is because these refugees would arrive back in their villages and the right-wing death squads would assume they must be guerrillas because they had been missing for some amount of time, and so they'd be assassinated quietly. And so we perceive the threat to these people's lives to be a real one— these people who are being deported. We also—the group of us who studied it—had come to the conclusion that the whole problem with Central America was poverty, not really Communist infiltration, and that we shouldn't be sending so much mass military aid down there. Rather, we should be looking at the causes of poverty, and how to help the people of the region to improve their living conditions. So we studied all that and then we became aware of a nationwide movement, which at that time had forty churches—none in New England—who were offering sanctuary to Salvadorans and Guatemalans, which meant that they would accept these refugees and care for them and help them find jobs. This was against the law because our government had decided that these people were not bona fide refugees. In the estimate of our government, these people were fleeing to get better jobs and they were economic refugees, but in our experience, and in our reading, they were really people who were caught in the middle of tremendous violence and usually were being persecuted by death threats and the like. So we decided to suggest to the congregation that we become a sanctuary site, and we went through some intense discussion with the church membership because the thought for many of them that the church would stand up and break the law was just more than they could bear. Church had meant to them a place to come to worship, and to stand up in that sort of sense really put us all in a lot of turmoil. After three weeks of intense discussions throughout the church, we decided to, in a sense, have a bit of a compromise. That is, the church voted, the total membership—well not the total—but at a congregational meeting everybody got together and voted. It was a unanimous vote to give a moral endorsement to any individuals in the church and to the Social Concerns Committee of the church to go ahead and offer sanctuary and declare Sanctuary. In this sense, the church gave its moral endorsement, but it wasn't really quite the church, it was the legal body offering it. So that was our compromise. But the church people went with that unanimously. So then we set up a sanctuary site and we let it be known. First the newspapers all flocked in and called up the INS (Immigration and Naturalization Service), and they told them we were breaking the law and we would go to jail for five years and all this stuff. Essentially the government, the INS, had said that "Yes, you're breaking the law, but we don't plan to prosecute any churches at this time." That basically was the answer we got. Anyway, we set up a sanctuary site, we began to help individual refugees who basically had been in the Boston area. We found that it was just overcrowded and they were all fighting for the same jobs and they'd like to get a chance to have a little safer life. So we've been helping people for four or five months now. I guess that's it. We help by getting them a place to live, usually with a family, and if they're minors, by helping them go to school, which is legal in Massachusetts. And if they want to work, we try to help them find jobs. That's a description of the project. There are churches in every denomination doing Sanctuary. So I don't think anybody can hide behind the thing of, "You Unitarians just do more of that," 'cause, really, the Catholic Church in Central America is leading the way. Yes, ours is the first New England church. I'll xerox all of the articles I have about it and mail them to you.

We go around to a lot of other churches now and basically we find a lot of interest, but everybody says, "Oh, we could never do this in our church." And the reason for all the hesitation is that there was, and there is, a danger of splitting churches on this kind of issue. In other words, half the people say, "I vote against it" and a quarter of the people are saying, "If you pass this, I'm going to leave the church." And if the church splits like that, then my job is in jeopardy, and even if they keep me, it's probably best if I move on. So there are real risks, and I had some sleepless nights over those risks because I happen to like my job.

I grew up in California and when I was eighteen I moved to Michigan for seven years. Then I went to Harvard for the Divinity School and I've been in New England ever since then, for the last eight years. I was part of the generation, I think, for whom our college years were more dissent demonstrations than classrooms. But I must admit that at the point when they started taking over the campus rooms and the ROTC buildings, that was a step too far for me at that time. I went to all the marches, I did some sit-ins, but when it came to taking over a building to make a point, that was too much for me to do. I had decided that if I was drafted, I would not go. I would rather be in jail than go to Vietnam. I had made that decision, but when my number came up in the lottery, it was so high I never got drafted, so it saved me that. I hadn't matured at that point enough to really understand what principled dissent was.

To me there are two types of principled dissent. I mean, everybody does principled dissent. They say, "I disagree with this on principle." But I think what we're talking about is what I'd call civil disobedience. And that is where an individual makes a choice, a conscious choice, to disobey a law because they feel there's a higher moral order at stake and that they have to be willing to accept the consequences of that choice, if there be consequences. That to me is what principled dissent or civil disobedience is. There should be enough principled dissent to keep the moral order moving forward, but not so much that chaos results. I guess by chaos I mean revolution. Yes, I would be opposed to violent revolution. There shouldn't be restrictions on people's opinions. Oh, certainly not. There should be a free marketplace of ideas. Would I permit the American Nazi Party to march? Oh God, I don't know. That's a tough one. I think probably yes, but I'd have to know that lives were safe in the process on both sides of the fence. No, we can't have that assurance, not all the time. So much of this I find hard to talk about in generalities because each case would be somewhat different. I mean, if we know that there's a bunch of assassins waiting around the corner for the President, you don't bring the President around the corner. If you know that there's gonna be a huge Nazi group and a huge anti-Nazi group all armed and all ready to fight, then I think you have some responsibilities there that will be different than if there was no prospect for open violence. I would not permit people to advocate just *anything.* I don't want somebody advocating masochism to my daughter. I mean, there's a point where tolerance ends and you have to say, "My life is committed to this value and this value and this value and I have to stand up for that."

I don't know much about the Puerto Rican situation. I'm more comfortable talking about Guatemala or El Salvador in what may be a roughly parallel situation. You are just poor for so long, and you watch a power establishment oppress your life for so long and you finally have aspects of the Catholic Church telling you you don't have to put up with this anymore, and then you have the right to stand up and say, "No more!"

I don't want to make a moral judgment for the people who are in that country. Me, personally, I don't feel comfortable participating in a violent overthrow, a violent revolution. I would prefer Dr. King's style, Gandhi's style, massive nonviolence, but if I had grown up a campesino in El Salvador and lived with it all my life and seen my relatives shot, who knows what I would do? So my feeling is, I don't send money to those groups to buy them guns, but I will certainly try to stop my government from sending guns to the government of that country, and I would help in medical supplies and that sort of thing. Yes I do oppose violence, though I must say I suppose there could be a situation where I could be so pushed to the edge where I could see that as an option. In my life so far, I have not seen that as an option. I would say there are probably some doctrines that are so sadistic and cruel that I would not want to tolerate them, like the Pol Pot government in Cambodia. I could not listen to a spokesman there and just say, "Isn't that a nice idea." I'd have to do something. I couldn't tolerate that, no.

I think that the Ku Klux Klan has a right to have its opinions heard but I draw the line at some point. When it advocates some sort of strong dehumanizing violence, then I'd draw the line. So if the Ku Klux Klan says, "I think we ought to meet next Saturday night and lynch a nigger," I'd say, "No, you don't have the right to enflame people like that." That would be like conspiracy, or whatever would be the word—planning to get 'em to do a crime. You don't have the right to do that. But if they go out there and just say, "Well, I just think white people and black people should live separately," well I guess they have the right to say that.

There are some basic values that I can't bend. It's not right to murder somebody, it's not right to molest somebody sexually. There's a whole series of things that it's just not right to do and if somebody's getting up there saying let's go do it, come along with me, I mean, I can't tolerate that.

I don't know a whole lot about other countries. I know that when I lived in Haiti, if you didn't stand up when Papa Doc came by you might end up in jail! I mean, we're better off than that! I know in El Salvador if you stand up too much too often for the poor you may get a bullet in your back at some point. I don't think this happens with that frequency in the United States, so in those comparisons we're better off than those countries. I think Americans will tolerate dissent to a certain point and then they get nervous. I think Americans allow dissent to a certain point, and then when it becomes too threatening we cut it off. I think it's a human trait to be ill at ease with dissent. What do I think most threatens the American collectivity? Oh my God, I'm just a small little country preacher! Well, let's see. It's interesting. I'll talk from our experience. Once our church took this vote to declare Sanctuary, what then upset the people was when we got a lot of publicity. It's like, well, if you keep things quiet, we'll give you the moral authority, but now all my neighbors know about it. They think, what kind of kooky church do you belong to? And anyway, we shouldn't be seeking this much publicity. I think it's when a person's sense of belonging to a social group is threatened that a lot of the anxiety comes up. So as the dissent begins to threaten our social status, there's a lot of anxiety. Some people write crank letters.

I'll tell ya, there's all kinds. In a place we used to live we were working on trying to show the town of Concord, Massachusetts, that it had racial problems. The minority population was so small there everybody thought we didn't have problems. So we hired this professional firm to do a real estate audit where they'd send in black couples and white couples to real estate agents on the same weekends to see if they got shown the same houses. And what they found was that they were shown basically the same houses but the black auditors said that the people in Concord were the most nervous people that they had experienced in all their auditing. So it was the social anxiety that essentially told the black couples that they'd never move to Concord 'cause everybody's so nervous with them. And so we printed this in the paper and made a big deal about it and then one of the people working on the project started getting all these death-threat calls. And they put a trace on it. Apparently when you get death-threat calls you can get them traced. It turned out to be one of Concord's leading business-

men. So that was a great education to me. That was a crank call. So some
of the cranks are people who are just out of it, you know, in terms of power,
and some cranks are people in power. I was in Concord for three and a
half years. I was the assistant in a large church and I decided I wanted to
give something to the Concord community during my stay there. I decided
my contribution would be to see if we couldn't get a little more ethnic and
racial plurality in the town. The town was 99.6 percent Caucasian and
basically upper middle class or upper class. So one thing had to do with the
racial study I talked about before, to see why blacks weren't moving into
town, and to let the people know why blacks weren't moving into town,
and why they were moving to Sudbury, which was the next town over.
There were plenty of rich blacks who were looking for places to live. I was
one of the three or four people who initiated that study. And then we got
concerned about the boat people and their tragic plight and we settled
about thirty in town. That was very curious because in some ways it was
easier for people to settle them because they were being the nice, helping,
white North Americans, but to have blacks who may be richer than they
were moving in as their next door neighbors, was hard to take!

Our cranks here know what we've done with Sanctuary, but they exag-
gerate all the implications of what we've done. And they think these weird
things. We're gonna flood Cape Cod with all these brown-skinned refugees,
or we're gonna flood Concord with black-skinned homeowners. You know,
a certain percentage found this very threatening. We're gonna become just
like X Y Z neighborhood and we all know the neighborhood goes down.
And then this whole thing about "Isn't this such a lovely town now, why
are you messing with it?" I don't know whether we're more irrational or
rational beings, but I think that most of what motivates us is irrational,
and we get fixated on a certain irrational idea that our security depends on
our neighborhood looking a certain way. When you start to change the
neighborhood, then there's a great deal of anxiety.

Sometimes the cranks identify themselves, mostly they're anonymous.
Some lady wrote that what made this town great was that it had a certain
colonial makeup. She was proud of the idea so she signed her name. These
people want an America that you can count on. Everything should have its
place and the whites should be nice and smile and the blacks should be nice
and smile and the brown people should stay down in Central America and
the Russians should stay in their place and this and this and this and this.
The world should stay this way and it's very threatening if it changes too
much. Very often these same people were refugees themselves. And it's so
weird. I mean, what we're arguing now is that we have a government policy
that allows refugees from Communist countries to come here because it
makes Communism look bad. But from other countries that may be awful
dictatorships, if they're our friends, we shouldn't let refugees in because
then that shows that we're really not friends with them and our government
isn't so good and we can't admit that. So we let in all these Vietnamese—
and we should let them in because we helped create that war not because
they're fleeing the awful Communist menace. But please don't let the Salvadorans and Haitians in because, gee, you know, those are friendly
governments.

Was I a youngster pretty much like other youngsters? Well, yes and no. I grew up in a household with four adults and five children. My father was a bit older, he retired when I was young. My mother was out there in an executive position in the school district and my father was home. This other couple that was living with us, they were black. They couldn't conceive children. So he goes out and he works at a job and she stays home. The woman helped my mother and my father at home. We called the man uncle, but he wasn't my uncle. You know, he's black and gone off to work and my mother's gone off to work, and the woman's black and my father's white, so I mean, I didn't realize it at the time. I just thought a lot of people lived like this. I didn't realize that it was unconventional. But you know, when I went off to play in the playground, nobody knew I was any different than anybody else. So it's sort of yes and no whether I was different from other kids.

My mother was a great social activist. She was banning the bomb as soon as it was created. She discovered that there was an East Palo Alto with black people about twenty years before the rest of the town figured it out. She decided that people weren't crazy, they were mentally ill, and that we should have a mental illness clinic in the town and that was a great embarrassment to people. She was really my role model with her social activism. People thought she was nuts for wanting to ban the bomb in 1954, or whenever it was. I mean, for the same reasons they think you're nuts now if you want to ban the bomb. So I saw that and I saw a lot of Third-World people come through our house. I didn't realize it was anything unusual until I got older. So she had a big impact on me in all these things. She's still alive and still banning the bomb.

My historical heroes would be Martin Luther King and Gandhi and Olympia Brown. There are some others, but those are the three that pop in my mind right now. Oh, and Jesus. The trouble with Jesus is you've got a whole religious issue. I'll present Jesus as a human being, but then that'll upset a lot of people. Jesus took on the legalism of his day. He had a loyalty to a moral order, a moral God, a moral belief that was more important to him than the letter of the state law. The letter of even the Roman law, or the particular Jewish statutes that may have been around. If that went against these moral principles, he had to stick with his moral principles and it cost him his life.

Olympia Brown is important to me because she is a sort of role model for me in my profession; but I think ninety-nine percent of the American public don't know who Olympia Brown is. She was the first woman in the United States to be ordained by a full denomination. The story of her going through all the malarky she had to go through in seminary and all the fights she had to fight, and her still believing in herself, to me, is a great example. That was principled dissent because everybody told her it was against the rules and she said, "It *shouldn't* be against the rules." And she pushed until there was a new rule. But I mean, as far as the general public, they know Gandhi and they know King and they know Jesus, though everybody knows Jesus differently. Those are the ones that have meant the most to me. Moses was a principled dissenter, for that matter. 'Course it's hard to tell what's legend and what's not legend, but that whole story that human freedom is more important than the pharaoh, then a dictatorship, is a huge image for our modern age.

I believe there is a moral law in the universe, and if there's a state law that significantly denies that moral law, then I have to choose the moral law. The modern interpretation is that, well, the President and the Pentagon must know best because they have all the information, so we should trust them because we don't have all the information. I think we have freedom of choice and I think we have the responsibility to try to choose between good and evil. We have to define good and evil, and we have to compare our definitions with one another's and see if what we say we believe is actually how we're acting. It doesn't matter to me if somebody's a humanist or a deist, or if it's Ghana or America, I think every culture has a set of moral codes. I believe there is a morality that transcends human nature, but I'm not going to try to stuff that down somebody else's throat. I believe there is a spiritual power in the universe and as that comes through human beings, it will have to be expressed through love and truth and service and peace and justice. That's my belief system, that's my religion.

What I was afraid of in the Sanctuary issue was that we'd come to this church vote and the vote would be fifty-eight in favor and fifty-nine opposed, or maybe worse, it would be fifty-eight in favor and fifty-four opposed. It would have passed, twenty-five people would have sent their letters of resignation in the next day, the board would have called me in the next week and said, "Hey, this place is falling apart. We've got to do something. We've either got to rescind the vote or we've got to change our social action philosophy or we're going to lose twenty-five of our stalwart members." And I'd be saying to myself, "God, you know, I really can't change how I do things. I'm gonna have to move on to another church."

Yeah, there were some people who disagreed with us. They recognized that we made a very strong attempt to find a democratic consensus on this issue and they were willing to abstain from the vote because they realized that those of us who were most concerned about the issue had been willing to compromise our position in order to keep the institution healthy. Maybe fifteen percent, maybe twenty percent opposed that the church should be doing it. There was a whole group of people who believed it should be done, but not done by the church. And so they wanted to vote in favor of it when it became a moral endorsement of the Social Concerns Committee doing it. There was another group who thought we shouldn't do it at all, either because they back the President and that's how they look at the world or because they just don't think a church should do this. That group was willing to abstain because they realized we were willing to compromise to some extent.

If the worst scenario had been realized I don't know what would have happened. Maybe I would have stayed and we would have lost ten or fifteen percent of the members and just gone on from there—that's a possibility, that would have been a shock. It would have taken really a year or two for the institution to recover from that. Whether or not I could have stayed after that time, I just don't know. I really don't know. But see, the point is, if our resolution was going to have any impact or power it had to find a compromise that would allow the entire church to stand up and make a moral statement. That's what brought some moral power to what we did because suddenly people saw a little New England church, which isn't known for radicalism, taking a civil disobedience vote giving moral authority to this idea, to this action even. So finding that compromise, to me, was a part of making a moral statement. Because if you make a moral statement just within your own little clique, it loses its power. If you can expand that moral statement to a larger consensus, it gains more authority in the larger community. I think this was easier for the general public to get behind than, say, if we'd taken over the city hall or something.

I think it's a part of American history. I mean, we were a sanctuary for persecuted religious groups in our beginning and we've been a sanctuary for different immigrant groups who fled either economic hardship or actual persecution. Sanctuary has been a part of our heritage. The Statue of Liberty is supposed to be a symbol of sanctuary for the poor and huddled masses. Now she's getting her face lifted with this credit card thing and everything. I mean, it's like the Establishment has taken over our huddled masses. We've had a lot of people call us an underground railroad because some of the refugees end up in Canada with political asylum and we're a stopping ground for them. I'd say we have somewhere between ten and fifteen new members in the church because of the stand we took. And some of those are active in the project.

The number of refugees has fluctuated because it's different from the Vietnamese situation. I settled thirty Vietnamese in Concord three or four years ago with a committee. I was head of the committee and they were legal refugees. But this is a kind of situation where people come and they might stay a week, they might say, "Oh, where do I go from here?" So people pass through. It's not like you get a group and you say, "Here's our group and they're living with us now." It's like people have been coming in and out. But from the beginning, we've never pretended it's any more than a small handful because we don't have the physical resources to handle lots and lots of people.

Some people don't come to some of our events. We had two of our refugees speak one Sunday morning and I noticed that maybe ten people that usually come to church didn't come, and they were ten who abstained from the vote and really didn't like the project from the beginning. To that extent they express their disapproval. But I think the general public has looked at what we've done and said, "My God, they are giving humanitarian help to some suffering human beings and somehow that's right."

Charlie Sabatier

"We don't need any laws, we don't need any constitution, we don't need the Declaration of Independence. All we need to do is treat people with respect."

□ □ □

We are not about to send American boys nine or ten thousand miles away from home to do what Asian boys ought to be doing for themselves.

LYNDON B. JOHNSON

Combat duty in Southeast Asia left Charlie Sabatier with a need for a wheelchair, but it is difficult for me to think of him as confined. The truth is, his mind is infinitely freer now than it was for most of his pre-Vietnam life. In that pre-Vietnam, South Texas existence, Charlie and I would probably not have had very much to do with one another. But in July of 1982 we met and talked in his suburban Boston home and he turned out to be civil, hospitable, direct, and a formidable raconteur. The talking and listening were facilitated by the array of thick sandwiches and cold beer he provided. Late in the afternoon of our day of talking and listening Charlie's wife, Peggy, phoned. He maneuvered his wheelchair out of the house they are remodeling, down the drive, and into his car and drove off to pick her up.

The May 1982 issue of the American Coalition of Citizens with Disabilities newsletter had carried a story about Charlie's successful battle with Delta Airlines over one of their policies regarding disabled persons. The story read, in part:

On March 17, 1982, in East Boston, Charles Sabatier fought with Delta Airlines over evacuation. Sabatier was arrested when he refused to comply with a Delta Airlines safety policy which stipulates that a disabled person must sit on a blanket while in transit so that he/she can be evacuated in case of emergency. . . . When Sabatier refused to sit on the blanket (which was folded), the flight was delayed, and Sabatier was eventually arrested for disorderly conduct.

The court in which he was charged was located in an inaccessible courthouse. Sabatier refused to be carried up the courthouse steps and was therefore arraigned on the steps. The location of the trial was then moved to an accessible courthouse. Charges against Sabatier were dismissed in court when the parties reached a pretrial settlement. Delta agreed to change its policy so that use of a *blanket to evacuate persons will be optional and paid Sabatier $2,500.00 for legal fee expenses, $1.00 of which would be for punitive damages at Sabatier's request. Sabatier agreed not to sue Delta over the incident.*

Vietnam is a central experience in Charlie's life and he spoke of it with excruciating candor. He, like many of the youngsters who fought in that Pyrrhic war, was weaned upon the mythical, Manichean, antiseptic cavalry romance of John Wayne. The appalling realities of the nonfilm firefight catapulted Charlie into two minority groups—the physically disabled and those who are determined to think for themselves. He is glad of the second transmutation but can never really be unmindful of the frightful cost he and hundreds of thousands of Southeast Asians and Americans paid for all of the ancient lessons retaught by that war.

———

You know, it was kind of interesting. I had been writing letters to Delta and to Eastern, who also had that blanket policy, to no avail. Not until I was arrested and I got other people to start writing letters to help me did I get anywhere. Then I asked the U.S. Conference of Mayors to write a letter to Delta because I was going through a training session for the U.S. Conference of Mayors as their consultant, you see, and so they were getting interested in the possibility of maybe being involved in a suit. And then I got the National Easter Seal Society to write a letter and I contacted the Paralyzed Veterans of America, who would be a natural ally because I was a National Advocacy Director for them about two years ago and so I had a lot of friends around the country. I sent out letters to everybody and told 'em what I needed. That if they knew anybody who had been subjected to that type of discrimination, please contact my lawyer, you know, to get affidavits done. We were really doing a lot of research. I'd come home from work and I'd just pound out on my typewriter for probably four to six hours every evening and write to everybody I knew for support. About every two days there was an article in the paper. And every time a new article would come out I would send it out to all the people. To keep the interest alive and let the people know what was going on. I contacted the American Coalition of Citizens with Disabilities because I was on their Board of Directors.

I think Delta just picked the wrong person. I was an assertive person, I knew a lot about my civil rights, and I had good contacts. I knew the General Counsel at the Architectural Barriers Compliance Board in Washington, who enforces the Architectural Barriers Act, and I knew a lot of people in and out of Washington and I was a disabled vet and that was great for media, you know. I think if I hadn't been a disabled vet I would never have generated as much media attention as I did. It was like, here he is, the disabled vet comes home, being subjected to this humiliation, this is not the humanitarian-type thing to do. And everybody started understanding that and empathizing with that idea about the humanitarian aspect, rather than the disability thing. I couldn't have planned it better. If I wanted to take something to show the sensitivity problems that disabled people were facing, I couldn't have picked a better thing than what happened with Delta.

And then immediately after I got arrested I found out that I was supposed to appear for my arraignment at a place that was inaccessible! So here I was faced with this attitudinal barrier, this policy by Delta, and I run up against the environmental barrier, and I'm telling ya, when you read these articles, you'll see it was beautiful. It just was exposed perfectly in the papers and on television and radio. Well, I'll tell you what I would have done if I hadn't been able to generate all that media. I would not have paid any fine. I had never raised my voice, I had never cursed anybody. I was never disorderly. I didn't do anything. I had two attorneys that were sitting next to me on the plane that wrote affidavits for me saying that I had conducted myself in a gentlemanly way. In my heart and soul, I knew that I was not a disorderly person. If anybody was guilty of anything, it was the airline, not me. I was prepared to go to jail over the thing. And if I was ever going to be guilty of anything, it was going to be contempt of court, not disorderly conduct. But I was ready, you know. Our Coalition here in Massachusetts was ready too. It was like, it would have been terrific to have been a martyr. It just would have been great. I mean, what could they do to me, my God, on a disorderly conduct charge! But I could have just generated more publicity if I were found guilty. Even if I hadn't been a disabled vet it would have been a big thing. Because here I would have been, in jail for refusing to sit on a blanket! I mean, that's beautiful. I was the Assistant Director for the State Office of Handicapped Affairs, so I was a bureaucrat or official of the state who was serving time for not sitting on a blanket. It was just too much for the media to pass up. And my wife, boy! God bless her. She could really turn into a PR person, I'm telling ya. She got the media out.

We had fifty disabled people outside the court with signs. We're in the Mass. Coalition of Citizens with Disabilities and the people are really getting excited, I think. They're realizing that their rights are being conditioned on a lot of things, because of Reagan. He's the glue that's binding us together and so they were ready. We have like a kind of hard-core group that calls themselves the National Liberation Front for Disabled People. You know, any time they can picket they're ready. They keep their signs in their closets! So there were signs and they were picketing the court. "Inaccessible court," the signs read, and "Unequal entrance equals unequal justice" and all kinds of stuff, and the television was great.

My wife and I are coming down the street and it's like I'm some kind of Mafia guy, you know. All of a sudden, man, it was like these TV cameras and these people were taking pictures and jumping in front of us and moving out of the way. I'm telling ya, it was a wave of people. It was beautiful. The judge knew nothing about disability law, nothing about Section 504 or reasonable accommodations, or the Office for Civil Rights Policy Statements on carrying people. He was totally ignorant of what he should have known about. And my attorney negotiates with him for an hour about coming down because I'm refusing to be carried up. I'm quoting the Office for Civil Rights Policy Statement and I *know* that Policy Statement. It says that I don't have to be carried up, but if they receive federal financial assistance, they have to provide me reasonable accommodations to their programs and activities to make them accessible to me. It doesn't mean they have to make the building accessible physically, but they can move the program to an accessible site, and that's all I wanted. I'm not going to be carried up, that's just further humiliation. I'm here because I refuse to be humiliated and I'm not about to bow down now. So just cancel this thing and set a new date in an accessible place. I said, "There happens to be an accessible courthouse in the town where I live." But the judge refused to do it. He took that approach, you know, that you're not going to come in here and tell me what the law is. It was the old condescending paternalistic thing.

This blanket thing had happened to me at least a dozen times before, and in the last three years I've flown at least three dozen times. I mean, I've been *everywhere*. I've been to Seattle and Los Angeles and San Francisco and New Orleans and Chicago and any place you can name that's on the map, practically, any major city, I've been there in the last three years. I've been subjected to that probably ninety percent of the times I flew Delta or Eastern. I would protest. I would get on just like this time. I would get on out of the wheelchair and into this aisle chair that Delta, by the way, likes to call the "invalid" chair—I've even written them letters about that. You know, about how language means things. Like you don't call black people niggers and you don't call women broads and chick and honey and you don't call disabled people cripples and invalids. You know, I told 'em what an invalid meant. That that's somebody in a bed, totally helpless. I said, "I'm not totally helpless and stop calling me names." And I'd write them nice bureaucratic-type letters. Yeah, they write back all the time, bureaucratic-type things. They got a standard-type letter, I'm telling ya. They hire somebody, you know, whose only qualification is—can you write a bureaucratic meaningless letter? You know, at least a one-pager. That guy's probably paid twenty-five thousand dollars a year to answer people like me. And I never got anywhere by it, but that didn't stop me from writing them. I had to write to get it out of my system, I think. One of the things I contended was that the whole damn policy was arbitrary and capricious because it happened to me a dozen times before and I always talked my way off the blanket! I'd get in there and argue with 'em and talk about my rights and all this self-worth, dignity, humiliation, and stigma and they'd go "Jesus Christ! Get him out of here. Forget about it." You know, "Just go sit down." They'd go, "Hey, we gotta take off, man!" So they'd say "Listen, forget it." And so that's what would happen. They would just forget about their dumb policy. And so I expected the same thing to happen this time. I mean, they're gonna subject me to this and I'll argue and get away with it. And this time I ran into a captain. The stewardess actually said forget it, and I went down—that's how I got into the seat. 'Cause this all happened at the door of the plane by the captain's cabin when I transferred from my chair to the aisle chair that gets me down the narrow aisle. And we argued and someone behind said, "Forget it." And so we went down. I got in the chair, got in the seat, had my seat belt on, they moved the chair out of the aisle and she comes down and says, "I'm sorry, the captain insists that you sit on the blanket." I said, "Look, you

tell the captain what I told you. That I'm not about to sit on this blanket."
And we went through this whole thing and I argued with every Delta person
in probably the whole terminal over the course of about forty-five minutes
and naturally, you know, this plane's going to Miami and everybody's
saying, "Let's get going!" Yeah, I mean, it's not like it's wintertime and
you're going to Minneapolis. They wanted to get going. Everybody's kinda
wondering. I think the people on the plane, who saw me coming on, see, in
this chair, they figured, this guy is sick or something and they were pretty
nice. Well, finally the stewardess got irritated about this delay and she walks
down the aisle and she used to like stoop down to talk to me but this time
she comes down and just stands there and says, "Look, if you don't sit on
the blanket, we're gonna have to de-board the plane and cancel the flight."
Out loud, see? So everybody said, "Wait a minute, this guy's not sick. This
delay's just 'cause he won't sit on a blanket." So some guy yells out, like
about five rows behind me, "You mean to tell me that this delay is because
this guy won't sit on a blanket?" And she says "Yes!" And he says, "Look,
man, if I sit on a blanket, will you sit on a blanket?" And I said, "No. But
if everybody sits on a blanket, I'll sit on a blanket." And he says, "Well,
why do you have to sit on a blanket?" And she says, "It's for his safety."
He says, "It's for your own good, do it." I said, "Look, seat belts are for
people's safety. *Everybody* gets one. If blankets are for my safety, I want
everybody to get one, Okay? If it's so good for my safety, it's so good for
everybody else's. But if I'm the only one that has to do it, it's like puttin' a
bag over an ugly man's head, you know? I mean, that's a stigma. So the
guy says, "Okay, then we'll all sit on blankets." Everybody says, "Yeah!"
So half these people started chanting, "We want blankets! We want
blankets! We want blankets!" I kinda enjoyed it, 'cause I was getting some
support finally. I was getting a kick out of it, but at the same time I was a
little bit nervous. It was funny except for the fact that the State Police
officer was comin' down the aisle at the same time they were chanting on
the plane. So he says, "Either you sit on this blanket or I'm gonna have to
arrest you." I said, "What charge? Where's the blanket charge?" He says,
"Disorderly conduct." And that got me mad. Disorderly conduct? *These*
are the people chanting "We want blankets," it's their conduct. I said, "If
anybody's being disorderly, it's them. And it's this airline that's treating me
like dirt who should be arrested." I said, "Besides, you don't work for the
airline. You work for the State of Massachusetts, just like me. You shouldn't
be arresting people that are violating some policy they have. This is not a
Federal Aviation Administration regulation. And even if it was, it should
be the feds making the arrest here, not you. You're out of your jurisdiction." Well, he didn't get ahold of all that and goes, "Oh well, I don't care.
Look, these people are gonna have to get off, you're interrupting and costing
them a lot of money. I'm going to arrest you. I'll worry about that later."
I says, "You bet you will, 'cause I'm gonna sue you for false arrest. I got
two attorneys sitting right here, right next to me, and I've got their cards
and they've already said that I haven't done anything wrong and they're
gonna be witnesses. You'd better write down your own witnesses 'cause
you're gonna need 'em." I found out later that I was right. That I wasn't
guilty of disorderly conduct.

But an ironic thing was that the guy who arrested me had a twelve-year-old son with multiple sclerosis who was in an electric wheelchair! When I was in his office taking care of the paperwork we were talking about his son and I said, "I'll tell you something. I feel better about taking a stand and doing this than I *ever* felt about my role in the war in Vietnam. I know that what I'm doing right here is right. I know right from wrong and I know that this policy humiliates people and irregardless of its intention to evacuate people in the event of a survivable crash, and that was even suspect if that was the real intention, it's categoric discrimination," I said. "Because when they see me as a nonambulatory person they categorically discriminated against me because they have me stereotyped as being helpless. I have no problem about how they get me out of the plane, *if* they get me out. I've got a problem about how they treat me *before* the crash. They could put the blanket above the seat in the compartment, they could put it under the seat. Do they think I'm gonna sit there and twiddle my thumbs in the seat waitin' for the stewardess to come back and get me on the blanket? I weigh two hundred pounds! Give me a break! I'm gonna be out of that seat just like I got in it, 'cause I know that when people start headin' for the exits, they're not comin' back for their purse, right? I mean, they're gonna be in the aisle, right down back, and there's gonna be this big cluster of people around the doors jumpin' out and I'll be right behind 'em. There are like eighty-, ninety-year-old people who get on that plane with the help of a walker and their grandson and they help 'em sit down and they kiss 'em good-bye. I'm telling you, if there was a survivable crash, those people, because of arthritis and age, couldn't get out. They'd be more helpless in a situation than I would, but they're ambulatory, you see, so they don't have to sit on a blanket. I mean, I had 'em cold, it was just unbelievable. I could have brought paraplegics in there who can lift five hundred pounds. I mean, I can prove that paraplegics are not helpless people.

If I had been in that pilot's place, of course I wouldn't have done what he did. 'Course not, because I think I have more common sense than he had. I mean, I think I'd realize that if there was really a survivable crash, you're just gonna grab somebody and try to drag 'em out, no one's going to think about which one. I'll tell you something that I've always suspected. In their minds, they didn't just see me as a helpless person, they saw me as an incontinent person. They had probably had experiences of people who were paralyzed and incontinent and they're trying to protect the upholstery of their seats. That's not unusual, that paternalism. You know, I lobby all the time. I'll talk to people a half hour in their office—senators, congressmen—and on the way out I'll get patted on the back like I'm a little kid. I mean, even very high officials. They're so far out of tune with what's goin' on in the disabled movement and the women's movement, the black movement, I mean, they're just so engrossed, I guess, in doing their job, that they lose contact.

I've got a blind friend who we see every once in a while. One day I'm walking down the street with this guy—and he's got dark glasses and a white cane—and a guy pulls over and says to me, "Hey! Could you tell me how to get to the Prudential Building?" Well, I had been here only a year and a half and I know the major roads, but I don't know the names of the streets so my friend starts talkin' and tells the guy how to get there and the guy pulls off and like five feet later pulls over and asks somebody else, 'cause he says to himself, "Blind guys don't know where anything is." But my friend can get around that town as well as anybody else. If anybody's gonna memorize how to get around, he is. But yeah, that's not untypical of the nondisabled population.

One of the things that happens when you stigmatize people is, you see, if I can call people "niggers" in my mind, I don't think of these people as human beings. There's not equality, you know. They're not my peers. If I call a Vietnamese a gook, it's easier to kill him than Mr. Hung Yung or whatever his name would be, right? So we do it. Americans do it, everyone, man. We call people krauts, limeys, gooks, niggers, the handicapped. People are refusing to recognize people as people, as having human traits. It's easier to just stereotype a large group of people than it is to deal with the problems and the need.

We always deal with problems in this country either technologically or monetarily, and that's how this country has decided to deal with disabled people. Hey, I get my butt shot up in Vietnam, I come back here, they're not interested in what I'm gonna do, you know. They're not interested in my head problems about Vietnam or getting over all that trauma. It's later for that. We'll dump some money on you, just like, stay home. But if I say, "Look, later with your money. Stop subsidizing my life, just allow me equal opportunity to make my way in this life to the best that I can and all I want you to do is provide me accessible transportation so that I can get to and from my job, or make that post office that's two blocks away from here accessible so I can mail a letter and maintain my dignity while I'm doing it, rather than have somebody go up and do it for me," they refuse to do that. They'll dump money on you though, so you can stay home.

I don't even know if I could really give an answer as to why I didn't sit on the blanket. I know good people, good friends of mine, who have sat on that blanket, and I consider them to be real advocates. They did it because, I guess, it was like the easiest course to take. Most people's lives, I think, probably are like water. Water runs to the easiest course and most people would prefer to go around a confrontation than actually confront somebody. Oh for sure I would have preferred that. I mean, nobody enjoys confrontation, really. I think you'd have to be sick to really enjoy confrontation. There's a lot that's gone on in my life that goes way back. There's building blocks, I guess, and you see things and it takes time. You are what you are today because of what you were yesterday and the day before. We are an accumulation.

I think by the time I got out of the army, I said to myself, "I'm gonna start making the decisions in my life." Because I was always saying, "I should have listened to myself." Well, I started really making decisions for myself for the first time when I was layin' in a bloody mess in Vietnam. It was the first time, okay? Up until then I'd always been doing these crazy things on the advice of other people. I grew up in a time where we saw too many John Wayne movies, okay? I was a World War II baby, I was born in July of forty-five and I grew up with all this Audie Murphy, John

Wayne type of thing. The good guy goes to war, gets a bullet in the shoulder, meets and marries the pretty nurse, and they live happily ever after. That was war to me—and besides, we always won. We were always the good guys and we were always moral and ethical and all that. That was the propaganda that I was fed all my life, through movies, television. When I was young, "Combat" was the big show. Vic Morrow, who just died, was the buck sergeant. I grew up in South Texas, my dad was a marine in World War II. I fell for it. I don't think that the movie industry really thought that they were propagandizing, but that's what it is. 'Cause you were subjected to only one side. I mean, the Nazis were always bad, every Nazi was bad, every bad guy had a foreign accent. The Japanese were the people who were always torturing people. My God, we'd never do a thing like that! Oh no! But I believed it. I mean, I was twenty years old and I believed it. I had *never learned* to question.

Actually I started questioning before I got shot but that changed my life completely. When I got shot I took a different road, I guess, from the one I might have taken. I probably would have come back from 'Nam and gone back to school and been workin' in a bank with a couple kids, probably divorced, I'm sure, that type of thing. But it's strange, you know. Being shot has made my life probably a lot more exciting. I would have probably lived a normal, average mundane kind of life. But it's like I entered a whole new field. I started learning real fast that disabled people were not considered the general population and I started wondering why.

I learned what things meant and the language and semantics got important to me. I was six foot two, a hundred seventy-five pounds, I'd never been disabled or in a hospital in my life. I had never seen anybody die before, then all of a sudden in a short period of time I'm killing people, people are trying to kill me, then I do get shot and almost killed. I get back and *then* I'm subjected to the worst bunch of crap I've ever seen in my life. I started being treated like dirt. It was ironic. Up until the time I got shot I was like Number One citizen. My country was spendin' *billions* of dollars for me. Thousands of dollars just to train me how to kill, thousands more dollars to send me halfway around the world to save us from "Communism." And they let it thrive ninety miles away! When I got in the army, that's when I started thinkin', wait a minute. Like I'm on this airplane and all of a sudden I realized, this is a one-way ticket! I'd been enslaved to keep this country "free." I'd been drafted for two years and if you don't think it's slavery, you just try to walk away from it! And so I said, okay, number one, I'm a slave, then I say, where am I? I'm goin' halfway around the world 'cause we had to pick a fight with some little Southeast Asian country to save the world from Communism! I had never even met a Vietnamese. I didn't even know what one *looked* like. I couldn't tell one from a Japanese and I'm going to go over there and kill these people? I thought, "This is ridiculous."

I was like twenty-one when I got there and the average age of everybody in 'Nam was nineteen. Which meant that the average age of the infantry, the guy on the line, was about seventeen and a half. And I just couldn't believe it. I just couldn't believe what was goin' on there. And we were goin' around in circles, you know, killin' people, and they were killin' us and it was like no war that we ever had. You never took ground, you never went north—you know, *that's* where the enemy is, Goddamn!

You would think, at least you would like to think, that the religious people would be your biggest dissenters, about things that are happening to the people, but instead they join the status quo! When I was in 'Nam we had this priest and he would never come out into the field because he thought he might get killed! Say, I can dig that. So the Jewish guy wasn't as afraid and he would come out and I went to services there and it was strange. I couldn't understand why *he* was even there, you know. I thought, hey, at least the Christians actually believe in the Ten Commandments. It says, "Thou shalt not kill." It doesn't say "Thou shalt not kill except for Vietnamese" or "Thou shalt not kill unless somebody starts a war in Lebanon." "Thou shalt not kill unless you're gonna defend the this or that." It just says, "Thou shalt not kill." Yet you know Catholics, man! I'm telling you. You know I'm a Catholic. They'll go off to war at the drop of a hat! We've even created "Holy Wars!" And all the priests go with 'em and say their rosaries and beads and bless 'em as they go into battle to kill the other half of the human race, many of whom are Catholics too! It's just nuts, because on the other side, there's another priest over there blessing *those* guys. Instead of the church saying these people got no business here, the church ought to be lettin' people come into their churches and protecting them from going out and getting themselves slaughtered.

There are some things really worth dying for, but it depends. It *depends*. It depends on a lot of circumstances that you just can't put in a hypothetical situation. After a while I think that there are just things that I refuse to compromise on. Those kinds of things are the things I was confronted with at Delta. There are things I've learned in my life you don't compromise on. I got that understanding from Lincoln. When he was debating with Douglas on the issue of whether slavery should exist in some places and not in others, would that be a "legitimate compromise." Lincoln said no, you can't compromise on that. You just can't compromise on slavery. We're finding that out in the disabled movement today. I don't think people understand that. Disabled people have rights with Section 504. Two years ago we had rights in the form of transportation regulations that would provide all new buses. New buses were going to be built and we were going to be able to get on 'em. Now the disabled movement has compromised on that and we got something called "local options," which means local discrimination. You know, they cart you around on a little bus called "The Ride." It'd be like Jewish people being carted around on the "Jew Bus." To me, it's not that you don't compromise during negotiations, but once you've got something, you don't accept somethin' less than what you've got.

I think employers have prejudices and stereotypes about disabled people and feel that they can't deal with somebody that has cerebral palsy who tries to come to a job. He might be intellectually a genius but slobbers on himself when he talks. They don't want that person in the building! And they don't want somebody comin' in there who's gonna make the rest of their people feel uncomfortable. Blind people make people feel uncomfortable, therefore, we have to keep blind people out of here, right?

It only costs less than one percent extra to make new buildings accessible for physically disabled people. But you know, they talk about cost effectiveness. When I grew up in the South, see, I'm old enough to remember seeing two water fountains. One with "colored," one with "white" marked on 'em. *Four* bathrooms, man, in the department stores. I've seen, you know, they had to sit in the back of the bus. They had different taxicab services. Blacks could not come to the theater. Everything, right down the line was segregated—separate systems. No problem with cost effectiveness there! You know, every regulation that comes out says "Not cost effective." It's prejudice. Outright discrimination.

To me, discrimination is like a current of electricity. People keep sending that current out. They keep wantin' to discriminate because people are different from them and they want to be around people like themselves. They discriminate against anything that's out of the ordinary, that's out of the status quo. They would *kill* to maintain that status quo. They will keep sending those currents of discrimination out and I'm tellin' ya, not until every individual principled dissenter blocks those currents will it stop. We gotta just *keep blockin'*.

People think negative. There's too many negative thinkers around here, man. Being creative and positive and trying to have model programs and really showing your commitment toward people, they don't think like that and they don't want to do it because it's a bureaucracy. "I don't have time to do that. I'm not paid to do that. I got too much work to do." Lay it off on somebody else. It's easier to deny somebody a job than it is to be creative.

I think I'm a real religious person, actually. But I'm a real anti–organized religion–type person. I think anytime it gets organized I don't want to have much to do with it. I just can't understand how anybody gets to be an adult and still maintains their hard-core religious beliefs. I mean, I know people *today* who think they're born with venial sin. I mean really! I know people who are still thinking that their relatives who ate a beef jerky on Friday in 1950 are still burning in hell! Hey! There've been wars fought over people disagreeing with concepts like that and then the Pope, you know, changes his mind! And says okay, never mind, all right. You all can now eat meat on Fridays. I just wonder, I mean, what about the guy that was burning for eons in hell? What about him? Is it retroactive? I mean, what's he got to say? Like well, exCUSE me, you know, like I've been frying my butt off around here, the hottest flame in the whole universe and all of a sudden you're gonna change your mind! Of course, I know most about the Catholic religion, but they've all got their hitches.

Priests always give you the same pat answer when they don't know the answer—"It's a mystery. It's a mystery. God works in mysterious ways." I went, just out of my curiosity when I got drafted, to this priest who said anybody was welcome to come see him anytime. So I took him up on it. I walk in there and I say, you know, "I got a couple of questions I'd like to ask you." And he says, "Yes?" Well, I asked him my question about the Ten Commandments. I don't know 'em verbatim, but I probably know 'em when I see 'em. I know 'em when I break 'em! And I says "What is this about 'Thou shall not kill?' What do you think about that?" And I got a piss-poor answer. He went on about, he evaded, never even came close to answering that question. Would not even really recognize that I had even asked it.

And the Catholics believe that their religion is the true religion. I was told if you were not baptized a Catholic and you died, you'd never go to heaven. And what does that do when you naturally think you're better than everybody else 'cause *you* have the true religion and *you* are going to heaven and you are going to see God and your buddy's not? So naturally they're lower than you are on the scale of life. Listen. A priest told me that soldiers could eat meat on Friday because they were soldiers. A special dispensation. Not only could they eat it but anybody at their table could eat it. Now that's boy, hey, big me. That makes me really powerful. I'm tellin' ya, "Thou shalt not kill" and justifying people to kill people and then giving them special rights. That's pretty cool too. If you kill for me, I'll wipe some sins away for you. I mean, that's the religion I was brought up in? Jesus Christ. And they wonder why I strayed from my religion.

I think that we are a nation of dissenters. Our nation was created by dissenters. Anybody that's ever made a major change in this world has been someone who was a dissenter. It's been done by somebody, you know, who you would call an unreasonable person. It was George Bernard Shaw who said the reasonable man looks at the world as it is and tries to adapt himself to suit the world. And the unreasonable man sees the world as it is and tries to change the world to suit himself. Therefore, said Shaw, all progress depends on the unreasonable man. I think that's absolutely true! And it's those dissenters that I think really are like a drumbeat ahead, you know, from the rest of the band. They are the people that are leading. Hey! If there were no dissenters, if there were no "unreasonble" people there'd just simply be the status quo. We'd still be goin' around as cave men. But somebody had to have a better idea. And it seems like every time somebody's got a better idea, the status quo is there to start callin' him names.

Like what I did. People would say, "Man, that was an unnatural thing to do." And it *is* unnatural, because thousands of people have sat on the damn blanket before me. I guess they didn't consider it unnatural. But I'm telling ya, people are going to *have* to start becoming more unnatural, if that's what you want to call it, more unreasonable; less tolerant with those greedy people.

I don't know what makes people principled dissenters. I'll tell ya, you're searching for somethin' and it's kinda like searching for something smaller than the atom. You *know* something's there, but it's those building blocks or the makeup or whatever that substance is that makes people good people or bad people. You know something's there, you're tryin' to search for it but I just don't think that we're there yet. I don't think we know what it is. I don't know. Everybody's different in their intellect, their ability. I'm no genius. I'm not really great with the books. I have to study real hard. I'm not super smart or anything, but I just think I was born with the right genes or something that just gave me good *common sense*. Good common sense to know right from wrong, good from bad and make good decisions in my life. And every once in a while we blow it.

I remember the first time I ever recognized discrimination in my life. I was on a bus and this great big, huge black lady gets on the bus and sits down and faces me and the bus driver stopped the bus and said, "I'm sorry, lady, you're gonna have to move to the back of the bus." And she says somethin' like, "Look I have a right to sit here. I don't have to sit back there. My feet are hurtin' me. I've been working all day. I don't want to walk back down there." Just like Rosa Parks. And he says, "Look, that's the law! Either you sit in the back of the bus or this bus don't go any-where." So she was at that tired, worn-out stage and says okay, I'm ready for a rest. So *she* was a principled dissenter as far as I'm concerned. First one I ever heard of. And she says, "Then you do what you have to do. I'm gonna sit here, I'm tired." So he got off the bus, went to the corner, and got this cop who was directin' traffic, and this cop come on and like put a handcuff on her and took her off the bus. Boy! I thought, what's goin' on here? I never realized, see, up until that time that black people had to sit in the back of the bus. I just thought, they wanted to sit there, that they liked it there. I guess I was about nine. I thought, well, I guess I'm always sittin' near white people 'cause I want to, but I never thought about goin' back there. I just never thought of it. And then, all of a sudden, boom! I started thinkin' about it. All the way when I was goin' home I was thinkin', what'd she do? I didn't see her do anything. I thought maybe she had pick-pocketed or robbed a purse. I didn't know. Why did they take her off the bus? I didn't know anything about it. And so I went home and I said to my mother, "What happened? This lady was arrested. I don't understand. Why couldn't she sit there?" And my mother said, "That's just the way things are. They've always been like that and that's the way they're always gonna be. Don't worry about it. Go outside and play." So I went outside and I remember sittin' on the porch for a long time and thinkin' about it, and *knowin'* that, now, I'm not getting the right answer here. Somethin's goin' on here, you know, like, even if it's always been that way and it's always goin' to be that way, well, why? Why is it that way? That's what I asked. I didn't get any answer to my question and back then that's probably the first time I started questioning like an adult would do. You know, I never thought of that again from that time on until after I got shot and I was in the VA hospital. The nurses were leavin' at four-thirty to go out and stand on the bus stop and take the bus and somebody said, "Why don't we go and take a bus and go down and have a drink with the nurses?" And every-body laughed. Ha. Ha. And there it went—boy! When that guy said that, I went back, back, seeing that person on the bus. And all of a sudden I went, "I don't believe this!" That's the first time that I had ever been discriminated against in my life!

I had been fortunate to live until that time as a white person in this racist society, and I'd never experienced any kind of discrimination, none. All of a sudden I realized—you know my life was so screwed up, it was like a big jigsaw puzzle and I had found one piece to start putting my life back together and I wanted to talk about it. Like, hey! There's a big puzzle out here and I know that if we can fit all the pieces together I'll understand everything that's happening to me. And that was the first significant piece of the puzzle I found out.

Listen, I'll tell you a story. This happened to me in New York. I came back from Los Angeles on TWA and I got to the terminal at Kennedy

International and I was getting a transfer to Delta, okay? It had nothin'
to do with the blanket, but another problem. Delta's terminal is in a
separate terminal. It's about a half a mile around. And there's no curb cuts
or anything. So I get there, it's midnight, and I get my bags on my lap and
I'm goin' out and I figure I'll catch a cab around. So I ask a guy about cabs
and he says, "Well, you're gonna have a hard time. Those cabbies have
been sittin' in line two hours and they want a big fare to go downtown." I
says, "Well, I'll get one." So I went out and I told this lady who was the
dispatcher. "I want a cab." She says, "Where ya goin'?" I said, "Delta
Airlines." She says, "Nope! Nobody'll take ya!" So I say, "Look, then if I
can't get over there, I want to go downtown, stay in a hotel overnight."
She says, "Okay." Cab comes up, I get in, the guy puts my chair in the
trunk and he says, "Where ya goin'?" "Delta Airlines." "Nope. I'm waiting
here for a fare to go downtown." And I says, "Well, I ain't goin' downtown,
I want to go to Delta Airlines." The dispatcher says, "You said you were
goin' downtown." I said, "I changed my mind." He says, "Get out of the
cab, I'm not goin' to take you over there. I've been sittin' here two hours."
"No, I'm not going to get out." So *he* gets out and he takes my chair out of
the trunk. I locked his doors. And he says, "Look, I'll call the police." And
I said, "Call 'em. You call 'em and then I'll sue *you*." I says, "If you call
'em you're gonna be involved the whole damn night, you won't get another
fare the whole night. Either you want to do that or take me to Delta. I
don't know specifically what the law is here but I guarantee you you can't
refuse to take me where I want to go. That's discrimination. Besides, if you
don't take me to Delta, I'm not gonna letcha back in the cab!" And he says,
"Look, man, don't make me break into my own cab!" I says, "I'm gonna
tell ya, take me to Delta or I'm gonna crawl over this seat and drive this
goddamned cab myself over there!" We went to Delta Airlines. That has
happened to me, like, three times! I've locked the door. I'm just not gonna
do that you know. And I know damn well ninety-nine percent of disabled
people would *never* do anything like that because the movement is in its
infancy stage. But we're getting there.

It *bugs* me that people in this country are always talkin' about civil
rights, you know. When I think of rights, I think of something more—a
civil right is something that is written in law and that's all bullshit anyway.
We don't need any laws, we don't need any constitution, we don't need the
Declaration of Independence. All we need to do is treat people with respect.

I grew up about twenty miles from this town called Alvin, Texas, and
there used to be a sign out there—I was in junior high school the last time
I saw it. I think since then they've had to take the thing down. It was a sign
out in front of the town that said, "Nigger, don't let the sun set on your
head." Not until I was twenty years old did I get out of South Texas. I'm not
a racist. I might have been. I remember one time I pushed the button on
the water fountain marked "white" and no water would come out of it, so
I pushed the button marked "colored" and water came out, but I would
not drink it. At that time we would think nothing about tellin' a racist joke
—and laughing. Maybe that's a way of finding out who's a real racist.
Something's happened to me. I don't think I've lost my sense of humor,
I'm pretty funny, I laugh—we've been laughing here—but I just don't

appreciate those kinds of jokes. The important thing was, I think, not just one incident, but I kept seeing incidents like that.

When I went into the army I was in Germany and I had never associated a whole lot with black people before, and suddenly I'm sleeping next to black people and showering with black people, drinkin' with black people and *fightin'* with black people. And I remember we were sittin' down on a cot and it was Christmastime and this one guy who was black got this big long bar of candy with these nuts all around it and he took this big bite out of it and handed it to me for me to get a bite of. Man! It was like somebody had handed me a piece of *shit* to take a bite of. Boy! Did that candy look good! But I hesitated you know, and he says, "Oh, forgit it!" And I said, "Hey, no, give it here." I still think of it and that was 1967 and Jesus! It makes you realize that, you know, they got me. They got a piece of me. There we were, havin' a good time, drinkin' beer and everything's great until I did somethin' like that, and I realized, well here I am, I'm a prejudiced ass. We grow though, we grow, hopefully.

What made me not like what was happening, those jokes, the water fountain, what made me dislike that or understand that it's not right, I don't know. I think that's what you're really looking for. Why would somebody young and immature know in his soul and his heart and his mind that this is not right? Actually I did think about it a lot then. When I would see things like that happening, I would dwell on them. And I could look in the eyes of people when they were being done a number on and I could see it. I could see the hate, frustration, anger and I could see that what was happening here, this policy that would create that kind of reaction by somebody, is a policy that should be eliminated. We should have no policies that create that kind of tension in somebody, that kind of anxiety, that sense of disaster. I think I probably always felt that way. Not just for the racist-type things I saw, but as I grew up if I saw some kid being punished by his father or something, you know, when the punishment far surpassed what was just, if I saw somebody getting beat up on the playground, I was just the kind of person that would kind of go help the person.

I remember one time. It got me in really bad trouble. I was in eighth grade and I was a big kid. I was six feet tall and we had this one guy who was the only disabled person I'd ever met in my life. He had CP and he couldn't talk very good and we were friends. Well, it had been rainin' on the playground and some kid threw him in this hole. Just for fun! Boy, I'll tell ya, when they threw this guy into the mud, it just made me sick and I ran over there to help him and these people were gonna throw *me* in the mud! And then we were both so muddy—it was raining like cats and dogs. And then when we were almost out of the hole, these kids kicked mud in our faces. So I told the kid, "I want to see you after school. I'll get you." And before I realized what I was sayin', I was talkin' to like one of the toughest guys in the school! And later I was sittin' in my class and my knees were almost shakin'. I'm thinkin', "I'm gonna get killed. What do I do now? If I back down now I'll be *dirt* for four years, all through high school." So I said, "Jeez, I gotta go get beat up." So I went over and met him at the drugstore. And I thought, "If I let this guy hit me, I'm gonna die, so I'm gonna get the first punch in anyway." So I walked out of this drugstore door, it was like eight steps down to the sidewalk and the glass door was framed in wood and it was closing behind this guy and he walked out and took that first step and I caught him in midair. I turned around and *smacked* this guy right in the face. I connected so good in his face that I could just feel the guy's nose crack. Blood went all over and he flew back and went right through the glass door. Just flew! And then all of a sudden I changed from being wimpo, like "I'm gonna get killed," to "Come on, man! Let's get going!" Yeah, I was *bad* you know. Next thing I knew, I was worried 'cause the guy wasn't wakin' up. And I'm goin', "Wheow! What power!" Next thing I know, they call the police and I ran. No one squealed on me. I got away with the whole thing. I mean, the guy was so bad, if it had ever been a fair fight, I would have been dead. But the guy had some kind of respect for that kind of power and I just didn't. I had no respect for myself, see, 'cause I had sucker punched the guy, right? I hadn't really used any kind of power and after that he's thinkin' I'm this bad dude, don't mess with Sabatier, man. I had this great big reputation for nothin'. I said, "Thank God, nobody else'd pick a fight with me!" So I never really had much respect, I think, for strength as far as authority over other people. Maybe those kinds of things that happen throughout your life kinda teach that just because somebody has authority over you, has the power to do a number on you, doesn't make them the kind of person you have to respect. I don't think, when you fight, there's anything fair about it. When you fight, it's kinda like war—you win. The *only* thing that counts is to win. You defend yourself by destroying another person, that's all there is to it. I don't care what anybody says.

Another time I was picked on myself. This was in the tenth grade. My mother's relatives lived in Nevada and so I went to high school there one year. Boy! All of a sudden, there I was, going to school in Las Vegas, Nevada, where I was out of the Southern culture and into this Yankeeland and it was quite different. I found myself being discriminated against. It was clear racism on the part of the blacks against me because of my accent! I had this accent, man, and I might as well be tellin' the racist jokes, just by sayin' "How'ya doin'?" And it was their own prejudices. They didn't know me. They never met me. They just wanted to beat up on me. So there I was. I stopped drivin' my car to school 'cause I was gettin' my tires slashed and having to get new paint jobs done. Every day I'd have to fight. Every day at lunch hour. See, I didn't have any friends. I didn't know anybody at the school. I was in quite a situation. I thought, "I'm never going to last out the school year." You know, my *body* can't take it! I can only take so much. And so I went to the principal and *that* was hard to do. Here I am, a strange person in the school. I know before I go there he's not goin' to listen to me. He'll say, "It can't be as bad as you say." And he did exactly what I thought. I said, "Look, just come out there and watch what goes on." And he wouldn't even do that. And every day at lunch I'd get in the line. I thought, "I know what's gonna happen, I mean, it happens every day." It's kinda like when you go out and it's raining, you know you're gonna get wet. Yeah, it's hard to face every day. I mean, it's heavy. It would be different if it was one on one but they'd just be like bees on honey! So one day I'm in the line and this *little* guy comes up to me, *little* black guy, almost a midget, wearing this little derby hat, you know, acting *bad*, acting *real* bad, going out of his way to be antagonistic and shovin' me and sayin' "Hey, hurry up, hurry up." And I thought to myself, "By God, if I'm gonna get killed again today, I'm gonna get a punch in. I know I'm one of these good one-punchers. I'm gonna get this guy." So finally I turned around and I said, "That's *it!*" And I turned around and the little guy had gone! He wasn't even there anymore and this guy behind me was a giant! The little guy had gone—he'd left—he wasn't even there anymore! Oh! They jumped on me and beat me up again and I'm layin' down there you know, and I'm goin', "I hope you guys get a kick out of this," I said, "I can't take it anymore, so just take my life." You know, the old sense of humor. I'm tryin' to make 'em laugh and maybe they'll stop beatin' up on me. I said, "I can't take it anymore, just kill me and get it over with." And you know, they laughed! They started laughin' and they never beat up on me again. They said, "How can we beat up on this guy that's got such a great sense of humor?"

And you know, all that time, I'm layin' there and *not one* white guy would come help me. I'd think, "Hey, I got these natural allies" and not one would help me. Later I'm thinkin' about this and I'm goin' "Wait a minute, I'm white, ninety percent of the people around here are white. This is a small group of black dudes kickin' the shit out of me. Why don't they come help me? I'd help them. And I started realizing I probably wouldn't help them 'cause they're white. I'd probably help them 'cause it's six against one. What is it that not *one* person in this whole cafeteria would come help me? And you know, I think it was a case of they never even considered my whiteness. They considered my foreignness. I was a foreigner. I was from the South. "After all, he is from the South, he's no kin to us."

Another time I had trouble when I left the parochial school and went to public school. So I'm new to that school and I'm goin' through the lunch line and I don't know anybody and some guy just grabbed my finger with a fingernail clipper, the flesh on the end of my finger and I'm goin', "Wha-what?" You know, this guy's got my finger in his fingernail clipper and I looked down and I said, "Er, what are you doing there?" You know, "With my finger?" I didn't start anything! Right? And he says, "Gimme a quarter." I says, "Give you a quarter?" You know, I'd never been exposed to any-thing like that before, I had grown up in a parochial school, see, and they don't do something like that there. And they were like demanding quarters and he's gonna *clip* the end of my finger off for a *quarter*, man! I'm goin', "What? You want a quarter? For my finger? Ooooh, Ooooh, Ooooh." I'm reachin' in my pocket, okay? And I don't *have* a quarter! I got a *dollar*. And I says, "Will you take a dollar?" The guy says, "Give me the dollar." I'm arguing with him, right? I'm sayin' will you give me change?" The guy says, "Yeah." So he takes the clip off my finger to give me change and I socked the shit out of him! Stupid, you know. I said, "This guy is stupid." So I say, "If you ever grab my finger with that fingernail clipper again, I'll kill you." Right? Nothing less than "kill you." So he jumps up and we get in this big fight and then the macho coach comes in, right? Coaches do things like this. "Okay, break it up, break it up, break it up." Here are all the Mexican guys and all the white guys and he says, "We're gonna settle this in the gymnasium." So I said, "No problem," because I was bigger than this guy. I said, "I'll take care of this guy" and actually the guy was a really good fighter. He had more experience, I think, than me. I was just a one-puncher. So he was a street fighter and he was really good but it was even-steven in the gym and the guy says afterward, he says, "I guess I taught you a lesson." And I says, "What are you talkin' about, man, I beat your butt!" And he says, "Bullshit!" And, boom! There we are fightin' again. So what do you fight about? "Yes, you did." "No, you didn't." Boom, you're fightin'.

I enjoyed the fighting and I enjoyed being able to defend myself. That's a nice thing—to know that you can defend yourself. That you don't take much guff. That's good and every kid needs that, at least men in our society need that. It was just demanded when we were kids. If you grow up wimpy, brother! People are going to start stepping on you so you have to be able to take care of yourself. No one ever really got hurt. That's the thing women miss most, I think, the fact that there's nothin' like winnin' a fight. If you get in a fight and you win, boy! The feeling of success and victory and power—there's somethin' about it that is a *good* feeling. And that's why when we get to be adults we get into violence. We like the violence.

It's kinda strange what happened to me. Just killing somebody, you know, is something that you never get over, and when I left Vietnam I think I was more committed to learning as much as I could and trying to understand and be empathetic about people and I gained more respect for human life than I ever had before. I was put in a situation that had little respect for human life—either on our side or theirs. We had free fire zones and in the free-fire zone, anybody walking, you kill. You know, no respect. You don't ask any questions, in the free-fire zone you just kill 'em. And I think killin' somebody close up is more of an experience than doing a number on somebody in a bush that you don't see. You just fire at the bush or something and you walk by and you don't know what happened.

I had some really close experiences where I have actually killed somebody *very* close. And I killed a woman who was unarmed and *that* was somethin' I will *never* shake. We had set up this perimeter and we were there eleven days and every day we'd run out, search and destroy, and come back. Well, it just so happened that there were about thirty Vietcong who were digging these tunnels, and we had caught them out in the open and didn't know it and when we set up our perimeter it was right on top of them. They hadn't dug the other entrance and so they were all closed in. They were like, after eleven days, tryin' to sneak out of the perimeter. They didn't have any food, they'd run out of water and they were on their way out. And it was about four o'clock in the morning. I'd just got off guard duty and I was going to sleep and I heard this guy on this tank next to my armored personnel carrier. He started yelling, "Infantry, there's somebody in the perimeter. There's gooks in the perimeter!" And I said, "Okay, we'll go check it out." So I jumped up, I took a couple of guys from my squad and I went to the other side of this tank and he says, "There's somebody in the bomb crater. I killed two on the side of the bomb crater." We saw their bodies, they weren't moving and we could hear someone in the bomb crater. I had this tunnel light, this big flashlight that we used when we'd go through tunnels, and I shined it in the bomb crater and this guy's got these two big old bullet holes right on each side of his neck and he's breathing, erh, arh, erh, arh, like that, and blood's burbling right out of the holes in his neck and he's *buck* naked and he's got a grenade in each hand and he's layin' on his back and the tanker yells, "Go get a medic." And I says, "There's no medic going to go down there. The guy's dyin', man," I says. "Besides, he's got grenades in his hands. What fool's goin' to go down there?" So the guy calls the medic and the medic wouldn't go down there and the guy ended up, like five minutes later he died. But I wouldn't have gone down there either. And so I said, "Look, let's fan out around this bomb crater." I'm right next to the bomb crater and there's a guy like two feet to my left and two feet to his left there's another and we're gonna walk around this bomb crater and then I realize, hey! I'm the guy that has the light! So I thought, I can use my power here, you know, I'm a sergeant. I could say, "Hey, psst, take this light." But they'd say, "Take *this*." So I didn't say that. I said to myself, "Wow! What am I gonna do?" So I held this light wa-a-ay out to my left and I could feel this guy's hand pushing it back over toward me, so I went way over to my right, where nobody was and I take one step and it was so dark I couldn't see anything and I took one step and this gal jumped up in front of me on her knees and screamed out something, two or three words, and I just *instinctively* pulled the trigger on my M-16 and I just used up a whole ammo pack, twenty rounds, just destroyed her. Blood flew on me and she like flew forward and then backward and she hit me as I jumped down. I thought any second, after that, everybody's gonna open up and this guy's gonna start shootin' back or his friends will or something, but no one did. I jumped down and when I jumped down I jumped on her and I rolled off and I reached over. I was ready to fight this person, right? And of course she was dead and I grabbed her and when I grabbed her I thought, "Boy this is a little person," you know, "this is like grabbing my little niece or something." So, it was real quiet. We just lay there for a second or two and then I took the light and I said, "Let's take a look." And I put the light on her and she had her hair all up on top of her head and I cut this string that she had tied it with and boy! She had beautiful hair. It went all the way down, like past her knees.

Beautiful long black hair. And I searched her and she had this wallet, the only thing in it was a picture of her and a guy that was probably her husband and two little kids and a razor blade, an old rusty razor blade. I don't know why she had that, but that's all that was in her wallet. So I took the picture. We went around and ended up killing three or four more people and capturing about eight others and the next morning, the sun came up and the CO called me over and said, "What's the statistics here?" And I told him how many dead and how many captured and he says, "Was there a woman there?" And I said, "Yeah, there was a woman." And he said, "Was she armed?" And I says, "No, we didn't find any weapons." But hell, I didn't have time to say, "Hey, do you have a weapon?" There were bullet holes in her ankles, in her arms, in her face, it was terrible. So he says, "Well, who killed her?" And I says, "I did." And this fool, he's got one of these guys that we captured and he happened to be her husband. He's in his tent and he's having this conversation with this guy with the interpreter and the interpreter tells the guy that I'm the one that killed his wife. So right away, man, the guy comes *runnin'* at me, you know, his hands are tied behind his back, and I just threw him down on the ground. And the guy just went berserk, you know, crazy. I mean, he was like a chicken with its head cut off. He wasn't comin' at anybody, he just went runnin' into everything, throwing dirt up into the air and kicking and hollerin' and screamin' and like he'd lost his mind, which he did. So there I was, you know, and that night everybody's callin' me the woman killer. Like it's a big joke. You know, the woman killer, it's a joke. That was the heaviest thing that's ever happened to me. And so I think, Jesus, I don't know whatever happened to that guy. Whether he ever got his mind together. I don't know what happened to her kids. I don't know if they're dead or alive. Unbelievable! The next day we ended up gettin' in a big fire-fight and burning down by accident, by all the fire and ammo and everything, all these hooches and stuff and the captain told me that that was the village that this lady lived in. So in a day I had killed an unarmed lady, seen her husband go crazy, and then burned down her village—and I'm the *good* guy! I'm the good guy? And I'm thinkin', I've gotta get out of here." God, she wasn't even armed. She was diggin' a tunnel, you know, carrying water back and forth for these people and what are they doin'? They're trying to get these foreigners out of their country, you know. That was us.

You know, I called them gooks. I used this term and everything. I played that game but I never, never really thought that I was going to be in a position—that's how stupid and naïve I was—I never thought that *I* would really have to shoot somebody and that I would get shot. It was just stupid, just so stupid. I am convinced, I've talked to all those guys, you know, *none* of those people ever thought that they were actually gonna pull a trigger on somebody or that they would ever get killed. You know, what happens is that the country confused the war with the warriors. We lost the war, therefore the warriors are losers. We can make jokes about them. They're psychos, they're nuts, they're baby killers, they're losers! We are discriminated against as much as if we had been the ones over there being killed.

I thought a *lot* about that when I didn't have nothin' to do except think. I was always in the field and sneakin' all the time and walkin' down trails and thinking, what am I doing? If I get killed today, will I go to hell or heaven? Am I guilty or innocent? Am I a war criminal? Am I violating people's human rights? Would I appreciate them in my country doing this? I'd walk in people's hooches and I mean, we'd go through a village at four-thirty in the morning. We don't knock on the door, we walk through and they're sleeping with their wives and babies and they're scared, you know, and you see these people, their faces. I felt like I was the Gestapo in World War II, walking in somebody's house without knocking on the door. 'Course that bothers me. I don't like doin' that. I'm not that kind of a person. But what am I gonna do? Refuse to go on a search-and-destroy mission? Jesus, so all I was hopin' to do was stay alive and get home and never find myself in that position again.

And so I *really* started thinking about all this right and wrong, good and bad and human rights, and what I would die for, what I wouldn't die for.

And I came to the conclusion that there's just human rights. Human rights, not civil rights. And human rights are not conditional. Any commitment to a *conditional* human right is no commitment at all. And that's exactly what we got, we disabled people. Here's a President who says he's committed to social justice and all this business and at the same time it's being conditioned on your ability to get on the bus, or on your ability to see something. Things that really shouldn't matter. And so a commitment for conditional human rights to me is no commitment at all. Exactly none. And I'll do everything in my power to make sure that people understand that if you're gonna be committed toward something you can't talk commitment and in your actions do something else. You can't say you're in favor of affirmative action and then go out and discriminate.

I mean all the people of the different populations should recognize things like that. Not many people look inward. They look outward to see where the problem is. They don't look in and say, "Yeah, I've wasted twenty people off the face of the earth and for what? You know, I'm guilty, okay, from there I'll make sure this never happens again and I'll try to stop it whenever I see it." You know, whenever I see that current of hate or that current of discrimination, or see that president or that mayor or the governor or somebody making bad decisions, whenever I see it, I got to stand up and stop it. At least I owe those people, or their souls that! I have to. I figure, if *I* don't, who will? I owe it.

Bob Sampson

"Unburdened by the torments of the time—
I reach for a happy heart, and pray."

□   □   □

God is my co-pilot.

When former probation officer Robert B. Sampson lost his job under dubious circumstances, much of his world fell apart. The loss of a place in his profession was more than the occasion of a decline in his economic circumstances. He lost his plane and boat, but more difficult to bear was the loss of his self-esteem and his faith in the essential justice of the social order. He feels that his lawyers "took the money and ran," having failed to pursue his case in a timely and vigorous manner. He was prepared to take his case all the way to the Federal Supreme Court, but was thwarted by legal technicalities. Forced out of his profession in his mid-forties, "the first probation officer in the history of Massachusetts to be fired," Bob, now in his mid-fifties, is still seeking full-time employment.

The emotional recall of the depths to which his reversal of fortune plunged him has been a part of every conversation of any length we have had. The equal and opposite reaction to that sense of loss and aimlessness has been an accentuation of his crusader's nature. Bob is a generally unabashed missionary and an indefatigable compaigner for justice and redress in his case. For some time he edited and published Justice, *subtitled "The Revealer," a newsletter designed to expose the machinations of the bureaucracy that blighted his life. He has poured his zeal and anguish into a book-length, privately published account of the history of his dismissal and the legal maneuvering attendant upon it called* The Massachusetts Judiciary Conspiracy?

One of the plates on Bob's 1979 Dodge sedan reads, GOD IS MY CO-PILOT, *and religious fervor is a dominant element in his personality. Bob is a tall, likable, blunt man who watches his diet and everyone else's. Strong, often conflicting triple currents of rebelliousness, conformity, and sentiment run deep in his character. His poetry, his flying, his sailing are all means of balancing these aspects. His standing up and out for justice is also pursuit of vindication from the very system he rebels against.*

———

I want you to feel free, John, to use anything and everything you want to use about me. I don't want to cover up nothing. I've nothin' to hide anyway. I mean, everything will be all right with me, you know. All I care about is when I die and I suck upon my last breath of life and I go before the Judge of Judges—it's not going to be handled in this world by you or me, it's going to be handled, I feel, eventually, when I meet my own death, when my own demise, my soul or my spirit or whatever you want to call it, brings me before the Almighty, He will give all the justice that we'll ever want in this world. I'm sure of it. Now some people will say, "Maybe that's a crutch." I don't know, but if it's a crutch, it's worked well for me. It's kept me going, I'll tell you. It's kept me going through my most trying, difficult times. This is why I think Jesus said why not turn your cheek because I think he realized that there's just no sense in each one trying to knock off the other. You're not going to get anyplace that way. You could go on forever and achieve nothing. There's no solution that way. Now I've found in my own case, since I've done nothing wrong to anyone, different things are taking place. One judge *died*, would you believe it? This judge in my case went off to Florida. He had very little time. Before he could really sit down there in that nice sun and surf and enjoy life and get a nice tan, he died! He was one of the youngest, most troublesome ones. I mean, he didn't care. He just went with what other people wanted. The other judge, the older man, he's got some kind of a very bad disease. He's dying. I just heard about that. And there are other people. There were three others that were giving me a hard time and one of 'em was a captain. He died before he got his pension. All of these people were people who were giving me the business for the benefit of the judges at that time. I'm not saying my own life was perfect but what I'm trying to say is, the Lord will do His own thing in His own time. Now what if I ran off in those days and I decided to kill 'em all? And that thought went through my head, and don't you think it didn't! But through my own belief, my own love, what held me back from the gun and the grenade, what held me back was I have a certain love for people. Like say, it could be my mother, could be my sisters, things of that nature. Because of that particular love—and I believe that my love of God is obviously on top—but in this hierarchy of love, I found that I didn't want to just kill someone or do any of these things. I felt like, you know, it says, what does God say? "Vengeance is mine saith the Lord." And He in His own way will make everything turn out all right for all of us.

I did lose a great deal of my self-esteem so I find it difficult to identify myself now. My experiences were so traumatic and they came like machine-gun fire, one after the other, that it was a miracle I could hold myself together. Even at this stage in my life, I'm just about having some sense of balance, you know. I used to be ambitious. I used to think if I worked hard, studied hard, you know, I would climb the ladder of success. Now all of that crashed down all around me. The only thing that saved my life at that time, really, saved me from a life maybe of alcoholism or doing something really destructive or bad, was my sincere one-to-one relationship with the Almighty Diety. I do believe in the Omniscient and Omnipotent Deity. You know, I'm almost ashamed, apologetic today to say that I love God and I believe in Jesus because we live in such a secular, materialistic world that it's almost a shame. If you'd say to someone today that you like sex and it's a beautiful thing, you can express yourself fully, they'll clap on the Johnny Carson show, but I think if you sit there and try to tell 'em that you love the Lord, that's a disgrace. And this unfortunately is the way our society is at present. Even the priests in the church are basically the same. They're not doing the job that they are supposed to do. But then again, I'm not gonna pick at them. How about all of us? I've been afflicted to such a degree that I find myself having great difficulty getting back within the system now, John. I have no faith in the system. I made the mistake of having faith in the system and that's not a good thing.

A lot of things are assimilated as you grow up. But without analyzing things, to the best of my knowledge, trying to look back and see how I grew up, my mother taught me many things. I mean this idea of love and justice and kindness. The same things I tried to do even to my people when I worked in probation. I did the same thing. I believe in putting myself out for people. Not because of their color or because of a political thing. I went out to help everyone. I got that from my mother. My mother used to say, "Even if there were not a God, Bob, I'd still want to live a good life and help people the best I could." Kind of a humanitarian outlook she had. That's another reason why I really didn't want to become violent. In a way, I had two forces fighting within me. The first one was this idea of my love for God and I had my love for my mother, her memory, you know what I mean. Why should I destroy that? She brought me into this world and tried to make me into some kind of a human being. And then my two sisters who are still alive today and my father—why should they have to endure me being picked up for knocking off three or four or five people? I didn't want to hang my problems on another person. Far better that I die in privacy than to make a situation worse than what it was. The second idea was that I felt that if someone does something bad to me—it's almost kind of a Christian outlook in a way—do I make the situation any better by going down to their level and doing it back to them? Maybe it has to do with pride, in a way too.

My mother was, without the slightest doubt, very important to me. I wrote a poem for my mother one time in anticipation of the day she might die. When I lost my mother it was another terrible thing for me to have to go through. I never thought I could make it, but I kept hanging on only because I figured that the Lord has something that He must want me to do in His own time in His own way. My father is still alive today. He lives with my two sisters. He's just celebrated his ninetieth birthday. He was a district fire chief and retired when he was seventy! My father was always a hard-working, ambitious, quiet, easy man. I remember growing up with him in the days when, not like now, performance meant more than money. They call 'em firefighters now, but in the days when they were known as firemen, they used to *work!* I was lucky if I saw my father four or five times a week! Because of his hours—they didn't work a forty-hour week, they had to go live in the fire station. So I didn't see my father. But my father was always an easy man to go to. He never criticized me for anything. He'd work and come home and give my mother his pay—right away. Every week my mother got the pay. She ran the house. She was the boss basically. My mother was twelve years old when she lost her mother and father, who had come over from Ireland.

If I had done what my mother said, I would have kept my job. She said you should always be in your job like a sycophant. She didn't know that word, but she said, in other words, Bob, give the judge cards on the Jewish holidays, give him little presents and things, and I wouldn't do that. She thought I'd make my job more secure and everything. Yeah, she was right. Oh yeah. I would have been a chief today. I'm sure it would have made a big difference. My mother really gave me damn good advice. Oh yes, the other guys gave the gifts and cards. Oh yes they did. One guy used to— you could check this with the Social Security—he worked in a liquor store. He brought cartons of booze out to the judge. The one who died. You should have seen the stuff he used to be stealing from the drugstores and giving to the judge. They were giving him all kinds of things. They were takin' care of all these people. Sure, I could have given him things. I didn't because I didn't feel it was right. They don't give *me* anything! Yuh, well, that's true, I had the job, but I kinda didn't see it that way, John. I didn't see it as a job for the gifts. No, I figured I had the job and I was doing my job. My job was to be a probation officer and help any of these people who came under my control and that's all I thought about. I had a captain one day—he died—he was always being a sycophant to the judge and this big guy came out to me and said, "Lookit," he says, "you're stupid, Sampson. What are you tryin' to help all these lowly bums for, they don't give a good shit about you?"—I'm pretty close to his words. He said, "They don't care about you. You ought to be like we're telling you, be like the others." I didn't do that and that was a big mistake. He's dead now, that captain. He was a big guy. I told him, I said, "I'm sorry, Captain, but I'm going to do what I have to do. I'm here, I'm going to take care of *everyone.*" My job was to help every person that come under my control. That's why I put the Code of Ethics together. They tried to stop me from doing my job, oh many, many ways, sure. They're responsible for *deaths* as far as I'm concerned. At this point in time, I'd say no, honestly and sincerely, there's no way you can rise in the system and have principles. I knew all these different people in public office. They don't have any basic principles other than to get money, have power, and enjoy a good time.

John Augustus started probation. He was a rich shoemaker and he had a great chance with what he was doing and it was purely altruistic in its nature. Then along come all the politicians, and down the tubes the whole thing went! My plans were to become the chief probation officer, right? And then with two secretaries and a lot of free time, I was going to try to put out a book on probation and a magazine. I wanted to lift us up to the status of a real professional association. And these are the things I wanted to do and I could have done them. Hey! There's another idea I want to tell you about that only God will know the answer to, but I'll just interpose it. I was sent to a meeting one time some time years back, and this man had a Ph.D. degree and I was the only one talking to him. I suggested that we need in probation a loose-leaf type of memorandum book for probation officers and all this stuff. And eventually within a year or two he came out with everything that I suggested. And then shortly thereafter he left and got a better position. Well now, that man was a Ph.D. and he took my idea and utilized it and it was exactly what I wanted done and I never even got a word. In my entire life I never got an ounce of credit for anything I've ever proposed, and yet all these ideas were mine. Yes, that has happened before, hundreds of times, lots of times. Why do I keep doing it? I don't know, 'cause I've got a big mouth maybe, eh? No one told me to bring in the Code of Ethics. I did that myself. I wanted a Code of Ethics because I just figured we should make ourselves professional. See, all of them were always looking for money and raises and all that at the State House. I said before we do anything we should first become truly professional. I thought we needed a good Code of Ethics to follow, something we can rely upon. So I composed the first Code of Ethics in the U.S.A. for probation officers. I posted the first one in my office, along with a prayer by St. Francis of Assisi; they both mysteriously vanished. After a fourth posting, I gave up. My chief of probation didn't like the Code and neither did another man, who was to get my job. He didn't want anyone stealing his thunder, as he was an officer at the time in the Probation Officers Association and very active in political clubs. I realize this now with hindsight. I didn't at the time. What I'm saying is, my Code of Ethics is a *historical* document in the field of probation. These were my first steps, that's all, toward our becoming a real profession, you know, regarding probation. It would have entailed a lot of better bylaws. Well they did that without me. I told them what to do. I wrote all over the country on that. I wrote up the different things to correct in the bylaws, and they did change all the bylaws and that made it much better. See, they used to have all these things, it was all a big farce when I was there, probably still the same thing 'cause it's so political. They would call up, you'd always know when the commissioner was gonna come to the court, things of that nature. Half the reports were all phonied up. They put guys on probation who were that thick with records, you know. That's not what probation is for.

The general consensus of opinion that I have seen is that everybody and his brother really is concerned about the law. They all feel there's a breakdown. The judges have gone down in their esteem, and this is what destroys every culture in every society, really. The minute people don't have faith in their law, this is where you find the cops are going to be crooked, all your politicians and most of your higher people are crooked. Every day you pick up the paper, John, don't you, and read about them stealing. Because if your top officials are bad, everyone down underneath them becomes the same way. I believe that very strongly. I believe that if you have your top people in the right jobs, you know, trying to do what's necessary, honest, and decent, everyone underneath them starts to slowly feel the same way. They say, gee, I don't mind doing this. If something goes wrong this man's gonna be fair, there's gonna be justice. I've found it to be true when I was a policeman that the lower some people were, the less money they had; the poor or the indigent, they are cryin' more for law and order. You take your black sections, or any other damn thing, they want law and order more than I do, or the wealthy or the rich people, 'cause they're the ones that are bein' ripped off. That's where all the damn drugs are and everything else. They want law and order more than ever. I used to go in all those sections way back there when I wasn't supposed to. They said they wouldn't go over to the black sections, who gives a shit, but I *always* went over there. I had no fear of anybody. If they're gonna kill me, fine. See, I didn't have any fear then because if I got killed I was insured—you know, my wife would have been taken care of. Right *now* if I get killed, that's different. But I mean, I had no problem because most of the places I went into everybody was clean, everybody was nice, it was fantastic. And I had my own guys where I had to go and check on them, and I tried to help these people. I didn't care who they were. I tried to get 'em jobs. I made no distinction between anybody or anything. That's the way I worked. When I was in the police I would never take any money. No one could ever accuse me of taking one nickel or anything that was legally wrong from anybody anyplace anywhere. I don't believe in it. Like when I was in a cruiser and there was an accident, we call a specific tow company. They would give you like ten dollars to call *them*. Simple things like that. I thought it was highly immoral. I called it blood money. So whenever there was an accident, everyone wanted to come with me when I was in the cruiser because they would have their share of mine. 'Cause I wouldn't take it. So they did better with me, see. But on the other hand, I would never tell on them either. So in my own way, I have my own things that aren't so perfect.

All of a sudden when I was in the navy I decided to write a poem. Just like out of nowhere. I had never written one before. Never! Didn't care about it. Hated English, everything. I don't remember exactly what that poem was but I wrote a poem. It was probably a very light type of love poem or something, I don't know. It just came out of nowhere. I just decided I wanted to write, and after that I started to think, well, it's a good way to get rid of a feeling once in a while, if you have a bad feeling. I even put one of my poems in my book on the criminal justice system. It's called "Hope," and I ended it as hopefully as I could, but I was very low then. The last lines are,

> Unburdened by the torments of the time—
> I reach for a happy heart, and pray.

But even in the navy I had trouble because they were trying to tell me what to do! I joined the navy because I thought there was a big war on and I had to get over there right away and do my part. It was as simple as that. I wanted to be a scuba diver. I loved swimming. I was an excellent swimmer and I was in good shape then and I later on did do scuba diving; but the navy wouldn't let me do it. So when they said they wouldn't let me do what I wanted to do, I said, well, hell, I won't do what *you* want me to do. So when the officers would try to tell me what to do, I just told 'em what I thought *they* ought to do! That got me in a lot of trouble. No, they did *not* take very kindly to that. I remember one time the captain of the ship said to me, "I can't send you over there 'cause I don't think you have the discipline. I think you'll kill our own men or something." That was a hell of a judgment for him to make. I could have killed *him* right there! They kept me on this ten-thousand-ton light cruiser. Near the very end, though, I said this is stupid. I'm not going to keep fightin' this system! So I *joined* for a while. I said yessir and nosir and did everything like that, and they said, "My what a good boy you are." So they ended up puttin' me on a goodwill cruise and they gave me an honorable discharge 'cause I did everything fine.

I've tried very hard all my life to be a conformist. I want to do like everybody else does. It just don't work out that way. I've always tried because I'm not stupid. You're outside the circle and you're looking in all the time. There's a big snowstorm out there and you're in here nice and warm and I'm looking in the window, freezing. Inside me, there's a little conformist trying to get out! I know a guy I consider a conformist. A friend of mine. My daughter, one of my daughters, is a real conformist. They do everything that you would expect them to do. You know, if it's go to church, they go to church. If it's to have a martini at five o'clock, they have a martini at five o'clock. To be a conformist is to be socially acceptable. I conform, believe it or not, every day. I'm wearing my clothes when I go out, for one thing, all right? Because of the law. See, I have to be practical! Where does conformity get to be cowardice? When you go against your own principles.

When I was a kid, often times there'd be different kids that might have said to somebody else, let's not talk to this kid; but I always did. I would never be a part of that. I always seemed to try to work for the underdog. I never in my life organized anything like that, no. I was never a victim either but I wouldn't become part of it. I didn't want to be part of it. Let's say there was a kid down the street and two or three would say let's not play with him, let's keep away from that guy. I would say, "No, I'm gonna do what I want. I'm gonna see him if I wanta see him. The hell with you!" Well, I can remember the last one. I remember when I had this little Jewish kid, he was smart, they were all tryin' to shun him. This was in the navy at Sampson, New York. You know, my own name. Sampson was the guy, I guess, who was takin' coffee at the Battle of Manila or something. He was sippin' tea when he should have been doing something. Anyway, I paid for trying to help that kid. They wanted to keep away from him because he was a Jew. It was a simple, stupid thing. But I think it was envy and jealousy because the kid made Officer Training School. So they said, what the hell, he's a Jew, and they started picking on him. So I started defending this kid, and these guys were stronger, you know. I'll tell ya, so they grabbed *me* and they said okay, you like it so much, you wiseass, and they got me into the shower in there and they had these big heavy brushes you know, and they gave me what they call a GI shower, which I didn't need, you know, I was clean!

It was upbringing, that's all. It's just the way my mother brought me up, that you don't do those kind of things. It would be hard to find a woman as good as she was. If you wanted a cup of tea, she didn't care what color you were. We had all kinds of people coming over there when I was a kid.

I know I have to work within the confines of society. But I figure that it's a big, wide highway. There's three or four lanes on that highway and I'm just choosing my own lane, that's all. But I'm still on the highway. I'm not trying to really go too far afield because you know, you can't live in the world when you're trying to fight it all the time. And I'm getting old now. I'm beginning to lose that sense of independence. I'm tired of fighting the system. That's what it really is. But I'm satisfied in my own way. My biggest wish is I want to communicate to masses of people so that I can try to get my thoughts across. People want to talk about it— radio shows, talk shows—but very few people want to become really involved today to fight against the politicians, the judges, and the attorneys, and this is the biggest problem I can see. It's gotta be done through the people in colleges in particular, because if you can get the idealistic kids while they're in school and in college, you know, in the younger grades, you might be able to instill in them a sense of justice whereby when they get out into the world they might be able to slowly but surely at least do something about correcting the injustices that do exist in our criminal justice system. My case is only just another example of the injustices going on around in the world. But I'm a prime example, if only for the fact that I tried desperately to try to solve the dilemma that existed in my society, and with very few people knowing about it, I went down the tubes. We might have had different ways of getting our judges, a different way of these judges administering justice, a better sense, a much, much better, more fearless equitable sense of probation. Probation is not run anywhere near the way it should be. I wrote the book and I'm doin' things now to the best of my ability, right? But it's like dropping little pebbles in the sea.

Sarah

"I don't think most people feel that they can question the Henry Kissingers of the world . . ."

□ □ □

Despite Reagan's "global limit" of warheads concept, tension is on the increase. The international implication on industry is a world-wide missile market in full expansion.—Conference Program, New Trends in Missiles Systems and Technology, Boston and Washington, December 1983

Out of regard for the feelings of some of her family members, Sarah chose not to use her last name. She is a small, pixiesque grandmother with a pleasant alto voice. Her husband, Ben, first acquainted me with her principled dissenting and later I read local press accounts of her activism and invited her participation. She arrived at my house in a pickup truck and as we talked we ate bowls of creamy, chunky fish stew and crusty bread while the forgotten platter of raw vegetables that my wife had prepared and left for us languished in the refrigerator. Inspite of, or perhaps because of, her particular upper middle-class rearing, much of the dead, defensive decorum of that class has yielded to a warm appreciation of the human condition. Though a guest in my house, Sarah served the stew, cut the bread, and found her own ashtray in a house where smoking is a failed addiction.

Sarah impressed me as a woman in whom the elements of reason and mild whimsy have combined to produce an amiable activist with the courage of her organic convictions. Her campaign against the increase and diffusion of weapons of mass destruction is being waged primarily for the benefit of her numerous progeny. Like so many other women I have listened to, she feels that the preservation of life-sustaining conditions upon the earth is a uniquely feminine responsibility. She is basically a proponent of what is loosely known as "the system," but she believes that important elements of that arrangement are seriously imperiling the global chances of survival. She feels a high responsibility for the exposure and abolition of these potentially fatal systemic imbalances. I have the impression that the exercise of those lofty obligations is still the occasion of no little chagrin for Sarah. Being in any sense a public person runs counter to a basic bashfulness that is an element of some considerable strength in her character. Tending her various grandchildren appears to be one of her more constant conventional activities, but this heavily engaged activist grandmother finds some time for the very private satisfactions of the piano. One morning as we talked on the phone it became apparent that when I called she had been attempting a Mendelssohn caprice "for her own amazement."

Shyness notwithstanding, Sarah has summoned the fortitude to address the quirky and contentious forum of a New England Town Meeting and has been dragged literally and very publicly through the mud for her beliefs. Nevertheless she appears to be in no way ready to quit the fight.

———

I come from what you might call an upper-middle-class background. I had a pretty conventional upper-class kind of childhood. Private schools, a kind of, I suppose, wealthy environment. My mother and father were very social people. We lived in a large house with servants. Except for a very few years of my life I was always in private school. I went to dancing school, I lived in a society where the children were debutantes and all that kind of stuff. I don't know much about poverty, shall we say. I was a spoiled brat is what I'm trying to tell you. That's my background. Pretty dull as a matter of fact. My memories of my childhood are a lot of being home with the maids and being alone a lot in the evenings when my parents were out or being upstairs when the company was there or in the kitchen, so I have a feeling that my parents' social activities were a big part of their lives. Looking back on that, I think it's motivated me in a lot of ways, so maybe in the end it didn't cost me anything. I think it did cost me time with them, but I don't remember regretting that at the time. I don't think that I longed to spend any more time with my parents because they always had neat maids that I liked to be with.

If I were to go back and think about some of the more motivating things that have gone on in my life, I think it was my relationship with the servants in our household. I was the youngest of three girls and I became so emotionally involved with these people that I just fantasized about going to live with them. They were going to take me away. The only reason I play the piano is that we had a, I don't know what you call him, a butler? Well, he wasn't a butler but he drove our car and took us to school, and he played the piano. And when my mother and father would go out in the evening, he'd play the piano for me all night long. I never was able to really play the piano, but he was handsome and he could play the piano and he was just my idea of everything a man should be. Money separates people. In my first marriage it certainly separated me from my husband, and I think people with money are distrustful. They never know whether they're being used or exploited in some way. There's just a lot of things that make it not all it's cracked up to be. I think that the foundation of a lot of the things that I do with my feelings about people and my life, as I've chosen to live it, has been my relationship with the servants of my family. And I didn't really realize that until a few years ago.

My husband left me with six children when I lived in Florida. I had this woman that came in who was black and she was a wonderful woman and I just realized how much I loved her. I was living in this very kind of snooty area where they weren't very nice to me because I had six children and there was no man around. So I began having her children and her grandchildren over. And I had a gardener too and he would bring all his boys over to my house and I had all these children and they had such a wonderful time. So the neighbors started to call my house—the address was Five Harbor Point—they began to call it Five *Harlem* Point. And I just was at odds with everything around me. And the more I was at odds with things, the more it became a game. My environment was really, really hostile toward me, and I felt a real identification with these people who really seemed to care for me. We had a lot of fun together and I would go to their houses, too, with my children. This area was in Miami, Key Biscayne, where, you know, Mr. Nixon lived. They didn't have any black people there and I became very upset because when I first moved there they wouldn't let my friend Lillie May sit at the lunch counter. My children and I, we all boycotted the drugstore and, anyhow, by the time I left that place, they just about ran me out of town. But looking back, I said to myself, well how come I feel so warmly about these people and so at odds with all these other people? And that's when it came to me that that's my background and the things that seemed to me warmest and most comfortable in my childhood were the people who worked for my family.

I grew up in West Hartford, Connecticut, and my father's family has a history of some note, I guess. Some money and prestige. I was brought up on family portraits and they tried to make me cognizant of my background, which I never was very interested in. I'm more interested today about where I came from. I suppose because you kinda obviously try to come to terms with yourself—why you do the things you do and all your biases and compulsions and whatever—when you get to be old. I'm fifty years old and I started to try to figure it out. I was a rotten kid! I was a bad kid. That's why I wonder whether I'm in the right context for your interviews because I'm not sure whether I march to a different drummer. I think to be against the nuclear arms race is pretty plain and simple and I think anybody who has one ounce of intelligence realizes that we're doomed. So that doesn't take a lot of individualistic thinking, but to be ready to jump up and down and run out and lay down in front of traffic about it all is probably the product of being a naughty child.

I didn't become really active in the disarmament issue until about three years ago. I was vaguely aware of the mounting dangers of the arms race, but I was too involved in my own life. I have nine children now, and they were all growing and going through teenage years, and my life was just so centered in their lives that I didn't really have any energy left over. I have a daughter who lives in Berkeley and three years ago she began to talk to me about disarmament. She was involved in things that go on at Berkeley and I was, at that point, going to be a grandmother, and I figured I was responsible for a lot of lives and, obviously, for the potential for an enormous amount of lives, so I just joined up with a group here that is really an offshoot of Helen Caldicott's Women's Party for Survival. I think they have a very real theme that has a lot of value and I think that women have a basic vested, real, essential interest in the survival of the race. I think that women need to be turned loose on this issue, on every issue. I think that they need to do it within the framework of their feminine understandings, rather than competing in a man's world. I think that there are certain essential traits that women can bring to bear on this issue. The other night there was an article in our local newspaper to the effect that, don't be fooled, those Syrians are not like us. Anybody who thinks they're liberal and that these people can be compromised with and we can all work it out, is crazy. I feel that may be true of the men, but I've spent most of my years raising my own children and grandchildren, and I bet my bottom dollar that Syrian women who are doing much the same thing as I have been doing have very much the same instincts. A lot of motherhood is instinct, so I would bet that I would have a great deal in common with most any Syrian woman who's raised children. On the other hand, I think men, because historically they don't do the child-rearing, can become very, I suppose, nationalistic, and they have become very different from one another in terms of cultural mores and culturally acceptable ways of thinking and acting. So I think men are much more likely to be different from one another, while women have this binding thing that cuts across not only the nationality but the cultural background.

One of the things that I think I was aware of very, very soon in my family was that we were not an emotional family. I was an extremely emotional child. I cried at everything. I was either caught giggling in the back of the classroom or crying. Nothing was just in the middle; but in my family we're not emotional. You just didn't cry, there was no talk about feelings. Oh sure, there were feelings, but I had a baby sister die and I don't remember anybody crying. I just don't remember how they dealt with it, although I remember how *I* dealt with it. But my father made it very clear to me that when you're grown up you control your emotions. I remember one time standing on a staircase and spitting at my father, which is a *naughty* thing to do! But you know, he would make me so mad! I just was full of emotion and there wasn't any allowance for that in my family. Still today I think that that's what makes me lose my cool with my family sometimes, even though they're lovely people and we stay close to them in some ways, except that we don't share our emotional lives very much. My father came from a navy family and I imagine it's due to the military mind, or whatever. I mean, how can you be thinking in terms of warlike things and be very emotional? I just don't see how you could do that. The two things don't mix. So I imagine my father came from a background of playing down that side of his life, and he certainly passed that message to me that emotionalism was childishness and to be grown up you'd better lock that up and stiff upper lip is being a grown up and being better able to get on with the serious things of life. I'm the big crybaby sap in the family. And I get angry too, so I'm kind of perplexing to my father, I think.

I have two sons now who would be eligible to be drafted, and they're so *young*! They're babies! And it seems to me when we start looking back on our whole involvement in Vietnam, we did it on the backs of kids who were so young that they were just programmed into a way of thinking, a way of *doing*, not thinking. That's it. They *weren't* thinking. My eighteen year old now is so young that I could see very easily how he could go to boot camp and learn the rules and regulations of what's expected of him and probably be guilty of the most horrendous crimes, because he's too young to be thinking about it much.

I don't think I'd put myself in that classification of people that you mentioned, of principled dissenters. There's certainly people here that are maybe not more active than I am, but possibly more effective than I am in the Peace Movement or whatever you want to call it. They're more knowledgeable than I am, better public speakers, and better at giving interviews and dealing with the press. I imagine that principled dissent is some kind of truth that you've come to feel is worthy of sticking up for, some kind of principle. It's interesting to be in the Peace Movement because of course we're always trying to evangelize and get more people to speak up, but it's just like getting people to come around to a religious point of view, you know, becoming a Born-again Christian, or whatever it is. It won't happen until it really becomes a truth that *they* are coming to grips with. We've had a terrible time getting new people to join in. I mean, you can show movies and you know the evidence seems to be piling up enormously in favor of the fact that we are heading toward annihilation by being such idiots. But you can't get anybody to believe that until they're really ready to believe it, and so I think that the idea of evolving toward a principle that becomes so real to you that you're willing to really stand up for it takes time. Nobody can figure out anybody else's way to arrive at it. I arrived at it just by being pushed into the realization that I was going to be a grandmother and that I had raised a lot of children, and that maybe I had no business raising so many! But the fact was that I had a lot of children and that they probably were all out there, you know, with the potential of multiplying, and that I had a lot to answer for in terms of not having stood up for what people have been telling us all along was the insanity of our nuclear arms build-up. I guess we've all been told that and the evidence was in way back when I was in high school in the fifties. But I became very wrapped up in my own sphere of life and I didn't do anything about it. So a kind of guilt, I think, got me going and right now I think that it kind of clears my conscience to do as much as I can. I'm not well organized and I'm not as well informed as I should be, but my intention is to spend more time with this issue because it makes me so angry. I would do anything, just about anything. I don't know how brave I would be in terms of risking my life, or whatever, but I suppose it is a principle with me.

When I first got into the movement, I realized that I was going to have to get over a deathly fear of getting up and speaking in public. I've been called upon to speak in front of school boards and town meetings and women's groups. I introduced the Nuclear Freeze resolution as an article in my town. I presented that and had a big run-in with our Town Moderator. At that time—I guess it was eighty-one—the concept of having to deal with such a national issue at a Town Meeting was really unfathomable to the moderators of the towns, and they didn't think that this belonged in this kind of a forum; so there was a lot of opposition from the people in authority in the town. My first time in making a presentation at our Town Meeting I got up and it was a very, very long meeting. I got up finally maybe at twelve-thirty in the morning and read our article, which was a resolution endorsing the Bilateral Nuclear Freeze. The Town Moderator was so incensed that he struck his gavel right down in the middle of my speech, saying that I had spoken too long. Then he dismissed himself from being Moderator and appointed somebody else to moderate in his stead. And he came down in the audience and asked to be recognized and got up and did a job on my presentation. He didn't think that this kind of thing had any place in the Town Meeting forum, that we were there to discuss and vote on local issues, and that if we allowed a precedent of introducing national or international issues into the town meetings, then who knows *what* we might get off on next year! In fact, the outcome of it was that people were so incensed about the way he had conducted himself that there was a movement in the town to have a special meeting to reconsider this issue all on its own. We had to gather signatures and go through a whole lot of hullabaloo, but we did it again and the second time, it passed.

The second time I've done what they call direct action was at Avco Enterprises, where they are making components for the Pershing and the cruise missiles that will be deployed in Europe very soon. I wonder about why you do such things. Why I would do such things as literally laying down in front of traffic to prevent the workers from going to their jobs, and being dragged away by policemen, who, you know, like to throw you in a puddle and when the minute they throw you in the puddle you get up and run right back, they pull you away again and say, "Lady are you crazy?" I have to laugh at this kind of thing because right then you're puttin' yourself really on the line. I mean, for instance, the day we did it, it was *pouring* rain. I mean, the rain was just absolutely awful. We were just the most bedraggled-looking group of people, and the police are out there, and I guess Avco had already decided they weren't going to make any arrests because that would be embarrassing. So they just hired an enormous amount of police. We had city police and state police and registered police, and there must have been maybe a cop for every two or three of us! You know, they've got dogs and they've got their battle gear on, and here we are, doing these outlandish things. You couldn't convince *anybody* of *anything* looking the way we did and I suppose acting the way we did. I mean, when you're standing there and the rain is drenching you and your hair is hanging in strings and you're running into traffic, you don't look like you've got too much of a straight line on anything! I think that appearances are certainly important in terms of the way people accept you and take your advice. One of the things we did at Avco was to bring a banner. We had been at a rally the day before and we had made a banner about ten feet long and eight or so feet wide. We had laid this large banner out in the park and all the children who were there at this rally came in with magic markers and they all drew pictures on it. "Boom Boom," "Missiles," "Ban the Bomb," and stuff, and everybody did their little part. It was all in colors and had all these kids' drawings and then we had written on it—I don't know, something like "Avco Works for War" or something. Well, we were gonna put this up on the fence, way up on the hill near the plant for the workers to see. So we had our banner and we were tripping up the hill and the police spotted us and threw us down on the ground and took our banner and threw it onto the ground, and that was the last we ever saw of it. Then they dragged us quite a distance down the hill and threw us into a puddle and by that time we looked kind of bedraggled. So I feel that there's only a limited amount of effectiveness to this activity. Unless we can talk a *lot* more people into doing this kind of thing, which I don't think we can. I'd like to be able to, but I've never been able to talk *anybody* into doing this kind of thing! The small numbers of people that are doing it now are having some limited effect, but even the press as they cover these direct actions don't really take them very seriously. No, I'm not going to stop doing this. I'm going to do it because it really makes me feel good. I feel empowered by doing it and I like to do it. And I feel so angry that it just feels good to get that anger out in that way. No, it didn't feel good when I was in the puddle, but emotionally it felt great. I think that we have done so much in terms of circulating petitions, standing around, you know, having yard sales to raise X amount of dollars to get our newsletter out, and all this kind of thing, and it seems like kind of pussyfooting around the real issues. But when you are really out there fighting you feel, ah, this is how I *really* feel about this. It's almost an indulgence for me because I don't think it's gonna convince a lot of people, but I do it for my own satisfaction, I guess.

As I say, I was an ornery child and I did a lot of things that probably had some roots in the fact that I was a dissenter. I remember going to the window where Brownie Scouts were meeting and making faces. I don't know where that came from. A lack of respect, maybe, for Brownie Scouts, debutantes, and things like that. No I didn't come out. I was supposed to but the whole business is just so awful. It's just *awful*. I had made that decision and my family went along. I guess I saved them a lot of money. Then I went to dancing school, Miss Ritchie's Dancing School. You wore white gloves and you had these little velvet dresses that had 108 buttons on them and you went there in the afternoons. You started maybe in the third grade or something. You learned to dance. You learned to go in your Mary Jane patent-leather shoes and white gloves. You were supposed to learn to go and curtsy and behave yourself. All the "nice" children in town went there. You learned that you weren't supposed to be goofing around in the cloakroom. Miss Ritchie had a little whip and if you did that stuff she whipped ya right across the you-know. So this was I guess, the nucleus of the group that eventually belonged to the Junior League and that were the debutantes. I don't know who decided on who could be a debutante. I think you were invited. And then I guess after you accept your family gives a party and they invite the appropriate people to come. Then it culminates in a big dance where all these young women are presented. Their fathers come out and present them to society. They all wear white dresses. Yeah, they present you to all these people who were picking their noses in dancing school! Then, I guess, technically you were able to date and be courted and all that stuff. Before then, God knows what happened! I think it's still goin' on today.

I probably don't regard not coming out as principled dissent. I didn't want to do it. Maybe there was some principle about it because I didn't like that whole scene then, but mostly I wouldn't have felt comfortable doing it. The dancing school was horrible too. Everything that had to do with that side of life, I guess, very quickly I learned to make trouble in it. In dancing school I was selling Double Bubble in the cloakroom.

When I was married for the first time I married a man whose family were somewhat into the social scene in a small town outside New York. That little town was the snootiest, awfullest place in the world, as far as I can see. It's, I guess, a preplanned town with all beautiful homes and everything was just perfect. The whole town, without exception, was just coiffured and outrageously wealthy. My in-laws came from that town and they gave us a membership to a club there and you had to dress in white. They played a lot of tennis and it's where you had receptions and played tennis and golf. And it was where all the attractive people went to do whatever they did. And I just couldn't stand it. All my bad self would come to the fore when I went there! They just seemed to be such an ingrown, snooty group of people, I just didn't like it. So that was a time where I used to maybe dissent somewhat. I don't think it was principle, but I certainly dissented. I'd come down there in outrageous outfits.

I dressed funny, I guess, just to show my disdain for all that money. *Dressing* was the main thing. Dressing inappropriately. My in-laws were friendly with some prominent people. We were supposed to meet them in New York at some very, very snooty men's club, and I remember coming into that meeting in sneakers and very inappropriately dressed. I think that in many ways maybe my dissenting wasn't very principled, maybe it was more naughty than principled.

You could name Gandhi or people like that as principled dissenters. I mean, having not known them personally, it's difficult to say. It is hard to evaluate the lives of people you don't know. For instance, someone like Jane Fonda is an interesting person. I'm realizing how ahead of her time she was and how much she really risked to do what she did through the Vietnam era. I know she went to Emma Willard, she had the boarding school background you know, and I know just how much she had to deviate to do that. And sometimes I wasn't even that sympathetic with her because she almost scared me with her vehemence. At that time she was a little harsh, to me. But in looking back on it, I really admire her gutsiness.

I guess I would permit the Nazis to march. I s'pose when you're just talking you can say a lot of stuff. When the Ku Klux Klan was marching you certainly could see why your sympathies would be with somebody who tried to run out of the crowd and strangle one of those guys, but I guess I agree with the principle of it all. I don't know how I would act if I had been there, or especially if I had had someone in my family involved.

I think we are in this awful situation that we're in now because we've just so long been conditioned to obey our fathers and the people above us and behave ourselves, and our school systems and our whole way of life has taught us how to not make waves and behave. I think Americans, particularly because we're not as well educated as we might be, feel insecure about speaking up. They feel that there's always somebody who knows more than they do and that they don't really have the *right* to say no. I think that that might be why I finally took action in the nuclear arms issue, because it suddenly came home to me that you don't have to be too brainy to know that this is just morally wrong in every precept. But I think that American people by and large have been intimidated by leaders and I think if you're well brought up you just don't dissent. Yes, I think what happened in Nazi Germany could happen here. It has happened here in a sense. In our hearts we know what's going on in Central America.

Right now you've got seventy percent or maybe more of the people polled in this country saying we don't want any more of these weapons being made. We want a freeze, and yet there doesn't seem to be any real outcry when our government goes ahead just like it planned to in the first · place and takes our tax dollars and develops the most incredible devastating war weaponry you could ever conceive of. It doesn't seem to really cross people's minds that we've said no, we don't want to, yet our government is going along as it pleases. There is a great contradiction here, and I think that people have just really been afraid to stand up and be counted. I think it just takes too much work. It's incredible when you realize that what makes our country go is money. Investments and big business and all these contracts—government contracts, Department of Defense contracts. They've all been made, they're in the works. I mean, who's gonna back out of 'em? You know, for the public to stand up and stop this thing is like stopping a boulder running down Mount McKinley. I think that the people are an awful lot better than they're willing to give themselves credit for. They know better. It's not just that they lack courage, they don't have the security or the faith in themselves.

The conference that we recently picketed was being held by a marketing company that I guess is located in California. It was a two-day conference with representatives from the Pentagon and Raytheon and some of the Route 128 technical industries. The subject of this marketing forum was how to market missiles to Third-World countries, how to compete in a market that's highly competitive, how to make missiles within the price range so that these countries can afford them. It was an astoundingly provocative program, to my mind. When you're talking about the so-called nuclear arms race, this is really, I suppose, the real nerve center of the whole situation. You could get a little glimpse of the commitment of these firms and the so-called military-industrial complex really at work. The Committee Against the Euro-missiles in Boston heard about this conference. We got word of it and decided to take part in this action. What they wanted to accomplish in this case was to let people know about this conference and what was going on there. But in terms of how each affinity group functioned there wasn't one overall leader or anybody calling the shots. Each affinity group on their own did whatever kind of disobedience they thought might be effective. I was prepared, I think, to endure some hardship in terms of being dragged or whatever. I was prepared to spend some time in jail. From a practical sense you have to kind of arrange your life. I mean, things like how long can you stay away from the rigors of home? My big commitment now is really to my grandchild, whom I have on a daily basis, and I had made arrangements with a woman who also is in the Peace Movement to sit with him. And I think my husband's very, very sympathetic and would have taken time out. I think obviously once you go this far in terms of getting involved with people that are intending to do civil disobedience, you've already kind of committed yourself to a certain amount of time and energy. That's a foregone conclusion. There will probably be a certain amount of inconvenience and time spent, whether it's in jail or going back and appearing at court or whatever.

I thought the Boston police were, by and large, quite gentle and reasonable, except the ones who initially threw us in the paddy wagon. We really had not committed any civil disobedience at that point, so I think they jumped the gun. When it finally came to trial they didn't have a case. I think that what they had meant to do was just clear the streets. In doing civil disobedience the big challenge is to really do it in the spirit with which you have initiated your action, which is out of a sense of caring, and to be confrontational really kind of defeats the purpose. I don't think the ends justify the means. I think the big challenge for me, really, is to keep my cool and be a lady and, you know, be gentle. And I think you can make a pretty good point that way. Being there was confrontational enough.

The morning of the action there was a sense of excitement. We drove over at about seven in the morning and we could see the minute we got down there that there were horses and paddy wagons all waiting for us. We had decided that we were going to sit down somewhere and block people from going into the doorway, but the whole exact strategy seemed somewhat cloudy to me. We hadn't had any practices. We heard that the police department was out in great numbers and were waiting for us with their horses, so we proceeded with our affinity group to walk down the sidewalk. There was one area where a policeman with a bullhorn stood up and said, "If you go beyond a certain restricted area you will be arrested." We got down almost to that restricted area, and there seemed to be some horses coming our way, so somebody in our group suggested, "Let's sit down." Wasn't that in the Gandhi film? You know, that was gonna be one way the horse wouldn't trample you. I don't know whether that was part of the rationale or not. Anyway, we as a group sat down and we hadn't even gotten to the restricted area. We were on the sidewalk and as I remember it we were singing, "We Shall Overcome." And then what happened next is rather a blur in my memory because they swooped us up so fast and literally heaved us, I think I was *thrown*, in the back of this paddy wagon. So it was a very short, short caper! And they apparently took us on quite a round robbin, circuitous route to the police station, where fifty of us sat in a cubicle that had no light, thank goodness, because it was terrible, full of I don't know what all over the floor, and it smelled and we stayed there for the day until they got around to booking us.

I think that the missile manufacturers, certainly some of them, are not mindful of what they are doing. Some of them justify it in a lot of different ways, but I suppose I feel that we give them another chance to rethink their allegiance to that kind of thing. I think that that's what civil disobedience is all about. It's communicating and making a strong statement and giving people who are inclined to a reason to rethink.

As I see it, civil disobedience is a discipline and I feel that it has to be done very gently. I think this is the way to get your point across. This was the first time I had been arrested. I just felt after the initial arrest and after being chucked into that paddy wagon, which was the only piece of a little bit of brutalness that I encountered that whole day, I found that otherwise the policemen I had anything to do with were reasonable. I felt that there were a few of 'em that were interested in what we were doing. I had brought a whole bunch of the seminar booklets. I had had them reprinted and I passed them out there at the police department. We all did. And I think that, by and large, there were some policemen who were very, very definitely sympathetic with what we were doing.

It was kind of interesting to be in that situation, and I was amazed to find that I wasn't particularly frightened. I don't feel it was particularly heroic. I didn't suffer any real discomfort or anything. There was a lot of media coverage and I went up to a meeting three or four weeks afterward to find out that they were going to be holding another one of these conferences at the Colonnade Hotel. The same group that had organized this civil disobedience notified the hotel that there would probably be some other actions taken and asked them to cancel out, and sure enough, they did. Yup, they did. I was prepared, if they hadn't, to go and do the same thing again. I felt like it would be kind of backing down, when we had said, don't do that! Once you start something you don't abandon it. Obviously there are things going on every day. I don't have that kind of energy level, but I think if they had come right around and set up another one of these conferences, it would be obvious we didn't make our point, we had to finish the job. I think that we'll probably see more and more people from this area taking part in these things because there's a core of really good people, mostly with a religious commitment, a real spiritual commitment.

I don't know about "lady." I don't like the term. It has a lot of connotations. Being a lady in the context in which I was using it meant being a gentle person, being respectful of others. It's not a term that I would use very often; my mother might, but I don't. I don't feel generally alienated by the system. I feel sometimes as if I don't fit in. My husband has got a wonderful big family, and they're just a wonderful group of six brothers and sisters. They are all married and have lots of children and it's just a wonderful family, and yet, when I'm with them, I feel a little out of step. These people are very conventional in their outlooks and the way they live their lives and their social customs. Obviously this nuclear issue is one I feel very strongly about, but I certainly haven't had a lot of luck evangelizing any of my friends and family. I don't see any of them getting particularly excited about it. I haven't changed anybody's mind. And sometimes I feel, you know, a little alienated from the mainstream of life, and disappointed that I haven't really been able to communicate my concern about these issues or my feelings about my values and so sometimes I feel a little lonely.

To me, it's clear as anything could possibly be and I have trouble bearing with people who apparently haven't noticed! This whole business of everybody going out and upgrading our colleges and schools makes me wonder what they think they're doing. Where are they upgrading them to? This whole mess that our world is in obviously has been devised and brought about by these wonderfully schooled people who have just got to be crazy in terms of talking about this "Star Wars" weaponry and all that. I just wonder what kind of world these genius types have gotten us into.

I don't think my opinions are unpopular in my town, but they certainly don't generate a lot of interest. I just think that the whole issue is too much for most people to cope with. I certainly opposed authority as a child, yes, for the fun of it. I hope there's more to it now! I have nine children and they're all multiplying. I have two grandchildren on the way and I have three now and two others by proxy, and I feel that I have a great responsibility to these dear children. I feel a real commitment to my children and their children and all the children, and I just feel like we're really playing a dirty trick on kids by continuing in this way. I think I'm more focused on this than I was.

Supposedly we have a democracy, but I think that probably that's in name only. I think that people are pretty apathetic and we have got ourselves into this mess because people really do not participate in the democratic process. We are letting ourselves be led down the road by, I guess, the corporate world. I guess those are the people that are really in charge, and I think that if we were to try to figure out who's to blame, I guess the people of the United States, myself included, have not really gotten involved in the process. I think it's a viable, workable process, but people don't participate. At this point, I'm not just sure who *is* the government. I don't think most people feel that they can question the Henry Kissingers of the world or the George Shultzes or the people making policies. I just think that we're pretty much conditioned to feel that they must have the answer. I mean, I didn't know anything about how presidents are made. You know, caucusing and elections and all that. It's pretty complicated stuff and I don't think that the average person knows much about it. It doesn't have to be that complicated. But it is and not too many people could even envision themselves getting in a role in government. I was a pretty uninvolved person. Politics hasn't been anything that was of interest to me. I was just going along in my life, kind of thinking whatever will be, will be. And then I was able to somehow energize myself to take a stand and say no, I think the world is in peril. I know what made me do it was my commitment to my grandchildren and realizing that I had obviously been pretty affirmative about the promises of a good life for my children and their children. And then I felt like I had maybe told them a lie. Living as if the world was going to go on was a living lie, that's all. And I had to kinda come clean and take responsibility.

Richard Schwartz

"The blood of a Palestinian child and the blood of a Jewish child are equally precious."

□ □ □

We have got clearly to distinguish between fact and desire.

W. E. B. DU BOIS

Professor Richard "Red" Schwartz is a law professor by profession, a sociologist by training, and a humanist by main inclination. The red hair that earned him the nickname by which he is still generally known is blond now. He is an affable, quick-minded man who walks with two canes. There is about him the air of the justice entering Shakespeare's fifth age. We talked for most of a brisk early May afternoon in the living room of his comfortable suburban home.

Professor Schwartz is an avowed pro-Israeli partisan deeply engaged in the pursuit of equity. The vexed questions attendant upon the mutual antagonisms of Arabs and Israelis leave little room for joint dialogue among American Jews and Arabs, but to that end, he has been instrumental in founding a discussion group in Syracuse devoted to the facilitation of dialogue and understanding among Palestinians and Jews.

There is a long-established Jewish community in the city of Syracuse, and a new blue-and-white gold-domed mosque rises baroquely amid large, wood-framed townhouses in an old residential neighborhood adjacent to the university. Prevailing opinion in both the expanding Arabic community and the Jewish population runs counter to the climate of reconciliation that the Middle East Dialogue Group is attempting to foster. Professor Schwartz did not dwell upon the general opposition to the aims of the group, but personal experience has taught me that the lot of the peacemaker varies from social discomfort to fully efficient shunning. The Middle East Dialogue Group is the seed of reason in very stony ground and I believe that all parties in it are principled dissenters in that they risk at the very least the opprobrium of their fellows.

I belong to a local discussion group—we use the word *dialogue*—and our purpose is to seek a solution to the conflict between the Israelis and the Palestinians. I have here a statement which may facilitate your understanding of our situation. Perhaps it would be worth my while reading some of it to you because I think you will get from it some considerable insight into the nature of our effort.

We have assumed that dialogue requires face-to-face, continuing meetings between partisans of the opposing positions. For this reason, we sought to form a group that included Jews who were committed to the Israeli cause and Palestinians who were committed to the Palestinian cause. . . . The basic assumption of the conversation is that all participants accept the legitimacy of both the State of Israel and self-determination for Palestinians, including the option of a sovereign West Bank–Gaza Strip state. The formulation of that initial assumption meant that many supporters of Israel and many supporters of the Palestinian cause could not conscientiously join the Dialogue. As a result, the group did not represent the "mainstream" of thinking in either camp. Rather it selected those who were inclined, distinctively and unusually, toward the path of reconciliation. This type of selection seemed to be necessary, if the group were to achieve its basic purpose: To provide a forum for Syracuse area residents from Arab, Jewish, and other communities to discuss a variety of U.S. initiatives furthering a peaceful accommodation between Israelis and Palestinians.

Okay. I subscribe to everything in here. From the beginning it was agreed that the members from each of the three groups ought to be roughly equal. Initially we had a small planning group that consisted of two, two, and two. Then we decided, after the deliberations of that planning group, that we would go to this equal number approach for a larger group. So we found five Jews, five Palestinians, and five others to participate in the first dialogue. The others are American Christians of non-Palestinian background. It happens that we do not have a Catholic member. Mostly our "other" people are Presbyterians and Methodists. No, there are no black people involved. We meet at various homes and occasionally in a church or a business. The first meeting was one at which we had an Arabic dinner at the Jerusalem Restaurant, appropriately, and we've had breakfast meetings which were meals. Now we usually meet in the evening about once a month, but that represents something of an increase. Earlier we had averaged about once every six weeks.

The Jewish participants are mostly Reform, perhaps even entirely Reform. There was one Orthodox and one Conservative, but both of them have dropped out. One dropped out because he said he really had not understood, upon joining, the nature of the assumptions on which membership was based. The basis of the conversation is that all participants accept the legitimacy of the State of Israel and self-determination for Palestinians, including the option of a sovereign West Bank–Gaza Strip state. The second dropped out saying that he had anticipated that there would be substantial discussion, including a discussion of these assumptions. Incidentally, the numbers have now increased to seven, seven, seven.

When we talk about Palestinians, we talk about people who were themselves born in Palestine or who are close enough to that so that we count them in the category. To my knowledge, all of our Palestinian members were born there except one, who is the son of a person who was born there. There are a few Muslims but most are Christians. I believe that all of the people who have entered this group have done so in good faith. When they said that they were accepting these conditions, I believe that they were indicating their belief in them. It was a sincere commitment on their part.

I drafted the statement. There are Jews in the area who disagree with me strongly and the position that I have taken, but not strongly enough, to my knowledge, to have refused to speak with me. At any rate, I've sensed no overt refusal to speak or to listen. Distaste, perhaps. There was, however, a suggestion of opposition to my being permitted to speak on a public platform. That was made rather quietly to the rabbi of a temple, and I don't know how he reacted to that. I believe either the rabbi or the suggestor communicated the thought that I ought not to be permitted to speak. But that was rejected, as I understand it, by the head of the organization within the synagogue that invited me.

Why do I hold these views? Peace is better than war. Freedom is better than the occupancy of territory by one power against the will of the people who live there. Those two objectives, I think, are intertwined in the situation. Peace could be obtained most readily if the people who do not want their territory occupied found themselves free of the occupation. I think it would be advantageous to both sides, if the arrangement of separation were effectuated in a way that was considered satisfactory and just by both sides. The tactics of how to accomplish this are not easy to discover.

I think that Sadat has given us an excellent example of how this can be done, namely, by a unilateral step forward by a person in a position of power. A step in the direction of peace which makes it possible then for the other side to respond. I think that those steps are not being taken by any of the people who are currently in crucial positions of power in Israel or among the Palestinians or in the Arab World. If you ask me what could be done to effectuate this outcome in the absence of those steps, I'm troubled. But I would say that the steps taken by the U.S. government with the Reagan initiative and currently Secretary of State Schultz's efforts to try to facilitate the implementation of that initiative represent moves in the right direction, and I hope vigorously for their success. If we turn to the level of ordinary people like you and me who are not in positions of power, then I would say that the chances of our being able to do anything effective to contribute to this kind of a solution are quite slim. Nevertheless, because of the importance of the objective, I think it's important for us to try what techniques are available to us. One that we have found worth trying and persisting with is the technique of exchanging views and increasing mutual understanding between people whose initial positions are as partisans of one side or the other.

Well, I think it unlikely that a Palestinian state would constitute a "dagger pointed at the heart of Israel." For one thing, I think the reason for the threat to Israel is because of the unsatisfied national aspirations of those Palestinians, or that's one of the reasons, and I think if that national aspiration were fulfilled in a way deemed by the people living in that territory to be satisfactory, then I do not think that they would support or sustain a military threat to Israel. For another thing, the Israelis are very strong at this time, and I think it unlikely that a military threat greater than what they currently already face would result from this kind of activity.

I don't think that war is inevitable. I don't think we know enough ever to assume that we can foretell the future. Even with all the social science and philosophy that we can muster about the future, man makes himself, as V. Gordon Childe says. And we have to assume in those conditions of uncertainty that various outcomes are possible. I'm not saying that the Israelis are inviting a new war by their present course, but I do not think that they would increase the chances of violence against them by withdrawing and permitting self-determination. On the contrary, I think that they would diminish the danger of war.

I don't find much substance in the argument that "God gave us this land," but if I have to I ask whether those who assume that Judea and Samaria must be part of Israel, whether they would be willing to concede the old territory of Philistia or Phoenicia, which would mean that the Palestinians or some other group would be more entitled than the Israelis to those lands, which were never occupied by ancient Israel. I don't think the ancient case is very important. Not nearly as important as the security considerations. The Israelis see Israel beset by enemies, justifiably so. They ask, "Why cannot the Arab World, with its great, enormous territory, absorb the Palestinians? There were only a limited number of them before the Jewish immigration began. Why can they not go elsewhere? And if there is a pan-Arab nation, why should not the other Arab nations make provisions for them, settle them down?" and so forth.

It's very difficult to say the extent to which my own orientation toward issues of war and peace, social justice, are affected by my Jewish background. But, subjectively, I feel that there is a direct connection between that background and these views. I have thought that the prophetic tradition in Judaism was one of the noblest products of human thinking and I take the prophets very seriously. The similarities among them are very strong, but I would be selective. That is to say, I would take Elisha less seriously, perhaps, than I would Elijah, Amos, Micah, or Hosea. Well, Isaiah was a prophet of the court, an aristocrat, and therefore, a little atypical in terms of the prophets who preached the social gospel. He certainly was not above criticizing the mighty and that is one of the elements in the prophetic tradition that appeals to me very much. It's almost certain that a person who is oriented toward a more just society will find himself in opposition to those who are in positions of power, where there is a substantial degree of injustice in the society. And it was true of Isaiah, although Isaiah was more concerned with the foreign policy issues than the social justice issues that concerned Jeremiah. At all events, yes, starting with Nathan, the tendency on the part of prophets to volunteer their moral messages—derived, as they thought, from God—was very strong, and it led them to criticize those in power wherever that seemed to be necessary. You're familiar with the story of Nathan, then? Well, I haven't said, "Thou art the man" to anybody in particular. I haven't said it in the sense that I have directly communicated it to anyone. But if you are asking me, do I feel that way? Yes. I feel that the government of Israel, when it announced that it knew nothing about the Shatila and Sabra massacres and that it bore no responsibility for them, was making two statements that are mutually contradictory. It's not possible not to know and yet to know that there's no responsibility in a situation of that kind. And that seemed to me to be so close to what Cain said to God, "Am I my brother's keeper?," that it was painful. I wrote something about it at the time that did appear in the press. It appeared in the two local papers and a truncated version appeared in the *Christian Science Monitor*. It appeared as comment under the heading, "Can Israel Make Peace as Well as War?" My suggested title for it was, "Can Israel Make Peace as Well as It Can Make War?" It was a somewhat different nuance. What was reproduced there is slightly edited down, but this is the gist of it.

The recent events in Lebanon bring anguish. They must not lead to despair. In our world we cannot afford to lose the hope that out of evil will come good and that out of war will come peace. As human beings, we must feel anguish for the suffering and death in Lebanon. The blood of a Palestinian child and the blood of a Jewish child are equally precious. The idea of one God means exactly that. Jews who have given the world that idea must feel anguish at the bloodshed in Lebanon. Each side has ignored its chances for peace. Together they have contributed to war. Each side must now consider its own moral responsibilities. As a Jew, my primary focus is upon the obligations of my own people. Self-defense justifies killing only when no other avenue is available. Only when there is no other choice. Did Israel have a choice? Could it have defended itself in any other way before taking recourse to this bloody campaign? Is not peace a nobler concept than a war of self-defense? Something else could have been tried before the Lebanese campaign. Either side could have advanced the cause of peace by coming forward with an offer. The basis for a just peace between Israel and the Palestinians is simple. Peace, recognition, territorial integrity, and self-determination. Specifically, the Arab countries surrounding Israel must agree to give recognition and peace to Israel. Israel must agree to Palestinian self-determination, including as an option the establishment of an independent state on the West Bank and the Gaza Strip. These two steps should be taken simultaneously. To implement these, Israel must, upon the signing of peace treaties, withdraw from the occupied territories to secure boundaries, leaving those lands to an international authority which would supervise a self-determining election. The campaign in Lebanon demonstrates that the Palestinians are too weak to threaten by their own arms or those of their supposed allies the existence of the Israeli State. For each side this fact could increase the tendency to move toward peace. The Palestinians could have moved and can still move toward peace by renouncing force and offering a political solution along the lines outlined above. There is already some talk in Beirut and on the West Bank of such a move. Israelis could, by offering such a political solution, also move toward peace. They should recall the advice of that most resolute of warrior statesmen, Winston Churchill, "In victory, magnanimity." This may be the historic moment when Israel can make its greatest contribution to peace. That depends, however, on the motives and the wisdom of Israelis. Either side can contribute to peace. Should either do so the other must respond in kind. If they do, then the day may not be distant when, in the words of the prophet, "Nations shall beat their swords into ploughshares, their spears into pruning hooks, nation shall not lift up sword against nation, neither shall they learn war anymore."

There might be people who might do violence to me for expressing those views. I doubt it. I suppose Meir Kehane might. But then, that wouldn't advance his cause. It might advance mine more than his.

I think that Gandhi and Martin Luther King were in their way magnanimous. Magnanimous means large of spirit, and they certainly were that. I think that what's needed is a leader who can speak in a way that is both morally inspired and politically practicable. I don't know where that's going to come from. I don't see anybody on the scene who looks as if he would be ready to do that.

I think that the move toward peace, to be successful, would have to have widespread support in Israel, and that should include the support of a substantial segment of each of the ethnic communities. There ought to be self-determination for the people who live there, including the possibility of a Palestinian state. According to an article by David Shipler that appeared in the *New York Times* last year, the Israeli government already lists as of that time more than twenty-five percent of the land as not belonging to Arabs. That is to say, possessed either by the government or Israeli Jews, and they have plans for the passing of title of an additional comparable amount. So that in a fairly short time, it's expected that the majority of the land will no longer be possessed by the Arabs of the Occupied Territories. It would be difficult to reverse, but the experience in the Sinai suggests that it's not impossible I would hope that there would be many moderate people in Israel who would be persuaded that territory is less important than peace. I think that there are many people in Israel who are of two minds on this subject. We can identify some people who are of one mind now and who are oriented toward peace. Peace Now people, perhaps even a majority of those 400,000 who showed up in Tel Aviv for the demonstration after the massacres. But there are also, I think, large numbers of people who are conflicted over the issue and the problem is to try to persuade them that peace is not only possible but that the road to it is a safe one, or reasonably safe at any rate. That the risks are sufficiently limited so as not to make the attempt a foolhardy one. We discovered in this area that it is possible for Palestinians and Jews to sit together like brothers and to understand each other. Trust has been established in this little group of ours. I think it is a real trust with a belief on both sides in the dependability of the motives and the actions of the other side. So that by now we hardly have sides. That demonstration seems to me very important, potentially, provided that others might go in the same direction. Whether they do so on the basis of this example is not important. That they do so is important because it seems to me that one possible movement toward peace, given the commitments to hostility of the leaders of both sides, can come from the grass roots. If people here and ultimately there could come to trust each other, that might change the situation. It is, perhaps, a necessary though not sufficient condition for the eventual arrival of peace.

In our group it started with hope, I think, but not much confidence, and that lack of confidence was there because some members on both sides were saying, "Well, what do we need to do this for? What's the good of this!" And there were issues that were raised that were very difficult to deal with. For instance, Palestinians were oriented toward the PLO and they wanted the Jews also to accept the PLO. My own view of that was expressed when I said, "You know, I don't know which PLO you're asking me to accept. Is this a PLO that might eventually be dominated by George Habbash? Habbash is clearly antagonistic to the existence of an Israeli state. He is a member of the PLO and the Palestine National Council. If, in asking me to commit myself to the PLO, you're asking me to be loyal to its leadership no matter what that leadership is, or to say that I think that they ought to be recognized even while they continue to take the position that they will not be satisfied until the State of Israel is destroyed, then I can't go along with that." "Well," my friends said, "All right. That's an issue we can't deal with. We believe that the PLO ought to be recognized. That it is a responsible group that represents the Palestinian people and their interests, but if we can't persuade you, we will nevertheless continue to work with you."

When the Golan Heights were annexed—or had their legal status changed—some of the Palestinians said, "Well, we have to know how our Jewish members feel about this." And we went around the room and we talked about how we felt about it. We Jews, I think, were able to say some things which led the Palestinians to understand that we were not in sympathy with what had happened. We varied to some extent, but the positions that we stated seemed to allay their concern. At the time of the Lebanese invasion there was another set of problems of mutual understanding. In some ways, the piece that appeared in the paper that I read to you was a response to that, a felt need to say what I at least thought about that Lebanese invasion. And then at the time of the massacres I felt very badly about that. I felt so badly that I invited the Palestinians in the group to come to my home and to join me as I broke the Yom Kippur fast. They did it and we talked about the personal feelings that this brought up.

We have a few times gone over the history of the conflict and it's been clear that we have different perspectives. They continue to see the intrusion of the large Jewish population into the territory between the Jordan and the Mediterranean as illegitimate, justifiable only by a League of Nations Mandate which was a product of the powerful nations of Europe, and that mandate as providing no justification for the Balfour Declaration establishing a Jewish national homeland. They don't see why that was necessary or justified, considering the dislocation of the rights and property of the Palestinians there. My response is, primarily, that if we argue over history we will never agree. If we ask the question, how can peace be brought about, considering and taking into account the strong claims of both sides, we may get somewhere. But the solution is one that requires a break from history and a relaxation of the tensions of that troubled history.

It's some kind of desire to contribute to the solution of human problems that makes me willing to take this unpopular position. Early, I think it was when I was a preteenager, I asked myself the question, What could be the meaning of life? I was troubled. I had nightmares. I don't really remember what they were, but I seemed to be troubled. I couldn't get to sleep at night and so forth. I needed comforting from father and mother and I ultimately began to ask myself that question and maybe this was the source of the trouble, or the expression of the trouble, I can't identify which it was. I think the experience of death may have contributed to that, you know. A grandfather died, others had died earlier, and the knowledge of death was troublesome. So I asked myself, If life is finite in this way, what can it mean! And I tried to figure out what it could mean and the nearest I could come to giving myself a satisfactory answer was that it must mean that we must be here in order to leave the world a little bit better than it was when we entered it. And I have held to that conviction ever since. Now, for me, that life be meaningful is very important! And therefore, such behavior as I can undertake that leads me to think something I do here might have that effect is comforting. It starts with the effort to find some meaning in life. The meaning that I found in it is the one that I've described to you. Namely, doing some good, to put it succinctly. Doing a balance of good as compared with evil. I remember probably at that age reading *War and Peace*. I read Samuel Butler, *The Way of All Flesh*. And I read a lot of nonfiction. We had *The Book of Knowledge* in multiple volumes and I would read about all kinds of things. Just go right through them. I was a reader of news magazines! My father was interested in foreign affairs and his attitude was always more conservative than mine. That became particularly clear as I reached the late teens when I went to college and read Marx and others. Then our positions were quite different. I remember him saying to me once in one of those sessions when I was having trouble getting to sleep, "Well, don't you worry, there are a lot of troubles in the world, it's true. Mussolini is invading Ethiopia and that's too bad, but it's far away and you don't have to worry too much about that." He was indicating that he was worried about it and he was pointing, perhaps not intending to, to that kind of thing as something for me to worry about, but he was also reassuring me by saying, "You can think about those things without being devastated by them." Yes, I could. Look! I can think about nuclear disaster and not be destroyed by the thought. One of the great stories in the Bible is the story of Job. That teaches me a very powerful lesson. You can contemplate evil but never give way to despair.

I think Israel should be a Jewish state in the way Brandeis is a Jewish university. That is to say, in its origins, but not in any kind of discriminatory policies.

A really good friend I can remember from my childhood was Billy Kilroy, who lived next door. His friendship was very important because he was my friend even though there was a boy down the street, also Irish

Catholic, who was either anti-Semitic or gave a very good imitation of it. And the boy down the street regularly beat me up on my way to and from school. I tried everything to avoid that, detours and all that. Ultimately, I couldn't succeed in avoiding him. He got the better of me in terms of locating where I was and also in terms of the exercise of the art of fisticuffs. But eventually my brother said, "Look, we have to put a stop to this." My mother tried to call his mother, who had been a classmate of hers in high school and that didn't help. No, and my father said, "Well, if you have a black eye, I have some salve that I can put on the eye and hide it." And my brother then said, "Look, we've got to do something about this," and he taught me to fight. And then we had a fight, this boy and I, in front of his house. And that was our last fight, because I at least managed a draw with him and may even have won if it had continued, but his mother at that point chose to intervene. Well now, you can imagine, you know, if you project these kinds of memories onto what I would think about the Israeli state, I would understand the need for the Israelis to defend themselves. I think there are Palestinians who cannot see beyond the interests of the Palestinians. Just as there are Israelis who cannot see beyond the interests of the Israelis.

In a strange way, one of the things which not only continues to motivate me, but even gives me a certain kind of hope, is that the realities of our world situation are genuinely, objectively dire. We find ourselves now for the first time, perhaps since the mythical time of Noah, in a situation where we as a race, the human race, genuinely face the possibility of extermination by our own hand, the possibility of suigenocide.

It is often said that there are very few instances in which, in this society, we have accomplished reforms without the prod of pain, but in the case of the nuclear problem we have not felt, fortunately, the prod of that kind of pain, except in our imaginations. But those who claim that we do nothing except when we are prodded by pain are generally thinking of something that is more direct than that. But now, in our reaction to the danger of a nuclear holocaust, we seem to have revived a vigorous imagination sufficient to substitute for direct pain as power for motivation. That's perhaps a source of hope, and if we then begin to reason back from that, we can ask ourselves the question, What state of affairs would we have to be in, for instance, thirty years from now, so that we could be secure against that terrible danger? And perhaps in light of that kind of a goal, we can then begin to analyze those elements in our culture, in our social structure, and in our individual experience that would be conducive to the peaceful resolution of all disputes.

I'm not at all ready to give up, I never will. But I think that the dial on the clock that is on the *Bulletin of the Atomic Scientists* is rather accurate. I would say this. To the extent that hopelessness is a short-term phase, that may be all right because one may be able to move from that hopelessness to some kind of legitimate effective action. But to the extent that it hardens into despair, then it is, to me, a self-fulfilling prophecy and it is an unjustified prophecy. Let us chose life not death, and work as hard as we can.

Sisters Catherine, Honora, Justine, and Mary Rita

"Save Our Sisters!"

□ □ □

*There is nothing more difficult to take in hand,
more perilous to conduct, or more uncertain in its
success, than to take the lead in the introduction
of a new order of things.*

NICCOLÒ MACHIAVELLI

*The four Sisters of Mercy who sued their Bishop for an explanatory hear-
ing after being summarily dismissed from their jobs as educators posed a
problem for me. We agreed to meet and discuss their principled dissent in
their home, the Convent of the Sacred Heart in Hampton, New Hampshire.
I was not certain about the conventions of convent decorum, but spontaneous civility was more than good enough. The Sisters Catherine and
Justine Colliton, Mary Rita Furlong, and Honora Reardon proved to be
amiable, intelligent ladies who have not lost their sense of humor, jocularly referring to themselves as the "suing nuns." Their wit and humor
enlivened the entire afternoon. My wife and I arrived at the convent in
the warm, brilliant forenoon of a late autumn day. The time, beguiled by
stacks of ham and chicken salad sandwiches, jocularity and profundity,
flew by and the sun was well down before we took the road again. Early in
the interview Sister Mary Rita had to leave for her part time Wednesday
afternoon job. Sisters Catherine and Justine sustained the dialogue with
vivacity, insight, and wry humor. Sister Honora acted as an able resource
person, and her quiet authority and power to reduce complex issues to
their cogent, irreducible nub was an indispensable element in the facilitation of the dialogue. A common Irish-American cultural heritage and
religious training and their joint insistence upon an explanation for their
dismissal have made them appear more of a piece in terms of personality
than they actually are.*

*The "suing nuns" are sadder and wiser for their experience. They plainly
miss the classroom, and it seems obvious to me that education is the
poorer without them, but their hunger for accountability and a just recognition of their formidable abilities is undiminished. These women are quite*

*prepared to invest an infinite amount of zeal, skill, and persistence to
attain justice. They have had a considerable measure of prominence thrust
upon them merely because they insisted on receiving a hearing from the
institution they have served for the bulk of their lives. Their inability to
secure what they feel is decent respect for their services and a definitive
statement of the reasons for their dismissal was the initial link in a chain
of interactions. This rich mix of conflicting small-town intrigues and
exuberances is compounded of ethnic antagonism and competition and
the factionalism that is endemic in our species, but more than an occasional
gust of the wind of change is plainly discernible in this controversy. The
reservations entertained by all disadvantaged populations about their one-
down statuses have probably never been anything but massive, but it is
the ambivalent fortune of both bishops and sisters to live in extremely
interesting times. This disorder in the diocese of New Hampshire is a
portion of the main question of the place of women in a socioreligious
system that cannot survive without them. It is in the light and heat of this
formidable question that the outrage, energy, and wry sarcasm of the four
Sisters of Mercy must be understood. Their legal action is but a round in a
sustained salvo against a long-established patriarchy.*

My name is Sister Catherine Colliton and I usually do most of the talking
so everybody looks at me. I'm the one who's most often quoted so I'm the
one who most often has the finger pointed at her for saying the outspoken,
or the wrong thing. But you know, that's the difficulty. See, for us, there
wasn't any wrong. The *whole* difficulty started when, unknown to us,
evidently there were some people in the school and in the parish who were
dissatisfied with us and our performance and our attitudes. And when the
Bishop of the Diocese of Manchester, which takes in the whole State of
New Hampshire, came on parish visitation to our Lady of Miraculous
Medal here in Hampton, they made their displeasure with us known to
him. And as I say, that was totally unknown to us. Then the next part of
the process was that the Bishop wrote to each one of us and asked us if
we would give the pros and cons of the difficulties that were apparent in
the school and in the parish. Meanwhile, the Sacred Heart School Board
had asked that we should have a meeting among the School Board and the
faculty and a facilitator. Come to find out, the facilitator that night just
happened to be the Superintendent of Schools. Now we didn't know he
was going to be there, but someone must have appointed him to be there.
So we had the meeting and even though I swore I wasn't going to say a
word, I didn't stop talking all night long! And others spoke also, others
on the faculty, religious and lay, and that was on the eleventh or the four-
teenth of December. Now then, that was in December and that Christmas,
before we went on vacation, the School Board gave each member of the
faculty a fifty-dollar bonus, which was unheard of in my twenty-five years
of teaching. Nobody ever gave me a bonus before! And we got a lovely
letter of appreciation for all that we have done for Sacred Heart School
in making it the tremendous place that it is. And it was signed by the

Chairperson of the School Board. And we had a wonderful faculty party in the convent. We invited the clergy from the rectory and so forth and as far as we were concerned when we went home for vacation, everything was fine. Well then in January Sister Honora, who was the principal of Sacred Heart School, got notice from the superintendent of schools that he wanted to see her. Then he called in a couple of days and he said, "I would like to see the Sisters of Mercy." All four Sisters of Mercy. And we were presented with what we call the "unsigned memo," which was a list of, we call 'em, charges, which were totally ridiculous. I mean, I didn't even understand them. They made reference to the staff and I always thought I was the staff. Well, come to find out, it's just the clergy who are the staff, and so on and so on. So at the last of this list of seven "charges" against us it said, "Therefore, I recommend that the Sisters of Mercy not be rehired." And it further recommended that we be given an opportunity to resign. Now these so-called charges consisted of things like we were "cliquish"—we are, after all, nuns living together in a convent, and we all get along together here very well—and our "autonomy." Things like that which really didn't have anything to do with our competence as teachers or whether or not we had violated any of the terms of our contracts—which we hadn't. Now in that unsigned memo there was no antecedent for the "I," so we didn't know who the "I" was, except that the letterhead said the Diocese of Manchester. So, was it the Bishop who fired us? Was it the Superintendent who fired us? Was it the School Board who fired us? Was it the clergy of the rectory who fired us? We never really got that straight. But anyway, it said, "Therefore, I recommend that you resign." And I said, "Well, I'll tell you one thing, I will *never* resign. Now what will happen if I don't?" And Brother Roger, the Superintendent, said, "The School Board will vote on Monday not to rehire you." This is all true. It's such a horror story. So anyway, I said to him, "Brother Roger, I know one thing. I am not going to fold my tent and go away quietly." So I left. I go into my classroom and you can imagine my condition. Eighth-grade homeroom. Kids that you love, you know, but it happened to be quarter of twelve, and this is during a testing period when they're all up in high G after a test, so at my door is the woman who at that time was Vice Chairman of the Sacred Heart School Board. "What's the matter?" says she. I says, "What's the matter, Doreen? You just fired me!" She says, "Sister, I don't know what you're talking about. I don't know anything about this." And I said, "Doreen, you're Vice Chairman of the School Board and you don't know anything about it?!" So that was on a Thursday and then I would say almost *immediately* the kids responded, and there was a parade in the corridor during noontime on Friday. It's just totally unbelievable, honestly, the whole thing.

SISTER HONORA   They came into school wearing pins saying, "Save Our Sisters!"

SISTER CATHERINE   Yes, "Save Our Sisters!" And the boys had these paper miters on their heads. How they ever connected the Bishop to it, it's just totally unbelievable. No, no, no. The School Board hadn't met and voted then, but the kids knew it when I came back into my classroom! They knew something was wrong. We didn't tell them. I mean, what was I going to say? I couldn't. And so the kids went home and said, "The nuns are fired, Ma," you know, "The nuns are fired, Pa." "Oh, that's ridiculous, that's ridiculous. You don't fire nuns!" So the whole thing just developed.

But you know, I just wanted to say at the very beginning that the whole process for us at the time was a purely secular, excuse me, for *me* at the time, was a purely secular reaction to what I saw as an injustice on the part of the School Board, 'cause it wasn't until later that we found out the Bishop was our boss. I never thought the Bishop was our boss. The School Board hired me.

SISTER HONORA   I thought *I* was the boss!

SISTER CATHERINE   And she thought she was the boss, so we never thought of it, and then, come to find out, if the Bishop was the boss, well, then they said we sued the Bishop, but we never, even then I never thought of him as a priestly bishop, I mean, the bishop as a religious person who was my boss. He was the employer and I was the employee and I was treated unjustly and that was my reaction. It was purely secular. But *since* then, and I would say since the settlement, it's almost like gone full circle in my mind and I have disassociated the secular from the religious. What is the settlement? Oh dear, someone else?

SISTER JUSTINE   My name is Sister Justine Colliton and the settlement is basically this. It's a document, probably two or three pages long. I would say most of it, actually the substance of it was drawn up by our attorney. We felt that the Bishop was the one who initiated the process to make a settlement. I mean, that was never our idea to do any settling. You know, again, we still didn't know *why* we were fired. It's a purely secular document and it's signed only by three attorneys, the diocesan attorney and our two attorneys. It said that we would seek employment elsewhere in the diocese and that the diocese would help us find other jobs. It said we could live here in the convent until July of 1984 and that's all public. And in addition to that settlement, which was passed out on the courthouse steps in Exeter, there's also what they called a "sealed agreement." We never wanted anything secret. We did not want a sealed agreement, we wanted the whole settlement open. This is the big thing. Right now we are available for work. We've been given full approval by the diocese, in print. By a letter. We are in good standing and we're on the available list but we're not being offered jobs. Oh, we know definitely there's a grapevine. "Don't hire them." I mean, even our own Community would not hire us. Our own sisters!

I taught five years at Sacred Heart School and I can say we've learned one thing. We speak now, "I." We were fired together so we've become very conscious of saying "I" because we didn't like the four of us grouped together. I had very good relationships with almost everyone on the School Board. I had taught one, two, three of their children. There's never been any problem whatsoever and if we had ever saved the notes that had been written to us as individuals from these same School Board members! We never found out what their complaint with us was. We never got our hearing. That's all we wanted. They refused. What we wanted was the right given to us through the Diocesan Handbook that said you had a right to a hearing if you were being dismissed.

I don't think they ever expected it to turn out the way it did. I wish we had worked for them, because we really could have done a better job with the whole thing. I'm serious! Anyone would have reacted the way we did. I went into Brother Roger and I just said a prayer, you know, "Dear God, give me the strength to say what I want to say, rather than just crying." And I did. I got the strength. And so he put down this paper, the unsigned memo, and he greeted me and so forth and I just pushed it aside and said, "I refuse to read that because I don't know who wrote it." And I said, "I don't read anything that's not signed." And he said, "I wrote it." "Then sign it," I said, So he signed mine and he also dated mine, put the twenty-eighth. I don't even know what happened to that, but some parent has that now for safekeeping.

SISTER MARY RITA   But then the Bishop, on May fourth, when we kept referring to the "unsigned memo" about the charges said, "Well those really aren't charges. Those are just topics for discussion." We said, "Well, Brother Roger didn't discuss anything." And we all said, "Well, we didn't discuss it, it was presented to us." And we still don't know why! And we don't know who either, except we have ideas and all, but we don't know. And now you notice, none of these are originals. We really looked to find out and none of us had an original, typed memo. We had a run-off, a xerox. And see, it's dated the eighteenth, but we didn't get it until the twenty-eighth!

SISTER CATHERINE   This is it. In the *whole* controversy, I think we might have received one piece of correspondence which was dated one day, sent the next, and received the next. Everything had this long space in between so we never knew where the letters went. See how that's unsigned? And poor Sister Honora was fired three times!

SISTER HONORA   Twice in one night and once in the afternoon. I was fired in an executive meeting over in the rectory, by the School Board in a secret session, and the next day I was presented with a letter saying I was fired. I was so shocked I probably didn't even think. I had been principal eight, nine years.

SISTER JUSTINE   Can I say this? We lost our, well, I don't even like to say job, but I mean, gee, I taught thirty years in the diocesan school system and I don't see any future for me. I don't think I'll ever be hired again here. And it's one fell swoop, all four of us and without any reason. We got along very well with the parents and the kids. The only thing was the School Board was terrible. When I walked out from, when I got my, when I was fired, I walked out of the nurse's office about quarter of twelve and my lunchroom mother was standing outside the door and I had the paper in my hand and I said, "Kathy, I've been fired" and I gave her the paper. Now that was Thursday. Friday when the children left the school at quarter of two, there were parents outside the school passing out envelopes to children with a copy of that unsigned memo and the announcement of a meeting Monday night to tell the parents to come. Now we did not know. No one believes us, but *we did not know* the parents had been out there at quarter of two passing these things out to the kids. We knew nothing! As God is my judge. It was mothers and fathers and eventually this group became SOS. It was "Save" at first, but then it became "Support." "Support Our Sisters." But it was an immediate reaction of the parents. Okay, so that Saturday night we went to a church supper and it was as if we had a big A for adultery on our chests because it had been announced from the altar that we were resigning and would be replaced. This was a Holy Name Society and they had given us free tickets and we went over and in my whole life I've never gone through anything like it.

SISTER HONORA   That Saturday after we received the unsigned memo there was a meeting and there must have been at least thirty people there and I think that was the foundation of SOS. And when we were at that meeting we were saying, "Don't worry about us, just save the school." We thought they were out to close the school, because the clergy really weren't that much in favor of the school. Financially it was a drain on the parish and the school was very successful and they didn't like that either. It was very successful, very happy. Every single classroom was filled, thirty children in each.

SISTER CATHERINE   I have this letter which was sent in October of 1981. That's the fall of the year we were fired. The school was evidently having tremendous financial difficulties, which is what put it in our minds that they wanted to close the school, not get rid of us. In fact, I can remember that Saturday morning we kept saying, you know, to the ladies, "Don't worry about *us*! Because we can certainly take care of ourselves. We always have."

SISTER HONORA   No problem. We can get a job anywhere.

SISTER CATHERINE   Yeah, famous last words. But in October they wrote this letter about how much they needed money, so finances were uppermost in our minds. The pastor was always talking about money, money, money. Even all the time, as I said to you when you came in, about the heat in the convent. 'Cause the school pays for the convent, so we were always worried about having too much heat on or, you know, saving money here, there, but not now!

SISTER HONORA   We've been replaced by lay teachers.

SISTER JUSTINE   Luckily no sister even applied, I guess. Oh they wanted sisters. 'Cause it's cheap help. It's at least half salary. Oh yes, Sisters of

Mercy. Can you imagine how that would have hurt? A sister in Chicago who's the head of a group of sisters called the National Coalition of American Nuns gave out a press release and said that any sister who took the place of any one of the four New Hampshire sisters of Hampton would be like putting a knife in the sister's back and a stone in her hand instead of bread or something like that. Her name is Margaret Traxler. We love her. We met her this summer. She is magnificent.

SISTER CATHERINE   What a woman! Dynamic. 'Course we talked to her and we became such good friends with these people. Of course we were delighted because where we *should* have gotten support, our Community, it was denied us. We were cut off from the church, we were cut off from our Community so these people from the larger community became our support and as Sister Justine said, she had national clout. *Nobody* knew us! It went to court in April. We've got the date. April Fool's Day. Imagine it! My dear!! Oh!!

SISTER JUSTINE   We didn't even know we had an attorney. We were fired on the Thursday and Catholic Education Week began Sunday and we had a whole lot of different activities going on that week. Like a luncheon for senior citizens and a potluck luncheon for the School Board and the clergy! And they *came*! We couldn't believe it and Katie said it was like sitting with Judas.

SISTER CATHERINE   We sat with the pastor. We sat right with him and of course we were so nervous. You know, we did everything right. I was in charge, so we said, we're gonna make this nice. I mean, nobody's gonna come. They won't come. The School Board won't come. We'll make all the food and eat it ourselves! It was, what do you call it, Valentine's Day. The table was smashing. There was a snowstorm that morning so we had plenty of time, delayed opening, and the kids were in helping set up the library with red and white and everything. Nobody had RSVP'd so we figured it would just be the faculty. When we had planned it we didn't know we were going to be fired.

SISTER JUSTINE   We sent invitations to everybody and no one responded, but they all came!

SISTER CATHERINE   My dear, the whole School Board showed! They trooped in together!

SISTER JUSTINE   And all the clergy.

SISTER HONORA   I couldn't believe it.

SISTER CATHERINE   Talk about choking. So I'm sitting back to back with Father Jerry and he made a remark, 'cause I'm eating all these desserts and my plate of course, was filled. I took all this food. "Oh my," he says, "eating." I says, "Yes." I says, "Father I don't even know what I'm eating." I said, "Can you imagine me sitting here having lunch with people that fired me?" And I says, "But I suppose Christ had to eat the last supper with Judas." He says, "That's right." He says that's right!!

SISTER JUSTINE   So anyhow, it was SOS, the parents' group, that got the attorney for us and the attorney drew up a position paper for Sister Honora to present to the School Board asking could we please have a hearing. Which is all we wanted. To find out why we were—whatever we were. They don't like us to say we were fired. Oh no. So we always say we were fired. So Sister Honora presented this Statement in Support of the Sisters of Mercy, God help us, and I'm sure John McEachern and Dan Thornhill, our attorneys, along with the rest of the world, had never had suing nuns.

SISTER HONORA   Singing nuns, but not suing. Reading that paper over was a big shock for the School Board because this was supposed to be their big secret meeting and Dan Thornhill came in with me—'course he practically pushed me in the door—and they said, "Who is he?" Then they really started dancing around, saying, "You can't have an attorney." We were thrown out. I mean he was. They wouldn't allow him in so we left the paper and we left. See, they make their own rules.

SISTER CATHERINE   As I said to someone—'course people get upset with us when we talk this way—we know there will be dire consequences before this is all finished. Oh, I'm sure. I'm sure we will be, we'll get the sign.

SISTER HONORA   Booted.

SISTER CATHERINE   I'm sure we will. I'm sure we will be eventually asked to leave the Congregation and I'm sure we will be excommunicated from the Church. Yes, I'm deadly serious. Because we are speaking against the Church. I mean, what else can you say it is? The Church has a two-thousand-year history of dominance. I mean, it's the year of Martin Luther and look what happened to him. But this is the way they see it and this is the way they've seen it from the beginning. The Church, the hierarchy. It's an uncharted course. My relationship with Almighty God will never change. I'm not that worried about the Church. I'll be embarrassed for my family when we're excommunicated, or bounced. I'll be embarrassed, I know I will. I'll feel bad for them, but I mean, God is God and I'm sure He's getting a good laugh out of all this. I see what's happening to us as part of a larger question. Oh *yes*, and we don't even know it. That's the sad part. I think we're instruments. I just think we're being used by Almighty God, if you will, as empty vessels and you know, He'll just move us where He will. I think it's all part of a Divine Plan. I think it is time for the Church to face up to what it has been telling us is justice and charity and Christianity for two thousand years; to practice what they preach. The sad part is, the four of us are just so insignificant. You wouldn't have known us before! Imagine having a professor of anthropology come to the convent to talk with us? It's unbelievable. That's what I said to somebody, a professor!

And you know, we're the same. We are the same people we always were and that will never be any different. So it's all like it's outside of us, or we're looking at this happening to us. We read about it and say, "*Isn't that interesting.*" "Imagine that!" You know, "Those bold things, saying that." But that's why I think it is a small microcosm of the revolution that is going on in the Church. Especially in the American Church. But see, we're the least likely to be in this position because we weren't flag raisers and we weren't rabble rousers and we're—

SISTER JUSTINE   Middle aged, except for Katie over there, the three of us are fifty-three and she's forty-nine, so we're the perfect age.

SISTER CATHERINE   Over the hill. And in *New Hampshire?*

SISTER JUSTINE   Did we tell you? Can I tell you this? In this same line, the whole thing is over and done with, settled. Every day we'll meet people and they'll say now, "Why?" "What was the real reason you were fired?" And that's, as God is my judge, what *we* don't even know. But I think it's very fortunate that it happened to us. We have nothing to lose because we have nothing to begin with. We have vows of poverty and we function in the Church. We do not have to support families, so no matter what happens to me, I mean, I know I can, I won't like it too much, ending up in a welfare home for the aged, because I've visited and I see what goes on in some of those places, but I'd be willing to accept that. I mean that I can go on in my old age if I'm privileged to reach old age. We have nothing to lose, see. We're not used to any big financial dealings. We work for a pittance. We don't need it. For thirty years I've lived simply. What made it easy was there were four of us. So if it had to happen to anyone, it's just as well it was the four of us. People think that we're simpletons and we aren't. You know, we have native intelligence. That's what I thank God for. I have the native intelligence that came to me through my parents 'cause otherwise I wouldn't have been able to take this. And they would have been putting stuff over on us left and right. I mean, I would prefer it had never happened to me, but if it had to happen, it's just as well it's us.

SISTER CATHERINE   We are an embarrassment to the Church. Oh definitely, and I think the worst part for the Church is, God forgive me for saying all of this, I'm saying the hierarchical church as it has developed down, not as Christ established the Church, the Church as it is. I'm not denying the faith or anything like that, but if they could get something on one of us that would blow our credentials, I'm sure that would be published. And thank God, again, we're poor innocents. And I'm sure they have researched every one of our brothers and sisters to see if there's anything. I am convinced of that. To see if they can't embarrass us.

SISTER JUSTINE   All we wanted was a little hearing. We hadn't done anything wrong. You know, we still have to deal with our Community, the Sisters of Mercy. See, we haven't straightened this out. I mean, I don't know how it will be resolved, but we couldn't just take it. *No one* could have taken it. It was just so insane. It was unjust. It was wrong! It was absolutely, one hundred percent incorrect.

SISTER CATHERINE   See, I hate to say it, but we knew, I knew I was a good teacher. I mean, I knew that. I've taught twenty-five years and I know I was a successful teacher. I *knew* there wasn't anything I had done that would make me a candidate for being fired. So I would never, I *knew* I wouldn't resign. So they had to fire me. Just like I will never leave the Community, the Congregation of the Sisters of Mercy. They're gonna have to *put* me out. And it's the same with the Church. I will never withdraw from the Church. They'll have to put me out and it'll have to be formal and it'll have to be in writing and it'll be public, see? 'Cause, I mean, forget it.

SISTER JUSTINE   Yes, I think a lot of people I know would have resigned. But if the School Board could have given me the reasons why I should leave and if I could accept them, I would have left. But again, they never could have come up, I'll be honest, they couldn't come up with anything against me personally. But if they could have come up with a reason, I'm a reasonable person, I would have left if it made sense to me. But see, they never gave us the reasons.

SISTER CATHERINE   And the Bishop kept saying, *"You know the reasons."* He called. He started calling here. And I said to him on the phone, "Okay, Bishop, supposing you did tell us the reason"—'cause he told us he told us the reason, which is a lie, but you don't want to say the Bishop lied, but he didn't tell us the reason! So anyway, I said, "Very well. Now supposing, Bishop, you did tell us the reasons, take that as a given, and I forgot. Will you tell me again? What they are?" Nothing. Nothing. No answer. There's no reason. So on May fourth, this was when we had the big meeting, oh, he kept asking for meetings. "We'd meet as sister and priest again." I said we'd be glad to come if we can bring our attorney. "No, we don't want any attorney. No attorney." Well finally he said we would meet and we could bring our attorneys. Well, my dear. We went. It was supposed to be in the diocesan office, it was in the Bishop's residence. *I am sure* he has never in his life before nor since been addressed this way. We went at him hammer and tongs. And one of the things I pointed out to him was, I said, "Name a thing. *Name a charge.* In front of all these people here, name one thing that I've done." He says, no he didn't speak, Father Christian, who is his secretary—what do you call 'em? Chancellor of the Diocese—he said, "You resigned from the Parish Council." I said, "Pardon me?" He said, "You resigned from the Parish Council two years ago." Or three years ago, I guess three years ago. "And you know the story." I said, "Wait a minute, what story? *You* tell *me* the story and then I'll let you know if that's the true story." So he proceeded to say that three years ago it was decided that the convent would become a fallout shelter.

SISTER JUSTINE   We have no basement.

SISTER CATHERINE   And I objected to the convent being a fallout shelter because this is my home. And again, in my innocence, you know, at the time how simple I was, I said, "And what about this cloister?" I mean, there is such a thing as cloister in a convent. The upstairs is not supposed to be open, it's supposed to be a cloistered area. And Father Roger, not the superintendent of schools, but another Father Roger, said, "There's no such thing as cloister with the revised canon law." 'Course I didn't know anything about that, but anyway, as far as I'm concerned, simple Sister of Mercy, I thought you weren't supposed to have men upstairs. Okay, so since I felt that I hadn't received backing from the Council membership, I resigned. I wrote a letter of resignation and I got a letter back from the Council accepting my resignation with regret. So that was the end of that. And I said, "Well, Father, you've told that correctly." And I said, "And I was fired for doing that three years ago?" And Justine says—

SISTER JUSTINE   Give *me* an example. And the Bishop, I think, said this. He said, "How do you get along with the sisters that you live with?" And I pointed to the other three and said, "*These* are the sisters I live with! And Sister Julie and Sister Doris and there isn't any problem." 'Course people think we're a little forward with the Bishop, but I mean, we know him. He's a local boy. He happens to come from New Hampshire and that's very unusual, to have a local boy become a Bishop. So I mean, he's just a common ordinary parish priest, that's what he is, Okay?

SISTER HONORA   It's because we didn't get along with the clergy.

SISTER JUSTINE   Basically, it's definitely the School Board Chairman. This is my idea. She used to like us, she liked us up until two months, I'd say, before. But she just wanted her way. And it wasn't just us, it was the lay teachers too. Now we had two lay faculty resign in protest over our firing. And the head librarian resigned in protest and the school nurse resigned. Most of the volunteers. Now they gave up their jobs. They risked their jobs. Luckily the teachers got other positions and the school nurse is working part time. She's a nurse, she'll get along, but we weren't the only ones. And we all felt the same way, that it was the School Board. They wanted an honor roll, the faculty didn't want an honor roll. They said we were too strict in marking. The School Board kept changing you know, over a period of six years, but they chose their own types and their friends and it was absolutely a terrible, terrible thing. Later seventeen members of the SOS ran for the School Board, you know, put in their résumés, and each one, well except for one, they all received letters saying that they were not eligible because they weren't Catholics in good standing because they supported us. And to think that the Bishop would permit that to be done. When we were fired, 97 children were withdrawn out of a student body of 240. Their parents withdrew them and kept them out. They've gone to public school. The parents wrote to the Bishop and said they'd put the children back when we'd been given a hearing.

Oh yes, ethnicity played a part, even though we're not supposed to say

it. But we know there's a difference. I'll tell you one thing. The clergy—
there were three of them—are all of French background. They have never
had Sisters of Mercy. They had had sisters of French background and
though Sister Mary Rita lost her certification because of a remark like
this—

SISTER CATHERINE Sister Mary Rita was not recertified as a teacher in
the Diocese of Manchester because of an ethnic remark which was published in the *Globe*.

SISTER JUSTINE What the remark was, well, the woman reporter from
the *Globe* came and she talked and was trying to find out why, why, why.
Why were we fired. And we didn't know. We didn't know. She said, "Is
it possible that it might have something to do with ethnicity?" And so
Sister Mary Rita said, "Well, if it's not our moral character and if it's not
our professionalism, and it's not this and that, maybe it is." And she was
quoted and she did say that. That's it. We've got the article somewhere.
And she was un-Catholic because she was suing the Bishop, which is
against canon law. She was an "un-Catholic Christian." We didn't know
what that meant!

SISTER CATHERINE Oh, the terms! And 'course people would try to supply
us with reasons and we'd say, well maybe that *is* a reason.

SISTER JUSTINE What is ethnic? Ethnic is nationality, okay? And I would
say that the Irish, from what I know, the Irish women are very strong in
the household, running things. And I think that's evidenced in the four of
us. Whereas someone from another ethnic background (without my saying
French), the men are used to running the show and they are used to
women being subservient. The four of us are very strong women, but we
never used it in an oppressive manner. We had a very nice atmosphere in
the school. The school was well run and yet loose enough. You could let
the kids be loose because they could be pulled back very quickly. So there
was a very comfortable feeling in the school. There was a lot of freedom
so we didn't lord it. But the pastor was a very nervous man.

SISTER HONORA He went to the Bishop and told him that he never felt
welcome and I remember speaking with the Bishop, saying, "I don't understand why he doesn't feel welcome. I certainly never did anything to make
him feel that way."

SISTER JUSTINE He was so nervous. You could never pin him down. He
could never come and just sit in my class. He'd come through the classrooms after school was out for the day. He could never sit and have a nice
conversation 'cause he was always jumping away. He was uncomfortable.
That's it, and God knows, we sure didn't do anything. And then, after we
were fired he cried and kept saying, "I'm so sorry." That he had done this
to us, or whatever. They all apologized at the end. The Bishop apologized.

Father Jerry apologized. Brother Roger apologized. They all went and shook our hands and said, "I'm sorry, I'm sorry." 'Course we didn't say, "I'm sorry."

SISTER CATHERINE   But the day that everything was settled, outside on the steps of the courthouse, they all apologized and that night we had to go to a meeting. A Sisters of Mercy meeting in Windham. We wanted to watch the evening news and so we were late for the meeting. We arrived and all the seats were taken.

SISTER JUSTINE   Talk about lepers!

SISTER CATHERINE   Here we had just settled this national event and they don't even say, "Hello, will you come in?"

SISTER HONORA   And they're not even watching the TV!

SISTER CATHERINE   So we go to the meeting, even though we didn't want to go and all the seats are taken, so they rush, rush, to get us seats and we sit down. They're in the middle of prayer and they can't interrupt the prayer to say hello. You can't, you know, recognize another human being. On the way to the grave, you keep your prayer. Oh no, it isn't over yet. We went to a meeting, Justine and I, in Windham. We don't go to parties but we'll go to spiritual or religious observances. So anyway, we went to the mass and 'course they're looking at the two of us going, "Oh! Look at the bold things" at the little procession beforehand and all. Well, it was just horrible. Just the thought of facing them, you know, you'd just as soon die as not, but you go and do it. So Justine is standing there talking to Sister Paula.

SISTER JUSTINE   She says, "How are you?" What do you say? What can I say?

SISTER CATHERINE   I mean, you're ruined for life, destroyed. You have nothing left.

SISTER JUSTINE   And she says, "How *are* you?" How are you?

SISTER CATHERINE   Exactly. It's like a Superior we had once. And they said, "Who'll be in charge of the sick?" She says, "There'll *be* no sick."

SISTER JUSTINE   And 'course I can imagine the look on my face because I just change all over. And Paula said, "What you did was wrong. I don't go along with it. I don't know all of it"—and didn't Mary Griffin say, "I don't know all the facts"?

SISTER CATHERINE   And we said, "Welcome to the group. We don't know all the facts either!" Then we were invited to lunch, if you can believe it.

SISTER JUSTINE   I said to them, don't be nice to me, because it's not over yet. I don't want them to think it's settled. It isn't. I mean, it's settled legally, but the Church still has to face up to what it did.

SISTER CATHERINE   One of the women told us that one of the clergy had said to her Thursday night, the night of the day we were fired, "They're nothing but big fat zeros in their own Community."

You know, a complete change in our life has resulted from our taking the stand. Especially that alienation from our friends. And it will never go back to what it was. For myself, and I'm just talking for myself, in the old days, when we entered the Community, having secular friends was frowned upon. You were only supposed to have friends in the Community. So for myself, all of my friends were in the Community, were other religious. Then, in the sixties and seventies, after the changes came about with Vatican II, so many sisters left the Community, all my friends left and I celebrated my Silver Jubilee alone. I was the only one in my band who persevered. But the interesting thing is that since this controversy, I think there isn't one who has left the Community who hasn't called and voiced her support of us and of what we've done. But the ones who stayed in don't. I'd say thirty out of three hundred have been vocal in supporting us. So see, that was very hard for me to have sisters that were friends that would just turn on me.

SISTER JUSTINE   They haven't even tried to investigate. I mean, they liked us before. And it's a very difficult thing to live through, John. I'm telling you right now. So it's no simple thing. I mean, it was a simple thing to say, "I will not resign," but it's very difficult to live day by day and meet up with people and every single day we're meeting up with people and very few will confront us. And all the time during the controversy when you'd meet people they'd just say, "How are you, how is your sister?" That sort of thing. They wouldn't even mention it.

SISTER CATHERINE   Some people take what we have done and what we're saying as being a deliberate effort on our part to destroy the Church. We just got a letter yesterday from a man in Somersworth, which is a small town around here, and that's just what he said.

SISTER JUSTINE   We do get what you'd call hate mail. It's terrible what they call us.

SISTER CATHERINE   The Bishop himself came and made a speech from the altar one Sunday and said that support for us was breaking the body of Christ.

SISTER HONORA   They tried all kinds of things.

SISTER CATHERINE   See, this was the difficult thing. They used religion in a secular argument. We were talking about employment and they used the Church. It was almost as if to scare us and we didn't scare. I never saw it as religious. That's why I said to the Bishop, "You have slandered us by innuendo. We have been sinned against." I would say this is what the lines were drawn up on. If you sided with us, or with our position, you were in opposition to the Church. I think that was the misuse of power.

SISTER JUSTINE   'Course you know a very *terrible* thing was that the priest stopped saying mass in our chapel. We always had mass every day in the chapel. And last year they just, nothing was ever said, but they just stopped, period. We were treated as if we were squatters here. It was terrible. Terrible, terrible, terrible. But Mr. Warren, our beautiful janitor, never changed. He came over and he fixed and did anything we wanted. He just said, "Now you just tell me what you need." He never gave up on us, never.

SISTER HONORA   You know, the day we went to Superior Court, he left a sign on our door saying something about "The truck is filled with gas"— just in case we wanted to sneak out in the middle of the night!

SISTER CATHERINE   'Cause we were evicted, you know, We'll tell you about that! But to get back to the court thing. In December 1982, right? Two days before Christmas, the Supreme Court of New Hampshire overturned the Superior Court ruling, saying that we did have a right to sue. So I'm sure from Rome to Washington to Manchester they didn't think where it was gonna go. Never, never. And the Bishop told us the Vatican was in on it. And the Apostolic Delegate. Archbishop Pio Laghi. It was a victory for us 'cause we had a right to sue the Bishop. See *nobody* could sue a bishop before. It said we could sue anyone we wanted to! It said that! Oh, it's tremendous. We could sue the School Board, we could sue the Superintendent. We could sue them all! And we did. And they sent it back to the Superior Court to give us the hearing.

SISTER JUSTINE   We never mentioned it in school, except that first day. And I had strict rules in my classroom regarding the big walk-in closet with the scissors and all and you cannot trust a kid for one minute, sixth-grader like that, with a ruler, or a pair of scissors, and they knew. They never would go into that closet without asking because that's where the stuff was and I couldn't trust them. I hate to say it, but the boys especially, you just couldn't trust them! So we had a silent reading period every day for twenty minutes and this was that Friday after we got fired and they were having that silent reading. All this hell has broken loose, but we have silent reading! So I was sitting there with my head down, reading. Well, I could feel such energy. The kids were always terrible anyway during the silent reading, but I could hear all kinds of activity. Kids just vibrate anyway, and I was up in the back of the room and I would hear the closet door opening and closing, staplers going, Magic Markers, and I kinda looked up and I said to myself, "Go to it kids! I deserve it! I deserve it!" They were making posters, "Save Our Sisters!" and all this stuff. And one kid made a, now they didn't know it was a miter, but it was like a bishop's miter. One boy, the biggest devil in the room, had gone right out of my classroom, into the next classroom! I found this out later. He had gone to the teacher and she helped him fashion this hat, which was a miter, and she's in there stapling it for him and he puts a big cross on the front and then they all had their rulers and they had like posters on the rulers. Banners and all this business. And I just sat! And then the classroom door opened and I sensed the whole thing and they're leaving the room! They are leaving! And I'm saying to myself, "Go to it kids!" And I kinda looked up and they're marching, this is the God's truth, up and down the corridor! The whole length of the corridor. 'Course when the bell rings for recess I rated no loyalty, they all ran back into the room, off came the miter—it was worth a million bucks! One of them said, "Sister, can we go walk in front of the rectory?" I said, "No, dear, no, no, dear. That's all right." On the board, afterward, in my classroom was a poster a kid had put up. I have it now up in my room here. I kept it. It says, "Save our Sisters!" Now, this child is not a Catholic, for the love of God, and he had gone back and it was all done in red and in ink he put, "Signed, Ben." So I have that and then I kept a little heart that someone made and it said something like, "Save Our Sisters. Save Them All." And then it had the four of us, our names, and 'course we're all misspelled! Worth a million bucks.

SISTER CATHERINE   At the end of that year we didn't go back but we still said we were under contract. That's what we said because our contract had been violated. It was summer and of course we weren't evicted, though we had been threatened with eviction in May. The reporters would say, "You gonna evict them?" And the answer was "Well, they can stay through the summer if they behave themselves." Because that was insane. You can't evict nuns. Can you imagine what publicity there would be, throwing us out bodily? From here? With valises coming down the stairs? Can you imagine that?

SISTER JUSTINE   Last year, that was hard, seeing the kids come in. This year it's not so bad. I go about my business in here and don't notice it as much. The person who took my place is a lay person. I don't know anything about her. Luckily I've never had to meet her. I don't even know where she comes from. Oh yeah, I'm sure she thinks she's saving the Church. I'll never forget the feeling that she is in there taking *my* class. Oh, it was terrible. Oh yes, I always knew I wanted to teach. From the first, oh yes, always. Never had any other idea, since first grade. That's the God's truth. It's my gift, I feel. I've always wanted to teach. And I still do. I miss teaching. I love teaching. I love the smell of chalk. I love the classroom. That's God's truth. Just to walk into a classroom. And I tutor just one day a week and I'm grateful for that, to still have my hand in it. I just love it. I work with one child and I wish I had more than the one. I'd like to have a whole group of 'em in there.

My mother and father were never meek. My father was a big union man and very active in the union. He was a very quiet homebody, but the reason we know he was active in the union was that he went to meetings every Monday night and that was the only night we could get out of the house!

My father would go to Dover for the union meetings and my mother would live for it 'cause she wanted us to be out having a good time. But he was very strict. He struck once when he was a very young man. No, he didn't strike, that's it. Everyone else struck and he didn't and he lost his job. And the ones who struck won and then maybe he joined the union after that, but he never struck again. I don't know why my father didn't go along with the others, but it was unfair that they were kept and he was fired.

My mother and father ran the household together. My mother was silently strong and yet she didn't lord it over him. He was not henpecked. See, I never thought about standing out against authority. I think just standing out, period. Like my mother would send us out. She had a saying, "Go out and be one among them." Now we never knew exactly what that meant. We might be uncomfortable with what we had on or with an assignment or something or some way that we had to perform in class and we felt inferior about it and my mother would say, "You go out and you hold your head high and you will be one among them." Later on we kinda caught on. We're supposed to assume our place, even though we might not be dressed as nice or be as well prepared, we should hold our head up high. But I never thought about standing out against authority. I liked people who would stand up for what was right, but not necessarily stand against authority. Basically, when you come down to it, I suppose it is the same thing sometimes, but I never thought about it in that regard.

SISTER HONORA   My father was a railroad engineer and he was strong in the union too. I can remember him saying, "Remember who you are. Your name is Reardon." Also I spent a lot of my childhood and in high school and college participating in sports, and I think justice comes in there too. The rules of the game and playing fair.

SISTER JUSTINE   When I say go out, I mean, just to go out on the streets around Newcastle. Out of the house, that's it! We would just *wait* for that car to go out of that driveway. My mother loved a good time and wanted us to have a good time. I don't know whether my father knew we went out or not but there was never any complaint. It was a very tiny, tiny town. And we had braids, we wore braids till we were a thousand and I came home one night from a dance and it must have been high school and I didn't have one dance. And I came home crying to my mother. And I said, "I know it's my braids. It's my braids." And my mother spoke to my father evidently that night, because the next day she told me I could get rid of my braids. Now, of course, I love braids on kids, but then we hated them. I suppose it kept us simple, I don't know.

SISTER HONORA   The Bishop will have everybody in braids!

SISTER CATHERINE   And then one time I remember when I was little we used to have a coal furnace down in the cellar and in the hall we had a big register. We'd have our hair washed and sit around that register and that way we'd dry our hair. And oh, the snarls, because there was no such thing as "No tangle, no tears" and I said to my mother when she was brushing my hair one time, "Hurry up." *And she did.* And the snarls! And there wasn't a thing I could do, see, 'cause I'd said, "Hurry up." Oh! So we were not really defiant, but whatever we did, we knew there was immediate consequence to the act. Another time I remember my cousin was over at the house and we must have wanted money. 'Course we never had any money or anything, and I'd hear things and I would repeat them. Anyway, I wanted some money to go somewhere or whatever and my aunt was there, too, and my cousin was the same age as me, and my mother must have said no to whatever it was that cost money. So then I said to her, "The almighty dollar." *I* got, it was my last slap, and I got it right across the face and I'll never forget it. 'Cause I was humiliated in front of my cousin and, see, I really didn't know what I was saying. I must have heard it somewhere and it sounded good at the time. No, honestly, I didn't think I was being fresh. No, not to my mother! But we always say that when we entered the convent, we didn't ever have to worry about superiors because we had my mother and my father!

And whatever you did, you had to report it anyway. Once I was cleaning upstairs in the bathroom and I must have been doing a thorough job and I *lifted* the bathtub, got the picture? up off the floor and disconnected the pipes! God only knows how, and I remember I had to stand at the door and wait for my father to come in and report that I had done this. The discipline in our house was always universal. Whatever we did, we did as a group. Justine was the ringleader. She had all the ideas, and then my brother would follow suit and I'd just go along anyway, 'cause I'd know they were gonna get caught and we'd all get caught. Oh I told, yes. It's really funny. That's why now if I have something on my conscience or whatever, I always feel better to say it out and then I don't have to worry about it anymore, see, 'cause, as I say, I always knew there was a consequence. You never had to wonder *what* was gonna happen. You were gonna get a spanking. And we always did. We all came from families where the mother was a strong influence, but I wouldn't call my mother overbearing. If you asked me who was the head of the house, I would say my father was the head of the house, he thought. And he always did. But we always knew if you went to my mother and told her, just like Justine with her hair, or asked her something, that night she'd speak to him and he'd change his mind. Absolutely, and we knew that. So that's the way we were brought up. See, the trouble with America is that it was founded on certain principles, and you were brought up as an American on those. The Bill of Rights and all of that was driven in. You know, human rights and the rights of the individual become a real part of you. But what we did was in opposition to the Holy Roman Catholic Church. And I'm sure some of them must think of us as heretics. I'm *sure* they must. And would love to see us condemned.

SISTER JUSTINE   Burned at the stake.

SISTER CATHERINE   Yup, it's true. Very, very strong feeling that what we did was anti-Catholic and anti-Christ. I guess that's one of the canons. You can't sue the bishop. You're excommunicated if you sue the bishop. There really is a canon. But that's my problem, I guess. I think obedience has to be free.

SISTER JUSTINE   I don't think God wants to be obeyed. I don't think He would even think in terms of being obeyed. We're the ones who think we should obey God.

SISTER CATHERINE   You should have heard the Bishop's poor attorney, trying to tell us about obedience. Saying that I had a vow of obedience to the Bishop. "I beg your pardon!" I said, "I never took a vow of obedience to the Bishop. I have a vow of obedience to *God*, not the Bishop! I never said I'd obey the Bishop!" They all thought that. This is all in the transcript. This is the whole misconception of authority.

SISTER JUSTINE   I want to go back, just in case God calls me to judgment tonight. Dear God, I'm not saying that I might not want to obey God, but what I really think is, I don't think God wants to be obeyed. I mean, that would almost do away with the whole idea of God. I don't think God would ever want to be obeyed. That's a weakness. If you want someone to obey you, that's a weakness. As soon as you get your wants, then what? So I couldn't even think in those terms. See, 'cause we're just simple— 'course I hate that word, simple, too. That just drives me crazy—people who say they're just poor, simple people, they don't want to get involved. One of our own sisters when we were at a wake a couple months ago said, "I don't want to get involved. I don't want to hear it." I said, "Listen, we *had* to get involved. Did you realize we never"—'course this is at a funeral, the casket is there and all the family's around and I'm trying to keep it low—"Sister, do you realize we have a clean slate from the diocese?" "Yuh, I don't want to hear it. I don't want to get involved."

SISTER CATHERINE   We had a boy at the Sacred Heart School and his father is in ball bearings, or something, and he goes all over the world selling his wares and one time he was in Indonesia in the airport and he's going through the Indonesian edition of *Time* magazine and he goes, "Oh, I know those women! That's Sister Honora and Sister Justine." Now if the article in *Time* magazine made it to Indonesia, you *know* it went to Rome! Plus again, from what we have been led to believe, no nun *ever* sued a bishop. In fact, one newspaper said we were suing God! "Nuns Sue God!" So it *must* have gone to Rome and Rome got upset about it because we had a case. And it will not go away, and neither will we.

SISTER JUSTINE   Now we have to think about where we do go from here. It's almost as if we're the over-the-hill gang. See, if they could have let us go quietly, we would have been gone in thirteen years anyway, we would have retired from the diocese.

SISTER CATHERINE   And we would have died and they wouldn't have known who we are. And now George Warren says, "See," he says, "I told you, on your tombstone they're gonna write, "She Sued the Bishop." So they should have left us alone, really. See, we thought, it's so simple. We kept *saying* that. You know, it's so simple, and either our contract— and I've included a copy of the contract in the packet for you—either that's a valid contract and the terms are valid or it isn't! So anyway, we have this new pastor and he said he would come twice a week and every time he gives a sermon I know it's for us. And I'm saying to myself, it's too late, you know what I mean? Don't tell us *now*.

SISTER JUSTINE   We were a captive audience.

SISTER HONORA   Equal opportunity, I think.

SISTER CATHERINE   He spoke of a person in the scripture and he had no name and no one would remember what he had done and he lived and he died anonymously. And then he said how the vast majority of the priests he had known over the years were unknown. And he said, that's the way it should be. Even if you do great things, they should be done anonymously. And I'm sittin' in my seat and I'm saying, "I'm gonna have it on my tombstone, 'She Sued the Bishop.' " You should have told us this two years ago, not be sayin' it now!" But the other day the girl came from UPI. And didn't she go to the rectory? Which we were afraid you would do. And she knocked on the door and said, "I'd like to speak to the sisters, I'm from United Press." And the pastor says, "Wa-a-a?" She says, "United Press International." "Why do you want to see them?" "We're going to have an interview." "Why are you having an interview?" "Well," she says, "it's Christmastime." 'Course we loved that. What that had to do with anything I don't know. Oh, she was lovely. Charming. We've met so many nice people. Well, my dear. The next sermon was on—

SISTER HONORA   United Press?

SISTER CATHERINE   No, on when we speak and the rippling effects that it has on others. It's too late now. They tell us all this stuff afterward.

SISTER HONORA   Like, "You can't sue the bishop."

SISTER CATHERINE   It dawned on us, after the thing was all over, part of the settlement was that we would abide in this convent for a year. The only names on that settlement are our two attorneys and the diocesan attorney. Which makes that a legal document. So, in effect, that legal document told the Church who would live on its property. I don't think that even dawned on them. I don't think the Bishop knows that. I don't think Archbishop Pio Laghi knows that and I don't think Pope John knows it.

SISTER JUSTINE   The Church needs to be told at times certain things. Let's say we were satisfied. We were very satisfied with the settlement. Personally I was. We were glad that it happened the way it did. And now, looking back on it, I think it's better than we ever thought it would be.

God knows what's going to happen in July. I can't even see. I have no idea what's going to happen. No idea. I don't know how much courage I have to do anything new. Whether I'll go and hide, I don't know.

SISTER CATHERINE   The only thing we're sure of is we're leaving here. We have to, that's legal. We said we would. That's part of the agreement.

SISTER JUSTINE   I know the reporters are gonna be out here and it'll be historical, to say nothing of hysterical.

SISTER HONORA   "Troublemakers leave."

SISTER JUSTINE   And we know one thing. We never, never asked any reporter to come or anything else. As God is my judge. We *never* called and said, "Hey, here's a hot tip." Oh, the media has been a great help to us. We would have been stuck without them, and everything that comes in the paper I'm delighted about. Every once in a while there'll be something—

SISTER CATHERINE   It'll be true, but we didn't necessarily want them to print it! And everybody says the press, oh they're terrible. Not us, we don't say that. *They* were our hearing. They were our forum.

SISTER JUSTINE   I don't think we were ever misquoted on what we said. They were very, very good, honestly. We are very, very grateful.

SISTER CATHERINE   And the Church hates them.

SISTER HONORA   'Course the SOS are responsible for a lot of support too.

SISTER CATHERINE   Oh, we wish someone would write about *them.*

SISTER JUSTINE   Yeah, the parents. They're the ones who should be written about. Oh, the organization they had—

SISTER HONORA   And the money they raised.

SISTER CATHERINE   And constantly calling up practically every hour on the hour to support us. The moral support.

SISTER JUSTINE   They'll drop in, they'll call. They're out of this world, the parents. But not one priest in the whole state came out for us.

SISTER CATHERINE   See, the difficulty is that we're such little fish in the stream. It's so insignificant. You know, this is the awful part of it, little did we know. You know, this is funny. One night we were here and we had such a good laugh. Maybe it was just the two of us and Sister Doris. And we were sitting here and Justine was working on her dolls and I probably was stuffing turtles, or whatever, for the church fair, beanbag turtles, that's my expertise, and here we are sitting, you know, in our nighties, and I always have an afghan on 'cause I'm always cold—

SISTER HONORA   Not this year.

SISTER CATHERINE   So we're just enjoying ourselves and all of a sudden Justine says, "Honestly, you know, if the Bishop could only see us in our natural environment, I mean, he was foolish to bother with us." You know, give them what they want and shut them up and then they'll go away. Give 'em a few beans—I'm always goin' into the store to get the cheapest beans and all—so we're saying to ourselves, if he only knew the *real* us, who we *really* are, and what was *made* of this. Again, by chance or by design, I prefer to think it was by design.

SISTER HONORA   He would probably like to go back to January 27, 1982, and change his mind, think it over for another week!

SISTER CATHERINE   This is the thing. I don't think that in Manchester on a diocesan level, they had any idea that it was going to have ramifications across the country, and we know more now than we did before about how far it could have gone if we had gone to court. And I certainly wasn't out to destroy the Church! Honestly I wasn't. And I wasn't out to destroy the whole federal aid to Catholic education either. On a university level? Not to mention the college and the little parochial school over here. No! All we wanted was a hearing! So that's been difficult. But I always held the Bishop responsible because he had the power. I don't think he ever started it, but he should have stopped it.

SISTER JUSTINE   We were an affront to the office of bishop. That's why they said, "Who do they think they are?" I mean, the Bishop is as human, as ordinary as the rest of us.

Alice Thompson

"An indecisive person is not a reliable person."

□ □ □

If God helps you, None can overcome you.

HOLY KORAN III.160

Tranquil, diminutive Alice Thompson and her lively, well-behaved thirteen-year-old, Tracey, met and talked with me in my office at Syracuse University. Our meeting was a dividend of a series of lectures and seminars I had given at LeMoyne College in Syracuse. The Reverend Frank Haig, president of that Jesuit institution, had attended the evening seminar and suggested Mrs. Thompson as a possible participant in my inquiry into principled dissent.

Alice remembered and reviewed her life for two absorbing evenings in the raw, rainy Syracuse spring. Tracey's presence was a positive asset to the climate of rapport. She diverted and diapered the youngest member of the seminar, her two-year-old cousin, and punctuated her mother's reflections with more than one pungent, pertinent observation.

To hear Alice remembering is not to come away with an impression of boastfulness. She is soft-spoken, so soft-spoken that it was necessary to put the tape recorder very close to her. As we got to know each other better, her voice became more animated, but never very loud. A persistent element in her self-perception is the view that she is often a kind of thin entering wedge of divine purpose. Although conscious of herself as a "tiny" person, she is resolute in her conviction that her Roman Catholic faith has made her whole and strong. So strong is her faith in God and His right that neither the august council of chiefs or the revered clan mothers of her Onondaga Indian Nation have prevailed against it. Armed with that certainty, she has challenged everything from racism to thuggery.

For Alice, principled dissent, standing up and out for what she believes is right, is a natural constituent of her faith. She has suffered for it, is cognizant of the possibility that she might die for it, but cannot conceive of the possibility that she will be moved from it.

I'm forty-seven years old but I don't look forty-seven, so I understand. I look a lot younger. I don't know how you want me to describe myself. Let's see, I'm tiny, four foot eleven in stocking feet, four foot ten and a half maybe, I don't want to tell any fibs here. I have green eyes and my hair is brown and my complexion is medium, probably fair because I'm a northern Indian. I'm not from the southern or southwestern area where they're a lot darker from the sun, okay? And my weight is probably about one-twenty, which is probably what? Pleasingly plump? No, I don't think so! But anyway, is that important? I think that I'm a strong-willed person. I think that like Father Haig said, I do live by certain principles. What is right is right and two wrongs do not make one right. I believe that every woman in her own right should be, can be a powerful person. By powerful I mean decision making, standing on principle.

If I feel that there is something that is right, then I'll go for that. If someone else comes along and tells me that what I feel is right is not right, or they're going to change it to their own benefit, then I will argue that point and I'll stand right on my ground. And nobody can make me budge. I don't know why, maybe it could be my bringing up, you know, the way my family raised me. My family is all a Christian family. There are Protestants involved and Roman Catholics. I'm Roman Catholic. My dad was Roman Catholic. My mother is an Episcopalian and then she switched over to another Protestant religion. But basically the family is Christian oriented. There are two kinds of religions on the Reservation. It's either the Christian religions or its the traditional Indian religion. The traditional religion does not believe in Jesus, and they have basic reasons for it. One of them is that they were not there at the crucifixion, which is true. So they feel that if there was such a person, they were not involved. So they are blameless of this. It's nothing to do with them. But I do believe in Jesus Christ and I believe in the thing that happened to him and I believe that we have to live by some kind of good moral code. The world requires a law to live by, and part of that is the Ten Commandments, before the birth of Jesus and after. I believe that if we didn't have these laws we'd probably be at everybody's throats or killing one another— there's a lot of that going on now, but I mean, it's controlled in a way. On the Reservation, in the Iroquois (this would include all the Six Nations) we also—I have to say *we* because I live under those laws—we also have laws that we live by to right and to correct the wrongs.

So whoever lives there knows what the laws are, or should know. Many times it is overlooked and not bothered with because it's not the State of New York and it's not United States law; but it's legendary law. So you can look at it that way too. But regardless of what kind of law it is, and it's all religiously based, I still respect that law because I live there under the Longhouse traditional Indian rules. When I was growing up, my family was able to teach me what those laws were, what I must learn, what I must live by. Oh yes, yes, there is a basic conflict with Christianity. Like I say, traditionals don't believe in Jesus Christ. And the other thing they stress is, do not go to church. *Do not go to church.* Stay away from the church. I can't abide by that. I tell them, "I respect what you say and what you think, but you can't take me away from the church. I have to go to church." And it doesn't matter what they do to me, I still have to go to church because I believe in it. About ninety-five percent of the Indians on the Reservation now do not go to church anymore. It used to be the opposite. Now they have all turned to the Longhouse.

I attend Longhouse meetings but I don't attend the rituals. Because being a Christian I can't do that and do the other thing too. I can be there at the rituals, I just won't participate. Traditional people do not associate their Great Creator with God. They associate God with the white people. I want to learn and listen and try to grasp what they're trying to teach me and anything like that. I mean, I have an open mind. I still have my own principles in my heart and mind. I want to learn everything that they do. I think it's good for every Indian to do this, if they're not weak. If they're weak, I don't advise it because then they won't be able to control themselves, see?

I think people have given up on attempting to force me. They said I should not believe in the Church, the Church is nothing. Or, "We're gonna burn the church down." Things like that. It'll come to threats. They mean any church on the Reservation. In the very beginning in the fifteen hundreds, there was a church that was on the Onondaga Reservation. It was a St. Mary's Roman Catholic Mission with a Roman Catholic following, okay? And they did burn that mission down and they also burned the priests with it. Put them on a stake, tortured them, and then burned them. What happened was that the way the Indians saw it is that the Jesuits betrayed them. The army came to the mission for food and a place to stay. The Indians looked at it like they were guests of the Jesuits. The Jesuits didn't have control of the army, naturally, and they don't turn people out. But the Indians didn't look at it that way and they retaliated and decided to get rid of them all during the night, and that's what they did during a surprise ambush of some sort.

Right now, the Longhouse Society of some sort will not allow a Roman Catholic Church on the Reservation or a Roman Catholic Mission. They would prefer that there are no Catholics on the Reservation. This bothers them from way back in the days of LeMoyne, okay? There are Protestant churches there. The Episcopalian church had a problem during the evictions* and I did the best I could to defend that church. The pastor of the Episcopalian church at that time was ousted from the Reservation for his interference with the Great Law, as they call it. So anybody who is not Onondaga, or who is not Indian, they say, they're a threat to the Great Law. But they do not say Onondaga anymore. They say Indians, because we got so many Indians out there from the different nations that they

---

* In March of 1974, the Council of Chiefs of the Onondaga Nation decreed the eviction of any white people living on the Reservation, even those married to Onondaga. This decision has been the source of continuing bitter, often violent division in that reservation community.

don't want to offend anyone. But I will say Onondaga because that's the law and that's the truth. And it should not offend anybody. Of course, I will say to them first, "No offense to all you other Indians who don't belong here!" That doesn't sound so good does it?

Well, I don't know if you should talk to that Klan guy or not. It depends. I don't know. The Ku Klux Klan, as much as I've read about it and know about it, I wouldn't. I defied them once myself. In Florida. It was, again, principle. When my husband was in the navy we were stationed in Florida and my husband had a friend in the service and he and his wife were black. And my husband's commanding officer sent word over that they were informed by certain officials in the city and of the community, and all this bit, that if we're going to be down there we have to abide by their laws and one of them is that the blacks could not associate with the whites and the blacks live in certain areas and the whites live in certain areas and there's no association whatsoever. It was stressed that we should live that way, go by their rules. They just said the community. But we were told by our friend that it was basically the Ku Klux Klan. They were the ones who were pushing the community to do that.

So then I said, "Gee I've heard of them." I had read about them in high school, but I didn't know they still existed. You know, I thought it was something of the past and that the thing was over with. I said, "I thought this place was civilized down here. Apparently it isn't." I associated the Ku Klux Klan with the barbaric, uncivilized brute because I'd read so many bad things and never read anything good about them. And another thing was that they were white and that's the only race that existed as far as they were concerned. My skin is light, too, but I'm also a Native American and I could argue with the Ku Klux Klan and tell 'em they could just get right out of this country and go back where they started from, back across the ocean. And then what we did, because I didn't like it and we said nobody can tell us what to do about this, this is ridiculous, I said to my husband, "We're gonna go to church and we're gonna go to *their* church." And he said, "All right, we'll go to their church." So we went searching for their church and we found out it was a Baptist church and we walked in their church. It was a big church and the place was packed and we walked in and the people just looked at us. Everything got so quiet you could hear a pin drop and nobody knew what to say. They just looked at us so we found a place to sit and we sat right in the middle of everybody and we waited and then the pastor or whoever was standing up there cleared his throat, started talking, gave his announcements and everything, and when he was gonna start the sermon he says, "I believe that we have company here and maybe we should get introductions first before we continue." We acknowledged that he was referring to us and he said, "We believe that you are in the wrong church. Maybe you've lost your way. You're probably looking for another church." And we said, "This is the Baptist church of such and such?" Yes. "You have a parishioner named so and so?" Yes. "Oh this is the right church. We're in the right place." And they said, "Well, no, you don't understand. White people don't come in church with black people. We'll get in trouble or you'll get in trouble." So then we stood up and said, "Well, we're not white people, we're Native

Americans. We're Indian people, we're not white and besides, what difference does that make? We're all Christian people. We're all God's people." But they became very nervous, the people in the church, because we were causing them a problem by being there. So then each one of us stood up, introduced ourselves, who we were, where we were from, and said if anybody didn't like it that we were there, they knew where to contact us. You know, it was like taking the whole world on! And so we said we intended to stay and have Communion with them and listen to their sermon and then go home. Needless to say, they made the sermon quite short and then they had their Communion and practically ushered us out—in a nice way. They were happy that we dared, I guess, to come in. Nobody does this and we told them how we were happy that they let us sit in with them and listen to their sermons, and that we had no desire to attend any other church except that one and we had walked the streets looking for this place. And I enjoyed that, the music, the gospel sounds, and everything kind of reminded me of back home because I used to sing in a quartet with my sisters. The very next day, we got a message that if we ever go into a church again like that the next thing would be a cross burning in our front yard. So then I cracked up. I laughed! And this guy, this officer says, "What are you laughing about, they're serious." I said, "This is ridiculous! This only happens in the movies! They don't actually do that here do they?" And he said, "Yes, they do." And I said, "This is really savage. I can't believe it! And they used to say that *my* people were savages! This is outlawed. This is modern times." So then I said, "Well, you can just go back and tell these people that we will go to any church we want to and we'll have friends, as a matter of fact you can announce to them that we're having our friends over for dinner again." But you know, after that we didn't have too many friends, see? The friends stayed away from us. And it ended up, that whole thing, that I was actually in a fight. A physical fight with a bunch of women, see, and I really believe that caused me to lose my baby 'cause I got pretty well shoved around. But I didn't give up! These were all white women. All of a sudden they turned against me. Like they were trying to teach me a lesson. But I fought back. They didn't know they were fighting with an Indian! I fought back. I was the smallest person there and I fought back. They were military wives and they were all Southerners. They didn't like the way I spoke, for one thing. They said I had the wrong accents and I said that's 'cause I'm a Northerner and I disregarded and ignored them. But my ignoring them after a while brought them out of their holes and they invited me to a party that they were having—an afternoon session. So then I reluctantly went to it. I said, well maybe I should go, maybe we can be friends. But it came up, you know, about how I was associating with a certain family and again I stood on my ground and said, "Whoever we wish to have company with, that's our business. Nobody tells us who to have company with. There's nothing wrong with that family. They're good people, they're good Christians. It's not right. You people are terrible. You're not Christians if you're talking like that." But after that, one thing led to another and there was a hair pulling.

I just took my glasses off realizing and knowing what was coming and rather than ruin my glasses, I took 'em off. And then one girl who was also a Northerner, she was from Connecticut and kind of defending my side said, "Oh Alice, Oh Alice! What are we going to do?" I said, "Just hang on to my glasses and shut up! Stay back there." And she was so scared. Wow, my God! I think, I don't know, I'll tell ya, when I was finished, I mean, when they came back and told me what happened, to this day, I don't know where I got the power and the strength, but every one of them got beat up by me! I don't know where it came from! All of a sudden I was the most powerful person in the world! And I'm tiny. There's one girl, she was so embarrassed she was crying because she was outside and she didn't have a stitch on. I threw her out of the trailer with not a stitch on. All her clothes were ripped to pieces. They said I went, I turned into a wild woman. They said I had ripped all her clothes right off her and pushed her right out the door. Out into the public! She was laying out on the lawn there with nothin' on. I told her, they said that I yelled at her, "If you want to be white so bad, go show your white skin off!" and shot her right out there. And she was a big woman. She was about five foot seven and I'm really short. And then there was this other girl. They sent a message to me that she had to go to the hospital because I had torn her hair out of her head! And I had her hair, you know, and she wanted her hair back! And I just sent a message back that I had it tied up to a lance, but I was just joking. See, they wanted to say things about me so I made it worse. I don't know how I did it. I don't remember. All I know is that this one girl kicked me in my stomach, she kicked me right in my tummy and then after that I just went crazy and cleared the whole place out. And there must have been about eight girls there that were ready to pounce on me. And they were all bigger than me!

So I think that when something happens to me like that, if I get cornered, well, I know that each human being has adrenaline that shoots up and makes you stronger. Unusually stronger they say. But I think that I was protected by the angels. I think that the angels came and gave me that extra strength. Again, we have that principle, right? Right is right and two wrongs don't make one right and that's all there is to it. I was defending a principle that I believe in. I believe that everybody is created equal under God. And I just said, to this day, if that came up again like that, I would still go by what I believe in. And that Klan down there means nothing to me. And if it's up to me, if they get to me they can take their crosses and step on 'em like kindling wood. And it's all according to what is right. And who says what is right? It's how you feel in your heart. Right is okay as long as it's not gonna hurt somebody else. Not if it's gonna cause any infliction on somebody else.

Like our Concerned Onondaga. Concerned Onondagas is a body of Onondaga women and men that was formed on the Reservation, and we went by the laws of the Great Law and the rules of the Reservation. We formed this group to become stronger during the eviction time. I said, "We have to form some kind of a group in order to be strong and powerful. You cannot be straggling here and there and being without somebody 'cause you have fear in you. But if we're all together, then you'll feel better. You'll feel stronger and you'll feel protected. This is what we should do." And this is what we did. The last time for this was when the meeting was going to be about Dennis Banks coming to live on our Reservation. They said, "Alice, you know very well this is going to cause a problem in the future. What do you think about this? Should we meet?" "Certainly we can meet. Any time you want to. And everybody can express their views." "Well, will you sign for him to have sanctuary here in New York State?" And I said, "Yes I will." "Well, how can you do that? We're to have peace on the Reservation and he belongs to the American Indian Movement and they're not a peaceful group." So then I told them, "Well, not necessarily. He understands the Great Laws. If he becomes a threat to the Great Law, then it means he has to be removed. But as long as he wants to live here and enjoy the peacefulness of the beautiful Reservation, or the creation that God gave us to find, he has that right to do that. Do not have a closed mind. He's a human being." And I did sign for him. I signed a letter going to Albany for him to have sanctuary here. I also went to the meetings to give him support that he would be pro-tected here under the Great Law of Peace, the Tree of Peace. He is now under that Tree of Peace, protected.

Well, what makes me strong is maybe my grandmother and maybe my grandfather. First, let's go back to the society of Indians. The Iroquois society is matriarchal and we young Indian women growing up were taught that the Indian women are the ones who made the rulings, had to stand tall and make decisions. Sometimes it hurts and sometimes it's for the better. Sometimes it makes everybody happy, but you have to be able to make decisions and do it according to what is right. And if you had a strong principle or strong feelings about something and it's good, then you stand by it, don't go back when they want to change your mind. An indecisive person is not a reliable person. I think that my grandmother would have told us that we should be like a good strong Christian woman. But we would still have our heritage as American Indian women.

But getting back to what you asked me before about the model, I think that basically the model that I took after was like some unseen force maybe, something supernatural, I would say, angelic. I'm not saying *I'm* an angel—I could probably be the farthest from it—but I mean, I really believe that we're just here to take care of the earth that God gave us. We're not here to own anything or take things away from other people. And what is given to us we just should take good care of and then keep passing it on. Teach our young ones to do the same thing in the future. Not to cause dissension between neighbors and peoples. I believe that each one of us was put on this earth for a certain reason. We all have a certain job, I think. It just seems that mine is kind of Christian oriented, reli-giously based. I do not project myself to other people that I'm greater or better than anybody else, but if there's something that I believe in and I've got a principle on that, I'll fight my ground and I'll stand right on it and nobody can budge me. But as a child I was a weakling! I was very sickly. Maybe I had courage then, I don't know.

We had a bad time in school. We had never gone to school before, but of course we could speak English like the rest of the kids. At first we thought it was kind of fun because there were other children there the same age, but as we progressed into another grade, we began to hear things like, we're Indians, and I didn't know what that was and neither did my sister. It was never discussed with us. Probably our grandparents and my mother just took it for granted that maybe we knew or maybe it doesn't even matter because everybody is a human being. They would make fun of us, you know, like, "You're Indians, we can't play with you and you can't play with us, you're different." I didn't know what an Indian was and I thought, "How come? Why are we different?" "Well, because Indians are 'redskins.' " Well, I looked at my skin and my skin wasn't red and I couldn't understand. Why did she say that? She said we have black hair and brown eyes and I looked in the mirror and I said, "My eyes are green and my hair's brown, so why would they say that to me?" I looked at my sister and I said, "You must be the Indian because your hair's black and your eyes are brown." And then she said, "No I'm not!" And she was getting all upset and everything like that. This was when we were in grammar school, because I remember we went home and asked my grandmother. At least I know I did. I said, "What is an Indian?" And she laughed! She thought it was funny. She said, "An Indian is *ungwehowe*, which means an Indian person and his land, you know, the true man." All Indians in the whole world, 'cause all Indians were all one person at one time. We weren't divided. Anyway, she explained to us—tried to explain to us—about this true man business, this *ungwehowe*, Indian. Well, we found out that we, our people, were the first ones on this continent and that we're caretakers of this good earth, our mother earth. Well, I thought that was something to be pretty proud of, but up until that time I didn't know.

When we went to school we had this problem where they would push us, you know, or they wouldn't talk to us. We were alienated because we were Indians and the teachers could see that this was happening and tried to talk to other students, and they'd say they can't play with us because we're redskins, we're Indians. So I was really getting furious. I thought it was terrible. I would cry and feel bad 'cause I had no more friends, just because I'm an Indian. I mean, I thought, why does God make me an Indian? Why can't I be like the rest of them? And now because I'm an Indian I have no friends. And, you know, this is awful and I don't look any different. My sister looked a little bit different, a little bit darker. Then the teachers came to us and told us why they were doing that. "It's not their fault," they said, "because they don't know." Their parents must have told them they couldn't play with us. So then I became, right then and there, I don't know if you would call it defensive, but I just denied them. I would ignore 'em. I thought to myself, when people want to be like that, then I don't need them. And as small as I was, thinking that way, I thought, "I'll go to school and learn, but if I have to go through school without friends and that's the way it's gonna be, then that's the way it's gonna be." It was frightening for us because we had never encountered anything like that before. We didn't even know that we were Indians. And then we found out we were and my grandmother said, "Of course you are." And we went, "Well how come you never told us before? Why is it important?"

Why should it make any difference in school? We spoke Onondaga and we spoke English. Both languages blended in together, but I didn't see any difference in either one of the languages, it was just blended right in together. We were speaking English and Indian, but I didn't know that's what it was, I thought it was just part of the language.

My sister and I were kind of fortunate because we had each other. We were in the same class, she was a year younger than I was and I was supposed to start earlier, but my grandmother decided that I would be kept back and start the same time my sister started. She wanted us together so that's what we did. Maybe my grandmother had a forethought, maybe this was in the back of her mind, but she never told us. We were together. We didn't need anybody, we had ourselves. We weren't always seated together, but we shared our lunch. I remember one time that I took a bread to school. They call it hot scones, and it's like a fried bread, and I had some of that in my purse and I ate one of them. And when they saw it, they thought it was some kind of Indian food and they all of them went into hysterics. They were laughing at me and they asked me what it was, and I told 'em it was hot scones and they said, *what is that*? And we were getting bent out of shape over it. And what they did, they pulled my purse and broke the bread up in pieces and threw it all over the place. And then when the teachers came in they said that I threw my bread all over the place. The teacher asked me if I did it and I said, "No, I didn't do it, I wouldn't take my bread and throw it—they took it away from me." So the teacher didn't do anything to me. They just came in and cleaned it up and took my sister and me back to class. Then the next thing was recess time. The bread business was the first episode, now we gotta have recess, right? And my sister and I are hearing the news now, people are telling us that we're gonna get beat up. So we went out and I told my sister, "We're gonna get beat up" and she says, "One of the girls told me that the biggest girl in the class is going to get us, what shall we do? We have to go out, if we don't go out we're gonna get punished." Okay? You have to go outdoors when they say you have to go outdoors. So I said, "I'll tell you what, we'll walk back to back. If you see anybody coming toward you or if I see anybody coming toward me, then we'll just have to fight." And we're just little kids! Can you imagine two little girls walking around outside back to back? No matter which way you go you're standing back to back and I'm sure it must have looked ridiculous. Then the teacher, like, disappeared. I don't know where she went. Then the great big, huge girl came along to me. She looked like a giant and my heart was up in my throat somewhere and I thought, "This is the death of both of us." And this girl, her skin was just like paste and she had short blond hair and she was built like an Amazon. All I could think of was a monster, a milky, sausage monster, and it was just awful. She had boney knees and I could see the bones and I could see her arms even had muscles in them like a man. And this was just a horrible-looking creature. "Well," I said, "I guess we're gonna get it" to my sister. And she started to cry. I felt like crying too, I was so petrified. I didn't know what to do and I said, "Well, we'll just have to take it." But I was saying little prayers, you know. We knew how to pray, and I asked for help, to protect us, and from that point on, I remember nothing except being in the principal's office. I don't remember anything. Every once in a while I would see maybe glimpses of students, girls on the ground, or running around or something, I could see these legs or dress or hair or something on the ground. Well, I guess what happened was, we were attacked by this girl and when she attacked us the whole bunch of them jumped right in on us. Well, the teacher could not tell who was doing the fighting, there were so many girls on top of us, but they all of a sudden just dispersed. All of a sudden they got off from us and were going every which way and we were just chasing them all and they became frightened of us, so we were taken to the principal's office for punishment and to be questioned. All these girls came in and said that we did all that and I saw that one girl, the whole front of her dress was ripped right in half, a whole piece of it was missing. She said, "My mother's going to be mad and some-body's gotta pay for my dress" and, oh! she went on and on and the principal looked at my sister and I and said, "Did you girls do all this?" And I looked at them—we were always told never to be tattletales, the truth will come out somehow, but don't ever tell anything—so I said, I did tell the truth, I said, "I don't remember." Which I don't. To this day I cannot really remember it.

Many times we prayed for help, and we'd receive that help somehow. I don't know how to understand it except something must just grab ahold of us and take care of us or give us that power or protect us somehow. I was six years old when that fight occurred, maybe I was seven. But we went through that ordeal and we had to make our stand and we did. The girls beat us up because we were Indians, I guess, and one thing built up on top of the other. Parents saying that you don't play with Indians and so on, blah, blah, blah, maybe built up within them and then they threw it on us. Then they probably enjoyed seeing us crying and they'd group together and laugh at us and intimidate us and push us around and cause us to feel bad and maybe that made them feel better, made them feel great, maybe. But then, after a while, you know you can just take so much pushing and it's time to push back. And if you know you're gonna get it, you're told you're gonna get it, and it's the end, well, then you gotta do your best. You've got to do your *best* going down!

Most of my bringing up was done by my grandparents. My mother worked a lot. We also had models in our family to look up to and my grandmother's a great believer in education. I find that I am too. My sisters and I all graduated from high school and college and they are married. I am the only one who is not married. I mean, I was married, got divorced, never remarried again. I would like to, but I don't know if I could handle it. One marriage is enough! I just don't think I could do it. It would demand that I would be in the kitchen all the time or probably at home sewing and doing all these domesticated things that I'm not used to anymore. Not saying that I wouldn't like to, but I have to work and I also feel that I have to have that security by working. I could never depend on anybody else to take care of me, financially or otherwise, because *I* have to do that. It's probably a pattern that I have and it's hard to break.

I expect to go to heaven, I got reservations there! There are so many things, like I can give you an incident. This happened two winters ago. I won't give you a date, but I know it was in the winter. It was cold and snowy out. I was on the bus. I'd just come from the hospital visiting my uncle who was very ill, had had an operation. I was sitting on the front right seat and a gentleman got on the bus at the Hotel Syracuse and he had a satchel, an attaché case. He had that in his hand and he sat in the front of the bus, diagonally across from the bus driver. He was a very distinguished-looking man about sixty-eight years old. I saw all these teenagers on the bus. I would say they were around eighteen, nineteen, maybe twenty. They were in the backseat making a lot of noise and I somehow had a feeling something was going to happen to that man, and I was getting kind of scared. Not scared like I'm gonna cry or I wish I could find a place to hide. I had a fear for him. I looked around the bus; it's like I was trying to see what the situation was. All this was happening quickly, within the next three blocks and they are long blocks. I see there were some other folks on the bus and there were a couple of men sitting almost across from me. And I said, well, I guess it'll be all right. Then this young guy comes up who was about nineteen or twenty years old and sat directly across from the man with the satchel, and I thought to myself, please don't do it. Don't hurt that man. He's gonna take the satchel. All of a sudden I just knew he was going to take it. That's what he was after. This guy kept looking at the satchel and he looked like he was very eager and he'd look at the man and he all of a sudden started looking at *me*! And I looked right back at him very, very stiffly and I thought to myself, whatever in the world. I started saying to myself mentally, saying my prayers, help! And the bus driver wasn't paying attention and the old man looked at me. He looked at the guy and I think he knew what was gonna happen, and he looked like he was frightened and I felt so sorry for him. All of a sudden this guy who was about nineteen or twenty stood up, and I stood up at the same time. I don't know why I did that. He just looked at me and he went right over to the man and sat next to him and grabbed the satchel and at the same time I grabbed this nineteen- or twenty-year-old guy's arm, his wrist. I was hanging on to his wrist and my nails were just going right through his skin! He says to me, "Lady, you better let go. You're crazy!" He said that to me! And I looked at him and I said, "Leave this old man alone and let go of his bag because I'm not gonna let go of you." And he said he was gonna punch me, so he pushed me and in turn I pushed him right back and he landed right on his seat and he got up and said, "You know, I could kill you." And I looked at him and I said, "Do you realize what would happen to you?" I wasn't going to argue with him. I just told him, if you take this bag, you're gonna go to jail. You'll have to answer for stealing and I said, "How would you like it if somebody did this to your grandparents? What if he right now died of shock, right here? What would you do? It's a terrible thing that you're doing." I said, "I want you to let go of that bag. Leave it there, give it back to the man, and I want you to get off this bus." The bus driver seemed like he wasn't aware of anything that was going on. So then he said, "I could take a knife out

and I could kill you." I just told him, "All I asked you to do is to get off
the bus and leave the man alone. 'Cause I'm gonna stand right here and
you stay right away from him." And I stood between him and the man and
I would not let him get near him and the kid said I was crazy and he just
looked at me funny. Looked like he was getting pale, but he did let go of
the bag and he went to the bus driver. The bus driver said to the guy,
"You heard the lady, get off the bus," and he told the bus driver that I
was a lunatic. The old man was petrified. But I stayed right on the bus
and I was like, like I really wasn't there. It was funny, the way I felt. I did
not get scared. I mean, I didn't show my fear.

I don't know why he didn't hurt me. He could have. He said he could,
but he didn't. I knew he wanted to. I could *tell* he wanted to, but he would
hesitate and I don't know what made him do that. I just believe that I
was protected again. I always believe that. I mean, not that I'll always be
protected, something might happen to me some day. Why did I do it?
Because I saw a defenseless man, an older man who could not match up
with this other person's strength. Oh I know, I'm just a woman, right?
Just a woman! I've often thought about that. Why did I do it? I could
have got hurt. But I think I did it because I saw somebody in distress who
needed help. And I looked around and nobody's gonna get up and help and
I thought, if I can help, I will help. But all these thoughts went through
my mind in a matter of seconds, not debating about it. Maybe it's just in
me to do that. I automatically got right up and went to his aid. He was
old, he was scared. But I wasn't afraid, I was furious. The other thing that
went through my mind was, how dare this person think he can go ahead
and take something away from somebody else or hurt somebody? Why
would I allow something to happen in front of me like that? I will not
allow it. I'll do the best I can and that's what I did.

I only told you that because things happen to me that I get involved in.
Situations where I swear I don't know how they start. But it just seems
like all of a sudden I'm at a situation that I gotta do something about it.
And I wonder about that. Why does God put me in these places or in these
situations? Maybe I'm one of His tools, perhaps, to help somebody. I
don't know. I don't see any reason why I should be because I'm a woman
and I'm not a very big person. I'm tiny and I treat people with kindness,
like I told you. I can be powerful in my mind and I stick to my rights and
stand on my ground, but I am not a physically powerful person that I
know of. You could even say I'm delicate. If somebody even bumps my
arm, it hurts! And I bruise easily. It's funny, though, that my physical being
and my mental being are two different entities almost. My mental being
is stronger than my physical being. Isn't that strange? Like my mental
being can get my physical being in trouble.

What I do, I think of God and I ask for help and I usually get help. I
just ask Him to please send His angels and I ask the angels to please wrap
their wings around me and keep me warm and protected. I feel something
and I hear something in my head. I don't hear a voice like a human voice,
okay, but I hear, I don't know if it's hearing or feeling, but it's mental.
Mouths don't move, but thoughts come into my head. If I'm saying a
prayer and there's some problem I know that God's listening to me. I

always thought that, you know, He's very busy too and I'm always bothering Him with my problems, but He has time to let me know something. I'll know when I feel good, then I'll know that everything's gonna be all right. They say that radiance will show up in your face, your personality, your character, or something like that. If mine does, if I have that kind of radiance, then my radiance came from the heavens.

Carolyn Thorburn

"Going along with the medical profession does not necessarily mean you are in good hands because drugs can have lethal side effects!"

☐ ☐ ☐

Science is not as scientific as people think it is.

NOBEL LAUREATE BARUCH BLUMBERG

I am reliably informed that, although in her forties, Professor Thorburn is very young looking and generally reckoned to be in her twenties. We first met at the amiable intellectual bazaar of the Association for the Study of Afro-American Life and History in Baltimore. She agreed to enlarge upon her brief account of her standing out against conventional medicine at some subsequent mutually convenient time. Months later we did meet and talk over dinner and well into the night in a New York hotel over-looking Central Park.

Professor Thorburn teaches Spanish at Upsala College in East Orange, New Jersey. Her dynamism and friendliness must enliven her classes. Intensity and amiability are still the aspects of her strong personality that come most readily to mind. True to her dietary convictions, she ordered a vegetarian dinner. She brought with her a number of books which she referred to occasionally to document her advocacy of the primacy of diet as a medical therapy.

Quite apart from her personal commitment to dietary therapy, Professor Thorburn espouses the recondite and delves into often obscure and generally neglected lore. She is willing to entertain the possibility of the Lost Continent of Mu, and the efficacy of spiritual alchemy. Hand in hand with her openness to a catalogue of baroque possibilities is her strong biblical faith. That faith seems to free her from some of the preoccupations that absorb many. I tried to schedule our conversation earlier in the day to free her from the peril of metropolitan nighttime travel. She assured me that she was not greatly concerned on that score and was in the habit of traveling at whatever time suited her convenience. She is not altogether in a world of her own. She is cognizant enough of the essential conventions.

She is observant of her injunction against preaching, at least in the first instance, but she defends her beliefs with spirit and animation. Challengers, especially those who question her faith in dietary therapy, can count on a sermonette in favor of vegetarianism from a youthful lady who appears to be a living advertisement for her dietary convictions.

———

I don't have a ready definition of principled dissent, but I can tell you what would be my interpretation of it. Dissent is any desire to not do something. Principled dissent would mean that you had thoroughly thought out all the ramifications of your actions and that you will not be swayed by any monetary or material compensation. You've decided that something is in disagreement with your ethical principles and you feel so strongly that you are beyond your ability to compromise. No, I don't think principled dissent is common. I would say no because a lot of people do compromise. Most people end up compromising in one way or another. It depends upon how strong your principles are. It also depends upon your entire belief as to why we are here. If you have a strong belief in God and you believe that certain things are definitely not right, for example, it's like Abraham. He was laying his only begotten son on the altar to be sacrificed and a possible allegorical meaning of that was that he was laying down his human consciousness to take up the Christ consciousness. In other words, he had perfect faith and trust in God. It was like an initiation. You had to perform the act to cement the fact that you are a servant of God. The important thing was that he had the will to do it. That's what a hero is. Not that you actually do it, but that you have the intention to do it. If someone's burning in the flames you want to rush in. The important thing is that you want to rush in even though they hold you back and you have to struggle. You are a hero because you wanted to rush in. Don Quixote is the epitome of the hero because you have to be somewhat slightly unbalanced to be a hero. In other words, if you want to think about it too much, you know—I might mess up my suit and maybe this is not the prudent thing to do—then you're not a hero. Don Quixote also epitomizes the fool. That's precisely what I'm saying. There's a little bit of the recklessness, I mean, he had total faith in what he was doing. He knew what he was doing. Oh yes, he was doing something! He was showing people the importance of faith. Something like what Abraham was doing in a different way.

You have to always want to surge higher. You can never be satisfied with your plateau. If you've achieved something, well fine, but if you're content to rest there, then that's no good. The goal must be worthy of being reached. For example, I certainly wouldn't think that being the perfect counterfeiter would be a worthy goal. Oh yes, I think it would make a difference if there weren't any principled dissenters. I mean, we would descend to the point where there were no standards or morals. I'm reminded, for example, of what happened during the blackouts. People just started looting because they saw everyone else doing it. They said, "Well they're doing it and getting away with it, so why can't I do it and

get away with it?" regardless of whether it's right or wrong or whatever.
I'm from Newark, and you know stores were just broken into at will.
That's the way it is when you just go along with whatever everyone else is
doing.

I think something happened in my early childhood which I felt strengthened my resolve not to go along just because everyone else is doing that.
There were a couple of things. The first happened when I was five. I went
to a day nursery because both my parents worked. Once in school a boy
said something uncomplimentary about my mother. I was shocked and
angry so I took off my boot and hit him over the head! He began to cry
and I felt vindicated and I marched home triumphantly. I told my mother
what had happened. I expected her to pat me on the back but she looked
at me and said, "Could you see me taking my boot off and hitting someone over the head?" And I said, "Well, truthfully, no." She asked me, "Do
you have respect for what he said? Do you think that what he said was
true? Do you have respect for him?" I said, "No, of course not!" "Well,
why are you lowering yourself below his level and acting so unladylike,
since you know that what he said was not true?" I was just shocked! I
looked at her and just went over in a corner and thought for a while. But
that gave me tremendous insight! I know what's true and I know when
what someone else is saying is a lie. So why lower myself? So that prepared
me for something that happened later on. I was in the school yard and
some girls were yelling at me. Actually one girl was doing this because I
had taken a basketball and shot it at the basket when I shouldn't have.
She proceeded to curse me, my parents, my mother, grandparents, back
to the eighth generation! I was just shocked because what I had done had
been done fifteen minutes ago! Why didn't she get angry then? Why did
she come back fifteen minutes later surrounded by ten people to help her
fight! It was just so incomprehensible to me, but because I had been fore-
warned, my skin was thick. She was yelling all these obscenities at me,
but because five years earlier I had had to consider that these obscenities
didn't mean anything, they only were real if I gave them weight, I could
handle it. Since I didn't give them weight, it was like dust falling on me and
I was shielded by this wall of previous experience. After she finished yelling
and screaming she said to me, "Well, what have you got to say about it?"
I just looked at her in disbelief. I saw myself floating above the situation,
I saw it in all its true absurdity. We were surrounded by forty people looking for a battle and all of a sudden I did the most comprehensible thing I
could do. I began to laugh hysterically. Not the kind of laughter where
you just chuckle, but the kind of laughter which makes your sides ache
and tears begin to come out of your eyes. She was astonished. If I had
hit her she would have understood that or even crying, but she couldn't
understand my laughing. So she said "Don't laugh in my face!" I walked
over to the wall about three feet away and continued to howl with laughter.
After about another minute I got control of myself and came back and
said, "You know, you're right, I shouldn't have shot the ball. I won't do
it again. Oh, by the way, I have to go home now, I'll see you, good-bye."
I just strolled off. Everyone was in shock and said, "You can't let her say

that! Go back and hit her!" I said, "You go back and hit her! I'm not interested. I've got other things to do."

Well, if she had hit me, I would have defended myself one way or another. But I grew up in Newark, in a section called The Valley, which was supposed to be pretty tough. And all through my life I never had a fight. I always got out of them with my wits. Either I talked my way out or I bluffed my way out. A girl in school wanted to fight me once, and I was on roller skates. I said, "All right, wait till I take my skates off." So I took my skates off. Then I said, "Oh, wait a minute, someone could take my skates. Let's walk and fight in front of my house." So we did that, but then I said, "Oh, wait a minute, someone could still take my skates. Just wait, let me just take them inside." She said, "Wait a minute, you might not come back." "What do you mean! Of course I'm coming back!" I said. "You'd better not go anywhere! You'd better be here when I get back!" and I went inside, laughing all the way. As soon as I got upstairs, I leaned out the window and said, "Oh, Lois, I have something to do. I'll see you later." I saw her two days later. We forgot, or she forgot, whatever it was we were upset about. So I always managed to talk my way out of all these fights.

One incident just caused me to think about how so many people just go along. I think this incident illustrates what I mean when I say that principled dissent is somewhat uncommon and not typical. I was about seven or eight years old. I was accused of cursing. We were in the schoolyard and we were told by the teacher to come in early. I wasn't very happy and I did make some comment, but it wasn't a curse word. One girl in back of me thought it was and she said, "Oh, you said a bad word!" I said, "I did not!" I thought nothing of it then. Later on, I came inside and realized that this girl had gone to the teacher and told her what I had said. Now that was pretty petty, especially since I hadn't cursed. Then when we got inside there were maybe fifteen of us sitting around the table and she accused me in front of the teacher again! The teacher asked, "How many of you girls heard Carolyn?" And do you know, *all* of those girls, every single one of them, raised their hands. None of them were even around! Laura, the girl who accused me, was the only one of them within five feet of me! The other girls weren't even paying any attention to me. They were at the other end of the playground. I just looked at them in disbelief and said, "They're lying. They weren't even there!" And the teacher said, "Why should they lie?" In other words, Laura was the leader of the clique, I was a nobody. I was a new girl, I had only been there a few weeks. I imagine they lied because they wanted to get in good with her. But for whatever reason, they did lie. Anyway, this whole situation was compounded when the teacher took me by the hand into the cloak room and gave me a beating. So here I was, being beaten for something I had not done. I ran home and complained and screamed. You know, you don't like being punished but when you know you haven't done it, you really feel injured. My parents later came to the school and told them look, if she does something wrong, don't beat her. My mother knew for me to protest that long and hard meant that I really hadn't done it. Well, anyway, to make a long story short, after that I never ever had any respect for any of those girls. And I thought about popularity, doing something just because someone else is doing it. I never came home after this and asked, "Can I do this? Can I wear this? Can I do this because everyone else is doing it, or everyone else is going?" I always thought that if what they're doing is worthy of being done, then that should be the reason for doing it, not just because it's being done and widely perpetrated. I think that incident has given me a clarity of perception. A lot of things we believe are just as untrue as the idea that the earth was the center of the solar system. But people believe these untrue things just because other people believe them, without really going in and analyzing these beliefs. Why did all those girls go along with the girl who accused me? Because it was comfortable. In order to dissent you have to take a lot of brunt and disagreement and it costs a lot of energy. You will be extremely uncomfortable if you dissent, but they make it easy for you to go along.

I think the easiest thing to do for you to get an understanding of what happened to me is to start from the very beginning. I was brought up in a household in which my father was somewhat interested in nutrition and we ate whole-wheat bread, brown sugar. We ate meat but it was sort of cut down and we took vitamins. We were sort of conscious of nutrition, although we didn't always practice it. I got married and I did not eat as healthy a diet as I had before my marriage. I ate a lot more doughnuts and cake and candy and spaghetti and macaroni, and I ate a lot more meat, too. I had a problem about meat when I was going to college. Seven months before I attended college, when I was about fifteen years old, my father came home and said, "Meat's not the best thing for us so we're not going to have meat anymore." Now, he paid the bills. I didn't protest and I didn't eat meat for seven months and I didn't mind at all. We ate a lot of soybeans and vegetarian things. But when I started college, I started to eat meat again. Nothing happened at first, but then after about a month or two I started getting these pains in my back. I was at school and I called home and they thought I should go to a doctor. My father mentioned off-hand, you probably can't handle the meat. I didn't really pay that much attention to it, you know, what did my father know? I'm going to the doctor, and she's going to tell me what's what. I went to a female doctor and lo and behold she said, "I think you're building up too much uric acid. You're eating too much meat. Stay away from it for a while." The very next day I didn't have any meat. The pain went away eighty-five percent! In one day! I said, Wow! In the next two or three days it just disappeared! After that I said, well why is it? I've been eating meat, as far as I know, all my life. It never bothered me before. I knew I was coming off a seven-month period of not eating any meat at all and then my mother told me later on that I didn't have meat when I was a baby until I had reached the age of three.

So anyway, I got sick shortly after I got married. It must have been within a year. I went to a doctor and he said I had a cyst. I had pain in my back and I had an ovarian cyst. The doctor said that I had a hormonal imbalance in my system and that he was going to give me something to correct it. He said that this medicine frequently worked and that I could avoid an operation. Now I wanted to avoid an operation at all costs! So I took the hormone pills. At the time, I had faith in the doctor so I took the medicine he gave me. When I filled the prescription I noticed that it said birth control pills! So I called him up and said, "Doctor, these are birth control pills. Do I have the wrong prescription?" He says, "No, it just so happens that the birth control pills are hormone pills. So you just take them as I said." At the same time my father had told me something else, he says, "Look, you're not eating as well as you should. You're eating a lot more junk food. Why don't you eat better and you'll get rid of this cyst. You don't need to take those birth control pills because they'll cause you problems." And I thought, "What does my father know, he's not a doctor." But I said to myself I know I'm eating a lot more junk food than I normally do, so I'm gonna eat better. So I ate a lot more fruit and vegetables and did away with the eating of ice cream, cake, and sweets. I lightened up on eating meat and went back to the doctor in a month. He said, "My God! It's eighty percent gone! That's fantastic! I've never seen anyone react so well so quickly!" So I asked him, "What about my diet? I've changed my diet. Do you think that could have any influence on the cyst?" "Oh no, diet's got nothing to do with it." I says, "Oh, really?" He says, "No, continue doing what you're doing and come back in a month." So I continued to take the pills, but because he had told me that diet had nothing whatsoever to do with my condition, I did not continue eating as prudently as I had been. I went back to eating a lot of junk food, but I did continue to take the pills for another month. I went back to the doctor at the end of this month and I felt worse. In fact, I was as bad off as I was when I was originally sent to him. So he said, "Oh, I have to give you a stronger pill." Now I thought to myself, "Are you sure diet has nothing to do with it? I haven't been eating as well as I should. These two months the only thing that has been changed was my diet." But he gave me a stronger pill to take. I said to myself, "Well, I am going to go on a better diet" but I took the stronger pill too. It was interesting. The *very day* I took the pill, I felt a pain in my chest and this was a strange pain, not a generalized pain or ache. This was a pain like the size of a dime. Right here in the middle of my chest. I said, this is the weirdest thing! I've never in my life had a pain like this. I had it for about twenty-four hours and then it went away. And I mention that because one thing those pills will cause is clots. If I have a clot, it could be because of those pills. I'm not prepared to speculate about it because I'm not aware of any negative effects yet. I went back to the doctor after six weeks of taking this stronger birth control pill. During those six weeks I'm on a good diet. I'm eating a lot more fruits and vegetables and no cake and candy. I came back to him in six weeks and he says, "Fantastic, incredible!" Again, a fantastic improvement. There's no more cyst. It's totally gone. Then he says, while he's examining me, "Oh, put down that she has a tumor." I says, "How come you didn't tell me I had a tumor six weeks ago?" "It wasn't there six weeks ago." I said, "Do you think it could be related to the stronger pill you gave me?" "Oh, no, no, no. Do you think that? Oh my God, no! Continue taking the pill for six months and then come back and see me."

Now I walked out a little perturbed because although I had gotten rid of the cyst, which was great, I've got a tumor that I didn't have before. I didn't feel well. I felt this sluggishness and this dull ache in the back and

I'm supposed to take these pills for six months and I do not like the idea of taking them that long. It's one thing to take them for six weeks, but now I'm supposed to take them for six months. After a few days the pain got worse and not only that, my *head* began to hurt! Now, I never have headaches. You know your body. Before this I had had two headaches in my entire life; once when I needed glasses and once when I was working on my thesis and I just had a nervous tension headache from writing all those philosophy papers. Now this headache was unusual in that every day it got worse. I called the doctor and said, "Doctor, I have this headache and not only that, I've noticed that my hair is falling out! I have a bald spot in the back of my head almost the size of your hand. And my hairline has receded one inch around! And it's getting worse every day!" He said "The headache and the hair loss have got nothing to do with the pill. Continue to take the pill for six months." I continued to protest, "Give me something else, give me something else. I'm going to come in, would you look at me?" I protested so much that he hung up on me. He called me a hysterical female. Meanwhile, I'm suffering. I kept taking the pill, but finally it got so I could hardly lift my head off the pillow. It felt so heavy and I said, "I'm not gonna take that pill today. I just can't. I can hardly walk around." I was teaching high school in Newark at the time and I had to teach two periods in the morning. Third period I was free and this one day I went to the teachers' room, I was so sick. Luckily nobody was there because I went through one of the most horrendous experiences I could ever have in my entire life. I couldn't stand! I couldn't walk! I was crawling on the floor. I was crying. It felt like I was a robot and someone had just pushed every single control at the same time. I started to sweat and feel chills. I felt this bubbling in my ankles and it was bubbling liquid and then it bubbled up to my knees, it bubbled up to my hips, it bubbled to my waist, shoulders, and then the bubbling reached my head! All of a sudden, at that particular moment, it felt like a hundred-pound weight had been lifted from my head. Then I touched my head and I realized that I could move the skin on it and I realized that before I couldn't move it because it was so tight. But then, I felt, my God! That pressure is gone. I felt like I was floating in liquid and I realized that bubbling probably was my blood. You know, I was twenty-four years old and I had this bald spot and my hair is falling out and the doctor's telling me these symptoms are nothing to be scared of! So that was my born-again experience.

After this happened, I didn't want to take any drug, not even an aspirin! I said to myself, I've been sick before, but I've never felt sickness like that! I mean, I can't even describe it to you. I felt weird! I felt I was from another planet because of the symptoms I underwent. I vowed then that I would not take another drug unless I was dying! In fact, I went back later on about this tumor that I had and did something that you wouldn't think was wise. I was so disillusioned, totally turned off. I said, if I'm going to die, let me die on my own. I'm not going to a doctor. I was thankful to be here after that experience, so why should I go to another doctor? I knew if I went to another doctor he would just want to give me another drug and that's what I didn't want. You might say I was unreasonable and that that was not the prudent thing to do, but I said, "I'm going to follow my father's advice from now on, which is to just eat better food." So I did this for about six weeks and you know what happened? I began to feel worse again! I felt more and more uncomfortable every day but I was so stubborn that I said, "I'm not going to a doctor. If I'm going to die, then *I* want to be responsible for my death!" It sounds irrational, or whatever, but that's how I was. I didn't even tell my husband that I was going through all this suffering. I didn't even tell my father. I told no one. I just said to myself, "Well, I'm just going to see what happens." I mean, I was just that angry. In the following months the pain got less and less. At one point I said, "Maybe I'm going to live." And finally, the pain was all gone! And I said to myself, "Gee, I wonder if I still have the tumor?" I went to my mother's doctor and he said, "No, you don't have a tumor." When I went out I was elated. My method had worked! By eating well, I had gotten rid of this tumor!

But you know what I did? Because I had been given a clean bill of health, I went back to eating junk food again! Things went along for a while until three years later I was having trouble with my digestion so I went to the doctor. I was mixing all kinds of nuts, and nuts are very hard to digest, especially when you eat a pound of them! Now I realize but then I was eating all these fruits and nuts and things and so finally my digestive system said, look, give me a break! Well, the doctor said I had a tumor, a fibroid tumor which was now the size of a grapefruit. A grapefruit! I said, "Oh my God, that's incredible!" So he said, "Go to a specialist." So I made an appointment with the specialist for one week later. And this specialist said, "Well, it's not that bad, have a child right away, get pregnant and don't worry about it. You're only twenty-six, I wouldn't recommend an operation." He told me not to worry, so I didn't worry. Then it got to be about the size of a six-month pregnancy. I mean, it's like three times larger than a grapefruit. Then I came across a book by Doctor Henry Bieler. He wrote *Food is Your Best Medicine*. In this book he maintains and details the idea that there is only one cause of disease. He talks about Hippocrates, the father of medicine, saying food shall be thy medicine. "Let food be thy medicine." Dr. Bieler says that when we eat improperly the toxins that we eat are in our blood and our blood wants to get rid of these toxins. And if it can't do that it shunts them off to a storage depot, which could be any organ of the body. Now where these toxins are stored is where you have the symptoms of disease.

See, I obeyed, I did exactly what I was told. I took the medicine and I suffered for it, so I began to study medicine. Some people said I should have sued him for malpractice. I said yes, I don't think he was right to tell me to take that same drug in an even stronger dosage after my symptoms. But I'm not quarreling with that so much. Any doctor coming out of med school and looking at my symptoms would have given me that drug. It was the so-called treatment of choice. But this time I began to read and I knew by previous experience that diet had helped me in the past so now I looked six months pregnant and I said, "I'm going to try it." So I went on a good diet for about ten months. The tumor just melted away. Before, it was just hard like a rock but now my stomach was no longer hard, distended, and bloated. It was flat and soft. I could put on a bathing suit. I felt good and energetic. I was writing my thesis that year and I went to Europe, but I was in such anxiety toward the end that I didn't eat well. I didn't take care of myself. I would just go for days and not eat proper meals. It got to the point where I just kept losing weight and I knew something was wrong. But I had all this pressure, I had to write my thesis in six months or lose my job! I got to such a point that when I sat down on a bench I had no more flesh to cushion me. Can you imagine sitting down on a wooden bench and you scrape because there's a bone and you're sitting on no padding? There's no flesh on your buttocks. I was so petrified when that happened I went to the doctor. I looked like something that came out of a concentration camp. I mean, I was a walking skeleton! I went to the doctor and he said to me, "What are you eating?" I told him I was on this diet. I was eating some weird diets. The problem was that I didn't have enough knowledge at the time to eat a vegetarian diet health-fully. I was eating cooked stringbeans for breakfast! It was terrible. So the doctor told me to eat meat again, so, to make a long story short, I went on another one of my roller coasters. I started eating meat again and for a while nothing happened. I came back to this country and I noticed the tumor was getting a little bit bigger, but I said, I can handle it. It's just like when you smoke and try to stop, you know, you think you can just smoke two cigarettes. You're not gonna fall if you just take two cigarettes! So I continued to cheat and eat wrong things. I had this craving for sugar and sweets. Two years, three years later, the tumor was back to its original size. I said, "Oh, my God! How did I let myself get into this condition!" Now the first time I went through all this I didn't go to a doctor, I did it all on my own. The second time it came back I said, "This time I'm going to go to a doctor to document what is happening." So I went to the doctor and told him that I wanted to go on this diet and that I had had the tumor before three years earlier but I had gotten rid of it through this diet of Bieler's. He listened to me as if I was totally crazy! He said, "That didn't happen!" I said, "What do you mean it didn't happen!" I started explaining my symptoms. He said, "Well, that's not possible. That's just not possible." I said, "I can understand your saying that because according to your books it is not possible, but I can tell you that this did happen to me and I'm just so intrigued by it, I'm going to see if it can be done again. Because if I have it out, if I choose to have children, I can never have them if I have a hysterectomy. Look, I choose to do this and I'm not that sick." He said "Well you are pretty sick." So I started asking him, "What do you know about nutritional therapy? What has actually been done? Have doctors actually studied a patient on a diet like the one I'm on?" He said, "No." I said, "What about nutritional theory like Bieler's? Have you read any of those people?" He says, "No." So I said, "How can you give me advice on something you know nothing about!" He wasn't very happy with my argument, but he did agree to monitor me for a while. Then I changed to a new doctor and he examined me and said I was so weak that he wanted to put me in the hospital for two weeks and give me blood transfusions because I was so anemic. He said he couldn't operate until my blood was built up. I said, "Well, gee I can build my blood up." He said, "No, that's no good." "I'd really rather do this nutritional experiment," I said, "because I'd like to see if it will work again like the other time." He said, "It didn't work." Just like the other doctor! "Well, I think it did work." Then he said, "Well, if you don't want to do what I want you to do, then I can't have you as a patient." "Well, where shall I go? I do want to try nutritional therapy." He said, "Go to a teaching hospital." Newark has a teaching hospital, so I said, "Okay, good, I'll do that." Before I left his office I asked him, "Doctor, if I am successful in getting rid of this tumor through diet, would you like me to come back and see you again? Because you say yourself that you do not know what causes these tumors." He said, "No, I don't want to see you again!" "Doctor, what do you mean you don't want to see me again? Aren't you interested in the fact that there may possibly be some connection between diet and the treatment of tumors?" He said, "No, I don't want to see you again." I said, "How can you say you're interested in pursuing truth or helping people? What kind of a man are you?" I was so upset I ran out into the waiting room and started to cry! You know, the fact that they were so arrogant to me. I don't know whether it was ego because I wouldn't accept his advice and that I had presumed to tell him that I had this disorder that I could possibly cure my way, but he wasn't interested in even knowing about it. So I went down to the teaching hospital. They examined me and of course they disagreed with my plan also, but at least they listened to me and I was happy for that. I found one doctor who said okay. I refused the operation that he was definitely strenuously recommending. But they said if I would sign this statement that I was going against medical advice and they had no responsibility for my decision they would follow me up on it. So I said, "Sure, sure! Of course I have responsibility for my body! I don't expect you to have any responsibility for it." So they agreed to follow me up on it, and I cured myself again. I've been fine ever since.

I was exactly the same as anybody else at first. I took the medicine. I did what I was told. It came to the point where I almost died! I mean, if I'd continued to follow instructions, my head would have burst! I can't see how it could have gone on like that. Something would have happened. It was like pressure building up in a steam engine. When I described these symptoms to a doctor later, he told me I would have had a stroke if I had not stopped taking the pills.

I think it got to be a matter of principle when I went to this doctor who was a specialist in the gynecology and obstetrics department of a major city university hospital. He threw me out of his office and told me he would not have me as a patient! The first doctor went along with me reluctantly, but I didn't stick with him because he was kind of lukewarm. But this doctor in the gynecology department was the first doctor who refused even to work with me. I stood up to him, stood my ground mainly because going along with the medical profession does not necessarily mean you are in good hands, because drugs can have lethal side effects!

You see, many doctors patronize people because they feel that they understand the body and patients don't. Many doctors get very upset if a patient even asks what they are prescribing. One doctor I went to wanted to give me pills to calm me down. So I said, "After my experience, I don't want to take any drug. Especially not a tranquilizer." I refused. In other words, you might say I became belligerent.

I feel that a part of medical science is based on misconceptions. I have been taking sciences for the past five years—biology, physiology, histology, biochemistry, organic chemistry—and I've come to the conclusion that chemists of today have come to a dead end. They were manipulating matter but without the spirit, and the universe does consist of both. Einstein's theory relates to that. Energy can be transformed into matter and vice versa. Food is really precipitated energy and affects the body in ways we do not completely understand. Energy is spirit. The atom bomb is an example of it. That's that energy, that sacred fire. That burning bush that Moses saw. That is the energy that is in our bodies. The energy which holds the solar system together and the energy which holds our molecules and cells in our bodies together is the same. It is the same force and to create or to destroy, you have to upset this plus/minus polarity. When you sever that you release a tremendous amount of energy, whether you're just taking one electron or you get to the nucleus! But the chemists and the scientists and the nuclear physicists don't know how to release this energy in a safe manner. You have to start with human questioning before you understand how the whole thing fits together. It takes a sincere desire for truth and not relying on concepts that "must be right" because they are written in books and accepted by everybody!

Right now I'm on a vegetarian diet. It consists mostly of raw food. In the morning I will have an energy drink consisting of bee pollen, which is somewhat of an animal protein. I don't take vitamins. I used to believe in them, but now I believe that you should get your vitamins in the food you eat. So this energy drink consists of bee pollen, chia seeds, and also brewer's yeast, or nutritional yeast. I'll take a teaspoonful of each one of these in some kind of apple juice and make a shake out of it in the blender and that'll be my breakfast. For lunch, if I'm hungry I might have an apple, or maybe two apples, or maybe no lunch at all. For dinner I'll have a raw sprout salad—mung, alfalfa sprouts—and I might have an avocado or any kind of vegetable. So I have a fruit for lunch and vegetables for dinner in raw form. I've been following this diet very strictly, especially strictly for the last few weeks, and I've noticed a tremendous change. You get younger, you rejuvenate. I'm forty years old and a lot of people tell me that I could pass for twenty-six or twenty-seven or twenty-eight. Some people say twenty-two, you know some people can't see too well! But people are generally astonished when I tell them my age.

There's no problem whatsoever! When I went to Russia, when I went to China I carried along my sprouts. I put them in a plastic bag. They don't weigh very much. In fact, it's so cheap to eat. I soak them overnight and then I grow them in a plastic bag spread out on my hotel desk or table and in three days I'll have a crop! You see they're so rich in protein.

Most of my friends understand me. I take strong positions about lots of things. Some of the other teachers in the school think I'm way out. You know, weird. They kid me about my diet. As I said before, I have a thick skin from that incident I told you about when I was five years old. Now, if I was doing something wrong, if someone caught me stealing or doing something that I know I shouldn't have been doing, I'd feel somewhat abashed about it. But as long as you feel that what you're doing is correct, then everything is fine. Of course, if they don't believe it, you feel kind of sad. Sometimes I feel, gee, it's too bad that they don't know how good it feels to be energetic. In fact, I've had my department chairman say to me, "You know, Carolyn, it's amazing, you've been here sixteen years and you and another teacher are the only ones who haven't aged! If anything you look younger!" Some of my students say, "Gee, Professor Thorburn, you look so well, what can I do to eat better?" They come to me for nutritional advice! So just do what you have to do and people either fall in line and don't say anything, or they kid you, or else begin to think, gee, maybe she is doing something right. Your actions have to speak louder. You just can't talk to people unless they come to you because you can't preach. You just state what you believe and the reasons why you believe what you do and show them the evidence.

Seiichi Michael Yasutake

"With a high level of honesty, there's a better
chance of people being able to face up to each
other and their differences."

□   □   □

What?
We
are losing the war?
Who is we?

MITSUYE YAMADA

*The Reverend Seiichi Michael Yasutake neither looks nor sounds like a
man of sixty-four. He has obtained the Third Rank, Black Belt, in Kendo,
a Japanese form of fencing, and moved like a much younger man as he
entered the Chicago hotel room where we talked and ate an early breakfast. The eldest son of a prominent Seattle family, his childhood home is
now an artifact in the Meiji-mura Museum in Japan. Internment in an
American concentration camp has quite naturally inclined him toward a
concern for the rights of prisoners in general and especially for the rights of
political detainees and prisoners of conscience. His participation in the
Civil Rights Movement, his assistance to Vietnam-era conscientious ob-
jectors, and his current ministry to the poor and homeless bear witness to
a life of humane, dissenting activism.*

*When Carmen Valentín, a colleague of his at the now defunct Central
YMCA Community College, was arrested, it was in keeping with his long-
standing concern for human rights to take a personal interest in her case.
A Puerto Rican nationalist, Ms. Valentín, with several colleagues, was
arrested and imprisoned on charges of seditious conspiracy. Probably one
of the most unpopular causes in the country today, the plight of these
prisoners moved Reverend Yasutake to assist in the founding of the Civic-
Religious Committee in Support of the Puerto Rican Prisoners of War.*

*For all his physical vigor, Mike Yasutake is not a very demonstrative
speaker. His vocal style is deliberate, without being monotonous. He is
very wary of that zeal which bore down traditional American canons of
justice and confined him and his family in concentration camps. Active
doubt is an essential part of his philosophical approach to the whole con-*

cept of advocacy. On the profoundest level, his insistence upon active doubt is an assertion of the caution that he feels humanity should reserve for the "self-evident" assumptions.

———

Seiichi is the name that I was given when I was born and the name I used through high school. Michael is the middle name that I acquired in my college years. I was born in Seattle in 1920 and ordained in the Episcopal Church in 1950 in the Episcopal diocese of Chicago. I was born of immigrant parents from the southern part of Japan and was brought up in Seattle, mostly among other Japanese families in a kind of Japanese colony. I was sent to Japan for about three or four years. My father's parents lived in a rural village in Kyushu called Nakashoji where my father was brought up and educated before he came to the United States. I went to first grade in a Japanese school. Then I was recalled back to Seattle by my parents to join my sister and my brother. I'm the oldest. It was a very traumatic experience because I was seven years old, a very impressionable age, and I didn't know a word of English. It was a very frightening experience to go to public school. In kindergarten all my classmates were one or two years younger than I was. Everything was in the English language, which I was completely unfamiliar with, so I had to begin from scratch. That was a kind of disorienting experience that probably affected me.

The two school environments were very different. In Japan it was very structured. We'd begin with calisthenics in the morning and then we'd go to the classroom. Even in the second grade they already had assigned room duties, like cleaning in the morning. They would mop the classroom floor by hand to keep it immaculately clean. Just when I was about to be advanced to second grade, that's when I came back. In the United States the life-style of Japanese-Americans was much more loose. It was, in comparison with Japan, very nondirected, as I remember. I don't remember whether there was any corporal punishment in Japan, but in Seattle, where there were many Japanese in the grammar school, there was corporal punishment by the principal for any misbehavior. There was spanking. I didn't get it but the others did. I was very, very, super well-behaved in school. But not that way at home. The teacher said that I was a very nice boy and my mother would always say she couldn't understand why the teacher spoke so well of me because I wasn't that way at home!

In school I didn't manage too well except that there were other Japanese in class and they would interpret for me. I would have to turn to them for help. The teachers were quite understanding because they were serving amongst Japanese. They were all Caucasians. One of them learned how— since my nose was dripping all the time, I guess I had some kind of a sinus condition—to tell me in Japanese to blow my nose. She would say, "How do you say blow your nose in Japanese?" and she learned it from the other Japanese students. I thought that English was difficult, and I was fearful of communicating because I wouldn't understand. I also had difficulty with English even when I was a freshman in college.

I have a sister who is a poet. She has published poetry and articles about Asian women. She also had a film which was shown nationally on Public Television. The film was called "Mitsuye"—that's my sister's name, Mitsuye Yamada—"and Nellie"—that's the name of a Chinese-American poet in San Francisco. They made the film together. Anyway, my sister was born in Japan. My parents went to visit and then she was left there for three years and then she was recalled back to Seattle before I was. She's three years younger than I am. By the time she was a freshman at the University of Cincinnati, where we both studied, she was writing on T. S. Eliot, and now she's teaching English at Cypress College in California. She's published poems about the war experience, the camps, and so forth. Her book of poems is called *Camp Notes*. It's published by Shameless Hussy Press.

Yeah, we were all in camps during the war because we were all on the West Coast. I was in Seattle then. I was in my early twenties. Let me see, going through my life, I graduated from high school in Seattle and then visited Japan for about a year and a half. That was just before the war broke out. I was in Japan during the Sino-Japanese War. I was fascinated by all the things that were happening in Japan. It was a little bit like homecoming. What I'd been reading about and hearing about through my parents and friends, I was able to see and I got reacquainted with my relatives. I contracted tuberculosis while in Japan and my mother came after me and I went back. I came back exactly a year before the war broke out. Otherwise I would have gotten stuck as many other Japanese-Americans were stuck in Japan. They were visiting or studying in Japan, sent by their parents. Then, after that, my father was taken by the FBI agents because he was very well known. He was one of the leaders in the Japanese community in Seattle. So the same day the war broke out he was taken away. He was a civil service worker, an interpreter in the U.S. Immigration Service. He interviewed people coming from Japan and interpreted for the Immigration Service. That was his full-time job. He was also active in all kinds of organizations. Among other things, he belonged to the Japanese Poetry Club. That was on the subversive list. All these things were on the subversive list. They still are, I think, today.

So he was in various different special camps. Department of Justice, FBI camps, and then finally released toward the latter part of the war. They didn't really have anything against him but they did incarcerate him. So he was taken the first night, then the rest of us were taken in April 1942, several months after the war broke out. We were all taken away to the assembly center first, and then to more permanent camps. There were ten of them located in various parts of the country. We were taken on the grounds that we were Japanese. The definition was that if you had, let me see, one thirty-second, or maybe one thirty-fifth Japanese blood, you were a Japanese. Hitler had a definition. I think it was about one-fourth Jewish, then you were Jewish. So it was far more strict here.

Our family—my mother, my sister, and my two brothers—was sent, and my father as I said before, was sent to the other camps. First to the Puyallup Fairgrounds, which is a county fairground that was changed instantly into a camp with barracks and so forth for the summer. In April we were evacuated from our homes. We could not take anything except what we could carry in our hands. Our house was rented. There was a real-estate agent and it was rented all through the war, but along with many other people, we lost a lot of property. Had to sell a car in five days and a lot of stuff was put in storage, which was vandalized or lost forever. The government would not give any insurance, and there was no way to protect any property, so it was vandalized. Just millions and millions of dollars were lost. But anyway, we were sent first to Puyallup Fairground Camp and then to Minidoka, Idaho. Sagebrush country mostly. We were all removed to Idaho by broken-down trains with shades down. They wouldn't let us see where we were going, so we could have been going to the gas chamber as far as we knew. We did not know where we were going until we got there. There was a great deal of apprehension. Everything was very, very secret. Military necessity was a big word. So that was my sister and I and my brother. I have two younger brothers and before we left, the older of my younger brothers volunteered for the 442nd infantry. I guess the young men thought that was a way in which they would prove their loyalty, in spite of what happened. Plus, they thought maybe their families would be treated better. Our camp, I understand, had the highest percentage of volunteers. However, in other camps there was a very low percentage of volunteers, and there were some military draft resisters in Heart Mountain, one of the camps. There were several hundred who resisted the draft, and sixty-six of them got sent to prison. I met one of them in Chicago, a man about my age, who was sent to prison.

Yeah, they were drafting young men in the camp, right. So these men said, "I'm not going. Hell, I won't go," way before Vietnam! And they got sent to prison. They said they were disloyal. But that was not too well publicized see, because the Japanese-American Citizens League (JACL), which is the main Japanese-American organization, projected itself as a very patriotic organization, and it was even opposed to these men. They didn't want to admit it. For example, Bill Hosokawa is a well-known associate editor of the *Denver Post*. He wrote a book called *Nisei*, which is a history of the Japanese-Americans, and it has a lot of stories about the JACL. He is a very gifted man. His book has a lot of good things in it, but he projects the Japanese-Americans as being very loyal and patriotic. The thrust of these men who resisted the draft, however, was, well, their perspective was quite different. Hosokawa was editor of a newspaper at the camp in Heart Mountain, and in his editorials in that concentration camp newspaper he severely criticized the attitudes of these young men who made everybody else look very bad. That is the way in which many leaders projected themselves. There were many kibei—teenagers brought up in Japan and recalled by their parents, who therefore were very good in Japanese—and many of them did rebel against the experience. They were recalled by their parents after they had been through say, high school, or the latter part of their high-school years, and I think they had a great deal of difficulty adjusting back. They were born here, they were U.S. citizens by birth, but they'd lived in Japan and been acculturated into Japanese culture and educated there.

Kibei means "returned Japanese." I imagine a lot of them had difficulty with their own parents. You know, the parents did not bring them up, they were brought up by their grandparents. I was brought up by my grandparents, but that was only for four years. Then there was this sense of disorientation. You know, for a long period as a young boy I used to dream about Japan, because it was so traumatic, my reentry into American culture. They were dreams of nostalgia I guess, and country life versus urban living in Seattle. To young children I guess the farm life has a certain attractiveness, earthiness about it.

When we were released from the concentration camp my sister and I went to Cincinnati. We were being released if we had jobs or if we were going to college. Many colleges and universities were rejecting Japanese just because they were Japanese. But many others did accept them. We found jobs to support ourselves and were admitted to the University of Cincinnati. I stayed there for a year; my sister stayed there longer. I was expelled because the University of Cincinnati had some defense work going on. I think it meant that they were training officers there. The government never gave the reason, but it may have been due to an interview that was conducted by either an FBI agent or an intelligence agent. Some governmental agent came and interviewed all of us to test our loyalty. There was a loyalty oath. He came and asked me if I would defend my country if it were attacked or something to that effect, and I said no. Because I did not believe in any war. So he was startled. So, that may have been one reason for my expulsion. Another may have been that I was in Japan before the war. I think the way they knew that was that we had all kinds of questionnaires. We had loyalty oaths imposed on us when we were in the concentration camps. That became a real stormy issue because, for one thing, these questionnaires were very confusing. My mother's generation was prohibited from becoming naturalized U.S. citizens by immigration laws, so they were Japanese aliens. The questionnaire said, "Would you renounce allegiance to the Emperor and proclaim loyalty to the United States?" And my mother would have to say yes, which makes her a person without any country. My sister was a Japanese citizen, she could not be naturalized because she was born in Japan. She wrote a poem about that. She's now naturalized. She married a Japanese-American. I think she still had to go and take an examination to be naturalized. But anyway, she was a Japanese citizen also.

Yeah, that's right, my brother served in Italy. He came back with minor injuries so he lived through it. That battalion was the most decorated one in the United States, I think. They had the highest rate of death and injury so it was almost a kind of suicide battalion. So my brother and I parted company. My sister had a boyfriend who was a Quaker and a Caucasian. They finally broke up but she was quite sympathetic to that view. So she and I basically are in agreement today on a lot of issues.

My family, like many Japanese, became Christians. They were Methodists. The Methodists did a lot of work among the Japanese in those years. They have Methodist Japanese-speaking ministers and we belonged to the Japanese Methodist Church in Seattle. I went to Sunday School there with my brothers and sister. My mother went there. My father did not go to church too much, although he supported the idea. Then, I came to

Evanston and went to Seabury-Western Theological Seminary for three years to get my divinity degree.

At the time of being released from the camp I must have answered in the way that the government expected me to answer, because we got out. Otherwise we wouldn't have. There were many thousands of others who did not. American citizens of Japanese ancestry were in a tough bind. I mean, how could I renounce my loyalty to the Emperor when I had no such loyalty in the first place? It made no sense whatsoever. So, some of them, many of them, were quite conscientious and answered the best way they could. They answered one "yes" and two of them "no," you know; why should I be loyal to a country that has got me in this jail here? They were placed among the so-called "disloyals." Some, many, somehow survived. I don't know how well. I think there would have been many who were damaged in a negative way because of the experience and probably a number of people did lose their mental balance. There were suicides. There were suicides from loss of self-esteem, of dignity, of life savings, and all sorts of things. All sorts of terrible things happened which are not too well documented. The loss of property, even that's difficult to estimate, I think. But anyway, my sister and I got out. Then I got kicked out of the University of Cincinnati with apologies from the dean of the college. He said the university had nothing to do with it, that he was very sorry, but it's the army order. So that was that. Then I went to Boston University. I read about Boston and I thought it would be interesting to go to someplace like Boston. That is where I finished my undergraduate work and there was no difficulty.

We didn't have any money by then. However, in the meantime my father did get out. My father got a job as a domestic, with my mother, and they worked for a Jewish family in Cincinnati for a while and then, eventually, he was called to Chicago to head an agency, which is a big agency now, that would help Japanese coming out of camps to find jobs. So he became the director of that. He died way back in 1950, at the age of sixty-three.

Some Americans were hostile to us, but some were not, once they got to know the individuals. Just like any other groups, I guess. It's not just Caucasians. There was some feeling against Japanese all throughout the war. Housing was impossible. Japanese moving to Chicago could not find any housing beyond certain limits. Housing discrimination was rampant so that there were no, absolutely no, Japanese living in the suburbs. Completely different from the way it is today. When I was ordained in 1950 I worked in Caucasian parishes. There was no Japanese church, although there were some Japanese-American churches in the Congregational denomination and a few other denominations. Then I worked as a pastor of a church in a white suburb in southwest Chicago. A clergyman is put in a kind of special class. At that time I was trying to help a Japanese family. Both of them were professional people from Japan. He was a chemist with an American Ph.D. The wife was a college graduate. They had a daughter and they wanted a house to live near where he was working as a chemist. It came to my attention that they were looking for a house; that was way back in 1956. I couldn't find a house for those Japanese. Real-estate agents would serve only whites, but we were living there as a clergyman in a church-owned house. There was no way that anybody could keep us out. So the prejudice was, I think it still is today, pretty extreme in a place like that in the suburbs. But it did not affect my work. I mean, I went on working just like anybody else and it was okay. I imagine there would have been some feeling against Japanese on the part of some people who would not associate with that church because there was a Japanese pastor there. That was way after the war, but there was nothing overt. But then, there were some other Japanese-American clergymen before my time, but they were all in charge of Japanese churches on the West Coast. Even today I think on the West Coast, Japanese ministers would find it difficult to get jobs in non-Japanese churches. Around here, it would be different.

We testified, we Asians, at a hearing of the Illinois Department of Human Rights, They wanted to have a hearing for Asians like those they have for Hispanics, and maybe blacks. They wanted Asians across the country to appear there and speak of their experiences with discrimination and other matters related to human rights. So we had one a couple of weeks ago and Japanese, Chinese, Indo-Chinese, all kinds of people came forward for a whole day and testified for five to ten minutes each about their experiences. Things like difficulty in finding jobs and so forth. I gave a testimony about employment and stated the difficulty of promotion and the experience of demotion due to race and the fact that Japanese-Americans and others like myself, who were born here and raised here and well trained, with all kinds of managerial and administrative skills, cannot get beyond a certain level. I spoke of how it feels to be put aside in the course of working in an institution, university, corporation, wherever it may be.

In one of these well-publicized articles, Hayakawa is called the super-American. It's not untypical of minorities and colonized peoples to have representatives like that. Well, he won't really be a representative, but he wants to project himself as somebody who's real loyal to the United States in a patriotic sense. He would be against redress. Many of us are claiming that we should be compensated for our experiences. He adopted the thinking of the United States white American. He is a Canadian. He was born in Canada. He came to the United States and then became naturalized. I understand that he almost didn't make it according to certain laws here, but somehow he squeaked in and came into the United States. He had some connection with the *Chicago Defender* then, a black paper here. He harks back to that, always. He also wants to project himself as a man who is very much in the know with minority problems in the United States. So here's a guy who knows everything and he's super-American. That's how he wants to project himself. He would say something like, "Yes, the United States was prejudiced in discriminating against minorities way back when, but look at me, you know how successful I am and this could not happen anyplace else." That's the kind of statement he makes from time to time. I know he referred to your ethnicity as "kurombo." That means nigger.

My experience in this country is that the people are very conformist. They want to go along with things as they are. If Reagan is in power, then he is very much respected, regardless of his ideologies or positions or evidence of beliefs. I guess it's a sense of insecurity, basically. You know, there is societal insecurity that makes people want to be like everybody else. I suppose that in that respect confrontation in various ways and shapes is effective because even a corporation would shiver at adverse publicity. Also, our society is based very much on image. It is lacking in substance. I think it's basically true of white Americans, and then it carries over into minority peoples when they true to be like the majority. Hayakawa being a good example. Many of my fellow Japanese-Americans tend to be that way.

Amongst immigrant parents the more white we are in skin color, the better looking we are, just like in the black community, I guess. There are shades. This was especially true for the looks of females. My sister, I think, was on the dark side, so that was not considered to be a good trait. If you were white as a white woman, that's a good trait. Women would talk amongst themselves. "She's real beautiful and white," you know and so forth. "Just like a Caucasian!" Something like that.

We were brought up with prejudice against blacks, against Filipinos, against Koreans, and so forth, by our parents. They brought us up that way, more or less. That prevailed in the Japanese community of Seattle and elsewhere, I think. It might have changed somewhat. Certainly with our generation there've been a lot of changes. Basically, prejudice is a matter of lack of exposure I think. With exposure on an equal basis on various levels all those things sort of vanish. How did I learn prejudice? Well, under that generation's influence. It was parental. It was pretty open. You'd catch it in table discussions and social circles. Women and men would be talking to each other and to their children and us and it sort of comes out. However, everybody was polite in the sense that there wouldn't be any open hostility against any group. But if the Japanese were hotel owners, say, of cheaper hotels—they certainly were not corporation hotel presidents—small hotel owners would say, "We don't take any blacks," you know. "We don't take any Filipinos because they're no good." The reasons were, you know, the usual things. Because they were lazy and they didn't have any money and they were unkempt and so forth. The usual things that prejudiced Caucasians would say.

I guess I began to question all that in college. Not courses in college, but by association. And maybe in high school. Also, when I was in Japan I was pretty well versed in what was going on in Japan. I read Japanese newspapers and engaged in conversations with all kinds of people. I was there for a year and a half. You pick up a lot of stuff. I could tell that there were all kinds of distortion in the image that they had of the United States, of the whites and all these things. I could tell. So as a young man I very quickly came to the conclusion that there is something wrong here, people are not seeing things as they are. So I had a kind of experience that lots of people wouldn't have had. Then too, the newspapers had all kinds of propaganda. There was much propaganda in Japan. Military propaganda about and against the United States. Americans were depicted as wallowing in luxury and very incompetent. Things like that. I cannot remember all the specifics, but I did recognize that there were many things being said about non-Japanese that were completely inaccurate. The stereotypes were almost the same as the anti-Japanese stereotypes that the U.S. press was projecting. You know, people dripping with avariciousness, and imperialists dominating other people, and so forth and so on. It may be military mentality. I see elements of that in the Pentagon. Some of the statements coming out of the Pentagon display that kind of mystique. It seems similar to the mystique of the military in Japan then.

My experience with dissent formally begins with the civil rights movement. When I left the suburban ministry I went into college work ministry, contacting chaplains and allocating funds to different college centers which get certain amounts of funds from the New York office. I was a kind of liaison officer. So I traveled around the country in the 1960s when the students' civil rights movement was really picking up, Martin Luther King and so forth. When Martin Luther King was marching I was already out of parish ministry in the suburbs. The white people I was serving there would have been the very people who were throwing rocks at Martin Luther King. At that time we were talking about integrating the white suburbs. We were just talking about it and I couldn't find a meeting place. The YMCA didn't want anything like that, the Roman Catholic priest said that's going a little too far, so we met in our parish. The parish that I was in control of. We had meetings with a Loyola University professor, an economist, I think, was a part of that group. That was the kind of place I was working in. It didn't cause trouble. It was not too well advertised, for one thing. It wouldn't have gone too well if I had pushed hard. I would not have gotten support from the diocesan headquarters, from the two bishops who were in charge. They were both white. But even if they had both been black, I'm sure it wouldn't have worked. There wouldn't have been much backing for that sort of thing. But anyway, I was willing to go as far as I could. In everything I do, I go to the edge, staying just this side of the jail. That's been my mode of operation. I never landed in jail, in spite of marching and all that sort of thing. Then, when I was in this college ministry, a regional coordinating ministry, I was traveling around all over the country, going to different conferences. I went to Mississippi one year after the three young men were murdered. They were murdered in the summer of 1965. That fall there was a conference in Atlanta. It was an Episcopal young people's student conference. After that I traveled to McComb, Mississippi. So I lived there for a couple of weeks and took part in voter registration and things like that and came back and related my experiences. I became more active in housing integration marches and picketing in the North Shore of Chicago, which is completely white. You know that Senator Charles Percy lives in Kenilworth, which didn't even have any Jews for a long time. We would picket the real-estate houses together with the college students who were back for the summer. They were very active. These white, Ivy League students were participants that summer in the civil rights movement there and in the South. The college students were quite prominent.

The other thing in the dissent experience is the Vietnam war. During the Vietnam War I was supportive of draft resisters and active in the peace movement at various levels. Yes, I am a total pacifist, whatever that means.

I am basically against organized violence; that would be my primary target, you know, the violence of nation against nation, large numbers of people in a group against another group. I would probably not be opposed to individuals defending themselves, probably not. But I have real questions about the basic value of survival. Christianity is certainly not based on the philosophy of survival. It's based on sacrifice, and if there is any survival then it's a very long-range term that would involve more than just physical survival.

I am linked to the Puerto Rican nationalist struggle, right. My reasoning behind that is that it is like supporting any revolutionary group. Most groups and individuals that I know believe in armed struggle when it's for a cause that is justified. There's no nation in the world that I know of that does not believe in armed struggle. The Puerto Ricans say that they believe in armed struggle, so in that respect, they are no different from the United States or Japan or any other country. On that basis alone, I would not withhold any support. It's a comparative and relative matter, the way I see it, although I think that organized violence of any kind is ultimately self-destructive. There are certain kinds of organized violence that are worse than others. And the organized violence that the U.S. government has imposed upon a colonial group like Puerto Rico is infinitely worse than what the Puerto Rican Independence people would be doing in their struggle.

Well, in the case of principled dissent, what is the meaning of principle? I'm not really sure what is meant by that, but I have a notion of what that might mean. I suppose you mean, what is the main thrust of the dissent, what is the main reason? That is the way I interpret your term. The way I understand meaningful dissent, there is a purpose for dissenting, and broadly defined, I guess it's for equality and justice. We want to see a society in which everyone is equal in practice, in actuality, rather than just in theory or in rhetoric.

In the definition that I have given, I guess I would say that the Klansman is a principled dissenter in that sense. There's something very human, there's something very touching about that dissent from my perspective. They could be completely wrong, but if they are believing in what they're doing, there's something very moving about that, a human element, and the person could be completely wrong. I do not see any inconsistency in your talking to the Klansman. I think it's a basic element in human relationships that is necessary. I mean, without that, life would not be meaningful. There could not be a relationship at a deep level.

The man who advocates incest is possibly a principled dissenter. I would say so, yes. That would be my definition of that. As I say, it's an element in human relationship and in beliefs. Well, superficially speaking, I suppose we are talking about the right to be wrong. I don't know, there are certain elements in our relationship experience that are very basic to life in society and individual growth. I think what you're getting at is that you are trying to identify a certain human quality without passing judgment upon the position that the person is taking. You see, with a high level of honesty, there's a better chance of people being able to face up to each other and their differences than there would be if these differences were passed over, which is the way relationship is usually encouraged. Yeah, refinement of human possibilities. That's a good way to put it. We can keep refining and that's a part of the struggle.

I would not put any restrictions whatsoever on the marketplace of ideas. Now if I'm faced with the actual situation, I may act differently. But off-hand, I would say there should be no restrictions. Oh! Well, the KKK has to be restrained! That's a dilemma, yeah. There's no clear-cut answer, but there's no division between thinking and acting anyway. I mean, that's very artificial. I do not endorse the actions of the KKK, but at the level of dissent I can respect a person's honesty in belonging to the KKK. In my own activity I would support the anti-Klan movement and I would try to do everything possible to restrain by legal means or by whatever means that would be acceptable, the activity of the KKK. Acceptable to me. I would not go assassinate him, for example. But I might put him in jail. I would have to weigh the pros and cons of the actual situation, at the same time understanding that person's position and respecting that, if that makes any sense. My understanding that person does not mean that I would allow that organization or that person to go ahead and do what they believe in if they're in conflict with my beliefs.

I guess it doesn't square. At a certain point, I'm not clear. There's always an element of doubt, whatever I do. In this respect if a person, if a Klansman or anybody else, is completely oversure of his position, I would be very suspicious of that. In other words, that verges on dogma-tism, and the genuineness of that belief becomes doubtful to me. There is always an element of ambiguity present, and we must accept that ambi-guity as a human condition. As a religious person I believe in certain foundations and in the long run justice prevailing in history. You know, I have that faith, that I accept on faith. But beyond that, in everything that is human, that is transitory, there are always elements of vagueness, elements of doubt. The understanding of justice is flawed. It's relative, but it does matter. Otherwise there is no sense in the struggle.

Justice and love and peace and whatever, those are the basic elements necessary for human relations, and these are what we are striving for con-tinually, but they are flawed. The understanding of them is flawed. Basically we're talking about justice, equality, and there is a certain mystique about it which motivates us, but that's enough for us to give our lives to without being able to spell it out, without being able to make a blueprint of what an equal society is. I have enough confidence in the coming of such a society and my being a participant of that to give my life to it. There has to be a great deal of confidence. There has to be depth—it's an almost unexpressed or inexpressable goal in human terms. But it has to be there, and it's constantly being tested, and one never knows when one might become a betrayer. I mean, it's another element of doubt. None of us know how strong we are until we're tested, and when the real test comes we may flip over. This has happened to people in the Puerto Rican move-ment and any other place. When that happens, I think I can understand why it comes about. It's a very human occurrence. Betrayal, out and out betrayal, to me that's understandable, and in religious understanding of human nature we take that into account. Therefore, that would motivate us to be as honest as we can be because you know, betrayal does not mean the end of everything in being human. There is a way of atonement. Yeah, punishment is also part, a necessary part of our social living. There can be no learning without punishment.

We don't all agree, and there's a constant struggle and debate, which in itself is a road to arriving at some kind of consensus. But it's all part of the genuine desire to understand what the depth of these things really is. Struggle means that there are certain restraints. Implicit in the meaning of the word itself is disagreement, weighing pros and cons of certain positions. Struggle in that sense is where we try to arrive at some truth in our life.

The way I look at it, the state has its own terrible force and violence, which it is quite capable of using, and does constantly. Whereas rebellious groups, including these Puerto Ricans, are not organized to the same degree. They say they believe in armed resistance. They have no army. Maybe they have a pistol or two, I don't know, but it certainly does not compare with the Pentagon. Yes, some people have died, but it wasn't like dropping a bomb on Hiroshima. That was very scientific and intentional. I make these comparisons when I support certain groups. Most middle-class people to whom I relate do not. So they misunderstand what the various levels of violence are. Well, for one thing, I think basically at the middle-class level, people lack self-awareness. They do not know the kind of government they are supporting or how their tax money is being used and how the United States is relating to other parts of the world. Those kinds of perspectives are completely lacking in most people.

As for my peers, I think they know where I stand in a lot of things, you know. I work for a social agency for the poor, serving food, providing clothes and shelter, assisting alcoholics. That's how I earn my living. On Sundays in a congregation situation, I work for a parish which is a pretty rich congregation. They know my views on a lot of these things. But I think they put me in the class of some sort of a house radical. That would sort of put me in a niche someplace. Whereas my intent is not to be stereotyped that way and be put in a closet someplace so that whenever they need somebody like me, then I would be put on the program and then they could feel a little bit better about it. That's not my intent. The sort of thing that I'm striving for is what I consider to be the very *human* elements necessary to social life. And it's necessary for everybody. Universal elements, that's the way I see it. Well, that's not the way they see it.

Yes, there are penalties. I was supporting Iranian students when they were being severely attacked by the Carter administration and by the Chicago police. I was supporting the teachers' union, which was very unpopular with the administration of the college because they were very nervous about that, so I got demoted. That was a penalty. It was run by a white board with a black president and black vice president. They were altogether co-opted. But I knew what the score was. I was not surprised. As a matter of fact, I learned a lot of things. By that experience I could differentiate better among different kinds of colonized peoples. I can understand puppet regimes much more personally than I had been able to understand them before just by reading about them. I know from personal experience why puppet regimes are necessary and why certain people become puppets in an oppressed society. So in the present situation it's not that tightly knit. Oppression is much more diffuse. In the white, comfortable suburban parish most people are a bunch of tourists, you know. They talk about other countries but they see things from the perspective of the tourist. You see retired people going and coming back and saying, "I've been to Italy," "I've been to Japan," but these experiences just reinforce their own narrow societal environments in which they were brought up and from which they derive their living. They have never been challenged to see the world in a broader perspective. I recognize that and I see my role as trying to break through that somehow. Sometimes I'm successful, but most of the time I'm not.

I was the one who hired Carmen Valentín. I was the head of the department at that time. We were not that close you know, but I had a very warm, very friendly, pleasant relationship with her and certainly that had a lot to do with my getting involved with the Prisoner of War movement. I didn't have the foggiest notion before Carmen was arrested that she was in any way involved in any kind of central independence movement. I knew that she was a person of very strong convictions, very intelligent, who was very skilled in her field as a counselor. Now before we hired her I checked her background, you know, because there was criticism that she had been on TV in that high school where there was a storm of controversy because there were certain pro-student administrators. This was in the late 1960s and early 1970s. There was a storm of controversy. Carmen became the center of it, in spite of the fact that she's basically a very quiet person. A very gentle, quiet person. Then, I figured that if a person was not in the storm of controversy in a very bad situation like that, then that counselor wouldn't be worth very much. That was my opinion, so I reached my own conclusions and asked her to come join the staff. I took it as a positive thing, and also I talked to several people and they were quite positive.

As for what we're doing right now, I'm part of a small committee that is interdenominational, with the top people of the United Church of Christ denomination involved. The main thrust there is to see that the prisoner abuse is stopped. We're trying to see the warden of that federal prison located right here in the Loop. So far we have been unsuccessful. Not having succeeded at that, we're having a Thanksgiving service on the day after Thanksgiving. A procession will march a few blocks and then an interdenominational worship service will be held right there in front of the jail to bear public witness in the midst of all the people who will be coming in. I belong to this group that is protesting the treatment of prisoners, you know, the prisoner abuse. Not permitting visitation to these prisoners as they do to other prisoners. Not permitting a spiritual religious counsel. Alex Torres's health is in danger now, so we're demanding that she be allowed to see a physician of her choice who will be a specialist, not a jail physician, and things like that.

During the Vietnam War, when these young men were being put in prison for resisting the draft or disobedience in the army, I used to visit these people in prison, because I was then traveling all over the country, and I got to know some of them quite well. Some of them did face the same kind of abuse, yeah. I had a newsletter. I worked for the district. It was not a prestigious position but it was a headquarters position and I used to write in those newsletters about my visitations to prisons. Also, I got my Ph.D. from Loyola University in the Department of Counseling and Higher Education and I wrote about Japanese-American history in my dissertation.

There was some criticism from some clergy about supporting terrorist groups, so I wrote a letter to the editor at *Witness* magazine. That's the main hang-up. They don't seem to be too concerned about Hiroshima and Nagasaki violence, or what's going on in the Pentagon, but let a few bombs explode here and there and one or two persons die and they become suddenly very concerned about terrorism, you know. Which to me, from my perspective, is just completely out of proportion. You know, it's paying attention to some very minor thing so you can forget about the real big problems, which is the typical approach to solving our social problems. So I responded to this criticism of support for terrorist groups in some kind of minimal way.

I see my life in that sense as being very consistent, evolving from, coming out of a couple of cultures, two or three cultures. The third culture is Japanese-American culture. In Seattle I felt like an alien. Maybe a little bit like these kibei that I told you about. In a sense, I identified myself with Japanese imperialism, you know, during the Japan Chinese war from the very beginning. One thing which impressed me a great deal was when I was having a hard time with the English—this was in high school speech class, and the teacher's name was Miss Hunter and it's very vivid. We had to make speeches, I think, so I decided to talk on—you know there was a lot of criticism of Japan's invading China—so I wanted to justify the Japanese invasion of China. I used to talk to my father a lot about it. He said, "Don't talk like that!" I said, "Why not? Aren't they right?" So I picked up a lot of stuff from the Japanese Chamber of Commerce in the Japanese Consulate in Seattle and I used that for my speech and gave a very good presentation. Okay, so the teacher listened to it and she said it was very good and she said she respected my views and that it was a good presentation and it sounded like stuff that I got from the Japanese Consulate! In that class I got an "A." The first time in my life that I ever got an "A" in English. I was a fairly good student in high school, but I never got anything close to that in English. That really impressed me! Here was a teacher who was completely disagreeing with me but she was fair and respectful and she was an excellent teacher and I still remember. A lot of things I have forgotten, but I still remember that. Those are the things that possibly made a difference in my life in trying to understand, you know, to size up what's right and wrong in society.

That was standing out, yeah. I think it was. Also it was against the white teachers and others basically. As a matter of fact, I still remember the speech that a teacher, I can't remember what his field was, but he came and spoke to the American history class and he was kind of making fun of, ridiculing the Japanese pilots. He said Japanese don't have any sense of balance. They make poor pilots because they're carried on the backs of their mothers and their heads are, you know, so they lose the sense of balance. And therefore when they grow up we don't have any-thing to fear from Japanese pilots. This was in high school and I resented that. I didn't say anything in the class, being a very polite Japanese student, but I was talking to some of my Japanese-American fellow students and one guy said, "If you feel like that why don't you tell him!"

I have a sister, as I said, who's a poet now. She's a feminist also and she just toured about ten Ivy League schools lecturing and talking to students. One of the professors she met was a Chinese-American woman who has been here for about fifteen years. She still sees herself as a foreigner here, unlike people like my sister who were brought up in this country, you know, all American. This woman has sort of adopted the mentality of the dominant culture. People like this woman have lost their identity in a sense and still see themselves as foreigners. Whereas we don't. We see ourselves as part of the culture here and if other people can't see it, well, we're gonna make 'em see it! All we're trying to do is project what is true about our U.S. society. Unless we do that we will not become a more wholesome society.

Right now, these Puerto Ricans, because they seem to be the ones who need as much support as possible, more than some other groups or liberal causes, are the ones I'm concentrating on. I've been in different peace groups of the church and I believe in everything they do, but I'm not as active as some. Usually I put my energy where I think there's not enough support and wherever whatever support I give would be a contribution. We sort of came together, a few of us, Joan Nicklin and myself and a few others, to form the Civic and Religious Committee in support of the Puerto Rican POW's. It's basically religion based people. What we want to do is build up a base emphasizing the human rights aspect. Independence, the self-determination of a group of people, the means that they think are necessary to achieve that end, and the abuse that they suffer because of that, are all of a package. People in this country, you know, the middle class and academics, are used to sectioning everything off. I'm not for independence. I'm not against it either, but I am against prisoner abuse.

In order to be human we have to recognize our limitations as human beings and the lack of clarity in what we do, no matter how right we think we are. Whatever we're giving our lives to, there's still an element of doubt. Ultimately, there has to be a kind of self-confidence that it is enough to give one's life to, without being dogmatic in the very narrow sense. One knows what one is getting into and the cost that one must be prepared to pay.

Most people believe in armed struggle. I don't happen to believe in it because I think it is counterproductive. I think the American Friends Service Committee, which is basically a pacifist organization, has a state-ment about this issue. It's not a very strong statement, but it indicates that they at least thought through it. They had to make a statement about their support of violent, revolutionary groups. It is a compromise statement. They themselves don't believe in violence, but that does not mean that they cannot support groups just because they are using violence. That would mean they would have to take the position that they would not support the U.S. government. I am ambiguous about the use of violence, but I do know for sure what the Pentagon stands for. What are you going to do, not pay taxes! I'm already supporting violence right now, so it's only a question of the *degree* of violence.

The Divine is working all through it. I mean, it just pervades the whole system. The Divine is not something that's imposed, it's in operation constantly. That is how It, or He, or She is understood! Our scientific tradition has taught us to divide everything up into compartments and we tend to do that in our religious thinking, our political thinking, and in many ways that creates unnecessary barriers to thinking of our lives as individuals in society as a whole, as a cohesive unit. And Divine and human are thought of as completely separate from each other. In some sense the Divine is completely outside of us and in another sense the Divine is very much inside. It is sort of in and out. In the midst of all this there is a constant struggle, there is an element of doubt continually. The more genuine the belief is, the stronger the element of doubt is, that is the way I would express my own experience. That's why I know that the KKK is not right because they are so sure! They would *kill* somebody not of their position. Now, I would not kill anybody. I'm not that sure.

ABOUT THE AUTHOR

JOHN L. GWALTNEY is an anthropologist and ritual wood carver. He was born in Orange, New Jersey and holds a B.A. from Upsala College, an M.A. in political science and sociology from the New School for Social Research, a Ph.D. in anthropology from Columbia University, and honorary degrees from Bucknell University and Upsala College. As a student of the late Dr. Margaret Mead, he wrote a dissertation on river blindness among the Yolox Chinantec of Oaxaca, Mexico, that won the prestigious Ansley Dissertation Award at Columbia and was later published as *The Thrice Shy*. His first book of narratives, *Drylongso: A Self-Portrait of Black America*, won the 1980 Association of Black Anthropologists Publication Award and a Robert F. Kennedy Book Award Honorable Mention in 1981. He is currently a professor of anthropology at the Maxwell Graduate School of Citizenship and Public Affairs at Syracuse University and divides his time between teaching, field research, and sculpture.